Technologies, Innovation, and Change in Personal and Virtual Learning Environments

Michael Thomas
University of Central Lancashire, UK

Information Science
REFERENCE

Managing Director:	Lindsay Johnston
Editorial Director:	Joel Gamon
Book Production Manager:	Jennifer Romanchak
Publishing Systems Analyst:	Adrienne Freeland
Development Editor:	Heather Probst
Assistant Acquisitions Editor:	Kayla Wolfe
Typesetter:	Travis Gundrum
Cover Design:	Nick Newcomer

Published in the United States of America by
Information Science Reference (an imprint of IGI Global)
701 E. Chocolate Avenue
Hershey PA 17033
Tel: 717-533-8845
Fax: 717-533-8661
E-mail: cust@igi-global.com
Web site: http://www.igi-global.com

Library of Congress Cataloging-in-Publication Data

Technologies, innovation, and change in personal and virtual learning environments / Michael Thomas, editor.
    p. cm.
 Includes bibliographical references and index.
 Summary: "This book presents a widespread collection of research on the growth, innovation and implementation of learning technologies for educators, technologists and trainers"--Provided by publisher.
  ISBN 978-1-4666-2467-2 (hardcover) -- ISBN 978-1-4666-2468-9 (ebook) -- ISBN 978-1-4666-2469-6 (print & perpetual access) 1. Educational technology. 2. Education--Effect of technological innovations on. 3. Digital communications. I. Thomas, Michael, 1969-
 LB1028.3.T396635 2013
 371.33--dc23
                              2012023349

British Cataloguing in Publication Data
A Cataloguing in Publication record for this book is available from the British Library.

The views expressed in this book are those of the authors, but not necessarily of the publisher.

Françoise Blin, *Dublin City University, Ireland*
Stephen Bronack, *Clemson University, USA*
Aaron P. Campbell, *Kyoto Sangyo University, Japan*
Mohamed Amine Chatti, *RWTH Aachen University, Germany*
Alice Chik, *City University of Hong Kong, Hong Kong*
Michael Coghlan, *TAFF, Australia*
John Collick, *Promethean Co. Ltd, UK*
John Cook, *London Metropolitan University, UK*
Cristina Costa, *Salford University, UK*
Edward Dixon, *University of Pennsylvania, USA*
Darren Elliott, *Nanzan University, Japan*
James A. Elwood, *Tsukuba University, Japan*
Ola Erstad, *University of Oslo, Norway*
Patrick Foss, *Tokyo Medical and Dental University, Japan*
Nicolas Gromik, *Tohuko University, Japan*
Sara Guth, *University of Padova, Italy*
Regine Hampel, *Open University, UK*
Mirjam Hauck, *Open University, UK*
Don Hinkelman, *Sapporo Gakuin University, Japan*
Jane Hunter, *University of Western Sydney, Australia*
Marcia Johnson, *Waikato University, New Zealand*
Tony Jones, *University of Melbourne, Australia*
Helen Keegan, *Salford University, UK*
Jeremy Kemp, *San Jose State University, USA*
Jaroslaw Krajka, *Warsaw School of Social Psychology, Poland*
Mark Lee, *Charles Sturt University, Australia*
J. P. Loucky, *Seinam Jogakuin, Japan*
Steve McCarty, *Osaka Jogakuin, Japan*
George MacLean, *Tsukuba University, Japan*
Dave Miller, *Keele University, UK*
Gary Motteram, *University of Manchester, UK*
Tony Mullen, *Tsuda College, Japan*
Diane Nahl, *University of Hawaii, USA*
Anna Peachey, *Open University, UK*
Nik Peachey, *ICT Consultant, UK*
Mark Peterson, *Kyoto University, Japan*
Thomas Raith, *University of Education Heidelberg, Germany*
Ken Reeder, *University of British Columbia, Canada*
Thomas Robb, *Kyoto Sangyo University, Japan*
Karl Royle, *University of Wolverhampton, UK*
Bernd Rueschoff, *Universität Duisburg-Essen, Germany*
Mathias Schulze, *University of Waterloo, Canada*
Kieron Sheehy, *Open University, UK*
Leslie Shield, *Open University, UK*

Table of Contents

Section 2
Innovation

Section 3
Change

Detailed Table of Contents

Section 1
Technologies

Chapter 1

Kikuo Asai, The Open University of Japan, Japan
Norio Takase, FiatLux Co. Ltd., Japan

This article presents the characteristics of using a tangible tabletop environment produced by augmented reality (AR), aimed at improving the environment in which learners observe three-dimensional molecular structures. The authors perform two evaluation experiments. A performance test for a user interface demonstrates that learners with a tangible AR environment were able to complete the task of identifying molecular structures more quickly and accurately than those with a typical desktop-PC environment using a Web browser. A usability test by participants who learned molecular structures and answered relevant questions demonstrates that the environments had no effect on their learning of molecular structures. However, a preference test reveals that learners preferred a more tangible AR environment to a Web-browser environment in terms of overall enjoyment, reality of manipulation, and sense of presence, and vice versa in terms of ease of viewing, experience, and durability.

Chapter 2

Gavin J. Baxter, University of the West of Scotland, UK
Thomas M. Connolly, University of the West of Scotland, UK
Mark Stansfield, University of the West of Scotland, UK

This paper investigates the implementation and use of an internal organisational blog by several departments in the HR division in a large public sector financial organisation in the UK. This qualitative study adopts a case study approach and examines the experiences of staff using the blog to explore whether it can facilitate organisational learning. The thinking and decisions that informed the pilot study are also investigated. Initial findings indicate that implementing an internal organisational blog does not revolve around the technology itself, but the work required to inform and educate staff about the idea of using a blog for working purposes. This paper has practical implications for the practitioner community with reference to organisational management informing them of issues to consider prior to implementing new technology in team environments. The paper also examines approaches towards maintaining technology initiatives (in this case blogs) once they are up and running. The unique focus of this paper is that it explores blog use from the perspective of individuals who have never used them before as opposed to a department that is already familiar with the technology.

Chapter 3

Rikke Magnussen, Aarhus University, Denmark

This paper examines the methodological challenges and perspectives of designing game-like scenarios for the implementation of innovation processes in school science education. This paper presents a design-based research study of a game-like innovation scenario designed for technology education for Danish public school students aged 13-15. Students play the role of company heads that develop intelligent music technology. This game-like learning environment was designed to develop innovation competencies through the simulation of a practical learning situation. The term "game-like" is used to denote that the scenario should not be considered an educational game, such as the educational computer games used in many schools today. The focus of the design is to include practices and tools from innovative professions and use game principles and elements to create a meaningful frame around the creative and innovative practices.

Chapter 4

Jyldyz Tabyldy Kyzym, Queens University, Belfast, UK

Decisions on both personal and public matters benefit significantly if uncertainties and risks are handled with more care and accuracy. It is crucial to refine and express degrees of confidence and subjective probabilities of various outcomes. Experience, intuition, and skills help make the most of uncertain information. This paper proposes a concept and design of a computer game which aims to train and enhance some of these skills. It is an online game, which allows players to indicate their subjective uncertainty on a numerical scale and to receive explicit feedback. The accuracy of the player is conditioned and motivated by the incentives based on proper scoring rules. The game aims to train accuracy and better calibration in estimating probabilities and expressing degrees of confidence. The "World of Uncertainty" (n.d.) project researched the learning effect of the game and its impact on players' attitudes towards uncertainty. The concept of this game can be adopted as part of an advanced and complex game in the future.

Chapter 5

Jerremie Clyde, University of Calgary, Canada
Glenn Wilkinson, University of Calgary, Canada

This paper contrasts the importance of procedural rhetoric for the use of games in university and college level historical education with the use of history themed digital simulations. This paper starts by examining how history functions as a form of disciplinary knowledge and how this disciplinary way of knowing things is taught in the post secondary history course. The manner in which history is taught is contrasted with its evaluation to better define what students are actually expected to learn. The simulation is then examined in light of learning goals and evaluation. This demonstrates that simulations are a poor fit for most post secondary history courses. The more appropriate and effective choice is to construct the past via procedural rhetoric as a way to use digital video games to make the historical argument.

    Rebecca Petley, LSN, UK
    Jill Attewell, LSN, UK
    Carol Savill-Smith, LSN, UK

MoLeNET is a unique collaborative initiative, currently in its third year, which encourages and enables the introduction of mobile learning in English post 14 education via supported shared-cost projects. Mobile learning in MoLeNET is defined by MoLeNET as "The exploitation of ubiquitous handheld technologies, together with wireless and mobile phone networks, to facilitate, support, enhance and extend the reach of teaching and learning." MoLeNET projects use a wide range of handheld devices with their learners including two handheld game platforms: the Sony PSP and Nintendo DS. A small number of projects have also experimented with educational and therapeutic use of the Nintendo Wii game console and experienced considerable success in engaging reluctant learners and supporting learners with difficulties and/or disabilities. This paper explores the impact that mobile game technologies have on teaching and learning for those involved in MoLeNET, including the development of academic and social skills and the improvement of mobility and health related issues.

    Paul Hollins, University of Bolton, UK
    Nicola Whitton, Manchester Metropolitan University, UK

This paper draws on lessons learned from the development process of the entertainment games industry and discusses how they can be applied to the field of game-based learning. This paper examines policy makers and those wishing to commission or develop games for learning and highlights potential opportunities as well as pitfalls. The paper focuses on ten key points in which the authors feel from experience in both commercial game development and education that parallels are drawn between the entertainment and educational games development processes.

Section 2
Innovation

    Billy Brick, Coventry University, UK

This article examines a study of seven learners who logged their experiences on the language leaning social networking site Livemocha over a period of three months. The features of the site are described and the likelihood of their future success is considered. The learners were introduced to the Social Networking Site (SNS) and asked to learn a language on the site. They were positive about two aspects of the site: the immediate peer-feedback available and the ability to converse synchronously and asynchronously with native speakers of their target language. However, there was universal criticism of the "word-list" based language learning materials and several participants complained about the regular cyber-flirting they encountered. Other aspects of the site including accessibility, ease of use, syllabus, activities, and relationships with other members are also considered. The potential for integrating some of the features of SNSs for language learning into the Higher Education (HE) curriculum and the implications of this for educators are also discussed.

Chapter 9

This paper describes the development of resources for a unit of work for the English National Diploma in Information Technology. These on-line resources are designed to support a personalised learning environment that maximises opportunities for students to achieve greater control of their own learning and progression. The resources are designed to promote metacognition, with the intention of encouraging students to think about how they learn and how they can progress most effectively. The resources were developed to explore ways forward in developing personalised learning environments and implications for research on wider implementation across all National Diplomas.

Chapter 10

Connected learning using video conferencing, the interactive whiteboard and Web 2.0 tools is possible in the new "interactive classroom" more than 2,240 New South Wales public schools will receive over the next four years. In Australia the New South Wales Department of Education and Training (NSWDET) is delivering $AUS 158 million of infrastructure and services to schools and technical and further education campuses for new technologies and applications to support teaching in the 21st century. The intention of the Connected Classrooms Program is to create a "large connected and collaborative learning community" of teachers, students and parents that can go online for information, resources and communication "anywhere, anytime" across a state that covers over 800,000 square kilometres. This paper describes the three projects in the program, the underpinning prior work and seven teacher professional learning platforms that reference anticipated learning outcomes and future directions. In its third year, this case study is a descriptive insiders snapshot. It provides an overview for project administrators and participants in other national and international education milieu who may be responsible for planning and implementing enhanced technology environments.

Chapter 11

Digital games can be powerful learning environments because they encourage active learning and participation within "affinity groups" (Gee, 2004). However, the use of games in formal educational environments is not always successful (O'Neil et al., 2005). There is a need to update existing theories of motivation and engagement in order to take recent game-related developments into account. Understanding the links between why people play games, what keeps them engaged in this process, and what they learn as a result could have a significant impact on how people value and use games for learning. This paper examines key research that relates to motivation, engagement, and informal learning through digital games, in order to highlight the need for empirical studies which examine the activities that occur in and around everyday gaming practice.

Chapter 12

Misbah Mahmood Khan, University of Hertfordshire, UK
Jonathan Reed, Neurogames, UK

Games Based Learning needs to be linked to good learning theory to become an important educational intervention. This study examines the effectiveness of a collection of computer games called Neurogames®. Neurogames are a group of computer games aimed at improving reading and basic maths and are designed using neuropsychological theory. The effectiveness of Neurogames was assessed using a matched pairs experimental design. Short exposure to Neurogames resulted in a significant increase in mathematical ability compared to control. The games resulted in a significant increase in reading ability. The study shows that brief exposure to computer games can result in significant changes to academic development. The implications for education and further research are discussed.

Chapter 13

Beat Döbeli Honegger, University of Teacher Education Central Switzerland, Switzerland
Christian Neff, Primary School Goldau, Switzerland

This paper describes the goals and first results of an ongoing two year case study in a European primary school (5th primary class) where the teacher and all students were equipped with a personal smartphone. Students are allowed to use phone and internet services at no charge and to take home their smartphones after school. In this project the students have access to an internet connected computing device which can be used for reading, writing, calculating, drawing, taking photos, listening or recording audio, and communicating. Does this setting help to achieve the goals of the official school curriculum? How do personal smartphones in primary school influence teaching and learning, especially weekly planning ("Wochenplanunterricht") and learning outside school? The paper describes the planning and introduction phase of the project as well as first best practice examples of using personal smartphones in and out of school after five months of use. The authors provide qualitative data from questionnaires with students and parents and quantitative data of phone and internet use. To date the results help to formulate specific research questions for further research and they encourage enlarging the case study to several classes in the near future.

Section 3
Change

Chapter 14

Sebastian H. D. Fiedler, Centre for Social Innovation, Austria &
University of Turku, Finland
Terje Väljataga, Tallinn University, Estonia

This paper reviews and critiques how the notion of PLEs has been conceptualised and discussed in literature so far. It interprets the variability of its interpretations and conceptualisations as the expression of a fundamental contradiction between patterns of activity and digital instrumentation in formal education on one hand, and individual experimentation and experience within the digital realm on the other. It is suggested to place this contradiction in the larger socio-historic context of an ongoing media transformation. Thus, the paper argues against the prevalent tendency to base the conceptualisation of PLEs almost exclusively on Web 2.0 technologies that are currently available or emerging, while underlying patterns of control and responsibility often remain untouched. Instead, it proposes to scrutinise these patterns and to focus educational efforts on supporting adult learners to model their learning activities and potential (personal learning) environments while exploring the digital realm.

Chapter 15

Making it Rich and Personal: Crafting an Institutional Personal Learning Environment 177

Su White, University of Southampton, UK
Hugh Davis, University of Southampton, UK

Many of the communities interested in learning and teaching technologies within higher education now accept the view that a conception of personal learning environments provides the most realistic and workable perspective of learners' interactions with and use of technology. This view may not be reflected in the behaviour of those parts of a university which normally purchase and deploy technology infrastructure. These departments or services are slow to change because they are typically, and understandably, risk-averse, the more so because the consequences of expensive decisions about infrastructure will stay with the organisation for many years. Furthermore across the broader (less technically or educationally informed) academic community, the awareness of and familiarity with technologies in support of learning may be varied. In this context, work to innovate the learning environment will require considerable team effort and collective commitment. This paper presents a case study account of institutional processes harnessed to establish a universal personal learning environment fit for the 21st century.

Chapter 16

Exploring Task-Based Curriculum Development in a Blended-Learning Conversational Chinese Program 193

Yao Zhang Hill, Kapi'olani Community College, USA
Stephen L. Tschudi, University of Hawai'i at Mānoa, USA

This paper brings task-based language teaching (TBLT) curriculum development principles into the blended learning context, presenting processes and outcomes from a project to develop a task-based thematic unit — asking and giving directions — in a hybrid web-based university-level class focused on listening and speaking skills in Mandarin Chinese. The authors follow the principled task-based curriculum design phases informed by Long and Crookes (1993) and Long and Norris (2000). Unit-based development made the workload manageable and provided an important experimental space for the instructors to best align task-based principles with online language instruction. First, the context of the project and its theoretical TBLT curriculum development framework are established. The distinct processes of needs analysis, materials development, task sequencing and teaching methods, and assessment methods adopted to meet the special requirements of the class are presented, along with a preliminary formative and summative evaluation of the teaching model. The conclusion discusses the theoretical and practical implications of the project.

Chapter 17

Mobile devices can motivate learners through moving language learning from predominantly classroom–based contexts into contexts that are free from time and space. The increasing development of
new applications can offer valuable support to the language learning process and can provide a basis
for a new self regulated and personal approach to learning. A key challenge for language teachers is
to actively explore the potential of mobile technologies in their own learning so that they can support
students in using them. The aim of this paper is first to describe the basic theoretical framework of Mobile Learning and Personal Learning Environments. Secondly, it intends to assist language teachers and
learners in building their own Mobile Personal Learning Environment providing a useful classification
of iPhone applications with a description and examples. The paper concludes with the proposal of ideas
for practical, personal language learning scenarios, piloted in an Italian language learning context.

Chapter 18

After speculation in literature about the nature of Personal Learning Environments, research in the design
and development of PLEs is now in progress. This paper reports on the first phase of the authors' research
on PLE, the identification process of what potential users would consider important components, applications, and tools in a PLE. The methodology included surveying "super-users" on their use of existing
tools, applications and systems and their preferences in learning, in order to enhance the development of
a PLE and reach a specification that potential learners will find useful and empowering in their learning.
The research resulted in suggestions on factors affecting technology use and uptake, human factors and
attitudes, and interface design that need to be factored in the design and development of a PLE.

This article reports on the implementation and impact of two blended models of teacher professional
learning that promote innovative classroom practice and improved literacy and numeracy in six school
districts in Ontario, Canada. The Advanced Broadband Enabled Learning Program (ABEL), situated at
York University in Toronto, Ontario, Canada, transforms how teachers learn and teach through a strategic blend of face-to-face interaction, technological tools and resources, online interaction and support.
Learning Connections (LC), its sister project, uses the same model to improve literacy and numeracy
in school districts. Research into the impact of both programs reveals increased student engagement
and achievement, enhanced teacher efficacy, and improved results in literacy and numeracy. This report
presents the findings from two participant surveys conducted in one large suburban board just north of
Toronto, and one large rural board in Northern Ontario, and demonstrates how the working definition of
literacy that teachers use in the classroom is being transformed by their use of technology in the classroom.

This paper examines the professional implications for teachers and managers in new and evolving forms of professional development using Web 2.0 tools in a European context. Research findings are presented from the "Creative Use of Media" learning event developed through a European eTwinning Learning Lab initiative in spring of 2009. The Creative use of the Media online learning event supported a series of initiatives celebrating the European Year of Creativity and Innovation and involved 135 participants from 27 countries. The key objective was to introduce a range of learning themes constructed around a phenomenon-based inquiry model, which supported interdisciplinary approaches and collaborative online learning methodologies to stimulate new teaching and learning rationales. Digital Web 2.0 technology was used as an independent creative medium and as a powerful facilitating tool to enhance and blend with the more traditional forms of visual, audiovisual and multimedia inquiry. In developing models encapsulating risk taking and experimentation this online learning project supported a general principle that future education models and professional development would be based on social learning and "customer-driven collaborative knowledge building" in relation to open source materials.

Preface

PROMOTING INTEGRATED TECHNOLOGIES FOR INNOVATION AND CHANGE: AN OVERVIEW OF THE IMPLICATIONS FOR VIRTUAL AND PERSONAL LEARNING ENVIRONMENTS

INTRODUCTION

The term Information and Communication Technology (ICT) incorporates two key aspects of the changing worldview associated with the network society. One is the easy access or increasingly overabundance of information, at any time or in any place (Baron, 2009). The second is the emphasis on communication. These new technologies are significant in terms of the opportunities they present for learners to build relationships with one another, the fact that they have achieved an almost "normalised" state (Bax, 2003), and that they aim to improve communication between individuals and organizations. The growing presence of ICTs in education since the early 1990s has been the result of an increasing awareness by national and international policy makers of the need to prepare learners for the challenge of 21st century skills (Economist, 2012). Today's students and educators are living through an information revolution, a process which reflects the transition to a globalised economy with a high degree of national and international interdependence (Lockard & Pegrum, 2007; Luke, 2003). Significant investment in ICTs by national governments is indicative of its increasing importance in policy terms. This investment reflects the idea that technology can enhance learning outcomes and the growing realization that students' ICT literacy skills have to develop in order for national economies to remain competitive in an increasingly interconnected world (Negroponte, 1995). Where once such a rationale was clear for more vocational disciplines and training purposes, now it is equally applicable to a range of other disciplines, where educators have sought to foreground the importance of cross-cultural skills and information technology alongside traditional content based learning (Neville, 2009).

In place of face-to-face or presence-based learning new forms of teaching and learning have been promoted alongside these new digital devices of the information age, from blended learning to e-learning, from mobile learning to second generation Internet or Web 2.0 applications (Bruns, 2008; Nivala, 2009). Technology is supporting the development of new approaches to lifelong access to education via a focus on anyone, anytime, anywhere learning (Ito, 2009; Ito et al., 2010; Jenkins, 1992). The new technologies support open and distance learning and the goal of realizing the type of flexible and reflective learning demanded by the information society that is available 24/7 (Kolb, 1984). If these visions are to be achieved, however, the challenge is to ensure that the new learning technologies promote rather than inhibit the spread of learning opportunities (Norton, Tiley, Newstead & Franklin-Stokes, 2001). While the new technologies have found a place in the mainstream, they are also being used to re-enfranchise elements of today's disaffected youth, subgroups, or minority cultures (Goodfellow, 2006). The tremendous investment in ICT projects and programmes around the world, from the European Union to the United Nations' UNESCO, attest to the role policy makers ascribe to its ability to narrow or span the so-called digital divide and to promote social inclusion (Oblinger, 2004; Oblinger & Oblinger, 2005).

New learning technologies generate a lot of excitement and a lot of funding and sponsorship as they are often driven by commercial rather than primarily pedagogical objectives (Buckingham, 2007). One-to-one laptop programmes around the world, as well as the use of Interactive Whiteboards and digital gaming (Squire, 2002; Thomas & Schmid, 2010), are two prominent examples of this. Through a lack of strategic planning and concern for appropriate integration, they also generate of lot resistance, failure, and often, a considerable waste of resources. ICT equipment can and often is increasingly made available to people disenfranchised from traditional modes of education, but this access to the physical equipment does little to improve real access if they do not know how to use it, and the trainers have never been properly trained. The shortcomings of many educational projects based on significant injections of funding stem from being high on good intentions but low on overcoming issues related to training and integration (Cuban, 1986).

Over the last decade there has been a growing focus on how learners use and experience learning in technology-mediated contexts. In this context, learners are typically perceived as creators of knowledge and content (Bennett, Maton & Kervin, 2008; de Freitas & Maharg, 2011; Palfrey, 2008; Pegrum, 2009). Nevertheless, more critical research is required on the diversity of student use of technologies in ICT enabled learning contexts, as well as their perceptions of computer-mediated learning, from digital gaming to virtual worlds (Bogost, 2007; Brown & Murray, 2005; Peterson, 2010, 2011). In technology-based learning, there has been a movement away from tutor-centred models of instruction to user-generated content and participatory and collaborative forms of learning (Gromik, 2012; Prensky, 2001, 2005, 2007).

An important aspect of this is to what extent digital age learners are acquiring the skills required to be effective at critical reading without the active participation of educators in the process (Purushotma, Thorne & Wheatley, 2008; Reinders, 2012). The role of the educator is not merely to satisfy learner expectations. Although the case for collaborative learning has been repeatedly made, pedagogical models have not emerged that clearly identify strategies for realising it (Rheingold, 2003). It is important to understand the growing awareness of the intersection of digital literacies and ICT skills, the importance of effective national policies on learning, and economic competitiveness within a globalized world (Lankshear & Knobel, 2008).

In this context, second-generation Internet applications in particular have been heralded as the harbingers of a radical transformation of pedagogy that replaces the "read-only Internet" (Web 1.0) with the "read/write web" (Web 2.0)—establishing increased potential for student participation, higher quality instructor feedback, as well as enhanced interactivity and collaboration through the development of user-generated content (Comas-Quinn & Mardomingo, 2011; Sykes, Oskoz & Thorne, 2008). Significant changes in the way people use the World Wide Web have occurred since the emergence of the second generation of the Internet in 2003 (Roberts & Foehr, 2008; Tapscott, 2009). As Warschauer and Grimes (2007) argue, "there is little doubt that the ways people make use of the Web have qualitatively changed in the last few years" (p. 2). The differences between the first and second generation of the Web are concerned with "an evolution from the *linking of information* to the *linking of people*" (p. 2). Web 2.0 is having a particular effect on modes of communication (Soloman & Schrum, 2007; Warschauer, 2011; Zheng, Young, Brewer & Wagner, 2009), especially in relation to new ways of interacting with one another, as well as how people participate and collaborate, both in and outside of learning environments (Sharpe, Beetham & de Freitas, 2010; Terdiman, 2010; Thomas, 2009).

In methodological terms these trends are associated with a shift towards social constructivist theories of teaching and learning, which foregrounds the importance of task-based learning (TBL), project-based learning (PBL) and personal learning environments (PLEs) (Selwyn, 2011a, 2011b; Selwyn, Potter &

Crammer, 2010; Thomas, 2011a, 2011b; Thomas & Reinders, 2010). Research by the British Educational Communications and Technology Agency (BECTA, 2006) identified that learning could be supported by the use of the new digital technologies in five main ways:

- Greater choice in learning opportunities and modes for all learners.
- Learners have increased motivation for and engagement in learning.
- Fewer learners under-perform or fail to succeed in education.
- There is improved child safety and protection.
- Practitioners collaborate and share good practice and learning resources. (see also, UNESCO, 2012a, 2012b, 2012c).

BECTA's research goes even further and attempts to situate this vision of a Web 2.0 pedagogy in a wider educational policy context of e-strategy. Web 2.0 social software can also help, it suggests, by:

- Tackling social equity by reducing inequality in educational opportunity, targeting technology for learning support and resources to those who need it most.
- Narrowing achievement gaps by applying technology to increase opportunity and engagement with under-achieving groups.
- Personalizing education—providing greater customization, match to individual needs and greater choice and opportunity for learners and developing more responsive and flexible arrangements for learning both in and outside of formal curricula.
- Exploring different and transformed models for delivering personalized educational services to users, particularly to under-achieving, hard to reach and disengaged groups.

When stated in such terms, this is a compelling vision of a new pedagogy mediated by digital technologies. Much of it however is based on assumptions about the ICT skills contemporary students are thought to possess and more specific and detailed research needs to be done in specific disciplines in order to map these new contours.

This collection of twenty chapters engages with some of the most important areas of research arising from this context and presents interventions from a range of international educators and researchers. The book is divided into three parts focusing on 'technologies,' 'innovation' and 'change' respectively and presents a snapshot of contemporary research in the field.

AN OVERVIEW OF THIS BOOK

Section 1: Technologies

In Section 1, there are seven chapters each addressing a range of technologies that have influenced the direction of presence-based and virtual education. In chapter 1, "Learning Molecular Structures in a Tangible Augmented Reality Environment," Asai and Takase focus on an area that has the potential to make a significant contribution to virtual environments over the next five to ten years (Dede, 2002). Using augmented reality (AR) technologies in a tabletop environment, the article explores how enables learners to observe three-dimensional molecular structures. The research highlights how the AR technologies aided the faster identification of molecular structures than students who merely had access to traditional PC environments utilizing a more limited Web browser experience. AR was shown to induce a greater level motivation and enjoyment on behalf of the students and they were able to achieve enhanced manipulation and presence of the biological structures as a result.

Since around 2005, Web 2.0 technologies have been associated with the issue of increased learner engagement. In a corporate work-based training context, wikis and blogs have been the two most frequently adopted Web 2.0 tools. In "Organisational Blogging: The Problem of Engagement," Baxter, Connolly, and Stansfield discuss this area with research on an internal organisational blog that is used with an HR division of a large public sector company in the United Kingdom. The research adopts a qualitative approach utilising case studies to explore how members of staff use the blog and its impact on facilitating learning within the organisation. Findings from the research underline the importance of staff training prior to implementation and the chapter outlines a number of insights about organizational management and behaviour in an environment in which technology is being integrated with new users for the first time. The chapter will be of particular practical value in the work-based training field in which Enterprise 2.0 solutions are being developed.

The remainder of the chapters in this section focus on digital gaming (Shaffer, 2008). In the first of these chapters, "Game-Like Technology Innovation Education," Magnussen explores the use of games in school science education in a Danish public school with students aged 13-15, focusing in particular on the challenges presented by these technologies in terms of methodology and design issues (Gee, 2007, 2008, 2011). Using a scenario in which learners are involved with playing the role of a company head whose role is to produce intelligent music technology, it was designed to examine how games can be used to simulate practical learning situations.

Games can also be used to enable learners to simulate their engagement with risk and uncertainty. In "'World of Uncertainty' Game for Decision-Makers," Jyldyz Tabyldy Kyzy outlines a proposal for a game in which the objective is to enable learners to examine their subjective uncertainty and receive digital feedback on their performance. Learners engage with a complex array of simulations in which they have the opportunity to estimate probability and improve their accuracy.

The theme of simulation is also evident in "The Siren Song of Digital Simulation: Games, Procedural Rhetoric, and the Process of Historical Education," in which Jerremie Clyde examines how digital games can be used to teach history in post-secondary education. Contrasting procedural rhetoric with that of history themed digital simulations, an evaluation of current practices in history education is articulated prior to a deeper engagement with how simulations are an ineffective way to realize learning goals. Clyde argues for a re-evaluation of the role of simulations and more research on how digital games can be used to involve learners in historical reconstruction and historical argument.

The use of mobile devices to promote digital gaming experiences is evident in an increasing number of research studies (Kukulska-Hulme, 2009; Kukulska-Hulme & Jones, 2011). Petley, Attewell, and Savill-Smith's chapter, "Not Just Playing Around: The MoLeNET Experience of Using Games Technologies to Support Teaching and Learning," describes a three-year research study exploring the potential role of mobile learning in English post-14 education. The MoLeNET project is a collaborative project that explores handheld devices and the use of three platforms, Sony PSP, Nintendo DS, and the Nintendo Wii to promote strategies for engaging learners who require support primarily due to learning problems or disabilities. Other aspects of the research suggest that these gaming platforms can also be used to aid the development of academic and social skills as well as having the potential to explore other issues such games for healthcare.

In the final chapter in this opening section of the book, Hollins and Whitton provide a thorough evaluation of research to date on the potential of gaming in education in their chapter, "From the Games Industry: Ten Lessons for Game-Based Learning." Drawing on research from entertainment games, the authors highlight a series of opportunities and challenges that will face educational policy makers and examines ways in which the field of digital games in education may evolve. In conclusion, the chapter is especially useful for identifying ten key points that can be used in the development of digital game-based learning in the future.

Section 2: Innovation

The second section of the book focuses on seven chapters that address areas of research including social networking sites, the use of learning platforms for collaborative learning, video conferencing, digital gaming, and personal learning environments.

In Chapter 8, "Social Networking Sites and Language Learning," Brick explores LiveMocha, a popular website that is based on the principle of social networking and enables language learners all over the world to develop peer-to-peer language exchange. Focusing on a small-scale case study that took place over three months, the chapter explores the features of LiveMocha and learner perceptions of them. Results suggest that learners valued immediate peer feedback, as well as the flexibility that enabled them to interact with native speakers in the target language utilizing both synchronous and asynchronous technologies. While learners also identified challenges in using a social network platform to learn languages based on LiveMocha's peer model, particularly the potential abuse associated with cyber-flirting, the study presents some valuable evidence of the potential role of social platforms in learning contexts.

Armitage's chapter, "Using Learning Platforms to Support Communication and Effective Learning," continues the focus on personal learning, describing the process that led to the development of online learning resources for the National Diploma in Information Technology in the UK. The chapter indicates how personal learning is a key theme at this level of education and how personalized learning is aligned with the objective of giving learners more control over the direction, progression and outcomes of their learning. A central element of the resources attempt to promote learners' metacognitive skills thus encouraging them to reflect on their learning as part of the learning process.

The importance of these themes is continued in Hunter's chapter, "Connected Learning in an Australian Technology Program: A Case Study," which discusses important developments in Web 2.0 and the digital classroom in an Australian context. The significant investment in digital infrastructure by the Australia the New South Wales Department of Education and Training (NSWDET) represents an investment of approximately $AUS 158 million spread over 2,240 schools. The target of this investment is to produce the "connected school" of the twenty-first century in which learners can engage in collaborative and communicative activity according to the principle of 'anywhere, anytime' learning. Hunter's case study provides a detailed overview of the implementation of the project, and it should be valuable for policy makers and those responsible for ICT planning and integration.

The focus on learner engagement continues in Chapter 11, in which Iacovides, Aczel, Scanlon, Taylor, and Woods from the UK Open University discuss "Motivation, Engagement, and Learning through Digital Games." The authors address the argument that digital games have the potential to improve learner participation, while also recognizing the inherent challenges they present in terms of being integrated into formal learning environments. Educators need to understand how games motivate and engage learners and the authors identify the need for more research that will guide this process in future.

The requirement for a more theoretical approach to games-based education research is also evident in the penultimate chapter of this section, in which Khan and Reed examine a group of computer games called Neurogames that focus on enhancing reading and basic maths. "An Evaluation of Neurogames®: A Collection of Computer Games Designed to Improve Literacy and Numeracy," presents research from a study using matched pairs within an experimental design. Findings suggest that the use of the Neurogames led to a "significant increase" in mathematical and reading ability compared to learners in the control groups and further research is called for to explore how this potential can best be harnessed.

The final chapter in this section examines mobile learning and the potential role of smartphones in personal learning environments. In "Personal Smartphones in Primary School: Devices for a PLE?" Honegger and Neff articulate the goals and initial results of a two year case study in a European primary school in which teachers and learners were provided with smartphones to aid learning. Costs were covered by the school and learners were given access to the web in order to facilitate learning. The research explored how the potential of the devices could be harnessed in relation to a range of skills including reading, writing, and communication using a phone's convergent technologies, both in and outside of school.

Section 3: Change

The final section contains seven articles in a range of topics covering future definitions of personal learning environments, task-based learning, blended learning approaches to course delivery, mobile learning, and the use of Web 2.0 tools (Lai & Li, 2011). In "Personal Learning Environments: Concept or Technology?" Fiedler and Väljataga provide a critical overview of research on personal learning environments to date, noting a series of rather contradictory approaches. These differences and contradictions are a result of the tensions between the possibilities offered by digital technologies and the restrictions and expectations offered by traditional learning contexts. In response, the chapter argues against the identification of PLEs with exclusively Web 2.0 technologies, a tendency that has been strikingly evident over the last few years, and to examine the underlying educational and curricula infrastructure which has remained unchanged. If PLEs are to be realized, then new forms of infrastructure will also need to be developed to match the innovative opportunities presented by the digital technologies.

This discussion is continued in "Making it Rich and Personal: Crafting an Institutional Personal Learning Environment," in which White and Davis consider the institutional resistances within universities to implementing radical changes such as those required for personal learning environments. While pedagogical change is driven forward by academic researchers, university services typically have more "risk-averse" philosophies due to the financial implications of such changes. White and Davis discuss a case study in which a strategy for overcoming these resistances was a crucial element in the process, as was the need to prepare learning environments fit for learners in the twenty-first century.

The turn towards to personalized learning has often been allied with task- or inquiry-based forms of teaching and learning (Lave & Wenger, 1991). In "Exploring Task-Based Curriculum Development in a Blended-Learning Conversational Chinese Program," Hill and Tschudi explore the use of task-based approaches in a blended learning context. Set in the context of task-based language teaching (TBLT), the authors present the results of their research from an online Chinese course (Van den Branden, 2006; Van den Branden, Bygate & Norris, 2008). Based on a rigorous engagement with the task-based approach in terms of needs analysis and task sequencing, the chapter demonstrates how online platforms can also be used to develop task-based approaches and such research will be important for the future of personalized learning approaches.

The focus on computer-assisted language learning (CALL) contexts (Beatty, 2010), where so much innovation with digital technologies is often apparent, is the subject of the "My Personal Mobile Language Learning Environment: An Exploration and Classification of Language Learning Possibilities Using the iPhone" by Perifanou. The author discusses how mobiles can be used to offer language learners a "self-regulated" and "personal approach to learning." Enabling learning in a variety of new spaces and places, the chapter presents a theoretical framework for establishing a PLE in a mobile language learning context. Moreover, the chapter presents a practical overview and classification of a number of iPhone applications that can be used in an educational context. In conclusion, a design for a PLE utilizing mobile learning for Italian language learners is outlined (Chinnery, 2006).

The design of a PLE is also the concern of the next chapter, "Factors Affecting the Design and Development of a Personal Learning Environment: Research on Super-Users." Fournier and Kop discuss their research on user expectations of PLEs. The surveys of users were comprehensive and sought to gain an insight into which features and tools are required by users and which they will be able to empower their learning. The findings of the research are now being used to design an interface for a future PLE.

In the penultimate chapter of the volume, Kitchener, Murphy, and Lebans engage with a number of themes from this section in their chapter, "Developing New Literacies through Blended Learning: Challenges and Lessons Learned in Ontario, Canada." The chapter discusses the implications of research arising from two blended models of teacher professional learning, each focusing on the innovative use of technology to enhance literacy and numeracy in the Ontario school district. The chapter explores the Advanced Broadband Enabled Learning Program (ABEL), situated at York University in Toronto, examining how a blend of F2F interaction, e-resources and tools, and online support can be used to enhance learning environments. The second project, Learning Connections (LC), explores the same mix of teaching methods but is focused on enhancing literacy and numeracy. Data from both projects is noteworthy in that it suggests enhancement gains in terms of both achievement and learning engagement in relation to literacy and numeracy.

In the final chapter, "Creative Networks of Practice Using Web 2.0 Tools," Orava and Worrall discuss the role that Web 2.0 tools can play in teacher professional development (Wang & Chern, 2008). Arising from a European eTwinning Learning Lab initiative in spring of 2009, the chapter reports on the creative use of the media online learning event, which involved participants from over 27 countries. Based on an inquiry led model of education that encouraged learning collaboration and creativity, the event introduced new ways of instruction with innovative Web 2.0 tools and facilitated a blended mode of learning that incorporated visual, audiovisual and multimedia types of enquiry. Such inquiry based model promoted risk-taking models of education within a social learning framework in order to engage learners in "customer-driven collaborative knowledge building" utilizing open source and open access resources.

These twenty chapters present a snapshot of the international research currently being undertaken in learning technologies, indicating the importance of trends in virtual and personalised learning. Including research from approximately forty educators and researchers from over ten countries, it is hoped the book will be of value to educators, academics, and policy makers working with digital technologies in education today.

Michael Thomas
University of Central Lancashire, UK

REFERENCES

Baron, N. S. (2009). *Always on: Language in an online and mobile world.* New York, NY: Oxford University Press.

Bax, S. (2003). CALL—past, present and future. *System, 31,* 13–28. doi:10.1016/S0346-251X(02)00071-4

Beatty, K. (2010). *Teaching and researching computer-assisted language learning* (2nd ed.). London, UK: Pearson.

BECTA. (2006). *BECTA review 2006. Evidence on the progress of ICT in education.* London, UK: Author.

Bennett, S., Maton, K., & Kervin, L. (2008). The 'digital natives' debate: A critical review of the evidence. *British Journal of Educational Technology, 38*(5), 775–786. doi:10.1111/j.1467-8535.2007.00793.x

Bogost, I. (2007). *Persuasive games: The expressive power of videogames.* Cambridge, MA: MIT Press.

Brown, M., & Murray, F. (2005). A culture of technology critique. In M. Cooper (Ed.), *Proceedings of the 33rd Annual Australian Teacher Education Association Conference, Griffith University, Centre for Professional Development.*

Bruns, A. (2008). *Blogs, Wikipedia, Second Life, and beyond: From production to produsage.* Frankfurt, Germany: Peter Lang.

Buckingham, D. (2007). *Beyond technology: Children's learning in the age of digital culture.* Malden, MA: Polity.

Chinnery, G. M. (2006). Going to the MALL: Mobile assisted language learning. *Language Learning & Technology, 10*(1), 9–16.

Comas-Quinn, A., & Mardomingo, R. (2011). Language learning on the move: A review of mobile blogging tasks and their potential . In Díaz-Vera, J. E. (Ed.), *Left to my own devices: Learner autonomy and mobile-assisted language learning* (p. 4765). Bingley, UK: Emerald Group Publishing. doi:10.1108/S2041-272X(2012)0000006006

Cuban, L. (1986). *Teachers and machines: The classroom use of technology since 1920.* New York, London: Teachers College, Columbia University.

de Freitas, S., & Maharg, P. (Eds.). (2011). *Digital games and learning.* London, UK: Continuum.

Dede, C. (2002). Augmented reality through ubiquitous computing. *Learning and Leading with Technology, 29*(8), 13.

Economist. (2012, June 26). *Let them eat tablets. Trying to stop the rot in Thailand's schools by giving out tablet computers.* Retrieved from http://www.economist.com/node/21556940

Gartner. (2011). *Gartner's hype cycle special report for 2011.* Retrieved from http://www.gartner.com/DisplayDocument?id=1758314&ref='g_fromdoc'

Gee, J. P. (2007). *What video games have to teach us about learning and literacy.* London, UK: Palgrave Macmillan. doi:10.1145/950566.950595

Gee, J. P. (2008). *Policy brief: Getting over the slump: Innovation strategies to promote children's learning*. New York, NY: The Joan Ganz Cooney Center.

Gee, J. P. (2011). *Beyond mindless progressivism*. Retrieved April 10, 2011, from http://www.james-paulgee.com/node

Goodfellow, R. (2006). From "equal access" to "widening participation": The discourse of equity in the age of e-learning . In Lockard, J., & Pegrum, M. (Eds.), *Brave new classroom: Democratic education and the internet* (pp. 55–74). Bern, Switzerland: Peter Lang.

Gromik, N. (2012). Cell phone video recording feature as a language learning tool: A case study. *Computers & Education, 58*(1), 223–230. doi:10.1016/j.compedu.2011.06.013

Ito, M. (2009). *Engineering play: A cultural history of children's software*. Cambridge, MA: MIT Press.

Ito, M. (2010). *Hanging out, messing around, and geeking out: Kids living and learning with new media*. Cambridge, MA: The MIT Press.

Jenkins, H. (1992). *Textual poachers: Television fans and participatory culture*. New York, NY: Routledge.

Kolb, D. A. (1984). *Experiential learning*. Englewood Cliffs, NJ: Prentice Hall.

Kukulska-Hulme, A. (2009). Will mobile learning change language learning? *ReCALL, 21*(2), 157–165. doi:10.1017/S0958344009000202

Kukulska-Hulme, A., & Jones, C. (2011). The next generation: Design and the infrastructure of learning in a mobile and networked world . In Olofsson, A. D., & Ola Lindberg, J. (Eds.), *Informed design of educational technologies in higher education: Enhanced learning and teaching* (pp. 57–78). Hershey, PA: Information Science Reference. doi:10.4018/978-1-61350-080-4.ch004

Lai, C., & Li, G. (2011). Technology and task-based language teaching: A critical review. *CALICO, 28*(2).

Lankshear, C., & Knobel, M. (Eds.). (2008). *Digital literacies: Concepts, policies and practices*. Bern, Switzerland: Peter Lang.

Lave, J., & Wenger, E. (1991). *Situated learning. Legitimate peripheral participation*. Cambridge, UK: University of Cambridge Press. doi:10.1017/CBO9780511815355

Lockard, J., & Pegrum, M. (Eds.). (2007). *Brave new classroom: Democratic education and in the internet*. Bern, Switzerland: Peter Lang.

Luke, C. (2003). Pedagogy, connectivity, multimodality, and interdisciplinarity. *Reading Research Quarterly, 38*(3), 397–413.

Negroponte, N. (1995). *Being digital*. London, UK: Coronet.

Neville, D. (2009). In the classroom: Digital game-based learning in second language acquisition. *Language and Education, 4*(6), 37–41.

Nivala, M. (2009). Information society strategies: Simple answers for complex problems: Education and ICT in Finnish. *Media Culture & Society, 31*, 433–448. doi:10.1177/0163443709102715

Norton, L., Tilley, A., Newstead, S., & Franklyn-Stokes, A. (2001). The pressure of assessment in undergraduate courses and their effects on student behaviours. *Assessment & Evaluation in Higher Education, 26*, 269–284. doi:10.1080/02602930120052422

Oblinger, D. G. (2004). The next generation of educational engagement. *Journal of Interactive Media in Education, 8*. Retrieved June 15, 2012, from http://www-jime.open.ac.uk/2004/8/oblinger-2004-8-disc-paper.html

Oblinger, D. G., & Oblinger, J. L. (2005). *Educating the Net generation.* EDUCAUSE. Retrieved June 15, 2012, from http://www.educause.edu/educatingthenetgen/

Palfrey, J., & Gasser, U. (2008). *Born digital: Understanding the first generation of digital natives.* New York, NY: Basic Books.

Pegrum, M. (2009). *From blogs to bombs: The future of digital technologies in education.* Perth, Australia: University of Western Australia.

Peterson, M. (2010). Massively multiplayer onilne role-playing games (MMORPGs) as arenas for language learning. *Computer Assisted Language Learning, 19*(1), 79–103. doi:10.1080/09588220600804087

Peterson, M. (2011). Digital gaming and second language development: Japanese learners' interactions in a MMORPG. *Journal of Digital Culture & Education, 3*(1), 56–73.

Prensky, M. (2001). Digital natives, digital immigrants. *Horizon, 9*(5), 1–6. doi:10.1108/10748120110424816

Prensky, M. (2005). What can you learn from a cell phone? Almost anything! *Innovate, 1*(5). Retrieved January 16, 2006, from http://www.innovateonline.info/index.php?view=article&id=83

Prensky, M. (2007). *Digital game-based learning* (2nd ed.). St. Paul, MN: Paragon House.

Purushotma, R., Thorne, S. L., & Wheatley, J. (2008). *10 key principles for designing video games for foreign language learning.* Retrieved February 25, 2011, from http://knol.google.com/k/10-key-principles-for-designing-video-games-for-foreign-language-learning#

Rankin, Y., Morrison, D., McKenzie, M., Gooch, B., & Shute, M. (2009). Time will tell: In-game social interactions that facilitate second language acquisition. In R. M. Young (Ed.), *Proceedings of the 4th International Conference on Digital Games* (pp. 161-168). New York, NY: ACM.

Reinders, H. (Ed.). (2012). *Digital games in language learning and teaching.* Basingstoke, UK: Palgrave Macmillan.

Rheingold, H. (2003). *Smart mobs: The next social revolution.* Cambridge, MA: Perseus.

Roberts, D. F., & Foehr, U. G. (2008). Trends in media use. *Children and Electronic Media, 18*(1), 39–62.

Selwyn, N. (2011a). *Schools and schooling in the digital age: A critical analysis.* London, UK: Routledge.

Selwyn, N. (2011b). *Education and technology: Key issues and debates.* London, UK: Continuum.

Selwyn, N., Potter, J., & Cranmer, S. (2010). *Primary schools and ICT: Learning from pupil perspectives.* London, UK: Continuum.

Shafer, D. W. (2006). *How computer games help children learn*. New York, NY: Palgrave Macmillan. doi:10.1057/9780230601994

Sharpe, R., Beetham, H., & de Freitas, S. (2010). *Rethinking learning for a digital age: How learners are shaping their own experiences*. London, UK: Routledge.

Solomon, G., & Schrum, L. (2007). *Web 2.0: New tools, new schools*. Washington, DC: International Society for Technology in Education.

Squire, K. (2002). Cultural framing of computer/video games. *International Journal of Computer Game Research, 2*(1). Retrieved March 20, 2011, from http://www.gamestudies.org/0102/squire/

Steinkuehler, C. (2007). Massively multiplayer online gaming as a constellation of literacy practices. *E-learning, 4*(3), 297–318. doi:10.2304/elea.2007.4.3.297

Sykes, J., Oskoz, A., & Thorne, S. L. (2008). Web 2.0, synthetic immersive environments, and mobile resources for language education. *CALICO Journal, 25*(3), 528–546.

Tapscott, D. (2009). *Grown up digital: How the net generation is changing your world*. London, UK: McGraw Hill.

Terdiman, D. (2010). *Where virtual worlds once ruled, FarmVille dominates*. Retrieved March 30, 2011, from http://news.cnet.com/8301-13772_3-10460293-52.html

Thomas, M. (Ed.). (2009). *Handbook of research on Web 2.0 and second language learning*. Hershey, PA: Information Science Reference. doi:10.4018/978-1-60566-190-2

Thomas, M. (Ed.). (2011a). *Deconstructing digital natives: Young people, technology and the new literacies*. London, New York: Routledge.

Thomas, M. (Ed.). (2011b). *Digital education: Opportunities for social collaboration*. London, UK: Palgrave Macmillan.

Thomas, M., & Reinders, H. (Eds.). (2010). *Task-based language learning and teaching with technology*. London, UK: Continuum.

Thomas, M., & Schmid, E. C. (Eds.). (2010). *Interactive whiteboards: Theory, research and practice*. Hershey, PA: IGI Global. doi:10.4018/978-1-61520-715-2

Thorne, S. L. (2008). Transcultural communication in open internet environments and massively multiplayer online games . In Magnan, S. (Ed.), *Mediated discourse online* (pp. 305–327). Amsterdam, The Netherlands: Benjamins.

UNESCO. (2012a). *Mobile learning for teachers: Global themes*. UNESCO working paper series on mobile learning. Paris, France: UNESCO.

UNESCO. (2012b). *Turning on mobile learning: Global themes*. UNESCO working paper series on mobile learning. Paris, France: UNESCO.

UNESCO. (2012c). *Turning on mobile learning in African and the Middle East: Illustrative initiatives and policy implications*. Paris, France: UNESCO.

Van den Branden, K. (Ed.). (2006). *Task-based language education: From theory to practice*. Cambridge, UK: Cambridge University Press. doi:10.1017/CBO9780511667282

Van den Branden, K., Bygate, M., & Norris, J. M. (Eds.). (2009). *Task-based language teaching: A reader*. Amsterdam, Philadelphia: John Benjamins.

Wang, S., & Chern, J. (2008). The new era of "school 2.0" – teaching with pleasure, not pressure. *Proceedings of World Conference on Educational Multimedia, Hypermedia and Telecommunications 2008*. Chesapeake, VA: Association for the Advancement of Computing in Education.

Warschauer, M. (2011). *Learning in the cloud: How (and why) to transform schools with digital media*. New York, NY: Teachers College Press.

Warschauer, M., & Grimes, D. (2007). Audience, authorship, and artifact: The emergent semiotics of Web 2.0. *Annual Review of Applied Linguistics, 27*, 1–23. doi:10.1017/S0267190508070013

Zheng, D., Young, M. F., Brewer, R. B., & Wagner, M. (2009). Attitude and self-efficacy change: English language learning in virtual worlds. *CALICO Journal, 27*, 205–231.

Section 1
Technologies

Chapter 1
Learning Molecular Structures in a Tangible Augmented Reality Environment

Kikuo Asai
The Open University of Japan, Japan

Norio Takase
FiatLux Co. Ltd., Japan

ABSTRACT

This article presents the characteristics of using a tangible tabletop environment produced by augmented reality (AR), aimed at improving the environment in which learners observe three-dimensional molecular structures. The authors perform two evaluation experiments. A performance test for a user interface demonstrates that learners with a tangible AR environment were able to complete the task of identifying molecular structures more quickly and accurately than those with a typical desktop-PC environment using a Web browser. A usability test by participants who learned molecular structures and answered relevant questions demonstrates that the environments had no effect on their learning of molecular structures. However, a preference test reveals that learners preferred a more tangible AR environment to a Web-browser environment in terms of overall enjoyment, reality of manipulation, and sense of presence, and vice versa in terms of ease of viewing, experience, and durability.

INTRODUCTION

Emerging technologies offer learners the ability to use three-dimensional (3D) virtual environments for learning. Computer-based systems that support 3D visualization, simulation, navigation, and interaction with a 3D virtual environment have given users various virtual reality (VR) applications such as virtual prototyping, training simulators, and digital museums (Vince, 1998). The synthetic worlds created by VR can improve learners' acquisition of theoretical knowledge

DOI: 10.4018/978-1-4666-2467-2.ch001

based on their interactive and individual learning with dynamic multimedia content (Bricken & Byrnes, 1993; Poland, LaVelle & Nichol, 2003; Schmid, 1999). Unlike VR, augmented reality (AR) superimposes virtual objects on a real scene (Azuma, 1997; Milgram & Kishino, 1994; Wellner, Mackay & Gold, 1993). One feature of AR is that it adds scene-linked information to make users' experiences more meaningful and it increases their understanding of the subject (Feiner, MacIntyre & Seligmann, 1993; Klopfer, Squire & Jenkins, 2002; Navab, 2004; Sharma & Molineros, 1997). Another feature is tangible interaction that provides users with an intuitive way of interacting with virtual objects (Poupyrev, Tan, Billinghurst, Kato, Regenbrecht & Tetsutani, 2002; Rekimoto, 1998; Ullmer & Ishii, 1997). Most AR applications using the latter feature enable users to interact with virtual objects through common physical objects such as tiles and paddles with no need for specific devices to directly manipulate the virtual objects (Kato, Billinghurst, Poupyrev, Imamoto, & Tachibana, 2000; Lee, Nelles, Billinghurst & Kim, 2004; Regenbrecht, Baratoff, & Wagner, 2001; Waldner, Hauber, Zauner, Haller & Billinghurst, 2006).

Multimedia systems have provided learners with new ways of interacting with various audiovisual resources. In molecular biology and biochemistry, up-to-date research results can be viewed through high-quality graphics that have been prepared using visualization tools. However, we think that multimedia and printed materials have been used as totally different media in distinct learning environments, each with their own advantages, where learners can only experience learning independently of one another. An AR interface has the potential to bridge the gap between multimedia and printed materials by superimposing multimedia information onto printed media. We believe that the seamless connections between virtual and real worlds can improve interactivity by creating a tangible environment that enables

virtual objects to be manipulated with the physical objects that correspond to them. The basic idea is the same as that in MagicBook, which consists of a transitional AR interface that uses a real book to seamlessly transfer users from reality to virtuality (Billinghurst, Kato & Poupyrev, 2001).

Many AR systems have been developed for demonstrations, with some applications having targeted education. An AR system explaining the Earth-Sun relationship shows seasonal transitions in light and temperature by enabling the virtual Sun and Earth to be physically manipulated with handheld plates that orient their positions to the viewing perspective of the learner (Shelton & Hedley, 2002). Construct3D, a 3D geometric construction tool for teaching mathematics and geometry, provides a basic set of functions for constructing primitive forms (Kaufmann, 2002). Augmented Chemistry is a virtual chemistry laboratory in which users view simple atoms and build complex molecules according to sub-atomic rules (Fjeld, Juchli & Voegtli, 2003). Another molecular-biology viewer augments physical models with molecular properties such as electrostatics, which are produced by computer auto-fabrication ("3D printing") (Gillet, Sanner, Stoffler, Goodsell & Olson, 2004). Even though a number of AR applications have been developed as demonstrations, we think that there has not really been a consensus on the effectiveness of AR within educational contexts.

An empirical study on AR-based applications for a car-door assembly revealed that the performance of tasks depended on the degree of difficulty in assembly and that AR conditions were more suitable for difficult tasks than manual conditions printed on paper (Wiedenmaier, Oehme, Schmidt & Luczak, 2003). In their performance tests, however, it took longer periods of time to complete the assembly tasks in the AR conditions than in the conditions under the supervision of an expert. Experiments related to geometry education found no clear advantages for AR-based geometry training in spatial abilities (Duenser, Steinbugl, Kaufmann & Gluck, 2006), even though the results for Construct3D (described above) preference tests demonstrated that AR conditions had advantages over the traditional desktop conditions in usability such as superior control, better learning, improved usefulness, and enhanced satisfaction (Kaufmann & Duenser, 2007). Augmented Chemistry also demonstrated a tangible AR interface had no significant effects on learning, compared to the traditional ball-and-stick model (Fjeld, Fredriksson, Ejdestig, Duca, Botschi, Voegtli & Juchli, 2007). Other qualitative evaluations of chemistry learning using think-aloud protocols and interviews indicated that virtual models tended to be treated as real objects in the AR environment, but they found no clear advantages that AR interaction had on learning compared to interactions with physical ball-and-stick models (Chen, 2006).

Although these empirical studies on the AR-based applications have demonstrated that the AR environments improved interactivity as a user interface, they found no evidence of the relationship between the advantages on a user interface and the effectiveness on learning. Besides, these results were based on the comparison of the AR environments with the real environments of manipulating physical objects, though many useful software tools have widely been used for viewing molecular structures. More empirical studies need to be carried out to deeply comprehend tangible AR environments before questions about the pedagogical value of the tangible AR environments can be answered and an AR interface can be effectively used for learning. The following questions were primarily examined in our work.

1. What is unique about the learning experience offered by a tangible AR environment to learners in comparison with a typical desktop-PC environment?
2. How is the tangible AR environment used for learning molecular structures?

CONCEPTUAL FRAMEWORK

Educational use of tangible tabletop environments produced by an AR user interface is embedded in a constructivist approach to learning, theoretically assuming that knowledge and concepts are created through experience and are obtained by interacting with information, tools, and materials as well as activities (Dede, 1995; Duffy & Jonassen, 1992). The constructivist learning environment places emphasis on the learner's rather than the teacher's or instructor's outcomes. Therefore, it is important to implement educational technologies based on learner-centered design (Soloway, 1998).

The AR environment offers advantages in visualization similar to those of the VR environment, encouraging multiple insights into complex information such as volume data, abstract concepts, and 3D structures through various visual methods (Salzman, Dede, Loftin & Chen, 1999). The AR environment differs from the VR environment in that it enhances the real world by superimposing virtual objects onto the real scene. AR obscures the lines between the reality the learner is experiencing and the content being provided by the system, while pertinent information is presented according to the objects in the scene. This information works as a trigger enabling users to extract memories matching the situation and cues associating the event with the memories (Neumann & Majoros, 1998; Shelton & Hedley, 2003). Spatial locations are considered to play an important role in reducing the cost of accessing information and supplementing memory (Alicea, Biocca, Bohil, Owen & Xiao, 2006).

AR technology also provides a learning environment that has unique features that enable viewpoint-based and tangible interactions. Viewpoint-based interactions in learning contexts enrich the real world with information related to scenes being viewed by a learner. The AR environment can allow him/her to interact with information from a first-person perspective by directly constructing knowledge, instead of through third-person symbolic experiences (Dickey, 2005; Winn & Jackson, 1999). Tangible interactions enable us to naturally and intuitively interact with virtual objects by handling their physical counterparts (Klemmer, Nartmann & Takayama, 2006). The embodiment of realistic sensations for virtual objects achieves seamless interactions between physical and computational worlds. The AR environment makes learning authentic by reflecting familiar situations in the real world (Rogers, Scaife, Gabrielli, Smith & Harris, 2002; Zuckerman, Arida & Resnick, 2005), which can establish a foundation for users to cultivate learning initiatives by enabling them to construct knowledge and concepts through dealing with experiential and realistic information.

SYSTEM OVERVIEW

The system that we developed in this work is a simple runtime viewer for visualizing molecular structures by overlaying them onto learning materials printed on paper. The viewer enables us to observe molecular structures with a minimum of functions in a tangible AR environment. Figure 1 has a typical example of viewer use, in which

a protein has been presented in ribbon mode. A learner can study molecular structures by viewing the 3D geometric model from his or her own preferred viewpoint and by reading articles on the paper materials.

The viewer is composed of modules for processing AR images and visualizing molecular structures through a user interface. The image-processing module detects identification markers in video images and recognizes patterns and their positions and orientations inside the markers. The visualization module includes a 3D molecular data loader and a molecular data-rendering system. The rendering system was designed to contain the minimal functions necessary for visualizing 3D molecular structures, i.e., for zooming in and out of molecules, selecting atoms (proteins, nucleic acids, and ligands), changing presentation modes (balls, ball-and-sticks, ribbons, and molecular surfaces), changing colors (amino acids, creatine phosphokinase, and acidity-alkalinity-neutrality), and presenting annotations. The specifications of the viewer system were listed in Table 1. A graphical user interface was designed in the viewer to enable learners to control the visualization functions.

Professors usually use commercially based visualization tools that generally require a high degree of skill for dealing with various functions such as calculation of molecular orbits, calculation of thermal vibration, and structure optimization

Figure 1. Tangible AR environment for observing molecules with ribbon mode

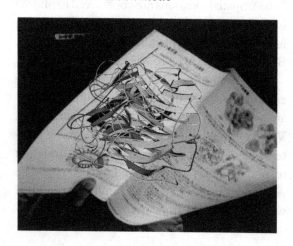

Table 1. Specifications of viewer system

Function	Specifications
Zoom-in and -out molecules	Based on local coordinates for all atoms
Select atoms	Proteins, nucleic acids, and ligands
Change presentation modes	Balls, ball-and-sticks, ribbons, and molecular surfaces
Change colors	Amino acids, creatine phosphokinase, and acidity-alkalinity-neutrality
Present annotations	On/off
Support file format	FiatLux MolFeat Presentation file

Figure 2. Framework for authoring and learning

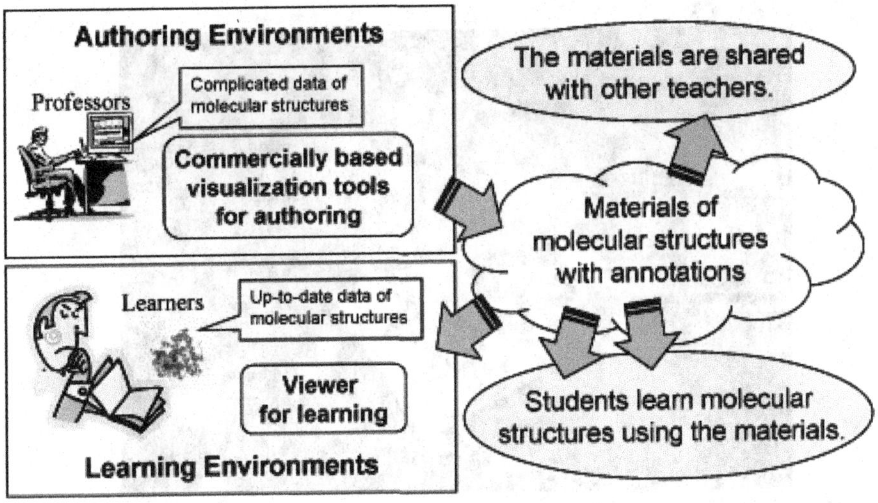

of the ground and transition states, and it is difficult for beginners to use these as a viewer due to complicated parameter settings for appropriately presenting molecular structures. We therefore tried to build a framework (Figure 2) that enabled learners to use a simple runtime program as a viewer for viewing molecular structures, with professors and/or researchers supplying the 3D data including comments and annotations prepared for research, by commercially based visualization tools (Asai, Kobayashi, Kondo & Takase, 2007).

Authoring/editing AR content requires expertise in computer graphics and knowledge about computer programming, which are two of the main reasons why AR has not come to be widely used. Virtual reality modeling language (VRML) is a kind of plain-text scripting language that is versatile for describing 3D objects. We have developed a VRML export function as an optional module in a visualization tool (Asai, Kondo, Kobayashi & Takase, 2006), so that the 3D data on molecular structures can be converted to a VRML format. However, this required us to make the style of visualization of distinct VRML data for the same molecules, e.g., in the presentation of atomic relations and bond conditions. Producing many VRML files per molecule is too

burdensome, and it is not convenient to change files to find a visualization style that a particular learner likes. Therefore, the molecular-structure viewer was designed to directly import the data on molecular structures from the visualization tools as well as enable molecular structures to be viewed with the basic styles. Here, we assumed MolFeat (FiatLux, n.d.) was used as an inexpensive commercial tool with the basic functions that enabled molecular structures to be visualized for research purposes and that enabled them to be authored for presentations and publications.

The viewer system was installed on a Windows PC that had a Web camera. The system requirements are Windows XP as an OS, and a CPU of Pentium IV 2 GHz with 512 MB main memory and 128 MB video RAM or higher is recommended as the specifications of the Windows PC. The system detects and recognizes square markers printed on paper learning materials that works to identify physical objects in the captured scene. ARToolkit (HITLab, n.d.), a set of open-source libraries, was used as an image-processing tool for tracking the objects based on the square markers. Figure 3 shows examples of visualization functions in the viewer: (a) a ball-and-stick mode and (b) a molecule-surface mode for the electrostatic field.

Figure 3. Examples of visualization functions in viewer

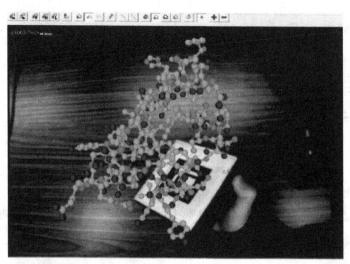

(a) Ball-and-stick mode

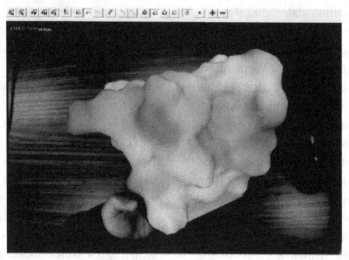

(b) Molecule-surface mode for electrostatic field

METHODOLOGY

The research methodology was based on a user study approach that aimed at empirically evaluating the user interface within the context of applications. The evaluation measures were composed of task performance and user preferences. To illustrate the potential that tangible AR environments afford for learning experiences, the AR system was compared to a Web-browser-based program in which users manipulated molecular structures with a mouse. Two phases of the evaluation were included to measure different aspects. The first phase (Phase I) was an investigation into how tangible AR environments work as a user interface for manipulating 3D objects. The second phase (Phase II) was an example of how tangible AR environments can be used for learning molecular biology or biochemistry.

Participants

Forty-two undergraduate students participated in this study. These students came from various departments and not all of them had molecular biology or biochemistry as majors. The characteristics of the participants are listed in Table 2. Although the proportion of males to females coincided with the ratio of experience they had in studying chemistry at high school or university, this did not mean that the male participants had experience and the females had none. All the participants had normal vision and had no previous experience with an AR system for viewing 3D molecular structures.

Materials

A Web browser with plug-ins for visualizing molecular structures was used as a familiar learning environment to enable a tangible AR environment to be compared. The plug-ins gave the Web browser the same functions as a tangible AR environment. The 3D position of molecular structures in terms of their position, orientation, and size was controlled with a mouse.

In Phase I, the task was to determine whether two molecules would be identical or different in structure and composition by using the Web-

Table 2. Characteristics of participants

Characteristic	Number	Percentage
Gender		
Male	23	54.8
Female	19	45.2
Experience studying at high school or university		
Yes	23	54.8
No	19	45.2
Frequency of computer use		
Everyday	40	95.2
A few times per week	2	4.8

browser and tangible AR environments. Seven sets of 10 pairs were created from 20 amino acids. The amino acids were expressed with colored balls and sticks and they did not have any annotations. As each amino acid was adjusted so that it had a different orientation, geometric rotation or mental rotation (Shepard & Metzler, 1971) was necessary for judging pairs even when they were identical. The position of the molecular structures was arranged in the Web browser by clicking and dragging with the left button of the mouse. In the tangible AR environment, on the other hand, two

Figure 4. Snapshots of tasks in Web-browser and tangible AR environments

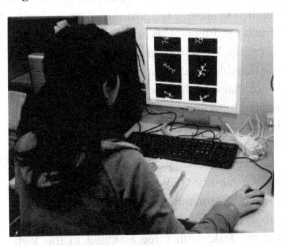

(a) Trials in Web-browser environment.

(b) Trials in tangible AR environment.

Table 3. Questions asked in Phase II

Topics	Questions
Aspirin	What are the chemical symbols in the two brackets? The side chains connected to the benzene in Salicin are modified to (1) and (2) in acetylsalicylic acid.
Insulin	Insulin has two chains (chain A and B) of amino acid, and they are combined by linked pairs of sulfur atoms. (1) How many pairs does the insulin have? (2) Which chain has the larger molecular mass?
Nitroglycerin	Look at the two chemical formulas, and answer the questions. What is the chemical formula put into (1) in Glycerin? What is the chemical formula put into (2) in Nitroglycerin?
Cholesterol	What is the difference between Mevastatin and Pravastatin in molecular structure? Hydrogen is changed to (1) in hexa-hydro-naphthol, and oxygen is changed to (2) in alpha-lactone.
Polyester	Answer the chemical formula in the brackets. Benzene in PET corresponds to (1) in PEN. PET and PEN have (2) in the main chain.
Polyphenols	Two side-chains OH of phenol in epicatechin change in number in epigallocatechin gallate. One side-chain OH of the Chromane ring in epicatechin changes to an ester bond to a phenol group with (2) hydroxyl group(s).

PET: polyethylene terephthalate, PEN: polyethylene naphthalate

palm-sized boxes with identification patterns were handled to arrange the position of the molecular structures. Figure 4 shows snapshots of the task in (a) the Web-browser environment and in (b) the tangible AR environment.

In Phase II, the task was to answer questions related to molecular structures after participants had read one-page documents that described the background, such as discovery episodes and biochemical functions of the molecules. Answering the questions required them to observe the 3D molecular structures in the Web-browser or tangible AR environment. Six topics were prepared for the task, with three assigned to the Web-browser environment and the other three to the tangible AR environment. The topics included aspirin, insulin, nitroglycerin, cholesterol, polyester, and polyphenols. Each topic involved two questions, and three possibilities were given as answers. The parts related to the questions were annotated in each molecular structure. The question items are listed in Table 3. The content in the one-page documents was not directly related to the questions, but was designed to interest the participants in the molecules. The molecular structures were manipulated in the same way as Phase I in both the Web-browser and tangible AR environments. Figure 5 shows an example of molecular structures being observed in a tangible AR environment.

An LCD monitor was used as a display device instead of a head-mounted display (HMD) because an HMD is not commonly used by most learners. A camera was statically mounted above a table in the tangible AR environment roughly facing the same direction that the user was viewing. Although one of the advantages of AR is viewpoint-based interaction that presents virtual objects based on the user's viewpoint, attaching a camera to a user's head makes the scene unstable due to him/her moving his/her head.

Procedure

Participants first read the instructions for the user study so that they could fully understand the sequence. The participants were then instructed on how to manipulate and observe the molecular structures and they had some time (roughly 5 to 10 minutes) to practice in each environment before performing a series of tasks. When the participants felt comfortable in the learning environments, they proceeded to the time trials. The tasks began with Phase I where the participants were required

Figure 5. Observing molecular structures in tangible AR environment

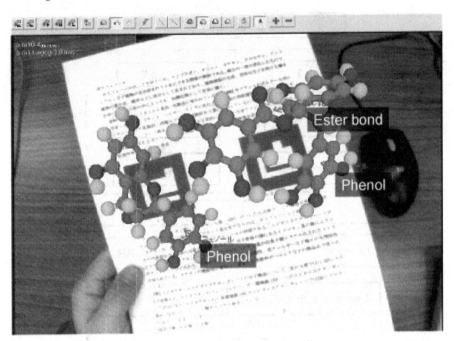

to complete the task as quickly and accurately as possible. The order of the environments was randomly chosen for all participants. To balance the effect of order, the participants were divided into two groups based on the sequence of the Web-browser and tangible AR environments, i.e., Group 1 had the Web browser for the first environment and Group 2 had the tangible AR for the first environment. After the seven sets of ten pairs of time trials were finished in either of the environments, another seven sets were performed in the other environment.

There was a break of 30 minutes after the Phase I task, and Phase II was then begun after participants had been given brief instructions. When the participants felt that they had understood what to do in Phase II, they proceeded onto the trials. Time limits of 30 minutes were imposed on the task for participants to complete reading the one-page documents and answer the two questions using either the Web-browser or the tangible AR environment. The participants in Group 1 had the

Web browser and those in Group 2 had the tangible AR for the first environment. Three topics out of six in the first environment were chosen by the participants themselves. After they had finished three topics with the trials in either environment, the other three topics were completed in the other environment.

After they had finished the trials in Phase II, a test in the form of a survey was conducted to evaluate their preferences using a Web-based questionnaire system (REAS). It mainly asked their impressions of each learning environment and tried to measure the difficulty they had in comprehending the six topics. The ratings consisted of a five-point Likert scale ranging from one (strongly disagree) to five (strongly agree). Open-ended comments were obtained as complementary opinions. The participants' behaviors during the user study were recorded on video. Figure 6 shows a block diagram of the procedure we used in the study.

Figure 6. Procedure for user study, repeatedly measuring dependent variables

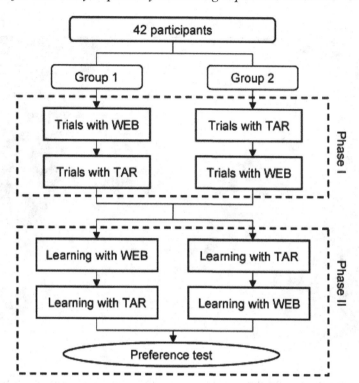

RESULTS

Phase I

Figure 7 plots the results for (a) the right-answer rates and (b) the completion times in Phase I. The plots indicate the means for the participants for the Web-browser and tangible AR environments. The seven different symbols correspond to the order for the seven sets of trials. The right-answer rates in the tangible AR environment as a whole were higher than those in the Web-browser environment, and the completion time in the tangible AR environment was shorter than that in the Web-browser environment. Table 4 lists the means, standard deviations, and paired t-tests for the right-answer rates and the completion times of the participants. The right-answer rates gradually increased with the number of trials until No. 3, and there were no statistically significant

differences (significance level $p > 0.01$) between the Web-browser and tangible AR environments. However, the rates deviated after No. 4, and there were significant differences (significance level $p < 0.01$) between the environments, with better rates in the tangible AR environment than those in the Web-browser environment.

The completion times gradually decreased with the number of trials until No. 3, and there were no statistically significant differences (significance level $p > 0.01$) between the environments. The time shot up at No. 4, and then decreased again with the number of trials. The environments were found to have significant effects (significance level $p < 0.01$) on the time after No. 4, with shorter times obtained in the tangible AR environment than in the Web-browser environment, which was, interestingly, the same trend as that for the rate results.

Figure 7. Right-answer rates and completion times in two environments in Phase I (WEB: Web browser, TAR: tangible AR)

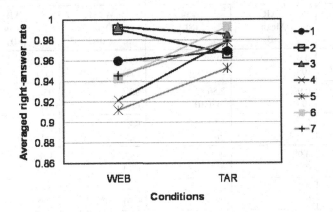

(a) Right-answer rate.

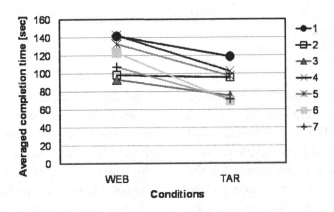

(b) Completion time.

Phase II

Figure 8 has a bar chart of the score count for the correct answers to each question asked about the molecular structures in Phase II. The black bars indicate the total count for the participants using the Web-browser environment and the white ones that for the tangible AR environment. The question numbers correspond to those for the six topics. Although the level of difficulty of the questions was observed to be quite different depending on the topic, the number of correct answers did not notably differ between the Web-browser and tangible AR environments. Table 5 lists the means and standard deviations of the total count over all the questions for participants classified by their learning experience in chemistry at high school or university. The maximum count goes up to six for each environment that had three topics with two questions. Analysis of variance (ANOVA) was used to find that the differences were not statistically significant for any factors ($F_{(1, 40)}$ = 0.267, p>0.05 in a within-subject factor (learning environment), $F_{(1, 40)}$ = 0.002, p>0.05 in a between-subject factor (learning experience), and $F_{(1, 40)}$ = 1.878, p>0.05 in the interaction effect).

Table 4. Means, standard deviations, and t-tests for right-answer rates and completion times in Phase I

No.	Right-answer rates			Completion times [sec]		
	WEB Mean (SD)	TAR Mean (SD)	t-value (SL)	WEB Mean (SD)	TAR Mean (SD)	t-value (SL)
1	0.96 (0.11)	0.97 (0.07)	-0.60 (p>0.01)	141 (52)	119 (51)	2.42 (p>0.01)
2	0.99 (0.03)	0.96 (0.06)	2.50 (p>0.01)	98 (39)	95 (46)	0.37 (p>0.01)
3	0.99 (0.03)	0.98 (0.04)	1.14 (p>0.01)	93 (42)	75 (31)	2.61 (p>0.01)
4	0.90 (0.08)	0.98 (0.07)	-5.58 (p<0.01)	142 (74)	102 (62)	3.15 (p<0.01)
5	0.87 (0.10)	0.95 (0.07)	-5.72 (p<0.01)	133 (56)	97 (45)	5.34 (p<0.01)
6	0.94 (0.05)	0.99 (0.03)	-5.45 (p<0.01)	123 (48)	69 (33)	7.16 (p<0.01)
7	0.94 (0.06)	0.98 (0.06)	-3.05 (p<0.01)	107 (37)	71 (34)	6.52 (p<0.01)

WEB: Web browser, TAR: tangible augmented reality,
SD: standard deviation, SL: significance level

Table 6 lists the means, standard deviations, and t-tests for the scores rated for the questions in the preference test. The results are classified into three trends for the subjective evaluations of the learning environments: preference for the Web-browser environment, preference for the tangible AR environment, and no preferences for either of the environments. The participants preferred the Web-browser environment to the tangible AR environment for questions 1 (ease of viewing), 2 (experience), and 4 (durability), whereas they preferred the tangible AR environment over the Web-browser environment for questions 3 (enjoyment), 5 (reality of manipulation), and 6 (sense of presence). The participants did not differ in their preferences for questions 7 (the ease with which they constructed the relationships), 8 (their ability to memorize the outlines), and 9 (their suitability as an introduction to biochemistry).

Figure 8. Correct answers in two environments in Phase II (black: Web browser, white: tangible AR)

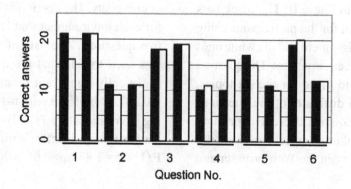

Table 5. Means and standard deviations for total count in Phase II

	LEX	MEAN	SD
WEB	Yes	4.52	1.04
	No	4.00	1.37
	Total	4.29	1.22
TAR	Yes	4.13	1.36
	No	4.37	1.26
	Total	4.24	1.30

WEB: Web browser, TAR: tangible augmented reality
LEX: learning experience with chemistry at high school or university, SD: standard deviation

DISCUSSION

The results for Phase I indicated better performance of tasks in the later trials in the tangible AR environment than that for the Web browser. We therefore estimated that users could benefit more from the tangible AR environment that enabled more interactivity with 3D molecular models after they had had some more practice. However, neither environment was expected to have any effects on the performance of tasks for extremely experienced users, because their performance may have saturated to similar levels for both environments (ceiling effect).

The results for Phase II indicated no differences in the total number of correct answers for the Web-browser and tangible AR environments. This implies that usability was not always reflected in user learning. Consequently, no evidence was found of relationships where benefits such as realistic sensations of virtual objects and human-memory support offered learning effectiveness, though these benefits had been expected in the tangible AR environments, as described in the conceptual framework section.

The overall results for the performance of tasks in Phases I and II suggest that the tangible AR environment is more suitable as a user interface

Table 6. Means, standard deviations, and t-tests for preference test

	Questions	WEB Means (SD)	TAR Means (SD)	t-values (SD)
1	The 3D structure was easy to view.	4.10 (0.85)	3.26 (1.33)	3.21 (p<0.01)
2	Prior experience was not needed.	3.86 (1.24)	2.76 (1.16)	4.51 (p<0.01)
3	The manipulation was enjoyable.	3.57 (0.86)	4.10 (0.91)	-3.06 (p<0.01)
4	It was suitable for long-term use.	3.57 (1.29)	2.93 (1.22)	2.20 (p<0.01)
5	It felt like I was handling the molecular structures.	3.40 (1.21)	4.12 (1.15)	-3.02 (p<0.01)
6	It felt like the 3D objects were actually there.	2.93 (1.30)	4.24 (0.96)	-6.28 (p<0.01)
7	It was easy to relate the molecular structures to the topics.	3.86 (0.84)	3.81 (1.06)	0.23 (p>0.01)
8	It was easy to remember the outline of the topics.	3.62 (0.96)	3.52 (1.11)	0.49 (p>0.01)
9	It was well-suited as an introduction to biochemistry.	4.19 (0.92)	3.93 (1.11)	1.32 (p>0.01)

WEB: Web browser, TAR: tangible augmented reality
SD: standard deviation, SL: significance level

for manipulating 3D molecular models, but it is not so different from that of the Web browser in terms of learning effectiveness. This trend is consistent with that in the previous work done for different purposes and in different contexts. Some user studies confirmed that the tangible AR environment could efficiently be used for manipulating 3D virtual objects. For example, the experiments on the assembly task successfully demonstrated the benefits of spatial cueing and direct manipulation in the AR environment (Tang, Owen, Biocca & Mou, 2003). However, the interface-design concept provides no proof of being effective or useful in practical situations, and the AR environment could hardly be extended beyond the design concept to become a usable system for practical applications. There have actually been a limited number of empirical studies that have tried to find learning to be effective in AR environments. Even user studies on education in geometry (Kaufmann & Duenser, 2007) and augmented chemistry (Fjeld, Fredriksson, Ejdestig, Duca, Botschi, Voegtli & Juchli, 2007) did not find performance that was quantifiable in AR environments, which was superior to that of traditional learning environments.

Our results for user preferences clarified some of the features that distinguished the tangible AR environment from that of the Web browser. The tangible AR environment gave the participants feelings of being able to intuitively manipulate 3D molecular models, because the interactivity of direct manipulation enabled them to interact with virtual objects as if they were manipulating real objects with their hands with sensorimotor feedback (Bowman, Kruijff, LaViola & Poupyrev, 2004). Our viewer system used paper materials as a tangible interface, which retained the physical affordance of paper as being handled in the real world. The reality was enhanced by improving interactivity, which was considered to result in the enjoyment of the manipulation itself. Factors such as enjoyment and reality are crucial to learners so

that they can take an active role in constructing knowledge and concepts, especially in the beginning stages of learning.

The open-ended comments revealed more detailed opinions about the Web-browser and tangible AR environments. The participants' comments on the Web-browser environment were clearly separated into positive and negative impressions they gained in manipulating 3D molecular models with the mouse. Most participants mentioned views of the 3D molecular structures were stable and the difficulty they had in manipulating their orientations with left-button clicks and drags of the mouse. The former was due to the stable viewing conditions the Web browser provided, and the latter was caused by the lack of experience the participants had in manipulating 3D objects with a mouse. Most participants in the tangible AR environment, on the other hand, mentioned, as an advantage of AR, that they could control the position of 3D molecular structures directly with their hands, and this was intuitive because it used the same metaphor as that in the real world. These opinions were consistent with the results for the preference test. In addition, two participants stated that it was easier to recognize 3D structures in the AR environment than those in the Web-browser environment, because the AR environment modeled the molecular structures with a real scene in the background rather than the uniform background color provided by the Web-browser environment.

Some drawbacks in the AR interface that were mentioned were that the views of the molecular structures became unstable due to sharp inclinations in the identification markers on the paper materials. The views were invalid at the viewpoint from the bottom because the identification markers could not be captured from the back side of the paper materials. It is known that instability in systems works as a distraction that reduces training and learning effects in virtual-learning environments (Dede, Salzman & Loftin, 1996).

One of the solutions to achieving stabilization is to provide learners with the option of indirectly rotating the molecular models. Another drawback was that the range of manipulations was limited to the field of view of the camera.

There are limitations to the current work. It is also important to point out that our user study relied on short-term tasks and a limited amount of content. We need to test the range in which AR environments can be applied by exploring the effectiveness of AR on various time scales and with different kinds of learning content. At present, we should be careful about generalizing the findings from our user study because of the small sample size, which should be addressed by expanding it in future work.

We did not deal with the aspects of collaborative learning implemented in AR environments. It is known that a collaborative AR environment enables communication behaviors to become more natural, social, and easier (Kiyokawa, Billinghurst, Hayes, Gupta, Sannohe & Kato, 2002) and this facilitates communication and information sharing among users (Wang, Gu & Marchant, 2008). We therefore plan to examine the effectiveness of learning in collaborative AR environments.

CONCLUSION

In this paper we have described a framework for learning molecular structures using tangible interaction provided by AR as a new type of learning environment in which professors use a commercial tool to create materials for presenting research, and students learn up-to-date research results with the viewer that we developed. The results from evaluations demonstrated that participants using the tangible AR environment performed better in tasks than those in the Web-browser environment in identifying two molecules. Although the tangible AR environment did not demonstrate any learning benefits, it did allow learners to intuitively observe 3D molecular structures and enjoy realistic interactions. The tangible AR environment has the potential to help change modes of learning from learners' passive roles to them taking the initiative, which could be accomplished by experiential and authentic learning environments where factors such as enjoyment and reality are essential.

ACKNOWLEDGMENT

Windows is a registered trademark of Microsoft Corporation. Pentium is a registered trademark of Intel Corporation.

REFERENCES

Alicea, B., Biocca, F., Bohil, C., Owen, C., & Xiao, F. (2006). Targeting and motor learning in augmented reality: optimal spatial positions for remembering. In *Proceedings of the Annual Meeting of the International Communication Association,* Dresden Germany. Retrieved July 10, 2010, from http://www.allacademic.com/meta/p93545_index.html

Asai, K., Kobayashi, H., Kondo, T., & Takase, N. (2007). Learning molecular structure using augmented reality. In T. Hirashima, U. Hoppe, & S. S. Young (Eds.), *International Conference on Computers in Education* (pp. 569-572). Amsterdam, The Netherlands: IOS Press.

Asai, K., Kondo, T., Kobayashi, H., & Takase, N. (2006). Augmented instructions for learning molecular structures. In Tzafestas, E. (Ed.), *EUROMEDIA* (pp. 63–68). Ostend, Belgium: EUROSIS Publication.

Azuma, R. T. (1997). A survey of augmented reality. *Presence (Cambridge, Mass.), 6,* 355–385.

Billinghurst, M., Kato, H., & Poupyrev, I. (2001). The MagicBook: a traditional AR interface. *Computers & Graphics, 25*(5), 745–753. doi:10.1016/S0097-8493(01)00117-0

Bowman, D. A., Kruijff, E., LaViola, J. J., & Poupyrev, I. (2004). *3D user interfaces: theory and practice*. Boston: Addison-Wesley.

Bricken, M., & Byrnes, C. M. (1993). Summer students in virtual reality: a pilot study on educational applications of virtual reality technology. In Wexelblat, A. (Ed.), *Virtual reality: Applications and explorations* (pp. 199–217). Boston: Academic.

Chen, Y.-C. (2006). A study of comparing the use of augmented reality and physical models in chemistry education. In *Proceedings of ACM International Conference on Virtual Reality Continuum and its Applications* (pp. 369-372). New York: ACM Press.

Dede, C. (1995). The evolution of constructivist learning environments; immersion in distributed virtual worlds. *Educational Technology, 35*(5), 46–52.

Dede, C., Salzman, M. C., & Bowen Loftin, R. (1996). ScienceSpace: virtual realities for learning complex and abstract scientific concepts. In *Proceedings of the IEEE Virtual Reality Annual International Symposium* (pp. 246-252). Washington, DC: IEEE Computer Society Press.

Dickey, M. D. (2005). Three-dimensional virtual worlds and distance learning: two case studies of Active Worlds as a medium for distance education. *British Journal of Educational Technology, 36*, 439–451. doi:10.1111/j.1467-8535.2005.00477.x

Duenser, A., Steinbugl, K., Kaufmann, H., & Gluck, J. (2006). Virtual and augmented reality as spatial ability training tools. In B. Plimmer (Eds.), *Proceedings of the ACM SIGCHI New Zealand Chapter's International Conference on Human-Computer Interaction: Designed-Centered HCI* (pp. 125-132). New York: ACM Press.

Duffy, T. M., & Jonassen, D. H. (1992). Constructivist: New implications for instructional technology. In Duffy, T., & Jonassen, D. (Eds.), *Constructivist and the Technology of Interaction: A Conversation*. Hillsdale, NJ: Lawrence Erlbaum Associates.

Feiner, S., MacIntyre, B., & Seligmann, D. (1993). Knowledge-based augmented reality. *Communications of the ACM, 36*, 52–62. doi:10.1145/159544.159587

FiatLux. (n.d.). *MolFeat*. Retrieved from http://www.fiatlux.co.jp/product/lifescience/molfeat/mol-index.html

Fjeld, M. Fredriksson, Ejdestig, M., Duca, F., Botschi, K., Voegtli, B., & Juchli, P. (2007). Tangible user interface for chemistry education: comparative evaluation and re-design. In B. Begole, S. Payne, E. Churchill, R. S. Amant, D. Gilmore, & M. B. Rosson (Eds.), *ACM Conference of Human Factors in Computing Systems* (pp. 805-808). New York: ACM Press.

Fjeld, M., Juchli, P., & Voegtli, B. M. (2003). Chemistry education: a tangible interaction approach. In Rauterberg, M., Menozzi, M., & Wesson, J. (Eds.), *INTERACT* (pp. 287–294). Amsterdam, The Netherlands: IOS Press.

Gillet, A., Sanner, M., Stoffler, D., Goodsell, D., & Olson, A. (2004). Augmented reality with tangible auto-fabricated models for molecular biology applications. In *Proceedings of the IEEE Visualization Conference* (pp. 235-242). Washington, DC: IEEE Computer Society Press.

HITLab. (n.d.). *ARToolkit*. Retrieved from http://www.hitl.washington.edu/artoolkit/

Kato, H., Billinghurst, M., Poupyrev, I., Imamoto, K., & Tachibana, K. (2000). Virtual object manipulation on a table-top AR environment. In *Proceedings of the International Symposium on Augmented Reality* (pp. 111-119). Washington, DC: IEEE Press.

Kaufmann, H. (2002). Construct3D: an augmented reality application for mathematics and geometry education. In *Proceedings of the International Conference on Multimedia* (pp. 656-657). New York: ACM Press.

Kaufmann, H., & Duenser, A. (2007). Summary of usability evaluation of an educational augmented reality application. In R. Shumaker (Ed.), *Proceedings of the Human-Computer Interaction International Conference* (pp. 660-669). Berlin: Springer-Verlag.

Kiyokawa, K., Billinghurst, M., Hayes, S. E., Gupta, A., Sannohe, Y., & Kato, H. (2002). Communication behaviors of co-located users in collaborative AR interfaces. In *Proceedings of the International Symposium on Mixed and Augmented Reality* (pp. 139-148). Washington, DC: IEEE Computer Society Press.

Klemmer, S., Nartmann, B., & Takayama, L. (2006). How bodies matter: five themes for interaction design. In J. M. Carroll, S. Bodker, & J. Coughlin (Eds.), *Proceedings of the ACM Conference on Designing Interactive Systems* (pp. 140-149). New York: ACM Press.

Klopfer, E., Squire, K., & Jenkins, H. (2002). Environmental detectives: PADs as a window into a virtual simulated world. In *Proceedings of the IEEE International Workshop on Wireless and Mobile Technologies in Education* (pp. 95-98). Washington, DC: IEEE Computer Society Press.

Lee, G. A., Nelles, C., Billinghurst, M., & Kim, G. J. (2004). Immersive authoring of tangible augmented reality applications. In *Proceedings of the IEEE/ACM International Symposium on Mixed and Augmented Reality* (pp. 172-181). Washington, DC: IEEE Computer Society Press.

Milgram, P., & Kishino, F. (1994). A taxonomy of mixed reality visual displays. *IEICE Transactions on Information and Systems, 12*, 1321–1329.

Navab, N. (2004). Developing killer apps for industrial augmented reality. *IEEE Computer Graphics and Applications, 24*, 16–20. doi:10.1109/MCG.2004.1297006

Neumann, U., & Majoros, A. (1998). Cognitive, performance, and systems issues for augmented reality applications in manufacturing and maintenance. In *Proceedings of the IEEE Virtual Reality Annual International Symposium* (pp. 4-11). Washington, DC: IEEE Computer Society Press.

Poland, R., LaVelle, L. B., & Nichol, J. (2003). The Virtual Field Station (VFS): using a virtual reality environment for ecological fieldwork in A-Level biological studies – Case Study 3. *British Journal of Educational Technology, 34*, 215–231. doi:10.1111/1467-8535.00321

Poupyrev, I., Tan, D. S., Billinghurst, M., Kato, H., Regenbrecht, H., & Tetsutani, N. (2002). Developing a generic augmented reality interface. *Computers, 35*, 44–50. doi:10.1109/2.989929

Regenbrecht, H., Baratoff, G., & Wagner, M. T. (2001). A tangible AR desktop environment. *Computer Graphics, 25*, 755–763. doi:10.1016/S0097-8493(01)00118-2

Rekimoto, J. (1998). Matrix: a realtime object identification and registration method for augmented reality. In *Proceedings of the Asia Pacific Computer Human Interaction* (pp. 63-68). Washington, DC: IEEE Computer Society Press.

Rogers, Y., Scaife, M., Gabrielle, S., Smith, H., & Harris, E. (2002). A conceptual framework for mixed reality environments: designing novel learning activities for young children. *Presence (Cambridge, Mass.), 11*, 677–686. doi:10.1162/105474602321050776

Salzman, M., Dede, C., Loftin, R., & Chen, J. (1999). A model for understanding how virtual reality aids complex conceptual learning. *Presence (Cambridge, Mass.), 8*, 293–316. doi:10.1162/105474699566242

Schmid, C. (1999). Simulation and virtual reality for education on the Web. In Hahn, W., Walther-Klaus, E., & Knop, J. (Eds.), *EUROMEDIA* (pp. 181–188). Amsterdamn, The Netherlands: SCS Publication.

Sharma, R., & Molineros, J. (1997). Computer vision-based augmented reality for guiding manual assembly. *Presence (Cambridge, Mass.)*, *6*, 292–317.

Shelton, B. E., & Hedley, N. R. (2002). Using augmented reality for teaching Earth-Sun relationships to undergraduate geography students. In *Proceedings of the International Augmented Reality Toolkit Workshop*. Washington, DC: IEEE Press.

Shelton, B. E., & Hedley, N. R. (2003). Exploring a cognitive foundation for learning spatial relationships with augmented reality. In *Technology, Instruction, Cognition, and Learning*. Philadelphia: Old City Publishing.

Shepard, R. N., & Metzler, J. (1971). Mental rotation of three-dimensional objects. *Science*, *191*, 952–954. doi:10.1126/science.1251207

Soloway, E. (1998). Learner-centered design: the challenge of HCI in the 21st century. *Interaction*, *1*, 36–48. doi:10.1145/174809.174813

Tang, A., Owen, C., Biocca, F., & Mou, W. (2003). Comparative effectiveness of augmented reality in object assembly. In V. Bellotti, T. Erickson, G. Cockton, & P. Korhonen (Eds.), *Proceedings of the ACM Conference on Human Factors in Computing Systems* (pp. 73-80). New York: ACM Press.

Ullmer, B., & Ishii, H. (1997). The metaDesk: models and prototypes for tangible user interfaces. In *Proceedings of the ACM Symposium on User Interface Software and Technology* (pp. 223-232). New York: ACM Press.

Vince, J. (1998). *Essential virtual reality fast: how to understand the techniques and potential of virtual reality.* London: Springer-Verlag.

Waldner, M., Hauber, J., Zauner, J., Haller, M., & Billinghurst, M. (2006). Tangible tiles: design and evaluation of a tangible user interface in a collaborative tabletop setup. In J. Kjeldskov & J. Paay (Eds.), *Proceedings of the Australia Conference on Computer-Human Interaction: Design: Activities, Artefacts, and Environments* (pp. 151-158). New York: ACM Press.

Wang, X., Gu, N., & Marchant, D. (2008). An empirical study on designers' perceptions of augmented reality within an architectural firm. *Journal of Information Technology in Construction*, *13*, 536–552.

Wellner, P., Mackay, W., & Gold, R. (1993). Computer-augmented environments: back to the real world. *Communications of the ACM, 36*, 24–27. doi:10.1145/159544.159555

Wiedenmaier, S., Oehme, O., Schmidt, L., & Luczak, H. (2003). Augmented reality (AR) for assembly processes design and experimental evaluation. *Journal of Human-Computer Interaction, 16*, 497–514. doi:10.1207/S15327590IJHC1603_7

Winn, W., & Jackson, R. (1999). Fourteen propositions about educational uses of virtual reality. *Educational Technology*, *39*(2), 5–14.

Zuckerman, O., Arida, S., & Resnick, M. (2005). Extending tangible interfaces for education: digital Montessori-inspired Manipulatives. In W. Kellogg, S. Zhai, C. Gale, & G. van der Veer (Eds.), *Proceedings of the ACM Conference of Human Factors in Computing Systems* (pp. 859-868). New York: ACM Press.

This work was previously published in the International Journal of Virtual and Personal Learning Environments, Volume 2, Issue 1, edited by Michael Thomas, pp. 1-18, copyright 2011 by IGI Publishing (an imprint of IGI Global).

Chapter 2
Organisational Blogging:
The Problem of Engagement

Gavin J. Baxter
University of the West of Scotland, UK

Thomas M. Connolly
University of the West of Scotland, UK

Mark Stansfield
University of the West of Scotland, UK

ABSTRACT

This paper investigates the implementation and use of an internal organisational blog by several departments in the HR division in a large public sector financial organisation in the UK. This qualitative study adopts a case study approach and examines the experiences of staff using the blog to explore whether it can facilitate organisational learning. The thinking and decisions that informed the pilot study are also investigated. Initial findings indicate that implementing an internal organisational blog does not revolve around the technology itself, but the work required to inform and educate staff about the idea of using a blog for working purposes. This paper has practical implications for the practitioner community with reference to organisational management informing them of issues to consider prior to implementing new technology in team environments. The paper also examines approaches towards maintaining technology initiatives (in this case blogs) once they are up and running. The unique focus of this paper is that it explores blog use from the perspective of individuals who have never used them before as opposed to a department that is already familiar with the technology.

INTRODUCTION

Organisations today often have to re-evaluate their internal ways of communication and information sharing as a result of an increasingly competitive knowledge economy. Though the concept of the knowledge economy (Webber, 1994) is not new the approaches that organisations are adopting via technology to share and disseminate knowledge among staff are becoming more widespread (Du & Wagner, 2006). The notion of 'Enterprise 2.0' refers to software that allows individuals to col-

DOI: 10.4018/978-1-4666-2467-2.ch002

laborate and share information in organisational contexts (McAfee, 2006). This type of software employs the same principles as "Web 2.0," which is often used to describe "the social use of the Web which allow[s] people to collaborate, to get actively involved in creating content, to generate knowledge and to share information online" (Grosseck, 2009, p. 478). The primary distinction between the two concepts is that Enterprise 2.0 refers to the use of social software in organisational contexts. Web 2.0 implies the use of the social Web in a general and more day to day social environment.

Weblogs or blogs are one example of Web 2.0 technology. This paper examines their use in an organisational context and explores how they can be used to internally share knowledge among teams and departments. Though there are numerous perspectives of what blogs are they can be described as being "frequently modified web pages in which dated entries are listed in reverse chronological sequence" (Herring et al., 2004, p.1). They can also be used to share graphics and audio. Blogs are not a new phenomenon; rather it is the way in which they are being applied combined with their evolving technological features that make them current.

This paper explores the issue that if used correctly, blogs can prove to be a beneficial communication, information and knowledge sharing medium. Though this has often been discussed in the academic literature a further objective of this paper is to analyse how blogs can promote the concept of "organisational learning."

The theory of organisational learning focuses on three central arguments. The first view is known as the functionalistic outlook which states that learning in organisations begins with the individual (Hedberg, 1981; Kim, 2004). This standpoint believes that it is the individual who learns on behalf of the organisation. The logic behind this debate is that knowledge initially resides in the individual and it is they who learn albeit through the supporting infrastructure of the organisation (Ortenblad, 2002). The second perspective of organisational learning is referred to as the interpretive view which advocates that learning is undertaken in organisations through the form of relationships, collectively and in groups. The final perspective pertaining to organisational learning is the stance that organisations can learn (Ortenblad, 2005). The logic behind this reasoning is the thinking that organisations learn, modify and adapt themselves internally by the knowledge channelled through them via their organisational members. We adhere to the interpretive view of organisational learning.

We agree that organisational learning is the "activity or processes (of learning) in organizations" (Ortenblad, 2001, p. 9) but within a social context. This view of organisational learning is described in more detail in a subsequent section of the paper.

Closely related to the concept of organisational learning is the term learning organisation. A learning organisation is "a place where employees excel at creating, acquiring, and transferring knowledge" (Garvin et al., 2008, p. 110). The phrase learning organisation is sometimes used interchangeably with that of organisational learning. Learning organisations are particular types of organisation that have a uniqueness in being able to sustain numerous organisational learning processes and activities for their organisational members to learn (Baxter et al., 2009). Learning organisations are theoretically able to adapt and modify their infrastructures which evolve as a result of the learning of their employees. This study contributes to the body of knowledge in the field of blog research by comparing the social uses of blogs with the social aspect of organisational learning and examining the two concepts to draw similarities between them. It is believed that at the time of writing this is something that has yet to be fully explored in the academic literature.

This paper contributes to the body of knowledge of blogs and Web 2.0 implementation initiatives in organisations through examining the initial implementation process and user experiences of an organisation that has begun using an internal division-wide blog. This study will help to inform the practitioner community about how such an approach began and explore the experiences and lessons learnt so that they can be generically applied to other organisations choosing to undertake a Web 2.0 collaborative project.

The remainder of this paper is organised as follows. Previous research covering the topic of organisational blogs is examined following which the main characteristics of blogs are discussed and are linked to the concept of organisational learning. A case study is provided where the authors have begun working with the HR division of a large public sector financial organisation that has recently piloted its own internal blog in the UK. Finally, the experiences that have been gained from the early findings of the study will be used to provide a set of generic criteria on how to sustain the use of an internal organisational blog after it has been piloted.

Previous Research

It has been argued that genuine empirical research on blogs is limited (Hall & Davidson, 2007). The main focus on primary research about blogs appears to be in the area of higher education where their potential to support project-based learning (Grippa & Secundo, 2009), participative learning (Agostini et al., 2009) and student reflection (Gomes, 2008) is being realised.

Research about the uses of blogs has however begun to be examined elsewhere with particular reference to blog use in organisational environments. Some examples of research that have explored the area of organisational blogging have included analysing why individuals use internal organisational blogs (Jackson et al., 2007) and examining internal corporate blogging communities (Huh et al., 2007).

The primary problem area that acted as the catalyst for the study described in this paper was internal communication. Blogs and their association to internal communication in organisations have already been explored (Kosonen et al., 2007). The theme of internal communication in organisations has also been widely investigated from varying perspectives. Some research issues explored include the role of management in improving internal communication in organisations (Robson & Tourish, 2005) and the examination of strategies on integrating multidisciplinary internal communications for the purposes of evaluating knowledge sharing in organisations (Kalla, 2005). The blogging initiative described in this paper was a response to a re-evaluation of the HR Division's communication channels in an attempt to implement a more centralised internal communication and information sharing structure.

There also appears to be a lack of empirical research on organisational learning as a lot of the theory associated with the subject area has yet to be tested in organisational settings. This paper argues that blogs seem to have a theoretical link towards organisational learning and dependent on their use might prove to be a suitable organisational learning approach. Examining the use of blogs to assess whether they can facilitate organisational learning might also assist in providing empirical evidence towards whether they are successful in doing so.

Though the study discussed in this paper reflects on the subject of an internal organisational blog it differs from previous studies on the topic. One main objective of this study is to analyse whether blogs can support the concept of organisational learning. This study is not primarily concerned with why the blog was introduced in the organisation but more about the initial impact it has had in the division it is being trialled in. In addition to this, this study describes the steps taken by company management to encourage staff to engage in the use of the blog.

Features of Blogs

The name "weblog" was first mentioned in December 1997 by Jorn Barger (Blood, 2002). It is important to remember that though blogs are often associated with the concept of Web 2.0 (Boateng, 2010) they are essentially pre-Web 2.0 tools. The creation and use of blogs have steadily increased with the phrase "blogosphere" being used to describe the interconnection of blogs on the Internet (Rosenbloom, 2004). This section of the paper identifies some of the key characteristics that are often associated with blogs that are illustrated in Figure 1. Though the key elements of blogs have often been addressed in the academic literature the aim in this paper is to link their features to the concept of organisational learning, which will be discussed in a later section of the paper.

Blogs and communication: Blogs are often associated with being able to promote communication (Lee & Trimi, 2008). Blogs allow individuals to reply to postings by adding comments to subjects or issues that are of interest to them. Though blogs can be used on an individual basis for the purpose of personal reflection it is their "conversational nature" (Lee et al., 2008) that makes them very suitable for engaging in dialogue and discussion.

Blogs, information and knowledge sharing: The communicative aspect of blogs also makes them very useful for sharing information and knowledge. Information can be added on a blog not only in the form of postings and comments but by uploading documents and files for users of the blog to read at times convenient to them. It could be argued that one of the main beneficial features of a blog, especially when used for collective purposes, is its ability to provide a central platform for users to contribute their personal experiences and thoughts. Blogs can allow the sharing of personal knowledge, or tacit knowledge, to occur. The capturing of this type of knowledge allows it to be presented in a readable, understandable and explicit format.

Blogs and knowledge management: Several definitions of knowledge management exist in the academic literature. One such definition that is suitable for this paper describes knowledge management as the "acquisition and storage of worker's knowledge and making information

Figure 1. Interrelated features of blogs with focus on communities of practice (CoPs)

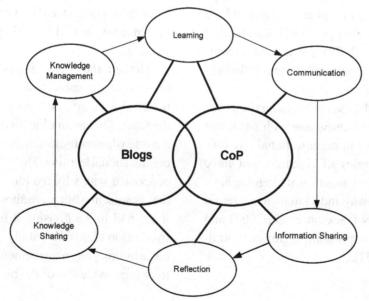

accessible to other employees within the organisation" (Martensson, 2000, p. 11). The link between blogs and knowledge management has already been identified in the academic literature (Kaiser & Muller-Seitz, 2009; Singh & Singh, 2008). Blogs allow postings to be stored and located chronologically under themed categories. Content that is centrally stored in a group blog can be searched and located by its users proving to be a useful knowledge bank.

Blogs and reflection: Blogs have also been associated with the concept of reflection through the idea that they allow blog users to think whilst writing (Nardi et al., 2004). Though there is no agreed definition of what reflection is one definition that is appropriate to the way in which blogs are used describes the concept as "the purposeful contemplation of thoughts, feelings, and happenings that pertain to recent experiences" (Kennison & Misselwitz, 2002, p. 239). When using a team or project blog working experiences could be reflected and acted upon that could benefit the individual concerned, the team and the organisation. Blogs also allow users to reflect on the context of their learning and practice which is in keeping with the concept of being a reflective practitioner (Schon, 1983).

Blogs and communities of learners: The social nature of blogs means that they can be linked towards the idea of community building and can accommodate what are known as a Communities of practice (CoP) (Wenger & Snyder, 2000) or in an educational context, a Community of Learners (COL) (Brown, 2001). Communities of practice often refer to individuals with similar interests or objectives that come together to work on or solve a particular problem. One example of a CoP might involve individuals in an organisation coming together to collaborate; share knowledge and expertise on a specific organisational project. It has already been argued in the academic literature that blogs can support several networks of CoPs in organisations (Roll, 2004) as well as communities of learners in the higher education sector

(Petersen et al., 2009). This it could be argued is due to the collaborative character of a blog and the fact that blogs allow people to network and share ideas regardless of where a community member is geographically located.

Blogs and Organisational Learning

Blogs have a strong theoretical link with the social aspect of organisational learning. The relationship between blogs and organisational learning has been previously identified by other researchers (Baxter et al., 2009). This section provides a brief overview of the association between the two concepts and explains why they appear to be suited towards one another. We examine the theory of organisational learning as it is important to the study outlined in this paper and one of our research questions is to investigate whether blogs can facilitate organisational learning.

Interpretivist perspective of organisational learning: Organisational learning is a complex subject area with many opinions and positions being presented about what the topic is about (Levitt & March, 1988). There is however no overall agreement about what the subject is (Cohen & Sproull, 1991). One viewpoint about organisational learning is known as the interpretivist perspective (Ortenblad, 2002), which proposes that learning in organisations is a social phenomenon due to the fact that individuals are social in nature (Wenger, 1991). Learning in organisations is therefore considered to be an interactive process that is dependent on a culture of collaboration to flourish. This outlook of organisational learning argues that organisations can be thought of as "social learning systems" (Wenger, 2000, p. 226).

Interpretivist organisational learning and blogs: The authors argue that blogs have a strong association with the social view of organisational learning. This perspective of organisational learning is also linked with the concepts of dialogue (Schein, 1993), shared knowledge and understanding (Fiol & Lyles, 1985), communities of practice (Brown & Duguid, 1991) and reflection (Hoyrup, 2004). Blogs used internally by an organisation can help to create a culture of collaboration, sharing of ideas and knowledge. An internal group or team blog would be a useful way to communally share knowledge in or between departments promoting a culture of openness and transparency. The feature of feedback that blogs support allows employees to reflect about issues impacting upon their working practices, department or organisation making blogs a useful tool for not only organisational development but also organisational learning.

When used in a team context or for the purposes of collaboration then it could be argued that blogs might be able to facilitate the social aspect of organisational learning. The inherently social nature of organisations means that the interpretivist concept of organisational learning appears to have a strong theoretical link to the principles of Web 2.0 and blogs. Figure 2 illustrates the theoretical associations between the two concepts. It could be argued that a lot depends on the culture of the organisation and purpose of the blog for collective organisational learning to occur. The information and knowledge shared among employees and through the organisation via an internal blog might further result in the organisation becoming a "learning organisation." There however appears to be a lack of empirical research about blogs (Hall & Davidson, 2007) particularly with reference to their application in organisations. The link between blogs and the concept of the learning organisation has already been identified in the academic literature (Roll, 2004, p. 10). Despite this fact the relationship between blogs and the "learning organisation" is one that has yet to be sufficiently empirically examined.

Figure 2. Diagram illustrating applicability of blogs, organisational learning

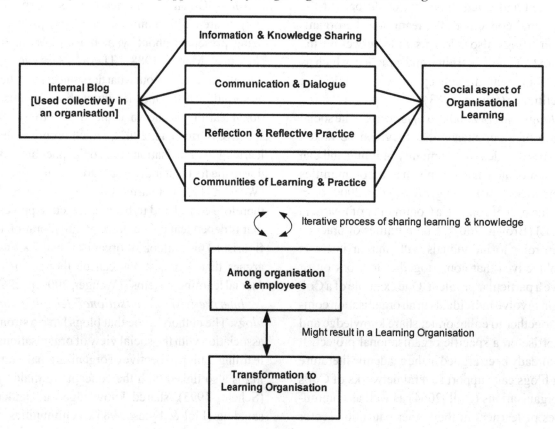

Research Objectives

In this section we outline a case study currently being undertaken by the authors about the use of an internal blog in the HR division of a large UK public sector financial organisation. The study focuses on one specific team in the company's HR division, the Organisational Development and Learning team (OD&L). The reason why the focus of this study concentrated on the implementation and use of an internal blog as opposed to a wiki or forum was because the company already used internal wikis and forums for the purposes of communication. The objective of the study was not to contrast these Web 2.0 technologies as communication tools. The aim was to provide an illustrative case study on why a specific division in the organisation implemented an internal blog and to explore the initial impact of the blog as a communication tool in the division.

The Participants of the Study

The OD&L team consists of: the OD team, the Learning team, the Employee Development team and the Internal and External Communication teams. HR is a separate team in the division but is not part of OD&L. The total number of staff for the HR Division is approximately 70 people who report directly to the CEO Office. The OD&L team has several key areas of focus: (1) providing organisational members with training to ensure that they have the necessary skills to do their jobs; (2) develop the leadership and potential of management in the company; (3) assess different ways of implementing organisational learning, team working and individual skills for staff. In addition to these aims another central objective of the OD&L team is to communicate the company's vision, mission and values.

The idea and motivation behind the creation of a blog for the OD&L team began as a result of research that is being undertaken by the authors

with the company's ICT division. The authors have initiated the implementation of practice area blogs in the ICT division to investigate whether blogs can allow organisational learning to occur in project-based environments. It was decided to extend the research into the OD&L team as they had expressed an interest to pilot a blog in their team. It was felt by management that the introduction of a blog in the team would fall within the department's remit of pushing new initiatives through the company. In addition, it was considered that the use of a blog might help to address some of the communication issues confronting the team. It was agreed within the team that there were too many internal communication channels in use for information and knowledge sharing. Various communication channels are used by the team including: telephone conferencing, e-mail, intranet, weekly team meetings and divisional team meetings via video conferencing. Both senior management and staff raised issues about the frequency, method and content of communication used by the team. One topic mentioned was the problem of finding and centrally storing information that would be of use to the team as a whole. The use of e-mails were criticised and were viewed as a contributing factor of this issue because it was viewed that they just get lost within the chain of communication and that the team had become too reliant on e-mail usage.

Another communication problem was the infrequency with which team information was updated and made widely available to the team such as through the staff intranet page. The team felt that there was a need to address how information was made available to all team members from a central location and how to ensure that team information could be made current through frequent updates. These particular problems identified by the team had an important bearing on their decision to trial its own blog. This study will further allow the comparison of blog use in different contexts and among individuals who are regarded as being technically proficient and those who may be less so. The findings from these studies will be used to further explore and contrast the steps each team has taken to promote their blogs among staff. The content of the blogs will also be examined for evidence of organisational learning from an individual, collective and organisational perspective. The results can help to inform management practitioners of other companies who are also wishing to implement a similar technology initiative but who might be unsure of how to do so.

Research Methodology

The principle research methodology used for this study is the "intrinsic" case study. According to Stake (2008) an intrinsic case study is used when somebody wishes to obtain a more comprehensive understanding of a specific case. This particular type of case study is undertaken not to generalise with other cases or to identify an issue in a certain research discipline. An intrinsic case study is performed when the case itself is deemed to be of sufficient interest to the researchers themselves and academic community as a whole. While we are aware of the criticisms that are often made about case study research, it is not the aim of the research to make generalisations about the case study itself but to report about the specifics of the actual case. It was decided to adopt a case study approach for the following reasons. Instead of undertaking research in a wide range of smaller companies it was decided to examine the use of blogs in a large organisation that has not used them before. This study is to be more focused than other blog-related studies that sometimes appear to be more wide ranging. The case study approach allowed the authors to work together with the OD&L team to explore the issues impacting upon the use of their blog.

Design and Procedure

Before analysing the steps the OD&L team took to start using their team blog this section will briefly describe and analyse some of the features of the blog. By discussing the rationale behind the decisions that informed the design of the blog it will be possible to assist other companies to reflect on things they may need to consider when implementing a similar blogging initiative.

It was decided by the team to trial Lotus Notes Domino as the platform for the blog because the company already used IBM server products. Though other types of blogging software such as Blogsphere were considered Lotus Notes Domino was used because it helped to address the issues of cost, security, administration and access of the blog. Due to the company's existing use of IBM Notes Client database it meant that everyone wishing to use the internal team blog could log in by default. This feature would allow the team to know who had posted on the blog. It would further aid the research because knowing who had expressed a certain view on the blog would aid further interpretation of staff opinions via one-to-one interviews. It was also considered to be easier to set up access rights based on every user's standard login and thus not require any separate user administration. These points are reinforced by the company's Lotus Notes administrator who explained why the Lotus Notes blog was used:

One of the reasons for piloting a Lotus Notes based blog is that it provides an identity management system out of the box (i.e., cost free).

In addition to the security aspect of the blog it was decided that to access the blog and leave a comment staff had to log in. The ability to track comments was considered to be important as stated by the Lotus Notes administrator:

It was deemed inappropriate to allow people to post blog entries and comments unless their identity could be authenticated via a spoof-proof login mechanism.

Another important reason why the Lotus Notes based blog was used by the company was because it did not take long to make it available for staff to use. This view was expressed by the technical analyst who helped to configure the blog:

It was quick to rollout and required 0 admin on my part.

One of the main considerations behind the design of the blog was to make sure that the user interface was as simple to navigate as possible to assist those who had never used a blog before. An example of the main user interface of the blog is shown in Figure 3. It was felt a simple interface would help to make it easier for a staff that was new to blogging to add postings and comments as well as find their way around the blog. The fact that the team was relatively techno phobic meant that this was a relevant issue to consider. It was important for the research because a plain interface for the blog meant that staff might be more

inclined to post on the blog. The features on the main blog interface were ones familiar to all types of blogs. These attributes included: notification of recent entries on the blog, themed categories of topics of interest posted by staff and searchable archive feature of posts dated in chronological order. The design characteristics of the blog were similar to those that have been addressed in the academic literature regarding blogging software (Wagner, 2003).

Standard blog characteristics as illustrated in Figure 4 were integrated into the blog for allowing individuals to create posts. Basic elements such as: limited formatting, the insertion of images from drives the adding of links and the ability to create categories was all considered and implemented. Changes could also be made to the blog at the HTML level though the use of the blog was considered to be easy enough for staff to be trained on how to use it. Effective usability features of the blog included: the ability to highlight or flag attractive or interesting posts to share among colleagues, the inclusion of podcasts and insertion of media files. The blog also provides a save feature that allows users to start a post, go away and reflect on it and then come back to complete it.

Figure 3. The main interface of the blog

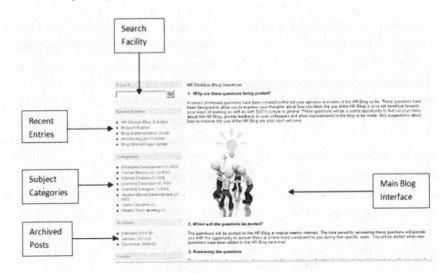

Figure 4. Blog post features

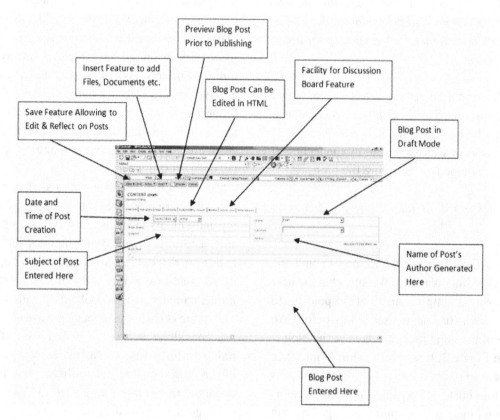

The Process

The introduction of the blog to the OD&L team was a gradual process. OD&L staff was first informed about the blog initiative through a "welcome note" post by the company's HR manager. There was no initial pre-defined purpose for the blog and the main theme that emerged from the welcome note was that the blog was viewed as:

A chance to share information and updates more widely and keep everyone up to date.

The blog was also seen as "an opportunity to kick-start a new 'self-service' approach" that would allow staff to learn about particular projects that the team was involved in or learn more about the day-to-day activities of the team and its individual members. After the posting of the welcome note it was decided by the OD&L team

manager to post weekly team updates on the blog. This was done to enable team members to practice commenting on the blog and to allow them to become familiar with its format. The thinking behind the trialing of the blog was to pilot it small scale in the OD&L team before moving it out to the other departments in the HR division. The objective in doing so was to bring the division together through communication and updated information posted on the blog.

The method employed by the OD&L team has been more moderate than the way in which the company's ICT division introduced the blogs to their practice areas. In contrast, the ICT division's approach was less structured with staff immediately starting to use the blogs for working purposes. This could be attributed to the fact that ICT personnel might be expected to be more comfortable in using technology whereas the OD&L team are slightly luddite in nature. In comparison however both divisions do have general blog administrators to assist staff with basic queries about blogging. Blog guidelines were created for the blogs but both the ICT and OD&L team decided not to refer to them at present because the main aim was to allow staff to interact with the blogs and not be deterred by blog moderation in doing so.

Though no pre-defined purpose was assigned for the OD&L team blog the initial thinking behind its use appears to be in keeping with some of the elementary reasons why some organisations decide to use internal blogs. The authors have reflected that through the early stages of the blog usage that organisational learning has yet to occur in terms of knowledge sharing and exchange of working experiences, although this may occur given more time.

Working closely with the authors the OD&L team took additional steps to inform team members about the benefits of organisational blogging. This was done because it was felt that if staff knew more about the concept of what a blog was and how using one might benefit their ways of working then they would participate in using it. The team therefore created a dedicated intranet page about the blog that contained blog information sheets provided by the authors. Some of the topics included: guidelines on how to blog as well as general information about what blogs are and their potential uses in internal organisational environments. Through consultation with the authors it was agreed with the blog administrator to post a weekly themed question on the blog to encourage staff to become familiar with commenting. The questions were designed to find out staff views about the team blog, provide feedback to management and suggest possible improvements to be made to the blog.

Presentation and Discussion of Results

Despite some of the early initiatives undertaken to get staff using the blog it has been acknowledged by team management that the blog is not having the immediate impact of centrally storing communication and information generated by the team. Though the blog has been disseminated throughout the HR division of the company many staff continue to use e-mail as their primary communication method and appear reluctant to post or comment on the blog. It was also recognised that the objective of bringing the team closer together through the use of the blog is currently not being achieved. The authors intend to explore the lack of engagement during the course of their research and have already identified further areas of investigation. One such area is the blog itself as staff has admitted having problems in accessing it. Some staff also felt that the format and design of the blog was a reason why some people were not using it. This point was iterated by one staff member who gave their view of the blog:

I find it very cumbersome and I think this discourages people from using it. The culture behind blogging was that it provided fast, simple and easy to use websites to allow anyone to write anything on the web - like instant news bulletins. I don't think the lotus notes blog does this. I think a blog is a great idea and could be used really well. But I don't think this is the blog we are looking for.

In addition to the accessibility of the blog being deemed as a possible reason for staff not contributing with posts or comments another issue raised in the team was the problem of trying to get older members of staff to use new technology. Combined with this point is the potential factor that some of the staff might still be unsure of what a blog is thus requiring further explanation about blog use. This issue was expanded upon via a post on the blog:

I think it's maybe important to point out that the people administering this blog for HR are not what we might consider webby or techy. These are people who don't blog, or have their own websites etc. and I think we should make this as easy and pleasant as we can for them.

A pre-test blog questionnaire was issued to the HR Division in June 2010. The results of the questionnaire have yet to be sufficiently analysed. Some of the open-ended questions have however produced interesting staff views accounting for potential reasons for staff disengagement with the blog. Some staff expressed reservations about the blog being introduced to the HR Division:

Not clear about what exactly the purpose is, and what controls there are over content.

I am unfamiliar with this form of communication so would not naturally use it - just a case of adjusting. Also would need to consciously think about what to put on it.

Certain staff also stated their concerns about the blog being one communication channel too many in the division:

Don't see the purpose of the blog, we have far too many different communication systems and none have been fully embraced by the execs.

Other staff appeared worried about posting anything on the blog due consequences of saying the wrong thing on the blog:

I would feel uncomfortable about putting down thoughts and feelings worrying about repercussions.

The following section of this paper examines how the OD&L team intends to alleviate the dilemma of staff engagement with the blog.

Though the OD&L Team blog is still in its introductory phase further research is required to progress this study to ascertain whether creating a blog to be used internally in an organisation for the purposes of communication and information sharing promotes organisational learning. This study has illustrated that the staff must be made more aware of why the blog is being introduced into their department and what the benefits of using it are. The purpose of the blog must be carefully explained and demonstrated. Once staff begins to feel comfortable in their understanding about the blog's introduction to their team then it could be argued they will start to use it more. As the research progresses we intend to investigate this further to determine whether this proves to be the case.

In order to encourage staff to use the departmental blog the OD&L team has devised a set of initiatives, which include:

1. Setting up instant messaging (IM) reminders for staff who have been identified as not having used the blog. Face-to-face demonstrations about how to use the blog will be provided to staff that are uncomfortable about blogging as a way of encouraging them to blog.
2. Creation of a series of demonstration eLearning videos to provide staff with an alternative option and format to learning more about their team blog. The eLearning videos will inform team members on a range of topics that include how to blog.
3. Management to send reminders to staff to regularly view the blog and contribute towards its content through the raising of work related issues and reflections.
4. Management to provide not only team updates on the blog but also their thoughts and reflections of their working experiences and therefore seen to be leading by example.
5. Hourly time periods to be agreed between management and staff to allow team members to familiarise themselves with the blog but with the mandatory requirement that they post work related content on it during that time.
6. Making the blog interface more user-friendly and providing the blog with extra functionality to ensure that the uploading of documents, images and the managing of categories can be easily achieved.

In addition to the initiatives for getting more staff to use the blog the authors will employ several research methods during the study that will allow them to obtain the views of staff about the blog and their experiences of using it. Questionnaires, interviews and focus groups will be undertaken to provide feedback from team members to determine whether organisational learning has occurred in the team as a result of blog usage. The findings gained from this study will be contrasted with the academic literature on blogs and organisational learning to compare similarities and differences with other empirical studies in these fields.

Recommendations for the Future

As a result of their direct experience of the research undertaken so far, the authors have proposed a set of practical criteria that management practitioners can follow or reflect on if they are experiencing problems in sustaining the use of an internal organisational blog. These guidelines can also be referred to by academic practitioners who may be encountering similar case study research dilemmas regarding the introduction and subsequent use of blogs in internal organisational settings.

Evidence of management support: It is important that management assume a leading role in using the blog. Devolving responsibility to staff for using the blog might be perceived as a negative sign that management have become disinterested in the new initiative. Management must reassure their staff that they continue to be fully committed to the use of the blog communicating this message through postings and comments.

Communicate usage of the blog: The purpose and vision of the blog must be clearly articulated to staff otherwise they will not see the value in using it. Staff might not interact with an internal blog due to a lack of understanding about why the blog was created. An important message to relay to staff is that the use of the blog will not displace but complement current forms of communication that the team currently uses.

Provide guidance to staff: Staff who has not blogged before will require support and instruction about how to blog. It is important that the support on the use of the blog is ongoing and that it runs beyond the introductory stages of the blog being launched. The creation of a blog administrator would be a useful way of providing staff with a central port of contact should they have any queries about using the blog.

Experiment with the blog: Allow staff to experiment with the blog as this will give them the opportunity to gain experience of postings and of adding comments. All support and guidance should be as learner-centred as possible. To facilitate collaboration and interaction on the blog staff should be encouraged to post work-related topics that will motivate colleagues to provide feedback. In doing so staff can learn more about one another's working experiences as well as their job roles.

Value contributions to the blog: Supporting contributions made by staff to the blog through the form of comments will influence them to continue posting on the blog if they feel that what they are publishing is being valued by the team. If there is a lack of feedback towards topics and issues raised on the blog then it is unlikely that individuals who were active in posting will continue to be so.

Develop your blog: When more staff begins to use the blog then greater functionality might be required to be added to it. It is important to remember that negative user issues might increase if staff thinks that their expectations are not being fulfilled through the use of the blog. It should be remembered that blogs are not only associated with text and that other forms of data can be embedded and integrated within them.

Review the blog regularly: One approach towards determining the success of a team blog is to review its usage at regular time periods. Analysing the number of hits to the blog, as well as the number of postings and comments will provide an indication of when and why staff is using the blog. If there is evidence that the blog is not being used that often then it would be sensible to seek feedback and opinions from staff to ascertain why this is the case.

CONCLUSION

This paper examined the implementation and use of an internal organisational blog in the HR division of a large UK public sector financial organisation. The characteristics of blogs were explored with the intention of linking them to the concept of organisational learning. This paper adhered to the view that blogs have common features with the interpretive outlook of organisational learning. Though this appears to be the case theoretically the study outlined in this paper aims to investigate this from an empirical perspective. The findings of the research will provide a good illustration of whether blogs in this particular study have been deemed as a suitable organisational learning approach. This case study has explored the concept of blog implementation in an organisation unfamiliar with their use. The initial findings of this study have highlighted that the successful running of organisational blogs do not revolve around the use of the technology. There appears to be work required to inform and educate staff about the idea of using a blog for working purposes.

This case study has revealed some interesting initial findings about internal organisational blog use. It appears that in this particular case study organisational learning through the use of a blog has not been immediately apparent. These findings will continue to be contrasted with the organisational learning and blog literature to compare with other empirical studies. However, at the time of writing this research area seems to be lacking in empirical evidence. Though the concept of measuring organisational learning is a complex one that is primarily interpreted through research issues being explored, this research will investigate attitudinal and behavioural change

in staff when using the blog. Thematic analysis of blog posts, interviews and focus groups will be performed and will be cross examined with the organisational learning literature to examine whether staff views correspond to the concepts associated with organisational learning. To move the blog study forward, we intend to continue working closely with the teams in the HR division of the company to alleviate the problem of staff engagement with the blog by holding information sessions on a series of topics about blogs, organisational learning and how to blog. The aim behind running these sessions will be to inform staff about the perceived benefits of using an internal blog for working purposes, the learning potential of blogs and their perceived applicability towards organisational learning. In addition, we will conduct individual interviews with staff to ascertain and capture their experiences of having used the blog. These views will then be analysed and themes extracted to determine whether they relate to the opinions expressed about blogs and organisational learning in the academic literature.

REFERENCES

Agostini, A., De Michelis, G., & Loregian, M. (2009). Using blogs to support participative learning in university courses. *International Journal of Web Based Communities*, 5(4), 515–527. doi:10.1504/IJWBC.2009.028087

Baxter, G. J., Connolly, T. M., & Stansfield, M. (2009). How can organisations learn: An information systems development perspective. *Learning Inquiry*, 3(1), 25–46. doi:10.1007/s11519-009-0038-8

Baxter, G. J., Connolly, T. M., & Stansfield, M. (2009). The use of blogs as organisational learning tools within project-based environments. *International Journal of Collaborative Enterprise*, 1(2), 131–146. doi:10.1504/IJCENT.2009.029285

Blood, R. (2002). Weblogs: A history and perspective. In Rodzvilla, J. (Ed.), *We've got blog: How weblogs are changing our culture* (pp. 7–16). Cambridge, MA: Perseus Publishing.

Boateng, R. (2010). When Web 2.0 becomes an organizational learning tool: Evaluating Web 2.0 tools. *Development and Learning in Organizations*, *24*(3), 17–20. doi:10.1108/14777281011037254

Brown, J. S., & Duguid, P. (1991). Organizational learning and communities-of-practice: Toward a unified view of working, learning, and innovation. *Organization Science*, *2*(1), 40–57. doi:10.1287/orsc.2.1.40

Brown, R. E. (2001). The process of community-building in distance learning classes. *Journal of Asynchronous Learning Networks*, *5*(2), 18–35.

Cohen, M. D., & Sproull, L. S. (1991). Editors' introduction. *Organization Science*, *2*(1), 1–3.

Du, H. S., & Wagner, C. (2006). Weblog success: Exploring the role of technology. *International Journal of Human-Computer Studies*, *64*(9), 789–798. doi:10.1016/j.ijhcs.2006.04.002

Fiol, C. M., & Lyles, M. A. (1985). Organizational learning. *Academy of Management Review*, *10*(4), 803–813.

Garvin, D. A., Edmondson, A. C., & Gino, F. (2008). Is yours a learning organization? *Harvard Business Review*, 109–116.

Gomes, M. J. (2008). Blogs: A teaching resource and a pedagogical strategy. In Jose Mendes, A., Pereira, I., & Costa, R. (Eds.), *Computers and education: Towards educational change and innovation* (pp. 219–228). London, UK: Springer.

Grippa, F., & Secundo, G. (2009). Web 2.0 project-based learning in higher education: Some preliminary evidence. *International Journal of Web Based Communities*, *5*(4), 543–561. doi:10.1504/IJWBC.2009.028089

Grosseck, G. (2009). To use or not to use Web 2.0 in higher education? *Procedia Social and Behavioral Sciences*, *1*, 478–482. doi:10.1016/j.sbspro.2009.01.087

Hall, H., & Davison, B. (2007). Social software as support in hybrid learning environments: The value of the blog as a tool for reflective learning and peer support. *Library & Information Science Research*, *29*(2), 163–187. doi:10.1016/j.lisr.2007.04.007

Hedberg, B. (1981). How organizations learn and unlearn. In Wystrom, C. P., & Starbuck, W. T. (Eds.), *Handbook of organizational design* (*Vol. 1*, pp. 3–27). Oxford, UK: Oxford University Press.

Herring, S. C., Scheidt, L. A., Bonus, S., & Wright, E. (2004). Bridging the gap: A genre analysis of weblogs. In *Proceedings of the 37th Hawaii International Conference on System Sciences* (pp. 1-11).

Hoyrup, S. (2004). Reflection as a core process in organisational learning. *Journal of Workplace Learning*, *16*(8), 442–454. doi:10.1108/13665620410566414

Huh, J., Bellamy, R., Jones, L., Thomas, J. C., Erickson, T., & Kellogg, W. A. (2007). BlogCentral: The role of internal blogs at work. In *Proceedings of the Conference on Human Factors in Computing Systems* (pp. 2447-2452).

Jackson, A., Yates, J., & Orlikowski, W. (2007). Corporate blogging: Building community through persistent digital talk. In *Proceedings of the 40th Hawaii International Conference on System Sciences* (pp. 1-10).

Kaiser, S., & Muller-Seitz, G. (2009). Acknowledging the innate impact of an information technology for engaging people in knowledge work: The case of weblog technology. *International Journal of Networking and Virtual Organisations*, *6*(1), 4–21. doi:10.1504/IJNVO.2009.022480

Kalla, H. K. (2005). Integrated internal communications: A multidisciplinary perspective. *Corporate Communications: An International Journal*, *10*(4), 302–314. doi:10.1108/13563280510630106

Kennison, M. M., & Misselwitz, S. (2002). Evaluating reflective writing for appropriateness, fairness and consistency. *Nursing Education Perspectives*, *23*(5), 238–242.

Kim, D. H. (2004). The link between individual and organizational learning. In Starkey, K., Tempest, S., & McKinlay, A. (Eds.), *How organizations learn: Managing the search for knowledge* (pp. 29–50). London, UK: Thomson Learning.

Kosonen, M., Henttonen, K., & Ellonen, H. K. (2007). Weblogs and internal communication in a corporate environment: A case from the ICT industry. *International Journal of Knowledge and Learning*, *3*(4-5), 437–449. doi:10.1504/IJKL.2007.016704

Lee, H. H., Park, S. R., & Hwang, T. (2008). Corporate-level blogs of the Fortune 500 companies: An empirical investigation of content and design. *International Journal of Technology Management*, *7*(2), 134–148. doi:10.1504/IJITM.2008.016601

Lee, S. M., & Trimi, S. (2008). Editorial: organisational blogs: Overview and research agenda. *International Journal of Information Technology and Management*, *7*(2), 113–119.

Levitt, B., & March, J. G. (1988). Organizational learning. *Annual Review of Sociology*, *14*, 319–340. doi:10.1146/annurev.so.14.080188.001535

Martensson, M. (2000). A critical review of knowledge management as a management tool. *Journal of Knowledge Management*, *4*(3), 204–216. doi:10.1108/13673270010350002

McAfee, A. P. (2006). Enterprise 2.0: The dawn of emergent collaboration. *MIT Sloan Management Review*, *47*(3), 21–28.

Nardi, B. A., Schiano, D. J., Gumbrecht, M., & Swartz, L. (2004). Why we blog. *Communications of the ACM*, *47*(12), 41–46. doi:10.1145/1035134.1035163

Oretnblad, A. (2005). Of course organizations can learn! *The Learning Organization*, *12*(2), 213–218. doi:10.1108/09696470510583566

Ortenblad, A. (2001). On differences between organizational learning and learning organization. *The Learning Organization*, *8*(3), 125–133. doi:10.1108/09696470110391211

Ortenblad, A. (2002). Organizational learning: A radical perspective. *International Journal of Management Reviews*, *4*(1), 87–100. doi:10.1111/1468-2370.00078

Petersen, S. A., Divitini, M., & Chabert, G. (2009). Sense of community among mobile language learners: Can blogs support this? *International Journal of Web Based Communities*, *5*(3), 428–445. doi:10.1504/IJWBC.2009.025217

Robson, P. J. A., & Tourish, D. (2005). Managing internal communication: An organizational case study. *Corporate Communications: An International Journal*, *10*(3), 213–222. doi:10.1108/13563280510614474

Roll, M. (2004, July 5-6). Distributed KM – improving knowledge workers' productivity and organizational knowledge sharing with weblog-based personal publishing. In *Proceedings of the BlogTalk 2.0 European Conference on Weblogs*, Vienna, Austria (pp. 1-12).

Rosenbloom, A. (2004). The blogosphere. *Communications of the ACM*, *47*(12), 31–33.

Schein, E. H. (1993). On dialogue, culture, and organizational learning. *Organizational Dynamics*, *22*(2), 40–51. doi:10.1016/0090-2616(93)90052-3

Schon, D. (1983). *Reflective practitioner: How professionals think in action*. New York, NY: Basic Books.

Singh, R. P., & Singh, L. O. (2008). Blogs: Emerging knowledge management tools for entrepreneurs to enhance marketing efforts. *Journal of Internet Commerce, 7*(4), 470–484. doi:10.1080/15332860802507305

Stake, R. E. (2008). Qualitative case studies. In Denzin, N. K., & Lincoln, Y. S. (Eds.), *Strategies of qualitative inquiry* (pp. 119–149). London, UK: Sage.

Wagner, C. (2003). Put another (b)Log on the wire: Publishing learning logs as weblogs. *Journal of Information Systems Education, 14*(2), 131–132.

Webber, A. M. (1994). Surviving in the new economy. *Harvard Business Review*, 76–92.

Wenger, E. C. (1991). Communities of practice: Where learning happens. *Benchmark*, 1-6.

Wenger, E. C. (2000). Communities of practice and social learning systems. *Organization, 7*(2), 225–246. doi:10.1177/135050840072002

Wenger, E. C., & Snyder, W. M. (2000). Communities of practice: The organizational frontier. *Harvard Business Review, 78*(1), 139–145.

This work was previously published in the International Journal of Virtual and Personal Learning Environments, Volume 2, Issue 3, edited by Michael Thomas, pp. 1-17, copyright 2011 by IGI Publishing (an imprint of IGI Global).

Chapter 3
Game–Like Technology Innovation Education

Rikke Magnussen
Aarhus University, Denmark

ABSTRACT

This paper examines the methodological challenges and perspectives of designing game-like scenarios for the implementation of innovation processes in school science education. This paper presents a design-based research study of a game-like innovation scenario designed for technology education for Danish public school students aged 13-15. Students play the role of company heads that develop intelligent music technology. This game-like learning environment was designed to develop innovation competencies through the simulation of a practical learning situation. The term "game-like" is used to denote that the scenario should not be considered an educational game, such as the educational computer games used in many schools today. The focus of the design is to include practices and tools from innovative professions and use game principles and elements to create a meaningful frame around the creative and innovative practices.

INTRODUCTION

One key-adage of our time is that Western countries will only survive based on their populations' abilities to be innovative, flexible and creative in a world of global warming and foreign industries that exploit cheap labour (Drucker, 1993). To meet these challenges, the primary task of educators has been defined as preparing learners to participate creatively in the knowledge economies that most Western countries have become (OECD, 2000). In spite of this being one of the main educational challenges of the 21st century, schools still teach students that knowledge is static, and as a result, students are being taught to become experts at consuming knowledge rather than producing new knowledge (Sawyer, 2006).

DOI: 10.4018/978-1-4666-2467-2.ch003

Past science and technology studies of actors in the field have led to a discussion of what is meant by "authentic science" in school education (McGinn & Roth, 1999). Rather than the traditional picture of the scientist as the isolated genius endowed with superior mental abilities, scientific knowledge in the field of science and technology studies is seen as emerging from disciplined ways of organising and making sense of the natural world, as well as being a construction of visual representations (Latour, 1999; Lynch & Woolgar, 1990; Latour & Woolgar, 1986). Visual representations such as graphs, x-ray images, maps, models, diagrams and hybrids of these are central in creating and communicating science and it has been argued that this view of scientific practice should have implications for how science is taught (diSessa, 2000; McGinn & Roth, 1999).

Games that simulate scientific practice have been mentioned as an approach for implementing innovation in school education (Shaffer, 2007). The game media is well suited for simulating complex rule systems and real-life settings. Game scenarios offer a medium equipped for complex simulations integrating many different aspects of real-life learning environments and framing them in a simulation a player can identify with and relate to. Access to a wide range of professional tools and representations supports authenticity and allows for players to tackle complex problems from professional contexts (Magnussen, 2008). Though the potentials of game media in technology innovation education are clear, how innovative practices in game-based environments occur has yet to be fully understood.

In this paper, the design of a game-like technology innovation scenario is presented. The scenario was developed as part of a design-based research study of how to implement innovative learning environments into cross-disciplinary science education in schools. I present the design, preliminary results and the methodological discussions that arise from the first application of the design.

GAME-LIKE SIMULATED PRACTICE

The empirical data in this paper is gathered from a technology innovation scenario, which is part of a new generation of theory-based educational games that simulate professional environments. One characteristic that these games share is that they simulate elements of the objectives and environments in a specific profession by using and making available the technology, tools and/or methods of that profession to students playing the game. Examples of simulations include environmental engineers trying to locate a polluted site (Squire & Klopfer, 2007), urban planners redesigning a central pedestrian street of a town (Shaffer, 2006), or criminal investigators investigating a murder using forensic techniques (Magnussen, 2007, 2008). The objective for creating these types of games is to use the game media to design complex settings based on the learning environments of real-life professionals, thus allowing students to engage in complex, creative, and innovative problem solving and learning processes of the professions. The motivation for developing these types of games stems from a critique of the teaching of standardised skills to children in today's school system. The skills acquired in this system do not prepare them for a future that involves a constantly changing, complex work life (Shaffer & Gee, 2005). Critics believe that, under the current system, students do not learn to deal with problems that do not have ready-made answers and do not solve problems using creative, innovative thinking or collaboration. As a result, the aim of this type of game is to use the game media to create environments with simulations of complex real-life situations where students have to think like professionals and solve problems in innovative ways as professionals do (Gee 2003; Shaffer, 2007). Simulating professions is not new. Commercial games such as Counter-Strike or the game version of CSI simulate the professional practices of counter-terrorists and forensic detectives. The primary difference between commercial games and the new generation of educational games is that the latter's designs are based on learning theories and/or detailed studies of the learning processes and the tools of real-life professionals. Some of these games are also designed to meet the goals of the formal school science curriculum (Magnussen, 2008), while others, "create the epistemic frame of a socially valued community by re-creating the process by which individuals develop the skills, knowledge, identities, values and epistemology of that community" (Shaffer, 2007, p. 164), also known as "epistemic games." Even though innovation is mentioned as an integrated part of the epistemic frame of professionals, the ways in which professional innovative processes may be implemented in game-like scenarios have not been studied in depth.

In the following, I present the design and play-analysis of a technology-supported scenario in which students play the role of company heads that develop intelligent music technology. This game-like learning environment was designed to develop innovation competencies through the simulation of a practical learning situation. The term "game-like" is used here to denote that the scenario should not be considered as an educational game, such as the educational computer games used in many school educations today. Focus in the design was to include practices and tools from innovative professions (IDEO, 2009) and then use game principles and elements such as roles and a winning state to create a meaningful frame around the creative and innovative practices. This design-research approach is based on an understanding of "game-like" as environments which are not constructed as games as such, but which are based on design experience with, and theoretical understanding of, learning in games such as described by James Paul Gee:

So the suggestion I leave you with is not "use games in school"—though that's a good idea—but: How can we make learning in and out of school, *with or without using games, more game-like in the sense of using the sorts of learning principles young people see in good games every day when and if they are playing these games reflectively and strategically? (Gee, 2005, p. 37)*

In this paper, I advocate that our understanding of games is currently so extensive that we should let design-research of learning environments be inspired by understandings of games, learning and play, rather than exclusively seek to develop new versions of educational computer games.

DESIGNING GAME-LIKE INNOVATION EDUCATION

The study presented in this paper is part of a four-year research project entitled, "Serious Games on a Global Marketplace" (2007-2011), which explores the design and use of educational games within various school contexts. The project was set up as a collaborative project in which academics work with companies to redesign, implement and explore the use of games in order to generate knowledge about serious game challenges and educational design, with the aim to develop new formats of serious games for school education.

The empirical case presented in this paper is a design-based research project, which involves the design of a technology innovation scenario for cross-disciplinary science teaching for students aged 13-15, in Danish public schools. The educational goal in the game-like scenario is to teach students how to take part in innovative thinking and the creative construction of new technologies that characterise professional designers and innovative companies. The scenario was designed to simulate professional innovators' innovation processes. Technological innovation was chosen to make the construction processes cross-disciplinary, since technology construction involves an understanding of social (e.g., user behaviour), technical and scientific processes.

The technology innovation education project is a design-based research project. Design-based research combines empirical educational research with the theory-driven design of learning environments (Brown, 1992; Design-Based Research Collective, 2003). Design experiments are therefore described both as a method to "engineer" learning environments and to develop domain-specific theories (Cobb et al., 2003). The design of learning environments and the development of theories of learning are closely intertwined and characteristic of the method, because they occur through continuous cycles of problem definition, design, enactment, analysis and redesign (Collins, 1992). In this paper, I present the first cycle of problem definition, design and intervention, and the different methodological reflections and hypotheses the design-research process was based on.

Being a design-based research project, there were two praxes design foci: to understand how game elements can be used in designs of technology innovation education; and the research focus—understanding how students construct and mobilise representations of knowledge in these scenarios. The design of the technology innovation scenario was to simulate professional innovation methods, but also to provide students with the tools of professionals. When entering the meeting places and workspaces of professionals in the natural sciences or creative and innovative businesses, we find a variety of visual representations and visualisation tools such as white-boards, tablets, mind maps, Lego process tools, etc. These tools are an integrated part of the generation and development of new ideas. Professionals such as scientists develop knowledge through sketching, and presenting models (McGinn & Roth, 1999; Latour, 1999). When entering a classroom and observing students' work processes, we see few of these tools used for visualising new ideas and thinking processes. Most student work is conducted with pen and paper, text processing tools, or by listening to a teacher who is standing at the front of the class, using a blackboard. One

hypothesis behind the project was that technology and visualisation tools are actors in professional innovative thinking processes, and if we want to integrate innovative processes in schools, we have to integrate the tools of professional technology innovators.

The main hypothesis behind the technology innovation design was that students' practices in using visual representations in game-like simulations of professional environments are formed by whatever artefacts are made available in their schools' workspaces, as well as by human actors and references to the profession that the game presents. Earlier, studies have shown that the way students create and mobilise visual "inquiry representations" depended on relations to the simulated profession, complexity in the game, teachers' encouragement, other students' design formats as well as artefacts such as boards, posters, whiteboards or interactive boards available in school workspaces (Magnussen, 2008). Providing students with these tools to create visual representations of their ideas therefore became central in the design of the technology innovation space.

The second hypothesis behind the design centred on the creation of a meaningful frame for the technology innovation tools and practices. Introducing innovation tools in classrooms does not necessarily spark innovative thinking processes. To ensure that these tools become an integrated part of the school practice, we have to create contexts where they can become possible actors in innovative thinking processes. To do this, we may draw on inspiration from the educational game field and its ability to frame complex professional practices and create meaningful game and learning experiences (Magnussen, 2009). The challenge is to design contexts that, through narrative elements or elements such as rules and consequences, frame highly complex creative contexts, but which are still open enough for flexible working processes that allow students to develop and approach a topic with their own process tools and creative ideas. We have to create a space where children are given inspirational demands. These demands should, however, not constitute rigid restrictions which limit innovative processes. Innovation processes need frames to develop, but may be obstructed by rigid rules. This is a difficult balance to strike, and part of the project is to develop design methods for the development and study of these flexible spaces.

THE SCENARIO DESIGN

The theme of the first game-like innovation workshop presented in this paper was "Development of future music technology." Students were given three days to develop and build prototypes of a future intelligent music technology. The design-based research study of technology innovation was part of the research conducted at the Playware Centre at the Technical University of Denmark, which is one of the partners of the Serious Games on a Global Marketplace research project. Playware Centre is involved in advanced digital products that create play and experiences among users of all age groups. The centre works with technology and physical user interaction, including play media developed on the basis of robot technology, modern artificial intelligence and mobile technology.

The three-day innovation camp was planned so that students would undergo three phases: user survey, brainstorm, and prototype building. The three phases had rules designed to stimulate innovative thinking and work processes at the different stages, such as "understanding needs of the user" and thinking "out of the box." The three-day camp was designed in collaboration with a professional innovation process consultant in Denmark, using, among other things, the Innovation Toolkit developed by the design consultancy company, IDEO (2009). The innovation camp was set up at the Science Talent Centre in Sorø, Denmark. The aim of this centre is to develop young science talents. The centre has recently opened and the facilities are very good; new laboratories with the latest technology, such as interactive whiteboards and flat screen PCs, which are set up in most rooms. The group in the first observations of the game-like technology innovation scenario comprised of 25 students aged 13 - 15. Students were selected from seven different classes at a school in Northern Sealand in Denmark. Together with their two teachers, who also participated in the innovation camp, students had designed a climate board game, which won a local competition in designing education materials. The teachers had invited 25 of the students that had participated most actively in the design of the winning project to participate in a four-day camp at the science centre, as a reward. The three-day technology innovation scenario was part of the four-day camp. The 25 participating students were described by their teachers as active students and 'above average' in science. Most of these students had a specific interest in technical and scientific subjects as well, and a few of them had creative interests outside school and played in bands or composed their own music.

The overall structure of the game was designed by the author of this paper, who also, assisted by two additional researchers, conducted video observations of student participation, throughout the three days. The camp was run by the director of the Science Talent Centre who played the role of local manager of the teams. She was assisted by the class' two teachers, who supervised the groups according to processes and rules in the different phases of the technology innovation. At the end of the camp, students presented their prototypes to a panel of four judges; two were from the Science Talent Centre, and two were from the Playware Centre (Lund et al., 2005).

In the following I will describe the structure of the different phases in more detail and report on the first results from the first test. These are the first studies in an ongoing design-based research study of technology innovation education in schools, and should thus be viewed as preliminary results.

Phase 1: Inspiration, Introduction and User Survey

The technology innovation camp was planned for three days with participating groups of students camped at the Science Talent Centre, participating full-time in the technology innovation camp. In the first day's evening, before the official introduction to the technology innovation camp, students were introduced to, and had a chance to play with, intelligent music technology developed by Playware as well as other types of robot technology. The idea was to introduce the concept of artificial intelligence to students, and inspire them to think beyond existing formats, such as those offered by iPod or YouTube. They were introduced to the Playware-developed "Beat Blocks" (Nielsen et al., 2009). These consist of coloured building blocks, where each block is an instrument, and different rotations of each block produces different expressions of an instrument. A user can play with the blocks to combine different instruments and tracks, and compose alternative versions of songs by famous artists. The idea was to inspire students to think "out of the box" and in intelligent formats that would help them produce and use music in new ways. Overall, students were enthusiastic in their play with the intelligent technology, and used extensive periods of time to experiment with creating alternative versions of songs by their favourite artists.

In the following morning, students were formally introduced to the camp through a narrative frame. Students were instructed that they would be innovative teams, who were to develop the future of innovative intelligent music technology in the course of the next two days. The target group was said to be young people, aged as participating students were, and the client was presented as the Playware Centre, which did not have the same intimate knowledge about the target audience as the students. To make these excellent new innovations, students would have to use the same techniques and tools as professionals. Students were shown an episode of the ABC Nightline show from 1999, where IDEO designers were given the task of developing a futuristic shopping cart. In the TV clip, the systematic user survey processes designers go through was shown, as well as brainstorm activities, and prototype building. The idea was both to give the students a visual understanding of the different phases of design, but also to introduce the visual representations and process tools IDEO designers use. This last point was verbally repeated following the TV clip demonstration. Students were encouraged to use whatever papers, coloured pens, pins and whiteboards they would find in their workspaces. Following this, the local manager, the director of the Science Talent Centre, introduced the first process: teams were to choose two members of their six-member groups and interview them about times of the day they listened to music and what problems there might be in the playing of or listening to music, at different times of the day. They were also asked to produce a time-line that illustrated music listening/playing timelines. The user survey was designed with the assistance of a professional innovation consultant who advised students to start with the user survey, because brainstorms without a basic understanding of the needs of users often produce poor results.

After the introduction, teams went to their workspaces to start working. Overall, groups were highly motivated and began making visual representations as part of their discussions and working processes; poster-size paper was put on walls, which students wrote and on with coloured pens. The groups were supposed to start with the user survey, but almost all groups went straight into the brainstorm phase and started developing ideas instead of investigating the needs of the users. Teachers had to intervene and get them to start with the user survey. It seemed difficult for students to focus on mapping the users' daily use of music, without letting this lead directly into designing technologies to meet user needs. These difficulties lead teachers to comment on how open innovation processes were fundamentally different from the processes students were used to work with in school. They said that most students are used to working with what they called "recipes." Both in science subjects as well as in other subjects, students are used to being told every step of a task, rather than working with open innovation processes. All teams eventually managed to produce timelines that mapped user needs as well as several ideas for technologies that could respond to these needs.

Phase 2: Brainstorm

The brainstorm phase was introduced to students in the afternoon of the second day, after teams had completed and presented their user surveys in the morning. The local manager (the director of the Science Talent Centre) encouraged students to start anew and put previous ideas in the background. Also, she introduced students to the set of rules they were to follow in the brainstorm process: 1. They must write as many wild ideas (the wilder, the better) as possible within 15 minutes, without talking to one another; 2. They must present ideas to the team—wild ideas should be encouraged, and team members must try to build on each other's ideas. Rejecting ideas was not allowed; 3. They must put ideas into different categories and vote – all members were given three points they could give to the different ideas they liked. All groups initially started out with the 15-minute idea development period, where they were writing down ideas on post-it notes. Following this, students began presenting their ideas to their team members by hanging post-it notes on the available boards and walls. Studying this process, it however became clear that it was difficult for students to follow the given rules of coming up with many creative ideas. To help, groups were encouraged by their teachers to go to the "inspiration table" where for inspiration, they could play with toys, music instruments and the Playware music technologies they had been introduced to earlier.

In most groups, there was also a dominant tendency to reject wild ideas, and the focus in team discussions within groups centred on what was technically possible, instead of the development of ideas. Later in the afternoon, the manager and teachers went around to the teams for a short briefing. The groups had been told that they should present their preliminary ideas and would have a chance to discuss problems with the manager and the supervising teachers. All teams went around to the different workstations to participate in this briefing and get inspired by the other groups' work processes. At the briefing, it became clear that most of the developed ideas resembled existing formats, such as those offered by iPod or internet music services. The manager again encouraged students to think of wild ideas and to more actively integrate elements of AI.

In spite of difficulties (and in one group, frustrations) experienced within the different stages of the brainstorm processes, teams worked intensely for the balance of day two—and some groups continued on, until late in the evening—on developing new ideas to intelligent music technology. This impression from the observations were supported by the teachers who stressed that students were highly motivated and eager to develop their designs further for the coming day.

Phase 3: Prototype Building and Presentations Before Judges

The third and final day of the innovation camp was initiated with an introduction to the prototype building phase. Students had been given the task to select the one idea they wanted to make a prototype of and present it to the manager and her team. The overall impression of the finished ideas was that they had greatly developed into being more wild and futuristic concepts, which included intelligent technology.

One group had developed an idea for a handheld wireless music player with a clay-like tangible interface for stress relief and in-build intelligent technology with sensors for response to the mood of the user. Another group had developed a music system shaped as blocks. One block was a music player and a watch depending on what side of the block was turned upwards. Another block could be used for making music by users shaking or twisting it for different sounds and instruments and a third block represented the speaker that could be turned and placed in a room depending on where the user was situated. The blocks could be used separately or combined for collective functions such as playing music made on the blocks. A third group presented the idea of a robot called a "Kaj" that would follow people around their homes and use voice recognition to respond to orders or go quietly to a corner if nobody talked to him. Kaj's brain could be removed and used as a wireless music player, outside the home. The fourth group of students had created an idea for a wireless micro player with no sound that was to be placed behind one's ear, where it would align with the brain through emission of electronic waves in a way that users would think that they are hearing music, without actually hearing any—essentially eliminating the risk of damaging ear drums. Teachers encouraged this last team to conduct research on whether this technology was actually possible and how. In general, it was at this stage that students started doing more specific research to specify the details of their idea. Students were highly engaged and almost ecstatic at this stage. In an interview with one of the groups, team members described the phase of having selected one idea for prototyping as "being in control again." This was compared to the more open brainstorm process where they had been discussing and debating pros and cons of many different ideas.

Students were asked to make models of their idea in paper, cardboard, dough and similar materials, to present the different aspects of functionality of the technology and how it would meet the user needs to a panel of judges from the science talent centre and Centre for Playware. By the end of the day, teams presented their prototypes and visual presentations of functionalities to the four external judges. Based on the criteria 1) ability to think new, 2) inclusion of intelligent technology and 3) usefulness to a potential user group the team with the modular block technology was announced as the winner.

CONCLUSION

In this paper, the first cycle of a design-research study of a game-like technology innovation education has been presented. As this is an on-going study with continuous cycles of problem definition, design, intervention and analysis, it is interesting to consider the possibilities for future developments, from this round of design studies. It became clear, from the above-described study, that participating in the various phases of technology innovation was both highly motivating and highly challenging for the involved group of children. In the observations of the different phases of innovation it was clear that certain processes of user survey and brainstorm were particular challenging to the groups. Students found it difficult to distinguish between the processes of user survey and brainstorming and by most went straight into the idea generating phase without understanding the process of identifying the needs of the user group. It also proved to be a massive challenge for most students to think outside existing formats and to develop ideas for intelligent technology. The members of the teams had a tendency to be too realistic with their own ideas, while rejecting other team members' wild ideas. We however saw how students over the course of the three days became able to think beyond existing formats and develop futuristic ideas for intelligent technology which would meet the identified needs of the user group. This ability of creative and innovative thinking within the given frame was a central result of the camp. Overall, the 25 students participated creatively and were motivated in the activities of the different phases of innovation. Also, they actively challenged themselves both to think of new and intelligent technologies that they had indentified user needs for.

To separate stages in innovative processes, thinking "out of the box," and not rejecting wild ideas is challenging, even to professional innovators (IDEO, 2009). With the aim to teach students these difficult processes, it is however central to future studies, that experiments with changing or developing elements in current designs, be carried out. One idea could be to appoint facilitators that are given the task to facilitate the different processes for each group. This is however a highly difficult job and including this element in the design would require reflections on the choice and role of facilitators. Another idea for future developments could be to build upon IT or technology-supported elements that would structure processes such as feedback from game characters or fictional clients. In designing for innovation, the balance between creating space for creative processes and instructing to make an activity meaningful is difficult to strike. The study however, shows that game-like scenarios, including narrative and competitive elements, and rules of play, create an interesting, meaningful, and engaging frame for integrating technology innovation in school education that can be developed more broadly for other types of school contexts.

REFERENCES

Brown, A. (1992). Design experiments: Theoretical and methodological challenges in creating complex interventions in classroom settings. *Journal of the Learning Sciences, 2*(2), 141–178. doi:10.1207/s15327809jls0202_2

Cobb, P., Confre, J., diSessa, A., Lehrer, R., & Schauble, L. (2003). Design experiments in education research. *Educational Researcher, 32*(1), 9–13. doi:10.3102/0013189X032001009

Collins, A. (1992). Toward a design science of education. In Scanlon, E., & O'Shea, T. (Eds.), *New directions in educational technology* (pp. 15–22). New York, NY: Springer.

Design-Based Research Collective (DBRC). (2003). Design-based research: An emerging paradigm for educational inquiry. *Educational Researcher, 32*(1), 5–8. doi:10.3102/0013189X032001005

diSessa, A. A. (2000). *Changing minds: Computer, learning, and literacy*. Cambridge, MA: MIT Press.

Drucker, P. F. (1993). *Post-capitalist society*. New York, NY: HarperBusiness.

Gee, J. P. (2003). *What video games have to teach us about learning and literacy*. New York, NY: Palgrave Macmillan.

Gee, J. P. (2005). Good video games and good learning. *Phi Kappa Phi Forum, 85*(2), 33–37.

IDEO. (2009). *Human centered design toolkit (2nd ed.)*. Retrieved from http://www.ideo.com/work/item/human-centered-design-toolkit/

Latour, B. (1999). *Pandora's hope: Essays on the reality of science studies*. Cambridge, MA: Harvard University Press.

Latour, B., & Woolgar, S. (1986). *Laboratory life: The construction of scientific facts* (2nd ed.). Princeton, NJ: Princeton University Press.

Lund, H. H., Klitbo, T., & Jessen, C. (2005). Playware technology for physically activating play. *Artificial Life and Robotics Journal, 9*(4), 165–174. doi:10.1007/s10015-005-0350-z

Lynch, M., & Woolgar, S. (1990). Introduction: Sociological orientations to representational practice in science. In Lynch, M., & Woolgar, S. (Eds.), *Representation in scientific practice*. Cambridge, MA: MIT Press.

Magnussen, R. (2007). Games as a platform for situated science practice. In de Castell, S., & Jenson, J. (Eds.), *Worlds in play: International perspectives on digital games research* (pp. 301–311). New York, NY: Peter Lang.

Magnussen, R. (2008). *Representational inquiry in science learning games.* Unpublished doctoral dissertation, Aarhus University, Copenhagen, Denmark.

Magnussen, R. (2009). Representational inquiry competences in science games. In Rodrigues, S. G. A. (Ed.), *Multiple literacy and science education: ICTs in formal and informal learning environments* (pp. 360–370). Hershey, PA: IGI Global. doi:10.4018/9781615206902.ch017

McGinn, M. K., & Roth, W. M. (1999). Preparing students for competent scientific practice: Implications of recent research in science and technology studies. *Educational Researcher, 28*(3), 14–24.

Nielsen, J., Bærendsen, N. K., & Jessen, C. (2009). Music-making and musical comprehension with robotic building blocks. In *Proceedings of the 4th International Conference on E-Learning and Games: Learning by Playing. Game-based Education System Design and Development* (pp. 399-409).

OECD. (2000). *Knowledge management in the learning society.* Paris, France: OECD Publications.

Sawyer, R. K. (2006). Educating for innovation. *Thinking Skills and Creativity, 1*(1), 41–48. doi:10.1016/j.tsc.2005.08.001

Shaffer, D. W. (2006). Epistemic frames for epistemic games. *Computers & Education, 46*(3), 223–234. doi:10.1016/j.compedu.2005.11.003

Shaffer, D. W. (2007). *How computer games help children learn.* New York, NY: Palgrave Macmillan.

Shaffer, D. W., & Gee, J. P. (2005). *Before every child is left behind: How epistemic games can solve the coming crisis in education* (Tech. Rep. No. 2005-7). Madison, WI: University of Wisconsin-Madison, Center for Education Research.

Squire, K., & Klopfer, E. (2007). Augmented reality simulations on handheld computers. *Journal of the Learning Sciences, 16*(3), 371–413. doi:10.1080/10508400701413435

This work was previously published in the International Journal of Virtual and Personal Learning Environments, Volume 2, Issue 2, edited by Michael Thomas, pp. 30-39, copyright 2011 by IGI Publishing (an imprint of IGI Global).

Chapter 4
"World of Uncertainty" Game for Decision–Makers

Jyldyz Tabyldy Kyzy
Queens University, Belfast, UK

ABSTRACT

Decisions on both personal and public matters benefit significantly if uncertainties and risks are handled with more care and accuracy. It is crucial to refine and express degrees of confidence and subjective probabilities of various outcomes. Experience, intuition, and skills help make the most of uncertain information. This paper proposes a concept and design of a computer game which aims to train and enhance some of these skills. It is an online game, which allows players to indicate their subjective uncertainty on a numerical scale and to receive explicit feedback. The accuracy of the player is conditioned and motivated by the incentives based on proper scoring rules. The game aims to train accuracy and better calibration in estimating probabilities and expressing degrees of confidence. The "World of Uncertainty" (n.d.) project researched the learning effect of the game and its impact on players' attitudes towards uncertainty. The concept of this game can be adopted as part of an advanced and complex game in the future.

DECISION MAKING UNDER UNCERTAINTY

Whether making small personal choices, or important public decisions, minor judgments without much awareness, or carefully thought-out ones, every day we face some level of uncertainty. Its role in our everyday life is increasing with the increas-

ing complexity, interdependence and globalization of the modern world and our knowledge about it. The interest in the problem of uncertainty is growing in economics, social and applied science; in areas such as decision analysis, game theory, politics, consumer choice, environmental risks and natural hazards, epidemiology, engineering, etc. On one hand, the demands and weight of the

DOI: 10.4018/978-1-4666-2467-2.ch004

problems we face are increasing. Too much risk in public decisions, or misleading forecasts, can have expensive and far-reaching consequences in both utilitarian and non-utilitarian terms. On the other hand, our knowledge of the world is increasing in complexity, and the amount of information we can relate to the decisions is constantly growing. The problems related to climate change, epidemiology, or earthquake prediction can illustrate this aspect well.

For important public and institutional decisions, various decision aids and techniques can somewhat mitigate this complexity. Expert systems, modeling and simulation systems can help to reduce uncertainties or to gain a better grasp of the situation. However, such techniques are not always applicable or efficient. And even when these techniques are useful, some human evaluation of uncertainties and risks might be necessary. Major strategic and policy-making decisions rely heavily on expert opinion about the uncertainties involved. Subjectivity in such probabilistic estimations is an unavoidable attribute.

Generally, uncertainties are better understood and accounted for in science. Confidence intervals, error assumption as well as probabilistic reasoning are regular features of the scientific approach. However, the problem remains when scientists and experts try to communicate their uncertainties to the policy makers or to the public. For example, the "science – policy gap" problem in ecology was discussed in detail in Bradshaw and Borchers (2000). Policy makers and the public are often confused with the lack of consensus in scientific opinion, so even when an issue achieves better clarity and consensus in the scientific community, it does not immediately transfer to the public opinion.

In contrast to a scientific approach to uncertainty, most of the ordinary people generally tend to avoid uncertainties and complexities. Unambiguous answers based on heuristics, or compelling but deterministic and oversimplified narratives (e.g., those presented in the media) are often preferred

to the more accurate probabilistic reasoning. Thus more information does not necessarily lead to better clarity and comprehensiveness in perception of uncertainties for non-experts. People feel even more confused receiving large amounts of contradictory information concerning personal or public goods (e.g., in financial, ecological or ethical terms) that can be brought about by their choices. Sometime simple heuristics seem to help with everyday small dilemmas such as opting for a new item in a restaurant menu or choosing to buy a lottery ticket. However, in many other situations our personal choices have far reaching consequences and should be taken more seriously. Especially issues concerning health and well-being such as dilemmas on child vaccination or opting for risky surgery require careful consideration of available information. Here, a doctor's or medical expert's evaluation of risks plays a crucial role. These examples underline the importance of expert opinion and suggest that experts are required not only to understand uncertainty but should also be able to communicate it to the other experts, policy makers, and to the public.

RISK, UNCERTAINTY AND GAMES

Although too much uncertainty is undesirable, manageable uncertainty provides an opportunity to make creative and safe decisions. Practical skills in dealing with risk and uncertainty are often overlooked in standard education. This problem could be best addressed in an educational game where players explore uncertainties and make risky choices in the safe environment. Computer game can be a perfect tool for training practical skills in dealing with uncertainty. Dempsey et al. (2002) defines a game as "a set of activities involving one or more players. It has goals, constraints, payoffs, and consequences. A game is rule-guided and artificial in some respects. Finally, a game involves some aspect of competition, even if that competition is with oneself." A rule-guided game with payoffs is very suitable for incorporating probability elicitation elements. Several researchers have advocated an approach to subjective probability elicitation consisting of five steps: motivating, structuring, conditioning, encoding, and verifying (Jenkinson, 2005). With their great potential for creating motivating and challenging environments, computer games provide an excellent setting to explore one's subjective probabilities. Scoring systems with rewards and penalties built into the game can motivate, structure, and condition the user. Computer games have a further advantage in encoding users' replies and feedback in visual, spatial, textual, verbal modes, as well as providing post-analysis of the elicitation process. While holding a story line and narrative, computer games need not follow a linear model. The narrative can be constructed by the player's choices during the game (Mallon & Webb, 2005). Important educational advantages arise when a game incorporates active learning, multi-sensory experience and interactive feedback (Amory et al., 1999; Mallon & Webb, 2000).

Since accurate estimation of one's own confidence is the key to making good decisions under uncertainty, it is useful to develop an environment where users can explore their subjective probability assessments. Detailed and structured feedback on their performance in a game situation should improve their decision-making skills—an improvement which is potentially transferable to the real life decision making. Accurate probability assessment can be encouraged by applying special techniques, such as proper scoring rules, based on the Bayesian approach to probability (Anderson, 1998; Dawid, 2007). As mentioned by Daneshkhah (2004), this tolerates subjectivity and facilitates the evolution of expert opinion; it can illuminate and quantify imprecise, ranked or ordinal judgments of probabilities. A main advantage of Bayesian analysis is that it suggests a constructive and practical approach for dealing with many important real life problems where standard statistical analysis is not applicable (Daneshkhah, 2004; Lindley, 2006).

THEORETICAL FRAMEWORK OF THE RESEARCH

The main factors to be considered when modelling decision making in our game we framed as following: 1) the uncertain event or situation; 2) utilities (payoffs— gains and losses); 3) judgement and decision; 4) feedback and learning. These factors or stages of decision making under uncertainty are further examined in our research from three perspectives: 1) real life perspective, 2) psychological perspective, 3) game or other interactive media perspective. The first perspective draws on observing the instances of uncertainty in the real life as well as current practice of decision-making and practical needs for training. The second perspective looks how each stage of thinking about uncertainty is reflected in a decision-maker's mind, i.e., the mental model of an uncertainty. We consider psychological issues around perceiving uncertainty and risk as well as the role of individual differences in judgment and decision making. And finally, the last perspective is on general issues of representing and communicating uncertainties and risks in the virtual environment. This is a game development perspective merging the previous two and considering opportunities and limitations of translating uncertain events into game where players can make decisions see the consequences and learn from this experience.

Statistical Analysis

We are employing mixed quantitative and qualitative research methods (interviews, questionnaires, and experiments) in order to test learning effect of the game as well as study the individual differences in performance. Player's performance records provide rich statistical material for analysing the trends in the quality of probabilistic estimations (coherence, consistency, calibration). The impact of the demographic and individual differences on the results is also in the focus of our research. Thus it is interesting to find if the game performance correlates with the indicators of decision-making,

Figure 1. Slider with payoffs

gaming, and gambling experiences of the players. We will also look at the group differences in terms of demographics (gender, age, occupation, etc.)

Game Play

The game uses multiple choice questions on a variety of subjects. However this is not just an ordinary quiz. Its main purpose is to improve and calibrate players' certainty and sense of probabilities rather than subject knowledge. Thus the topic of the quiz or difficulty level became irrelevant so long as the player enjoys the quiz and is motivated to achieve higher score. In addition to the questions based on academic courses, we have been mainly using multiple choice general interest "almanac" questions. In future more image-based questions, questions on cognitive abilities and math questions will be included.

On answering each question, the player has to indicate his/her confidence as accurately as possible using interactive probability slider (Figure 1).

As a player adjusts the slider, corresponding payoffs for correct and incorrect outcomes will be shown. This payoff function is based on proper scoring rules and designed to encourage the honest and accurate confidence judgment. In addition to immediate feedback, players receive brief overview after each set of questions and also

can access the results of previously completed quizzes. On the basis of several quizzes the calibration charts are available in the personal profiles (Figure 2). Detailed feedback helps to monitor own progress adjusting for over/under confidence across a variety of subjects and difficulty levels.

CONCLUSION

Some degree of uncertainty is involved in almost any decision. Moreover, according to Oreskes (2004) there is no such thing as certainty in decision-making. However we can operate with degrees of certainty. The diversity of origins, levels and manifestations of uncertainty leads to a wide range of approaches in understanding this concept. A probabilistic Bayesian reasoning is one of the most conventional ways of expressing uncertainties according to the literature. This comes especially natural in the case of repeated events and games of chance. When probability distributions are not as obvious, an expression of uncertainty in terms of subjective probabilities was suggested as an alternative. Although this is a disputed area in the literature we conclude that uncertainty of any type can be theoretically expressed by subjective probabilities.

People are not very good in probabilistic forecasting; we are prone to biases and heuristics (Kahnemen et al., 1982). However, the ability to give accurate probability estimates is one of those intuitive skills which come with experience and can be trained. Considering that the computer games are very convenient means of gaining such experience, we have developed an online game presented in this paper.

We are still in the process of collecting and analysing the statistical data from the game, the majority of which came from the student players. Participants found the game appealing; the containment of the interest was very much dependent on their personal interest in the subject

Figure 2. Calibration chart

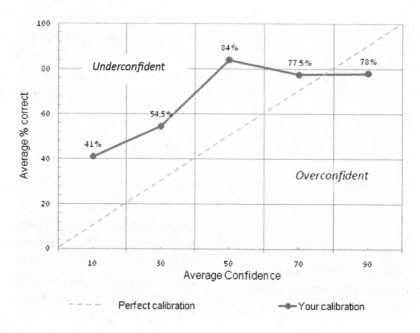

of the quizzes. The research involves collecting data from online players as well as experiments in the observed groups. The preliminary results indicate that there is some overtime improvement effect with the majority of the participants. However, in the study with the repeated task, before and after quiz, the learning effect might be subtle. On the other hand it is expected that the players with some professional experience in decision-making or interest in gambling will show different pattern in the game progress. The details of the experiments, analysis the data and results will be reported later.

The set of skills involved in dealing with uncertainty are very complex and based on both rational and non-rational cognitive processes, where players' individual differences and attitudes to the uncertainty influence plays an important role. In order to be able study these skills we needed in some sense "pure" game, meaning certain simplicity and straightforwardness of both tasks and motivators. Hopefully, in future this concept will be developed to be part of the more complex and challenging computer games for learning and entertainment.

ACKNOWLEDGMENT

This research is supported by EPSRC. The project also involves: Dr. David Newman (QUB), Prof. Philip Dawid (Cambridge University), Dr. Melissa Cole (Brunel University), Tony Elliman (Brunel University), Bride Mallon (DKIT), Dr. Emiliya Lazarova (QUB), and Damian Green. For more information see http://www.worldofuncertainty. org, http://quiz.worldofuncertainty.org

REFERENCES

Amory, A., Naicker, K., Vincent, J., & Adams, C. (1999). The use of computer games as an educational tool: Identification of appropriate game types and game elements. *British Journal of Educational Technology*, *30*(4), 311. doi:10.1111/1467-8535.00121

Anderson, J. L. (1998). Embracing uncertainty: The interface of Bayesian statistics and cognitive psychology. *Conservation Ecology*, *2*(1), 2.

Bradshaw, G. A., & Borchers, J. G. (2000). Uncertainty as information: narrowing the science-policy gap. *Conservation Ecology, 4*(1), 7.

Daneshkhah, A. R. (2004). *Psychological aspects influencing elicitation of subjective probability.* Retrieved from http://www.sheffield.ac.uk/content/1/c6/03/09/33/Psychologypapers.pdf

Dawid, A. P. (1982). The well-calibrated Bayesian. *Journal of the American Statistical Association, 77*, 605–613. doi:10.2307/2287720

Dawid, A. P. (1997). The well-calibrated Bayesian. In Hamouda, O. F., & Rowley, J. C. R. (Eds.), *Probability concepts, dialogue and beliefs* (pp. 165–173). Cheltenham, UK: Edward Elgar.

Dawid, P. (2007). The geometry of proper scoring rules. *Annals of the Institute of Statistical Mathematics, 59*, 77–93. doi:10.1007/s10463-006-0099-8

Dempsey, J. V., Haynes, L. L., Lucassen, B. A., & Casey, M. S. (2002). Forty simple computer games and what they could mean to educators. *Simulation & Gaming: An Interdisciplinary Journal, 33*(2), 157–168.

Jenkinson, D. (2005). *The elicitation of probabilities: A review of the statistical literature.* Yorkshire, UK: University of Sheffield.

Kahneman, D., Slovic, P., & Tversky, A. (Eds.). (1982). *Judgment under uncertainty: Heuristics and biases.* Cambridge, UK: Cambridge University Press.

Lindley, D. V. (2006). *Understanding uncertainty.* Cambridge, UK: Cambridge University Press. doi:10.1002/0470055480

Mallon, B., & Webb, B. (2000). Structure, causality, visibility and interaction: Propositions for evaluating engagement in narrative multimedia. *International Journal of Human-Computer Studies, 53*, 269–287. doi:10.1006/ijhc.2000.0387

Mallon, B., & Webb, B. (2005). Stand up and take your place: Identifying narrative elements in narrative adventure and role-play games. *ACM Computers in Entertainment, 3*(1), 6–6. doi:10.1145/1057270.1057285

Oreskes, N. (2004). Beyond the ivory tower: The scientific consensus on climate change. *Science 3, 306*(5702), 1686

World of Uncertainty. (n. d.). *Welcome to the World of Uncertainty.* Retrieved from http://www.worldofuncertainty.org

This work was previously published in the International Journal of Virtual and Personal Learning Environments, Volume 2, Issue 2, edited by Michael Thomas, pp. 40-45, copyright 2011 by IGI Publishing (an imprint of IGI Global).

Chapter 5

The Siren Song of Digital Simulation:
Games, Procedural Rhetoric, and the Process of Historical Education

Jerremie Clyde
University of Calgary, Canada

Glenn Wilkinson
University of Calgary, Canada

ABSTRACT

This paper contrasts the importance of procedural rhetoric for the use of games in university and college level historical education with the use of history themed digital simulations. This paper starts by examining how history functions as a form of disciplinary knowledge and how this disciplinary way of knowing things is taught in the post secondary history course. The manner in which history is taught is contrasted with its evaluation to better define what students are actually expected to learn. The simulation is then examined in light of learning goals and evaluation. This demonstrates that simulations are a poor fit for most post secondary history courses. The more appropriate and effective choice is to construct the past via procedural rhetoric as a way to use digital video games to make the historical argument.

INTRODUCTION

This paper suggests a different approach to game based learning for history and challenges the more common and popular use of digital simulations. This builds upon our previous work on a digital mode for history, with the use of procedural rhetoric to author scholarly history in a gamic form, by applying it directly to historical education and student learning. Due to our emphasis on procedural rhetoric, this paper is based largely, although not exclusively, on the North American work done into game based learning over the past few decades. It will start by examining how history

DOI: 10.4018/978-1-4666-2467-2.ch005

functions as a form of disciplinary knowledge and how this disciplinary way of knowing things is taught in the post-secondary history course. The manner in which it is taught will be contrasted with its evaluation to better define what students are actually expected to learn. The simulation, a very popular tool for digital game based attempts to teach history, will be then examined in the light of learning goals and evaluation. This will demonstrate that simulations are in fact a poor fit for most post secondary history courses. The more appropriate and effective choice is to construct the past via procedural rhetoric as a way to use digital video games to make the historical argument. While our focus here is on history as a discipline, our conclusions are applicable to learning in other academic disciplines where the focus is on how arguments are constructed and truth is created, as opposed to merely memorizing and conveying content.

The digital mode results from the application of procedural rhetoric to scholarly history to produce a valid argument that optimizes the use of computers for university and college level historical studies. The digital mode of history was first presented as a way of communicating scholarly research at the *Seventy Years On: New Perspectives on the Second World War* in the Fall of 2009. The paper discussed how history as a disciplinary form of knowledge is not mode dependent, where mode is the technological medium through which the scholarly argument is constructed and conveyed. For example historical arguments can be conveyed through the printed scholarly article and monograph, the oral classroom lecture, documentary film or computer video game. History is not mode dependent because it is defined by its epistemologies which are dependent upon a series of creative processes such as empathetic re-enactment, limited counterfactual, and narrative reconstruction. The point of the digital mode is not to replace the textual mode found in print, but to offer a multi-modal approach to presenting valid scholarly interpretations of the past, whether

they are constructionist, de-constructionist, or re-constructionist histories. In the realm of education it does what Karras (1994) has stated is essential in an approach to teaching historical argumentation, in that it can be explicitly taught, performed, and evaluated. The digital mode of history allows new questions to be asked, old questions to be addressed in new ways, and constructions of the past to be communicated more effectively. The digital mode offers exactly what students want; challenging content, exciting methodologies, and engagement with the material (Russell & Pellegrino, 2008).

This paper considers the application of the digital mode to historical education, and describes how arguments are created in the digital mode using Ian Bogost's ideas of procedural rhetoric. Procedural rhetoric becomes a significant tool to understand how the digital mode constructs an argument in a way that is relevant in the context of historical education.

CONSTRUCTING THE PAST AS HISTORY

In order to express knowledge in a different format, whether that format is a digital simulation or a gamic representation of a scholarly argument, it is important to know how that knowledge exists. It is crucial to make that decision intentionally because it shows an epistemic awareness that we also want to see in students as critical thinkers. Epistemic cognition is particularly important for history students as valid representations of the past are constructed radically differently depending on the epistemic choices made. Epistemic cognition is the process that enables individuals to develop the criteria for limits and certainty of knowing (Maggioni, VanSledright, & Alexander, 2009), which enables a constructive approach to ambiguity as opposed to the common student misapprehension that historical certainty exists.

While there have been many attempts to address the epistemological question, "what is history?", Alun Munslow provides a functional answer that is useful for analyzing digital expression of the past. In his works *Narrative and History* (2007) and *The New History* (2003) he defines three broad epistemological approaches for historical scholarship: reconstruction, construction and deconstruction. This paper will borrow these categories to understand the nature of history and place it as a form of disciplinary knowledge in the post-secondary history classroom. Munslow's (2003, 2007) three epistemological approaches make it clear how some expressions of the past, such as history-themed commercial digital games and simulations, are fundamentally different from the scholarly history that is often taught.

Munslow (2003, 2007) suggests that the majority of historians working today are constructionists, where the past is constructed as history through reasoned argument. Constructionist history relies on empirical methods and analyses as well as narrative to create adequately justified true claims and theories about the past. Such claims and theories function as the basis of both historical knowledge and the traditional epistemology of history. As a form of history, constructionism recognizes that "history" is not the past. Constructionism builds up knowledge of the past and expresses the past as history by both analyzing how and what individual pieces of evidence can do, and what conclusions about the actions of historical agents (be they individuals or corporate entities) can be established through the relationships between fact, evidence and interpretation.

In this case, evidence itself is separate from a notion of historical fact, despite these terms often being used interchangeably, as the fact only becomes evidence based upon its relationship to the question at hand. This differs from popular approaches to history where one often hears claims of factual accuracy as basis for veracity, a claim often made in conjunction with digital simulations of the past such as *Making History* series

by Muzzy Lane. The constructionist approach to history, while allowing almost any question to be asked, provides constraints around how the question can be answered.

This is in contrast to a deconstructionist approach which is more open to how a question is answered and at first glance seems a more flexible approach for a digital mode or gamic version of history. The deconstructionist idea of an unknowable past, or past that can be known in a multitude of ways, suggests the digital mode of history could be almost anything as long as it could be shown to have some sort of expressive power or meaning. Taking a deconstructionist approach then might be simpler, or at least offer more freedom to the scholar working in the digital mode who wants to create entertaining history games for their students, than a more valid constructionist approach to history. However, this approach would also be contradictory to most historians' aspirations for themselves and their students to achieve something approaching objective truth in historical scholarship. In addition, for a history (as an expression of the past) to have meaning and achieve adequately-justified true claims and theories about its subject matter, these claims and theories must be recognizable as history and be part of the scholarly discourse at all levels.

Reconstructionist history is a third choice for the digital mode of history, and like deconstructionist history does seem to present some benefits to educators working in the digital mode of history. The reconstructionist historian attempts to recreate the past as it actually was through the use of sources, which by their nature as facts are considered objective. The potential to use computers to collect, compile, arrange and present a vast array of historical data seems to hold the promise an accurate recreation of past. Of course the utilization and arrangement of facts or data, is an interpretive activity and even the use of a computer to compile and present them is, to some degree, tainted by subjectivity. Like deconstructionist history, this also taxes the historian's ideal of objective scholarship and then becomes a significant problem for education. The reconstructionist mode is now commonly that of the popular historian, the entertainment-documentary and many digital video games, where an attempt is made to tell the "real" story. It is clear that they are reconstructionist forms of history as the main claim to authenticity is based on the volume of data used. Reconstructionist history claims that history is the past, as opposed to a constructionist view where it is the past as history.

Irrespective of the epistemological choice, there are no hard and fast rules in history as to what constitutes evidence, the limits of evidence, or the relationships between fact, evidence and interpretation. Even simply reading existing historical arguments students find it extremely difficult to understand this process and "it is likely that many students will be stopped at the beginning of the learning process" (Pace, 2004, p. 13). Rules are established by the student or scholar in the creation of the argument itself, its use of facts as evidence, and the relationship between evidence interpretation and conclusion. That argument is generated by the scholar or student even if the decision is made to convey the argument through a computer-mediated gamic format. Even though constructions of the past as history can be computer mediated, it is not the case that process of constructing the past as history can be automated. It is only within a given historical argument that we can find the rules that govern that particular construction of the past. It is that argument and the process of its formation (including historical imagination and empathetic re-enactment) where we find the rules used to construct the argument. Those rules are then used to produce the procedural version. The rules of the given argument or construction of the past are dependent upon the question being asked, the known facts and methods applied. In order to be considered "good history," these three factors must be interdependent. Once the relationships are set the logic of the argument can be used to generate a set of rules and procedures that are then

mediated by a computer. That set of computer mediated rules and relationships are the digital version of the historical argument.

HISTORICAL TEACHING AND EVALUATION

The instructional goal of the post-secondary history course is the creation of the historical argument, which is the process of establishing the relationships between facts, evidence, interpretations, and conclusions. The essay is traditionally used to evaluate student ability to create a historical argument using these processes. In fact, the American Historical Association (1998) in its "Statement of Excellence in Classroom Teaching of History" states that the final evaluation of student learning should include written or other work that provides evidence of analysis and interpretation of the factual information those students collected to address a significant historical question (American Historical Association, 2010). However, instead of interpretation and analysis, what most students seem to focus on is the content of the course, dates, persons, places and things rather than process of constructing arguments about the past as history. When course lectures or readings try to contextualize those facts in different constructions of the past students see those only as alternate opinions, and secondary to the facts themselves with the main issue at hand being that of whether something happened or not (Voelker, 2008). Often how courses are organized re-enforces this separation of content and process with a minimal amount of class time given over to the construction of historical arguments and essay writing. Even essay writing is often treated as the mechanics of presentation rather than a heuristic process that is used to form the historical argument. It is usually relegated to being dealt with outside of class, by teaching assistants, sessionals, librarians, writing centre tutors, or through online tutorials, special lectures or drop in seminars, and written guides. The mechanics of presenting the argument in essay form and the lecture as a model of the process of constructing an argument are rarely brought together for the student.

Faculty want students to learn facts as both the building blocks of history and the basis of cultural literacy (Maxwell, 2010), they also want the students to learn the process of constructing narrative interpretations of the past based on those building blocks. The research of Russell and Pellegrino (2008) suggests that the lecture and reading combination is an efficient way to transmit a great deal of factual information but fails to promote notions of how historical meaning is constructed. While professors imply the process of constructing the past as history through the structure of their lectures, students focus primarily on that which is being explicitly taught: people, places, and things in the past. It is only those students who are aware of this implicit modeling of process through lecture and course readings will be successful. It could be argued that most history teachers are not even aware of this failure by students to connect process and content, but they are aware of many of their students being unable to produce a reasoned historical argument for their term papers.

In essence there is a disconnection between the main evaluative tool of the history course, the essay, and what students are being taught in the classroom. What students most often come equipped to do from Secondary School is to summarize the factual content, and while "eager to learn but relatively unable to initiate or carry out projects on their own" (McClymer & Moynihan, 1977, p. 360). It is important to recognize and address this disconnection because merely changing the mode or introducing digital learning objects, such as simulations or history games, will not result in effective student learning of the process of history. The essay as an evaluative tool does not just measure historical knowledge, but also the construction of the past as history. Indeed, it is the quality of the argument that receives the most scrutiny, as factual accuracy will not necessarily

gain marks and inaccuracy will *cost* them. What the essay evaluates in student learning is the process of constructing the past as history despite this only being implied by the instructor (Beaufort, 2004). This process is generally only taught indirectly through modeling via the students' readings and through lecture, rather than constituting a major part of the courses content.

Student demonstration of that implied knowledge often takes place through the practical application of their assignments, not before, which is a high stakes process of trial and error from the students' point of view. So while the students are evaluated on their understanding of the processes of reasoned argument, and evidential attributes and relationships, they are not directly taught it. They are rarely able to play with the process to gain a better understanding of how it functions.

There are other techniques in history courses, such as annotated bibliographies, document analyses, seminars, and class presentations that are used to better equip students to construct the past as history. The document analysis assignment is designed to encourage students to think critically about primary sources. They are given a primary source, which is a document produced in the time period under study, and asked to interpret its value as a historical source with respect to such concepts as authorship, intentionalality, context, reception, and significance. Document analyses exercises have been used to help develop students' historical imagination and can also be merged with the final paper, asking students to comment on the context of their primary sources within their essays (Tobin, 2001, p. 499). The outline and annotated bibliography assignments are given to students in advance of their term paper as a way to check the students progress on their research, the logic of their thinking, and to encourage them to get an early start. While both these assignments do encourage students to think about the nature of historical evidence and the structure of their argument, they are rarely integrated into their term papers, being seen instead by many students as discrete exercises. In addition there is some evidence to suggest that without significant support students are not even adequately prepared to deal with these initial scaffolding exercises (Britt & Aglinskas, 2002). Unless class time is given over to teaching the process of building historical arguments, these assignments are no better than the term paper for expecting students to engage in trial and error learning (although fewer grades are attached, and so have lower risk) based on implied concepts from their lectures and readings. These assignments are intended to help build skills so that students are better equipped to deal with a term paper, but they do not necessarily teach the process of constructing the past as history. Instead, they focus on discrete parts of the process and it is no wonder that student see them as such. All of these issues can be ameliorated by class discussions, tutorials and seminars, but the use of these tools is unfortunately often impractical in the face of shrinking budgets, large classes, and too few teaching assistants.

In response to student inability to write an essay, the difficulty of reaching the hundreds of students enrolled in history courses in any one semester, and the instructor's inability to teach these skills in the classroom, a number of online learning objects have been developed to help students write a more effective essay. For instance, Workshop for the Information Search Process for Research (WISPR), developed at the University of Calgary, was based on Dr. Alex Hayden's (2003) phenemological research into how students handle the research and paper writing process (Rutherford & Pival, 2006). Even excellent learning objects such as this one do not deal with the process of creating knowledge in a discipline specific way, thus failing to teach students to construct the past as history. It does teach a student to write a paper and do research effectively, but fails to introduce students to thinking historically, to consider the process of historical construction.

The increasingly popular digital response to the problem of student inability to write a historical essay, engage with history, or think historically utilises everything from online discussion groups around a course to online learning objects like *Heaven & Hell on Earth: The Massacre of The "Black" Donnellys* (Pettit & Street, 2007), *Salem Witchcraft Trials* (Hurter, 2003), *The Estate Inventories of Early* Virginians (Phillips, 2002). In most cases they do one of two things: in attempting to teach the process of historical construction they become exercises in the mechanics of paper writing and/or research; or they end up teaching content and not process. They tend to either explicitly or implicitly use the metaphor of historian as detective searching for existing clues and solving a mystery by finding out the truth behind it. This is the popular metaphor of documentary media, such as the History Channel's series *Battlefield Detective,* or fiction such as Josphine Tey's *The Daugher of Time.* The idea of historian as detective only works as a metaphor for re-constructionist history, where the historian is uncovering a truth that is already there, as opposed to constructing a valid interpretation of the past. The current process of historical education concerns teaching this process via modeling it through lecture and readings. It does work for a limited number of students, but instead of trying to find a way to make that modeling more effective, instructors are turning to very different approaches. For example, the computer-based *Salem Witchcraft Trials* (Hurter, 2003) which continues to emphasize content over process and models an obsolete way of reconstructing the past. This misplaced emphasis and modeling are particularly evident in the case of digital historical simulations for education; whether they are scratch built or modified commercial-off-the-shelf (COTS) digital games.

DIGITAL SIMULATIONS OF PAST

In the end, the history that is taught in most courses and that most students are evaluated for creating is one that constructs the past out of an argument, instead of attempting to recreate or simulate the past. Attempts to simulate the past through digital video games are exercises in re-enactment that are outside scholarly history's epistemology for assigning truth attributes. Prensky argues convincingly that "*whenever* one plays a game—video, computer or otherwise—and *whatever* game one plays, learning happens constantly, whether the players want it to, and are aware of it, or not." The question then becomes, what is it exactly students are learning? What one should actually be creating in a digital mode is in fact the digital version of the valid empirical reasoned argument that is taught to students, and is more commonly communicated by the mechanical means of print or through the oral presentation of the lecture rather than in the digital simulation.

Kurt Squire has suggested that "the important question is not *can* games be used to support learning, but *how*" (Changing the Game, 2004 p. 1). Within the context of game based historical education the most important question is actually *what* is being taught, as the how will be predicated on that. While there has been an explosion of interest in the field of history education regarding the use of games and simulations, a thorough consideration of what is actually being taught in the post-secondary history course does not seem to have taken place. There have been a number of articles focusing on the classroom use of non-digital simulations, where the students take on the role of historical actors during a particular time "to get into the shoes of historical people and to move around in them" (Monahan, 2002, p. 74). Monahan claims that "a simulation comes closer than any other tool to helping students understand the past from the perspective of those who lived it"(Monahan, 2002, p. 74). Despite this and claims of student enjoyment he does not explain how a simulation creates student understanding, how that understanding is a valid form of history, and what learning is actually evaluated. This raises the question as to whether or not what they are learning is history or another form of knowing. The valid

history course focus on the process of constructing the past as history in student assignments suggests that most historical simulations, digital or otherwise, are a poor fit for academic historical education. Monahan's (2002) implementation of simulations also involves a great deal of instructor mediation to ensure for whatever learning there is to take place. Simulations fail to do what Royle and Clarke (2003) suggest games should be doing in education to be effective, namely to put the individual at the centre of the learning experience; to focus on the students interacting with the content to create knowledge; and to match what is actually being taught. At best for simulations to be effective in post secondary historical education they require instructor mediation, through discussion, seminars, reflective writing and the like. This suggests that the learning is not taking in or through the simulation but as a result of the follow up exercises. This in turn means they are failing as game based learning since the learning is not taking place during the play experience. It would be better if the game mechanisms were developed "where players literally perform the kinds of understandings we want them to have" (Squire, Giovanetto, Devane, & Durga, 2005), which is the point of the digital mode of history.

By focusing wholeheartedly on simulation based learning objects and exercises, while possibly having significant value in primary school education and heritage education, instructors are likely to take secondary and post-secondary historical education down the wrong path. There are several examples of the use of simulations for teaching history at different levels, including Squire and Barab's (2004) use of *Civilization III*, Aaron Whelchel (2008) using *Civilization III* and *Age of Empires*, and Julian Del Gaudio (2002) scratch building role play simulations such as *Eunice: A Captivity Simulation* and *In Search of Freedom: Navigating A Slaves' [sic] Journey*. More recently in Canada, the Social Sciences and Humanities Research Council of Canada has funded *The Simulating History*

Project: Best Practices for History Simulations (Kee et al., 2009) which focuses on historical simulation through games to be used in teaching. Even if the Simulating History Project and others like it were able to develop good history simulations, it brings to mind Prensky's (2003) exhortation regarding digital games and education when he says "just because one learns *how* to do something, it doesn't mean one has learned *when* or *whether one should* do it." When one considers what is actually being taught, or more to the point, evaluated in most academic history courses and what a student would need to learn to function as a history scholar, these simulations are of limited to no use. They are exercises in historical re-enactment, which is not even a new way to teach, as it has been used in role play in the classroom or visiting historical sites, particularly those with costumed interpreters. As paradigms of constructing the past re-enactments are flawed because their accuracy is based on their ability to replicate historical events (Monahan, 2002). This is problematic because there is nothing in how we observe or interpret the past that enables us to declare events unfolded as they had to, we can only say they unfolded as they did. Kurt Squire in his 2005 perspective paper points out that "it is increasingly clear that simply replicating existing paradigms of instruction is unwise in the information age" (p. 18).

Digital historical simulations may seem to do historical re-enactments and counterfactuals differently than their live action counterparts. They allow replications, one to record and review, to include more role-players or larger environments than would otherwise be possible. However, making the reconstructions bigger, better, and faster, is not changing how they express the past, they still fail as expressions of scholarly history. The students need to know how to construct the past as reasoned historical argument. It might very well be the case that there are ways to use these computer mediated re-enactments as sources to greater conclusions, but students still need to know how to come to those conclusions, how to move that experience from event to evidence, to relate it to other pieces of evidence, move from evidence to interpretation and finally to conclusion. Epistemic challenges aside, computer games, even commercial quality games like *Civilization III*, are not immediately motivating for students because it is not always clear to them how a computer game can teach history (Squire, 2004). The game should allow for the performance of disciplinary ways of thinking that provides a more active interpretative role to students (Anderson & Hounsell, 2007). This means it must focus on the process of constructing the past as history, where student interaction with the game creates knowledge of this process, rather than requiring supplemental learning activities. Their success in exploring the gamic procedural rendering of the reasoned historical argument should be the arbiter of their understanding of how to construct the past as history.

GAMES AND PROCEDURAL RHETORIC

Since simulations are not a legitimate expression of the past as history and are out of synch with what is being taught in the history class, it begs the question as to whether or not computers should even be used. It requires one to consider, as has been outlined above, how the past as history is constructed as a reasoned argument. Applying Ian Bogost's (2007) ideas of procedural rhetoric to how history is constructed suggests a possible method for the creation of a digital gamic scholarly expression of the past as history. Historians construct the past as a series of evidential relationships, which are procedural within a given argument. Those procedures can be expressed as rules that govern how the parts of an argument move towards a verifiable conclusion with a reasonably established truth attribute. In order to do that and still construct the past as scholarly history, one has to look at how procedural environments construct arguments. Ian Bogost argues convincingly that procedural environments make arguments in a sufficiently different way than classic text-based forms of rhetoric. Bogost calls this new form of persuasion "procedural rhetoric." The notion of procedural rhetoric demonstrates how one could build the digital mode of history that creates computer mediated gamic scholarly constructions of the past. The gamic nature of which allows students to explore and interact with the process of historical construction within a given argument.

The historical narrative offers explanations of events by constructing relationships and placing them in an order and context. Narrative explanation is dependent upon the idea that order and relationships are explanatory and it is in the ordering and constructing of relationships of the historical narrative that one finds the processes. In order to identify the process of a given argument one has to consider how facts are evidence, the relationships between individual pieces of evidence, the way in which evidence builds towards inference, and lastly how inferences lead to a conclusion and the formation of a justified belief. This is exactly what professors expect and assess in student essays. Pace (2004) argues that students tend to be unable to read the historical narrative and understand the process of how it constructs the past seeing it instead as a series of historical facts. His responses to this challenge include six steps such as using hyper links and audio files to make his own thought process knowable to his students while doing the assigned readings or reformatting them to emphasize those parts of a reading that are most important.

In the digital mode of history Pace's (2004) six steps can be addressed as the evidence and resulting arguments are explored as a multi-modal rule set. In addition, by having a computer mediate those rules for the player, it allows a deeper exploration of the historian's thinking through trial and error (as opposed to allowing for trial and error only at the point of evaluation). In this

way, students can gain a much deeper and more critical understanding of how the past is constructed as history. They can explore parts of the historical process that normally take place within the historian's mind before anything is set down on paper, such as the use of evidence, the limits of empathetic re-enactment and the explanatory narrative. Since the historical process is taught through modeling, allowing students to explore the process itself, as opposed to just the historical facts or mechanics of writing, the emphasis is placed on the construction of the past as a reasoned argument. Students have an interest in the past and learning about history but how it is taught causes them to lose this interest. What is required is a way for students to be engaged with the material, such as readings, in an insightful and meaningful way (Russell & Pellegrino, 2008). In the digital mode of the argument itself they are explicitly engaged in the process of historical construction. This interaction enables them to understand how the past is constructed as history and as a result better able to meet the requirements on which they are evaluated.

Allowing students to read and, better still, author their own work in this way will result in less focus on flowery prose and hollow rhetoric and more focus on the logic and structure of the well reasoned empirical argument about the past. Tsui (1999) found that it was not a particular discipline that encouraged the development of critical thinking in students but writing assignments and instructor feedback. While authoring in the digital mode may seem intimidating, the work of Gee (2010) suggests that most students can handle the technical aspects of authoring in this way. From the instructor perspective "the inclusion of computer games within formal learning is a necessity" and is now "an issue of curriculum and teaching methodology rather than a technological issue" (Royle, 2009). One does *not* require an entire games studio, professional programmers, artists and game designers in order to produce a high quality serious game (Blackman, 2005). Authoring in the digital mode can be done in a number of ways, including creating original code, modifying a COTS game with its bundled editors, or using a commercial game engine licensed at a nominal cost for educational use such as *Source SDK* or *The Hero Engine* (Valve, 2008, Whatley & Harris, 2010; Clyde & Thomas, 2008). Students working in the digital mode, expressing their arguments via procedural rhetoric, have to make all the evidential and interpretive relationships of their historical narratives clear through translating them into an interdependent set of rules. Working in the digital mode creates the learning environment that Dickey (2005) states is the ideal for using digital video games for teaching where the "learner plays an active role in the construction of knowledge, while the role of the teacher is to provide materials and environment that support learner's engagement in the learning tasks." Students authoring in this way are forced to think deeply and intentionally how they define and construct an argument. By reviewing the evidence, rule set, design, and finished product the educator is better able to evaluate student understanding of history.

If at least some of the course "readings" are in the form of a digital game and students can construct their own assignments in the same way, they will be introduced not only to historical skills, but also to procedural literacy. Procedural literacy is "not limited to the abstract ability to understand procedural representations of cultural values, it also uses that understanding to interrogate, critique and uses specific representations of specific real or imagined process"(p. 246). It is an important skill in a world where media are increasingly dominated by all types of digital video games. It is also a critical literacy for academic work in other disciplines regardless of mode because it is an abstract approach applicable to all reasoned arguments. It provides students with a means to determine what counts as evidence such as empirical observation or predicative models and how reasonably justifiable truth is being created. As the thinking skills that are encompassed by procedural literacy are

really the attributes of critical thinking, it provides students with a way to develop critical thinking skills in a media context they are familiar with. While defining critical thinking can be problematic for some, most definitions include the ability to recognize important relationships, make correct inferences, evaluate evidence or authority and deduce conclusions. Critical thinking has been touted by institutions of higher learning as the main benefit they offer society, as they claim it ensures a thinking citizenry and competent work force in an increasingly complex world (Tsui, 1999).

CONCLUSION AND FURTHER CONSIDERATIONS

The digital mode of history is a way to avoid the siren song of digital simulations which, while fun, only seem to offer student engagement. They fail to address the important issue of how the past is constructed as history. The digital mode provides an engaging way to introduce the process of scholarly history to all students, particularly those new to the university environment. This is more effective than digital simulations and even current classroom practice at universities where historical methods and process are often taught only at a senior level in courses primarily aimed at history majors. While the digital mode of history, like course readings, would benefit from additional in-class discussion or seminars, it does not require them, unlike digital simulations. This means that the digital mode of history is particularly practical for engaging large first-year classes in the process of constructing history because it does not require seminars, class discussion, or tutorials to be effective.

There are other benefits of the digital mode for teaching the process of constructing the past such as peer learning through digital palimpsests and graffiti. Digital palimpsests are seen in games like *Demon's Souls* (Miyazaki, Takeuchi, & Nakajima, 2009) where the server automatically records a player's actions and makes them available for others to see. In *Demon's Souls* they have an instructive role as they show a player the last moments leading up to another player's demise. In this context graffiti refers to the ability to leave behind notes and comments, often context specific for other players by writing them in the game environment, acting as a form of virtual class participation. The potential for peer learning and more effective evaluation of student participation and learning offered by the digital mode of history is the topic of a future paper. Drawing upon the conclusions in this paper, our current research is moving in the direction of the application and testing of procedural rhetoric in the post-secondary classroom. Our own epistemologies suggest that one can create reasonably justifiable truths through reasoned argument, which we have done here. We are aware of the benefits of quantifiable data and that other scholars have epistemologies that require it. In light of this, we have created a game focusing on the construction of the past as history and tested it as part of our paper at the LOEX of the West Conference at Mount Royal University in June of 2010. We will be using that game in the post-secondary classroom in the near future and testing the more practical aspects of using procedural rhetoric as an approach to game based learning. In addition, over the next year we will be taking an existing scholarly historical argument and translating it from explanatory textual narrative into a scholarly game in the digital mode using procedural rhetoric.

REFERENCES

American Historical Association. (1998). *Statement of excellence in classroom teaching of history*. Retrieved from http://www.historians.org/teaching/policy/ExcellentTeaching.htm

Anderson, C., & Hounsell, D. (2007). Knowledge practices: 'Doing the subject' in undergraduate courses. *Curriculum Journal*, *18*(4), 463–478. doi:10.1080/09585170701687910

Beaufort, A. (2004). Developmental gains of a history major: A case for building a theory of disciplinary writing expertise. *Research in the Teaching of English*, *39*(2), 136–185.

Blackman, S. (2005). Serious games ...and less! *Computer Graphics*, *39*(1), 12–16. doi:10.1145/1057792.1057802

Bogost, I. (2007). *Persuasive games: The expressive power of videogames*. Cambridge, MA: MIT Press.

Britt, M. A., & Aglinskas, C. (2002). Improving students' ability to identify and use source information. *Cognition and Instruction*, *20*(4), 485–522. doi:10.1207/S1532690XCI2004_2

Clyde, J., & Thomas, C. (2008). Building and information literacy first person shooter. *RSR. Reference Services Review*, *36*(4), 366–380. doi:10.1108/00907320810920342

Clyde, J., & Wilkinson, G. (2009, Fall). *The digital mode of history*. Paper presented at Seventy Years On: New Perspectives on the Second World War, Lake Louise, AB, Canada.

Del Gaudio, J. J. (2002). Creating simulations for use in teaching lower division U.S. History. *History Computer Review*, *18*(1), 37–52.

Dickey, M. D. (2005). Engaging by design: How engagement strategies in popular computer and video games can inform instructional design. *Educational Technology Research and Development*, *53*(2), 67–83. doi:10.1007/BF02504866

Gee, J. P. (2010). *New digital media and learning as an emerging area and "worked examples" as one way forward*. Cambridge, MA: MIT Press.

Hayden, K. A. (2003). *Lived experience of students searching for information.* Unpublished doctoral dissertation, University of Calgary, Alberta, Canada.

Hayden, K. A., Rutherford, S., & Pival, P. (2006). Workshop on the information search process for research in the library. *Journal of Library Administration, 45*(3), 427–443. doi:10.1300/J111v45n03_08

History Channel. (2003-2006). *Battlefield Detectives.* USA: The A & E Network.

Hurter, S. R. (2003). Elusive or illuminating: Using the web to explore the Salem witchcraft trials. *OAH Magazine of History, 17*(4), 60–61. doi:10.1093/maghis/17.4.60

Karras, R. W. (1994). Writing essays that make historical arguments. *OAH Magazine of History, 8*(4), 54–57. doi:10.1093/maghis/8.4.54

Kee, K., Graham, S., Dunae, P., Lutz, J., Large, A., & Blondeau, M. (2009). Towards a theory of good history through gaming. *The Canadian Historical Review, 90*(2), 303–326. doi:10.3138/chr.90.2.303

Maggioni, L., VanSledright, B., & Alexander, P. A. (2009). Walking on the borders: A measure of epistemic cognition in history. *Journal of Experimental Education, 77*(3), 187–213. doi:10.3200/JEXE.77.3.187-214

Maxwell, A. (2010). Assessment strategies for a history exam, or, why short-answer questions are better than in-class essays. *The History Teacher, 43*(2), 233–245.

McClymer, J. F., & Moynihan, K. J. (1977). The essay assignment: A teaching device. *The History Teacher, 10*(3), 359–371. doi:10.2307/491847

Miyazaki, H., Takeuchi, M., & Nakajima, E. (2009). *Demon's Souls.* Foster City, CA: Atlus & Sony Computer Entertainment.

Monahan, G., W. (2002). Acting out Nazi Germany: A role-play simulation for the history classroom. *Teaching History, 27*(2), 74–85.

Munslow, A. (2003). *The new history.* Toronto, ON, Canada: Pearson Longman.

Munslow, A. (2007). *Narrative and history.* New York, NY: Palgrave MacMillan.

Muzzy, L. (2007, 2010). *Making history: The calm and the storm & making history II: The war of the world.* Retrieved from http://making-history.com

Pace, D. (2004). Decoding the reading of history: An example of the process. *New Directions for Teaching and Learning, 98,* 13–21. doi:10.1002/tl.143

Pettit, J., & Street, K. (2007). *Heaven & hell on earth: The massacre of the "Black" Donnellys: Great unsolved mysteries in Canadian history.* Retrieved from http://www.canadianmysteries.ca/sites/donnellys/home/indexen.html

Phillips, J. (2002). The dinosaurs didn't see it coming, but Historians had better: Computer-aided activities in the history classroom. *History Computer Review, 18*(1), 27–36.

Prensky, M. (2003). Computer games and learning—digital game-based learning. In Goldstein, J., & Raessens, J. (Eds.), *Handbook of computer game studies* (pp. 97–122). Cambridge, MA: MIT Press.

Royle, K. (2009). Computer games and realising their learning potential: Crossing borders, blurring boundaries and taking action. Retrieved from http://www.gamebasedlearning.org.uk/content/view/67/

Royle, K., & Clarke, R. (2003). *Making the case for computer games as a learning environment.* Retrieved from http://citeseerx.ist.psu.edu/viewdoc/download?doi=10.1.1.110.2561&rep=rep1&type=pdf

Russell, W. B. III, & Pellegrino, A. (2008). Constructing meaning from historical content: A research study. *Journal of Social Studies Research, 32*(2), 3–15.

Squire, K. (2004). *Changing the game: What happens when video games enter the classroom? Innovate.* Retrieved from http://www.innovateonline.info/index.php?view=article&id=82

Squire, K. (2005). *Game-based learning: Present and future state of the field.* Retrieved from http://www.mendeley.com/research/gamebased-learning-present-and-future-state-of-the-field/

Squire, K., & Barab, S. (2004). Replaying history: Engaging urban underserved students in learning world history through computer simulations games. In *Proceedings of the 6th International Conference on Learning Science* (pp. 505-512).

Squire, K., Giovanetto, L., Devane, B., & Durga, S. (2005). From users to designers: Building a self-organizing game-based learning environment. *TechTrends, 49*(5), 34–74. doi:10.1007/BF02763688

Tey, J. (1968). *The daughter of time.* Scarborough, ON, Canada: Bellhaven House.

Tobin, K. (2001). To think on paper: Using writing assignments in the world of history survey. *The History Teacher, 34*(4), 497–508. doi:10.2307/3054202

Tsui, L. (1999). Courses and instruction affecting critical thinking. *Research in Higher Education, 40*(2), 185–200. doi:10.1023/A:1018734630124

Valve Corporation. (2007). *Source SDK.* Bellevue, WA: Valve Corporation.

Voelker, D. J. (2008). Assessing student understanding in introductory courses: A sample strategy. *The History Teacher, 41*(4), 506–518.

Whately, D., & Harris, N. (2010) *Hero engine simutronics corporiation.* Paper presented at the Harris at Game Developers Conference, San Francisco, CA.

Whelchel, A. (2007). Using civilization simulation video games in the world history classroom. *World History Connected, 4*(2), 1–14.

This work was previously published in the International Journal of Virtual and Personal Learning Environments, Volume 2, Issue 2, edited by Michael Thomas, pp. 46-58, copyright 2011 by IGI Publishing (an imprint of IGI Global).

Chapter 6
Not Just Playing Around:
The MoLeNET Experience of Using Games Technologies to Support Teaching and Learning

Rebecca Petley
LSN, UK

Jill Attewell
LSN, UK

Carol Savill-Smith
LSN, UK

ABSTRACT

MoLeNET is a unique collaborative initiative, currently in its third year, which encourages and enables the introduction of mobile learning in English post 14 education via supported shared-cost projects. Mobile learning in MoLeNET is defined by MoLeNET as "The exploitation of ubiquitous handheld technologies, together with wireless and mobile phone networks, to facilitate, support, enhance and extend the reach of teaching and learning." MoLeNET projects use a wide range of handheld devices with their learners including two handheld game platforms: the Sony PSP and Nintendo DS. A small number of projects have also experimented with educational and therapeutic use of the Nintendo Wii game console and experienced considerable success in engaging reluctant learners and supporting learners with difficulties and/or disabilities. This paper explores the impact that mobile game technologies have on teaching and learning for those involved in MoLeNET, including the development of academic and social skills and the improvement of mobility and health related issues.

DOI: 10.4018/978-1-4666-2467-2.ch006

INTRODUCTION

The Mobile Learning Network (the MoLeNET programme; www.molenet.org.uk) uses a shared cost funding model with the Learning and Skills Council (LSC, now the Skills Funding Agency: www.skillsfundingagency.com) providing capital funding to procure handheld and supporting infrastructure technologies to introduce and embed mobile teaching and learning. The participating institutions contribute to the cost of the LSN (www.lsnlearning.org.uk) support and evaluation programme which provides training, support, mentoring, research resources and systems. Over twenty thousand learners and four thousand teaching staff took part in phases one and two of MoLeNET (2007-2009). In the third and current phase (2009/10), a further eighteen thousand learners and three thousand teaching staff are expected to take part from over seventy colleges and schools across England.

Throughout the MoLeNET programme, the projects involved have purchased a range of mobile devices and technologies depending on their individual aims and objectives, and the project participants. Such technologies include mobile phones and Smartphones, personal digital assistants (PDAs), ultra mobile personal computers (UMPCs), MP3 and MP4 players, digital still and video cameras, specialist scientific survey equipment, voting systems, handheld games devices (Sony PSP, Nintendo DS) and, in some cases, Nintendo Wiis. They have also purchased the wireless technology and servers required to maximise the potential of the mobile equipment. The number of games technologies purchased by MoLeNET projects (Figures 1 and 2) increased substantially after the first year in which they represented only 3% of all handheld technologies purchased. In year two 22% of all handheld technology purchases were games technologies.

The MoLeNET programme is far reaching and diverse in its application and impact (Attewell, Savill-Smith, & Douch, 2009). However the research findings reported in this paper specifically relate to the use of games and games technologies for teaching and learning. In particular five case studies are presented in which MoLeNET projects used the Nintendo DS and Nintendo Wii to support teaching and learning and to enhance experiences and outcomes for learners.

Further information about MoLeNET and the projects involved can be found at www.molenet.org.uk.

Figure 1. Pie chart to show range and spread of devices purchased in MoLeNET phase 1

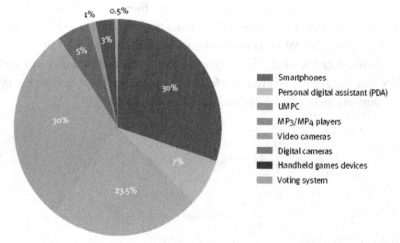

Figure 2. Pie chart to show range and spread of devices purchased in MoLeNET phase 2

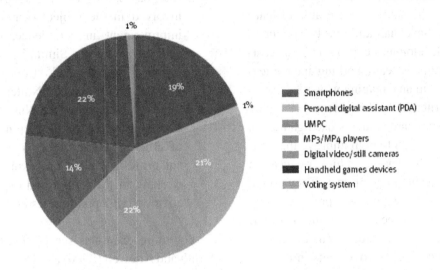

DIGITAL GAME-BASED LEARNING

Digital game-based learning is very much advocated by authors such as Prensky (2001, 2006) who asserts that digital games can support the development of an array of skills, including decision making, communication, memory and spatial awareness. He explains that the main reason why learners voluntarily play games for extended amounts of time is because they enter a state of "flow" (Csikszentmihalyi, 1990) whereby the level of play challenges the player such that they become highly involved but is not so difficult that the player loses focus. Therefore, with a combination of opportunities for skills development and probable high levels of engagement, digital games have the potential to be very effective teaching and learning tools. Furthermore, Oblinger (2004) explains that factors that promote learning, such as individualisation, feedback, assessment and social involvement can be seen throughout digital games. For example, digital games provide individualisation through levels of difficulty and variety of content; feedback is often given in the form of actions, text or spoken words, is often instant, and the player is very aware of the

consequences of their behaviour in the game; assessment opportunities are clearly presented to the player in the form of progression from one level/zone to another or in the form of points scores, time taken to achieve a task etc. so the player is easily able to measure improvements and then reflect on possible reasons for these; and social involvement is now becoming a particularly strong factor in complex games as multiplayer games are no longer confined to players using the same console but can be accessed online by many players regardless of location.

Successful cases of game-based learning can be found within the health and military sectors as well as primary, secondary, further and higher education. The following are just a few examples of the diverse ways in which digital games have been used for learning purposes in these areas:

- Bristol Secondary School (Facer, Joiner, Stanton, Reidt, Hull, & Kirk, 2004) conducted a project with their year seven students, investigating the Savannah environment. They created a virtual Savannah that students were able to interact with via Personal Digital Assistants (PDAs) and

Global Positioning System (GPS) functionality. The students were able to learn about the Savannah and lion behaviour as well as developing decision making, cost-benefit analysis, team working and navigation skills, in an engaging way.

- At Bournemouth University (Pulman, 2008) social care students used games on the Nintendo DS to help improve their numeracy skills as part of a higher education assistive technology project. They found that the games helped to improve not only their numeracy recall skills but also their confidence with the subject, and this resulted in noticeable improvements in the calculations they carry out in their daily lives.
- Kato, Cole, Bradlyn, and Pollock (2008) investigated the impact of game playing on management of self-administered cancer medication. They found that adolescents and young adults who played a game focusing on cancer treatment demonstrated an improvement in adherence to self-administered medication compared to a control group who showed no change.
- Giles (2009) describes a case study in which an individual with Parkinson's disease demonstrated improvements in movement, walking and coordination since he started playing games on the Nintendo Wii for three hours each week.
- The Consolarium ("the Scottish Centre for Games and Learning, established by Learning and Teaching Scotland to explore the world of computer games and how they can impact on teaching and learning in Scottish schools," www.itscotland.org.uk) have documented numerous examples of effective game-based learning in Scottish primary schools. For example, in 2008 two Aberdeenshire primary schools used "Nintendogs" on the Nintendo DS as an inspiration for a whole range of cross curricular study, including story writing,

role-playing, art and numeracy. Learners involved in the project demonstrated an improvement in confidence, enthusiasm and self-esteem. Similarly, Lairdsland Primary School used "Cooking Mama: World Kitchen" on the Nintendo DS and "Endless Ocean" on the Nintendo Wii as a starting point for developing a variety of skills including money-handling, internet browsing, word processing and team working in the former and exploring creative writing opportunities in the latter.

For more examples see De Freitas, Savill-Smith and Attewell (2006) and Douch, Attewell, and Dawson (2010).

Issues with Digital Game-Based Learning in Formal Education

The evidence from the literature as discussed above, indicates that digital games have great potential as learning tools, however the use of these games beyond simplistic edutainment/learning drill and skill style games within the education sector is by no means wide spread. The following reasons may play some part in this:

1. **Curriculum coverage:** Although research evidence indicates that digital games can support the development of a range of useful skills, there are currently very few complex games that provide good curriculum coverage. Games that are specifically designed to focus on particular learning objectives tend to be less engaging for the player as they are often drill and skill style or simplistic games. Leddo (1996, p. 24) suggests that these "edutainment" type games may be preferable to standard instruction, however that students "would never voluntarily play such a game outside of class" because they do not promote "flow" state as discussed above.

2. **Timetabling and lesson structure:** Timetabling in schools, colleges and universities is often inflexible. However, because the types of complex games that are enjoyed by many learners often take several hours to complete, require intense sessions of gameplay, and may suit some learners better than others in terms of level and content; they do not necessarily fit well with such structured plans (Clark, 2003).

3. **Negative conceptions:** Findings from Becta's 2002 schools survey (Kirriemuir & McFarlane, 2003) indicate that there are preconceptions amongst some staff that digital games that are console based are purely for entertainment purposes, and there are also concerns regarding appropriateness of the content in some of these games. Some staff also expressed apprehension regarding the time commitment that may be required for training and integrating game-based learning into lesson plans and schemes of work.

4. **Funding:** The financial implications of purchasing games technologies or software or of designing and creating games may be too great for many institutions to manage, particularly considering the rate at which technologies become outdated (De Freitas, 2006).

However, it is possible that some of these issues are beginning to be overcome. With the introduction of games technologies such as the Nintendo DS, there are now learning games available that address a number of curriculum areas, but that can be played for short amounts of time and that individuals actually engage with voluntarily. Furthermore, the MoLeNET programme has enabled participating colleges and schools to purchase games technologies and has provided the necessary support to help staff to consider the potential teaching and learning benefits and pedagogical applications of these devices. Some MoLeNET projects are also moving on to consider using learner owned technologies and other solutions to overcome funding issues and the ever changing technology scene.

MOLENET RESEARCH APPROACHES

MoLeNET involves many projects working with the common goal of supporting and improving teaching and learning through the use of mobile technologies. The projects vary in terms of their size and focus, involving learners from different subject areas, studying at different levels and working in various locations. The projects procure mobile devices based on their specific aims and objectives, and use these technologies to support teaching and learning in ways that are appropriate and relevant for the teachers and learners involved. It was evident that a context sensitive approach to the research element of the MoLeNET programme was necessary, and practitioner led action research was chosen as the main research approach.

Practitioner led action research is "concerned with social practice, aimed towards improvement, a cyclical process, pursued by systematic enquiry, a reflective process, participative and determined by the practitioners" (Kember, 2000, p. 24). It is also appropriate "whenever specific knowledge is required for a specific problem in a specific situation; or when a new approach is to be grafted onto an existing system" (Cohen & Manion, 1995, p. 194). The MoLeNET programme definition of practitioner led action research is: "A research approach with the fundamental aim to help professionals (teachers, managers) to improve practice and to understand change processes. Using a cyclical process to diagnose issues for investigation, plan research strategies, implement, review and reflect upon findings." With an aim to maximise opportunities for improving and recognising improvement in practice, as well as gathering meaningful research data from this diverse community, practitioner led action research was deemed as the most appropriate strategy for investigating and promoting impact for the following reasons.

- Practitioner researchers can take ownership of the research in their own 'real-life' educational settings, making it appropriate to their particular context and people involved.
- Action research involves cycles of planning, acting, observing and reflecting, all of which teachers do naturally as a matter of course in their classrooms.
- Action research focuses on the process of understanding and improving practice, which is of interest to other practitioners, and can lead to a continuous cycle of improvement.
- Action research can contribute towards staff professional development.
- Action research has been identified as being particularly well-suited to the study of innovations, and, in particular, the use of Information and Communication Technology (ICT) in Education (Somekh, 2000).

However, there are also a number of challenges with large scale practitioner led action research including:

- The fact that final outputs do not necessarily produce data which is easy to quantify or generalise from.
- It can be difficult for people to work in a way that is research-focused if this is new to them (e.g., collecting data in systematic and rigorous ways, and being reflective and impartial about successes and problems) so extensive support and training is required.
- Conducting the research can be heavily influenced by external factors/pressures such as inspections and staff changes.

- It takes time to plan, undertake, analyse and reflect on research, and time is a precious commodity in busy colleges and schools.

In addition to the action research, further evaluation activities are carried out by LSN gathering data concerning all projects, e.g., individual learner record data on achievement, retention and progression.

In order to facilitate practitioner led action research in the MoLeNET projects, in addition to a project manager, each project selects a lead practitioner researcher (LPR) to take responsibility for the action research aspect of the project. These LPRs receive training and face-to-face and online support from LSN and develop action research plans to investigate the impact of mobile technologies on teachers, learners and the institution and to support and inform those involved in improving practice. The findings and conclusions from the action research are reported to LSN at the end of the project in addition to information from a project management perspective.

A broad range of research methods have been employed by the LPRs taking part in MoLeNET to gain evidence of impact and feedback from those involved (students, teaching staff, support staff, managers, employers, assessors, etc.). These methods include pre and post paper and online questionnaires; structured and semi structured interviews; focus groups; formal and informal observation; online forums/blogs/Wikis; minutes of meetings; text and video diaries and critical incident logging; statistical information relating to achievement, retention and attendance; and virtual learning environment (VLE) traffic and access information. The most popular research method was questionnaires, which the practitioner researchers found quick and easy to administer and to analyse, however lower response rates than anticipated were an issue for many of the projects and most recognised that qualitative methods such as interviews and/or focus groups were also needed to provide more detailed evidence. Many found that both teachers and learners responded better to focus groups, as opposed to interviews, as they found these less intimidating and also were able to share experiences and ideas/concerns with others in a similar position to them. Observations provided useful evidence of good practice and learner engagement and behaviour, though some teachers found these rather formal and were concerned about being observed using new and unfamiliar technologies and teaching methods too early on in the project. Statistical data was used in a number of cases to form a clearer picture of impact, though it was often difficult for the practitioner researchers to collect actual as opposed to predictive data and to make valid comparisons with learners not using mobile devices. Although the action research approach has been well received by the participating institutions, with the majority indicating that it has helped to promote change and propel the project forwards, and with a wealth of data being produced, it was necessary for the practitioner researchers to combine a number of research methods in order to get as detailed and accurate a picture of impact and reactions as possible. It is also recognised that much of the data provided by the individual projects to LSN relates to specific cases (i.e., individual cohorts of learners on a particular course, using mobile devices in specific ways to address various aims) and it is difficult to generalise from these, nevertheless "a holistic consideration of all of the data and direct involvement of practitioners in the research process does provide some confidence in apparent impact." (Attewell et al., 2009)

To find out more about the impact of MoLeNET phase one see Attewell et al. (2009). Publications relating to phase two of MoLeNET include a detailed overview of impact (Attewell, Savill-Smith, Douch, & Parker, 2010) and a case study based report exploring mobile learning in work-based and vocational learning (Douch, Savill-Smith, Parker, & Attewell, 2010).

MOLENET ACTION RESEARCH FINDNGS

MoLeNET projects have utilised many handheld technologies to support teaching and learning, including handheld games technologies (the Sony PSP and Nintendo DS) and the Nintendo Wii games console. Case studies from MoLeNET phases one and two's action research demonstrate how colleges and schools have used these games technologies for learning with real benefits for learners and teachers. These benefits arise from both their use as gaming devices and from their additional functionality including internet access, image/video/audio capture, and communication functions. The following table summarises the ways in which these three games technologies have been used for teaching and learning in MoLeNET (Figure 3):

Key findings from the action research indicate that handheld games technologies can help to improve learner motivation, focus, and behaviour. This is particularly interesting as the initial reaction from many of the teachers involved was fear that the introduction of games technologies would lead to behavioural issues. Teaching staff have noticed improved achievement, particularly in mental maths, and improved confidence and self-esteem. Both learners and teachers have also been able to monitor learner progress and reflect on tasks more easily. Furthermore, the games technologies have been used to provide more personalised and relevant learning experiences, enabling learners with different needs to work at their own pace and in a way that suits them. Learners have shown far greater levels of engagement when utilising the games technologies and previously unpopular sessions such as key skills have seen a rise in attendance levels. Learners have enjoyed using games on the Nintendo DS so much that break time clubs have been set up in some projects and in others teaching staff have reported that learners have worked during their break times

Figure 3. A summary table of the ways MoLeNET projects have used games technologies for teaching and learning

Device	Game-based learning	Additional functionality
Nintendo DS	Games such as "Dr Kawashima's Brain Training," 'Professor Layton's Curious Village' and Professor Kageyama's Maths Training' have often been used by projects as lesson starter activities to focus the learners and to provide a warm up activity. The games are also often used as a plenary activity for consolidation and assessment, and as an incentive/reward. The games have been used with learners of all levels with a particular focus on developing numeracy and literacy skills in lower ability learners and also English skills for ESOL learners. Learners have used the games independently, monitoring their own progress, and also competitively and collaboratively. The devices have been used during lesson time, at break times, at home and in transit.	The PictoChat tool on the Nintendo DS has been used widely to enable learners to practice reading, writing and communication, as well as social interaction skills. Learners are able to send written and pictorial messages privately to their peers or their tutor, including asking and replying to questions, completing grammar and spelling tasks, constructing sentences etc. The teacher is also able to assess individual students' responses and provide immediate feedback via this tool. The Nintendo DSi also has a camera function, which some learners have used to record their tutors or themselves completing tasks for later instruction/revision or proof of progress respectively. Internet access has also been used for course related research purposes.
Sony PSP	The Sony PSP has rarely been used by MoLeNET projects for its gaming capacity as the Nintendo DS is seen as being able to offer more in terms of variety and suitability of games. One project, however, very successfully constructed a numeracy scheme of work for ex-NEET (not in education, employment or training) learners using the games on the PSP. The learners used the time, speed and score data from games such as 'Pro Evolution Soccer' to learn how to calculate totals, averages, differences etc. This was so successful in engaging the learners and making learning relevant for them that an unprecedented 100% success rate was recorded. For the scheme of work for this project visit MoLeShare (www.moleshare.org.uk) and search for Numeracy Uplift Project.	MoLeNET projects have principally purchased Sony PSPs for their recording capacity and large playback screens, and these have been particularly useful for learners in workplace environments. Learners have been able to collect video and photographic evidence of themselves performing tasks for their portfolios. They have also been able to record the tutor performing a task so that they can play this back as a tutorial and work at their own pace using the pause and rewind functions as necessary. Recordings of their own performance have also been used for peer and self reflection and assessment purposes. Learners have also used the PSPs to browse the internet to research a subject or to access online learning resources and materials both inside and outside the college. And some have used the Skype function to communicate with their peers and teaching staff.
Nintendo Wii	There have been a few purchases of the Nintendo Wii by MoLeNET projects, and these have been used principally to enable/encourage learners to engage in sports and exercise activities. Learners involved have mainly been learners with learning difficulties and/or disabilities or learners disengaged with traditional sports and PE. The Wii has also been used in one college as a means of generating data for learners to work on, as opposed to providing data that has no relevance for the learners.	

because they are eager to improve on their scores. Finally, learners with learning difficulties and/or disabilities have taken great pleasure in being able to access what they would consider to be 'main stream' technology and being able to get involved with activities that perhaps they may have missed out on previously.

MOLENET CASE STUDIES

The following summaries of case studies from Douch et al. (2010) describe the ways in which the Nintendo DS and Nintendo Wii have been used to great effect by institutions involved in MoLeNET phases one and two. For more information about games technologies in MoLeNET and to view 35 case studies of good practice (Douch et al., 2010).

Ashton Under-Lyne Sixth Form College: Measuring the Effect of Using the Nintendo DS to Improve Short-Term Memory Skills

Ashton Sixth Form College currently has approximately 2000 students enrolled on a range of academic and vocational courses, and provides for around 1000 part-time adults students each year. "The 'Learning in the Mobile World' project at Ashton Sixth Form College involved 32 staff and over 180 students with allocated mobile devices. The whole student population benefited from the installation of the Wi-Fi network across the entire college campus. The project further developed and embedded the use of mobile devices across a wide range of curriculum subjects, from levels 1 to 3, and included the use of iPod Nanos, iPod Touches, iPhones, Nintendo DSs, XDA Mantles, ASUS eeePCs, Flip cameras, digital voice recorders and Palm Treo Pro PDAs. On the whole, teachers have identified improved student engagement and attendance, with particularly pleasing increases in self-esteem and motivation in the level 1 and

additional learning support learners" (Attewell et al., 2010).

Twenty-five learners took part in a small experimental trial, as part of Ashton's MoLeNET project, investigating the impact of the Nintendo DS on short-term memory. All learners had been diagnosed with a specific learning difficulty (such as dyslexia, dyspraxia or Asperger's syndrome) and were studying at levels two and three. Each learner's short term auditory and visual memory capacities were tested at the beginning and end of the trial using the Turner and Risdale (1994) Digit Span test and the Smith (1973) Symbol Digit Modalities test. The learners were able to use "Dr Kawashima's Brain Training" on the DS as often as they wanted, including, but not restricted to, during their weekly additional learning support sessions. At the end of the two month trial the learners showed a significant improvement in their short term memory post test scores.

Walsall College: Using the Nintendo DS Lite to Engage Young People Not in Education, Employment or Training and to Improve Literacy and Numeracy

Each year Walsall College supports over 3000 14-19 year old learners in accessing vocational courses and delivers education and training to more than 4000 adult learners on the college campus and in the workplace. "Walsall College and its partners, with the help of MoLeNET, aimed to improve teaching and learning by developing a programme of study within Achieving Together and for learners with severe learning difficulties and disabilities, concentrating on using Nintendo DS Lites and their educational games. The project also aimed to improve teaching and learning by adapting SRS systems, recording equipment, E-PCs and MP4 players in lessons as well as outside college. The project involved 350 learners and 30 staff" (Attewell et al., 2010).

Walsall College distributed over 300 Nintendo DS Lites to learners (Figure 4), many of whom were disengaged learners working towards their GCSEs. The initial set up and logistics of handling such a large number of devices took some time but once ready the teaching staff began to use the DSs as starter, warm up and plenary activities in at least two literacy and numeracy lessons each week. Teaching staff witnessed a major improvement in learner behaviour and classroom disruption, with learners becoming more focused on their work.

The head of mathematics at one of the partner schools commented "Using the 'Dr Kawashima's Brain Training' regularly has improved pupils' metal ability to think quicker and has also allowed them to develop strategies to improve short and long term memory, which will assist in their GCSEs" (Douch et al., 2010). Learner feedback was equally positive with learners commenting that "it helps me to build my confidence in maths, it's better than worksheets because you have to be quick" (Douch et al., 2010).

Following this success Walsall College plans to expand provision to skills for life and key skills learners.

Figure 4. Learners at Walsall College

The Manchester College: Using the Nintendo DS and Wii to Enhance Learning and Promote Positive Behaviour

The Manchester College was formed in 2008 following the merger of Manchester College of Arts and Technology and City College Manchester, and has several sites across the city. "The MoLeNET 2 project carried out at The Manchester College involved four main cohorts, with an immediate effect on over 100 learners and 12 staff with the potential for a possible 400 learners and 40 staff to become involved as the project progressed. Based on sites across urban Manchester, the project targeted learners with learning difficulties or requiring additional learning support or whose first language was not English; media, IT and Diploma students and ex-NEETs. A wide range of equipment was used including headcams, DS-Lites, PSPs, MP4 players, Netbooks, iPAQs, iPod Touches to deliver personal resources, provide self-evaluation tools and enable interconnected activities. Learner engagement, interaction and cooperation were notably enhanced in all cohorts with consequent behavioural and achievement improvements" (Attewell et al., 2010).

As part of their project, The Manchester College used the Nintendo Wii to support 16 learners in their level 1 application of number key skills sessions. The main programme of study for these learners was level 1 construction and motor vehicle, and although they appreciated the value of the key skills qualification, some learners found it challenging working in a non-vocational classroom environment. The purpose of using the games devices, therefore, was to enhance the learner experience with a view to promoting positive behaviour.

The Nintendo Wii and Wii Fit became the focal point of an application of number session on introducing Excel spreadsheets. Learners had previously found these sessions boring and teachers had struggled to keep them engaged. In a new game-based approach, learners used the Wii Fit board to carry out a series of ski jumps to generate data (e.g. length of each individual's jumps) for their Excel assignment. The lesson involved recording the data, carrying out calculations and creating graphs.

The college found that by using the Nintendo Wii to create the data for the session, the learners were encouraged to take greater ownership of their learning. They were engaged throughout the ski jumping activity and recorded the data responsibly, with the tutor taking on more of a facilitator role. It was felt that because the learners had greater control over their learning they showed a much stronger determination to complete the assignment accurately and on time.

Learners' reactions:

At the close of the session learners were asked to evaluate whether the Wii had enhanced their learning experience and many learners suggested that it had. They enjoyed generating the facts and preferred this method to reading data off a piece of paper. Using the Nintendo DS and Wii has had a very positive impact on the learner experience. The games devices enabled learners to take control of their learning; they engaged and stimulated them, and improved concentration, which in turn had a direct impact on the promotion of positive behaviour within the group (Douch et al., 2010).

Teachers' reactions:

The tutors involved in the case study were impressed with the positive impact of the games devices on the learners' learning and are keen to use them in future sessions (Douch et al., 2010).

The Manchester College intends to continue to use the devices in these ways and would like to explore other game-based learning opportunities.

National Star College: Supporting Therapy Routines Through the Use of the Nintendo Wii

"The National Star College is an independent, specialist college providing for learners who have physical disabilities and/or acquired brain injuries alongside associated learning, behavioural, sensory and medical difficulties" (Attewell et al., 2010). National Star College addressed the area of physiotherapy as part of their project. The physiotherapists involved investigated the use of both the Wii and Wii board for specific therapy support, with an aim to engage learners in their physiotherapy routines and to enhance their experience of these. Staff had previously reported that some learners were reluctant to attend physiotherapy sessions because they found these boring.

The Nintendo Wii had a significant impact on the work of the physiotherapists at the college. Previously limb movement would have to be prompted by the physiotherapist; however the Wii enabled learners to voluntarily coordinate movements in response to the game's requirements.

"One student used a downhill skiing game by sitting on a Wii board and voluntarily rotating his torso to navigate down a slalom route on screen. He was able to practise this routine regularly in his own room outside the therapy sessions and when he returned home in the holidays. This sustained the therapy, was enjoyable for the student and because it was a game, his response times and level of accuracy could be measured over time" (Douch et al., 2010).

Staff in the project explained that it was important to develop structured plans for how to use the Wii in ways that were appropriate for each learner in order to make the most of this gaming technology for physiotherapy routines. See www. moletv.org.uk/watch.aspx?v=UWRAE

Trafford College: Wii Fit for Students with Learning Difficulties and Disabilities

Trafford College was formed in September 2007 and has four sites across Greater Manchester, with approximately 11,000 students in total, studying both academic and vocational courses. The Trafford MoLeNET project aimed to strengthen their existing use of mobile technology and to expand provision into the areas of skills for life, Train to Gain, and teacher training. "Building on areas of good practice developed in MoLeNET 1, this project investigated methods of engaging learners on skills for life level 1 programmes, and developed a model of excellence for Train to Gain programmes using mobile technology. They also created a bank of mobile materials (video clips) for use in teacher education delivery; 'Talking Points'" (Attewell et al., 2010).

During their MoLeNET project Trafford College found an unexpected use for games technologies with the Supported Learning Department with learners with learning difficulties and/or disabilities. They explored the use of the Nintendo Wii Fit as a means of enabling these learners to access physical activities within a safe and familiar environment. It was hoped that this would enrich their learning experience, providing health and mobility benefits that may also lead to improvements in self confidence.

Two Wii machines were set up so that learners could use them during lunch breaks, with about 15-20 students dropping by each day. Staff at Trafford College were thrilled by the positive impact of the Nintendo Wiis on learners' physical abilities as well as social communication skills and self esteem. The learners who had experience of being excluded from some activities enjoyed by others appreciated having access to mainstream and popular technologies and were keen to discuss their use with peers and at home. They were able to select from a range of activities on the Wii, providing them with greater choice than previously

Figure 5. Learner at Trafford College

available (Figure 5). The activities linked well to the life skills programme being undertaken by the students and also helped them to develop social skills such as turn taking and communication. See www.moletv.org.uk/wtch.aspx?v=KEF3T

The college principal reported "This is an exciting development for our Supported Learning students, and the Trafford College leadership team are delighted that our students and staff have the opportunity to engage in such an innovative project" (Douch et al., 2010).

Leading on from this success Trafford College reported that they are now keen to further explore the Wii Mii application and have already found that by creating personal avatars some students have revealed valuable information about their internal desires or conflicts that had previously gone unrecognised.

CONCLUSION

LSN have received numerous reports detailing examples of how teachers and learners have used mobile games technologies to support teaching and learning and research evidence from a range of quantitative and qualitative research tools illustrating the positive impact these technologies have had on the learning experience. The case studies described above illustrate just a small number of these examples, however a cross case analysis of the evidence provided by the projects involved in MoLeNET clearly points to games technologies playing a strong role in improving teaching and learning, leading to positive outcomes for both teachers and learners. These benefits include social as well as academic skills development, with devices such as the Nintendo DS enabling much easier integration of game-based learning into the curriculum, and observed and reported levels of engagement and motivation being massively improved through the use of familiar technologies, and interactive, personalised and enjoyable learning opportunities.

There have been very few reported barriers to using the games technologies by MoLeNET projects, with many staff explaining that they are easy to use, especially as many of the learners are already confident in their use. Because there are a number of games that address curriculum areas, there has been little extra preparation in terms of creating content, and where the devices have been used for their additional functions the photos and videos collected by the staff and learners can be used as learning resources in the future. A number of staff, however, mentioned that they would like there to be a wider range of games available so they could better match sessions to curriculum requirements. The devices have been used with a range of learners and teachers comment that it is essential to plan carefully and to ensure that the learners are clear of the learning objective, as with any session. One obstacle that was noted with the Nintendo DS was that where a learner had poor hand writing or a speech impediment the DS may not recognise the response and mark a correct answer as incorrect, thus resulting in frustration and a lowering of self esteem on the part of the learner.

MoLeNET research to date demonstrates that handheld games technologies have an important part to play in education whether they are used for playing games or for the affordances offered by their additional functionality, and research findings from MoLeNET phase three will further explore the extent to which projects have utilised game-based learning and handheld games technologies in 2009/10, and the impact this has had on teachers, learners and institutions.

REFERENCES

Attewell, J., Savill-Smith, C., & Douch, R. (2009). *The impact of mobile learning; examining what it means for teaching and learning.* London, UK: LSN.

Attewell, J., Savill-Smith, C., Douch, R., & Parker, G. (2010). *Modernising education and training: Mobilising technology for learning.* London, UK: LSN.

Clark, D. (2003, November 20). *Computer games in education and training.* Paper presented at the LSDA Seminar: Learning by Playing: Can Computer Games and Simulations Support Teaching and Learning for Post-16 Learners in Formal, Workplace and Informal Learning Contexts? London, UK.

Cohen, L., & Manion, L. (1995). *Research methods in education* (4th ed.). London, UK: Routledge.

Csikszentmihalyi, M. (1990). *Flow: The psychology of optimal experience.* New York, NY: Harper & Row.

De Freitas, S. (2006). *Learning in immersive worlds. A review of games-based learning.* Retrieved from www.jisc.ac.uk/media/documents/programmes/elearninginnovation/gamingreport_v3.pdf

De Freitas, S., Savill-Smith, C., & Attewell, J. (2006). *Computer games and simulations for adult learning. Case studies from practice.* London, UK: LSN.

Douch, R., Attewell, J., & Dawson, D. (2010). *Games technologies for learning; more than just toys.* London, UK: LSN.

Douch, R., Savill-Smith, C., Parker, G., & Attewell, J. (2010). *Work-based and vocational mobile learning: Making IT work*. London, UK: LSN.

Facer, K., Joiner, R., Stanton, D., Reidt, J., Hull, R., & Kirk, D. (2004). Savannah: mobile gaming and learning? *Journal of Computer Assisted Learning, 20*, 399–409. doi:10.1111/j.1365-2729.2004.00105.x

Giles, J. (2009). *Physios recommend a healthy dose of gaming*. Retrieved from http://www.new-scientist.com/article/mg20227145.700-physios-recommend-a-healthy-dose-of-gaming.html

Kato, P. M., Cole, S. W., Bradlyn, A. S., & Pollock, B. H. (2008). A video game improves behavioural outcomes in adolescents and young adults with cancer: A randomised trial. *Paediatrics, 122*(2), 305–317. doi:10.1542/peds.2007-3134

Kember, D. (2000). *Action learning and action research: Improving the quality of teaching & learning*. London, UK: Kogan Page.

Kirriemuir, J., & McFarlane, A. (2003). *Use of computer and video games in the classroom*. Retrieved from http://www.slideshare.net/silversprite/use-of-computer-and-video-games-in-the-classroom

Learning and Teaching Scotland. (2009). *Game-based learning*. Retrieved from http://www.itscotland.org.uk/

Leddo, J. (1996). An intelligent computer game to teach scientific reasoning. *Journal of Instruction Delivery Systems, 10*(4), 22–25.

Prensky, M. (2001). *Digital game-based learning*. New York, NY: McGraw-Hill.

Prensky, M. (2006). *'Don't bother me mom – I'm learning!' How computer and video games are preparing your kids for 21st century success—and how you can help!* St. Paul, MN: Paragon House.

Pulman, A. (2008). *Mobile assistance – the Nintendo DS Lite as an assistive tool for health and social care students*. Retrieved from http://www.swap.ac.uk/docs/casestudies/pulman.pdf

Smith, A. (1973). *Symbol digit modalities test*. Los Angeles, CA: Western Psychological Services.

Somekh, B. (2000). New technology and learning: Policy and practice in the UK, 1980-2010. *Education and Information Technologies, 5*(1), 19–37. doi:10.1023/A:1009636417727

Turner, M., & Risdale, J. (1984). *Turner and Risdale digit span test*. Retrieved from http://www.dyslexiaaction.org.uk/

This work was previously published in the International Journal of Virtual and Personal Learning Environments, Volume 2, Issue 2, edited by Michael Thomas, pp. 59-72, copyright 2011 by IGI Publishing (an imprint of IGI Global).

Chapter 7
From the Games Industry:
Ten Lessons for Game-Based Learning

Paul Hollins
University of Bolton, UK

Nicola Whitton
Manchester Metropolitan University, UK

ABSTRACT

This paper draws on lessons learned from the development process of the entertainment games industry and discusses how they can be applied to the field of game-based learning. This paper examines policy makers and those wishing to commission or develop games for learning and highlights potential opportunities as well as pitfalls. The paper focuses on ten key points in which the authors feel from experience in both commercial game development and education that parallels are drawn between the entertainment and educational games development processes.

INTRODUCTION

The conception of computer games in education dates back to the 1950s with the integration of war-gaming and computer science research, coupled with the emergence of educational theories that emphasise active learning. The first computer games were developed in the 1960s and soon after they were being used and developed for educational purposes (Wolfe & Crookall, 1998). Educational games and simulations have been used for many years in business, training staff in financial and economic skills, and in the military for combat and strategy training. Americas Army, published in 2002, is arguably the most successful serious game produced, and the health sector

DOI: 10.4018/978-1-4666-2467-2.ch007

has used simulation and visualisation techniques for many years, for example through the use of virtual patients. However, rigorous academic study of digital games, from a variety of perspectives and disciplines, is still very much in its infancy.

The development of appropriate games for learning, in which the gaming and learning outcomes are closely aligned and are fit-for-purpose for specific teaching situations, is difficult. Commercial off-the-shelf (COTS) games often have too much irrelevant content and a steep learning curve while, at the other end of the spectrum, the creation of new games specifically for learning requires expertise and expense. There are problems also in the attitudes of institutions, parents and professional bodes towards the use of games for learning as they can be seen as trivialising the curriculum in an increasingly target-driven and scrutinised environment. If games are to be taken seriously as an educational tool it is essential that development models emerge that enable high-quality games to be produced—in terms of educational value, game play design and appropriateness for the target audience.

Educational games are commonly produced by specialist game-based learning and e-learning development companies, or by enthusiastic teams (or even individuals) based in educational institutions. Entertainment games companies rarely venture into the field of educational games because the potential markets are smaller than for entertainment games but many of the lessons learned from the industry could be equally applied to the processes by which games for learning are developed.

This paper aims to highlight some of these lessons. It is aimed at those interested or involved in the creation of games for learning as well as those developing policy in the field and commissioning educational games. It considers what might be learned from the entertainment games industry in terms of the development of educational games, focussing on the process of game creation, and specifically not on the design elements. A great

deal has already been written on ways in which to harness the motivational and engagement factors of entertainment games to enhance learning (Malone & Lepper, 1987; Garris et al., 2002; Dickie, 2007) so that will not be dwelt one here; this paper will focus on the development process rather than the product. Also, while the authors recognise the rich history of paper-based games, the scope of this paper is limited to digital games. The points that are made in the following sections do not purport to be unique to the entertainment games industry, but they are simply areas in which the authors feel that those creating and commissioning games, might learn valuable lessons from a related industry.

BACKGROUND

Games consoles, personal computers and other games devices are becoming ubiquitous items within most homes in western society. Over 65% of US Households play video games, globally over 138 million Playstation 2 consoles have been sold and over 155 million console games are sold each year (Online Education, 2009). The video games market in the UK now outsells the film industry (Wallop, 2009). Commercial games designers have the ability to create highly engaging, immersive experiences where players keep coming back to for more (something that is sadly rarely the case in formal education). What constitutes a "good" computer game is arguable; (Koster, 2004) suggests that "fun" is an essential criteria (Prensky, 2007) talks about engagement and immersion, indeed it could be argued (sic) that sales volume measurement is a useful indicator of a good game. Suffice as to say the question of "goodness" is outside the scope of this paper.

In much of the academic literature on games-based learning one of the key reasons given for using games to teach is their motivational qualities (Oblinger, 2004; Prensky, 2007). However, this assumption that digital games are inherently motivating is challenged in reality. While games may motivate some learners, they are off-putting for others, who see them as a waste of time or inappropriate for academic learning. This may be particularly true the case of older learners who may have more limited time and are perhaps more strategic in their learning aspirations (Knowles, 2005). It also cannot be assumed that because an individual is motivated to play games in his or her leisure time that he or she will want to play them to learn something, or that the types of game played by choice will be appropriate for formal learning (Whitton, 2010). So while the motivational appeal of games may be present for some people, the primary reason for their use in teaching and learning must be because they have pedagogic value. Computer games offer the opportunity for players to explore, collaborate and problem-solve in massive virtual environments with immediate feedback and support as they move from easy to progressively harder tasks.

Research has suggested (McFarlane et al., 2002; Sandford & Williamson, 2005) that the use of games in formal teaching situations may present problems because it can be difficult to find appropriate games for specific teaching situations and they can be time consuming to learn and complete. The link between the game outcomes and the learning outcome must be strong because otherwise, while students could be engaged in playing the game they may not learn what was intended. Educational games also need to be designed in such a way that the focus is on learning from the game, not in learning the game itself, and learning processes such as reflection and collaboration need to be explicitly designed into the game play (Whitton, 2010). For these reasons, it can be challenging for teachers and other educators to find appropriate games with learning outcomes at the right level, which fit within the practical teaching constraints of a given situation.

There are a range of approaches to finding appropriate games: from using commercial games, either those designed for entertainment (Squire & Barab, 2004) or those designed explicitly for learning (Whitton & Hynes, 2006) to those created using modifications of commercial games (Robertson & Howells, 2008) or those developed from scratch (Ebner & Holzinger, 2007). However, each approach has its drawbacks: there are a limited number of commercial educational games available, games designed for entertainment may not map closely to the desired learning outcomes and curricula and the cost and expertise required to create bespoke games may prohibit this option for the majority of teachers.

There are historically several differences between games designed for education and those console and PC games designed purely for entertainment. One major difference, however, is still the amount of money spent on design and production: entertainment game budgets typically run into the millions of pounds, while that spent of educational games is significantly less. Major commercial entertainment games companies are unlikely to be prepared to invest equivalent sums on games for learning as there are simply not the same potential markets (although there is also now a growing market in the development of amateur or cottage industry web games with low budgets and simple production values, but focussed strongly on game play and originality).

The recognition, belatedly, by the industry of the social impact of gaming and the potential positive contribution it has to make to society is leading to the growing acceptance of educational games as having a legitimate place in the industry as they can be shown to have commercial potential. The market for educational games is at present small but the rise in popularity of "casual" games, which allow players to engage in bite-sized chunks, are challenging the notion that there is "no market," which has been the default position of industry for many years.

However, commercial educational games have tended to be based on the tried-and-tested task-reward structures and behaviourist principles, which relying on extrinsic motivation rather than learning integrated into the game design itself (for example Nintendo's Dr Kawashima's Brain Training). This means that the full educational potential of games to create exploratory learning environments where players can actively engage in problem-solving and creative tasks is not being reached by the majority of educational games produced commercially for the mass market.

While educational game developers are certainly paying more attention to the games industry over the last decade than previously, there are still problems with bridging the gap. These include academics concerns regarding the application of disruptive technologies not necessarily embedded in existing academic research and teaching practise, the levels of risk typically associated with commercial games development being unacceptable in academia, and the prohibitive costs and/ or expertise required to produce a game with the appropriate production values and game design quality to be acceptable by some target learner groups.

This paper suggests ways in which the educational games development community could learn from the entertainment game design community, although the metrics applied to define success by the games industry and education sectors differ markedly, which presents a challenge in making the transition. It highlights some of the harsh realities of an industry that is sales-driven, as the metric for success historically has been the number of unit sales (although this business model is currently being challenged by contemporary commercial models, such as the use of micro-payments and digital distribution, which advantage smaller developers).

An area in which the creation of games specifically designed for learning is becoming more feasible is in small companies that specialise in the design of educational games or rich media to support computer-enhanced learning, or in similar departments based within educational institutions. In many cases the individuals working in these units have a background in other areas—such as learning design or online learning development—and may have little or no experience of the commercial entertainment games industry. This paper considers the game development process and agues that there may be things that educational game designers—and those commissioning educational games—can learn from looking at what is common knowledge in the games industry.

LESSONS LEARNED FROM THE ENTERTAINMENT GAMES INDUSTRY

This section presents a list of ten areas in which the authors feel that educational game developers, and those commissioning games for learning, could have something to learn from the processes of the entertainment games industry. The list was created as a result of the authors' experiences of over twenty years in game development coupled with extensive experience in education, pedagogic design and research. This list does not purport to be complete or to be elicited from first-hand research, although it is grounded in relevant contemporary literature. It simply aims to provide practical guidelines to those involved in the development of educational games, highlighting that can themselves learn something from a different discipline.

1. Appreciate the Importance of a Known Brand

The sales of entertainment games have historically been entirely dominated by expensive licensed well-known brands, either characters native to the games industry or those taken from the media and film industries. Particularly in the context of games for children, it is important to recognise the endorsement these characters give a game, both in terms of establishing the credibility of the game and in setting and meeting learner expectations. While a connection to a known brand may not ensure that a game will be engaging over long periods of time, it will certainly contribute to the initial motivation to play the game.

However, the use of existing characters, licenced properties or established intellectual property in educational games is prohibitively expensive. They may also be off-putting to learners who have preconceived notions of what games involving these characters and properties involve, for example arguably sexualised characters such as Lara Croft or overtly masculine licensed properties such as Call of Duty or FIFA.

The lesson for educational game designers is that association with a brand can help to ensure an audience, but that selection of brands for the specified target audience must be appropriate. Players are sophisticated in their affiliations and will be unlikely to be fooled by using a copycat version of a popular character to make a game appear motivating—at best it is likely to be amateur and derivative. Creation of original characters is by no means trivial and getting it wrong could mean that learners will not even start to engage with what is otherwise a good learning game, but a focus on original character development can provide one solution if carried out robustly and with a deep understanding of the target user group.

2. Focus on Adding Value

The practice of creating online materials and interactive learning content from scratch is still common in education. While this is a waste of resources for the creation of learning materials, when it comes to the design and development of computer games, which are expensive in terms of development time and expertise, this can become ridiculous. Creation of computer games requires specialist skills, is extremely time-consuming and expensive. It is simply not sensible to develop every aspect of a game from scratch, particularly

when easily-available middleware, modding engines or existing multi-user virtual environments (MUVEs) such as Second Life will probably do the job better at significantly less cost (both financial and in terms of team sanity).

The focus of educational games development needs to be on adding purpose and value rather than creating the underlying game mechanics (e.g., a new physics engine or rendering algorithm). Use of existing middleware where possible will allow developers to focus on adding new value, specifically being able to focus on creative game design, interaction and learning design, and not re-inventing the wheel. Instead of devoting energy to recreating the underlying game mechanics, additional resources such as example case studies, or suggestions for how to integrate games within the curriculum, could be provided with games and increase both the likelihood that they will be used (more widely) and that their use will be more effective in educational terms.

3. Remember the Reason for Creating a Game in the First Place

It is important not to lose sight of one of the reasons for using a game to learn in the first place—as well as providing pedagogically-sound active learning environments, computer games also have the potential to motivate and engage learners (Whitton, 2010). However, in the case of game-based learning (a sub-set of so-called "serious" games) it is often the case that the *serious* is over-emphasised at the expense of engagement. While it can be a difficult balancing act to create a game that retains its engaging qualities and is not seen as frivolous or inappropriate for formal education by at least some of the target learners, it is important to acknowledge that serious need not equate to boring.

Many educational games or edutainment titles produced are reliant on extrinsic motivation factors, through "game" rewards for the completion of "learning" tasks. While extrinsic rewards are an integral part of the rules of play (Salen & Zimmerman, 2004) fostering intrinsic motivation, where the game play and learning outcomes are intrinsically linked, is to the game experience (Crawford, 2003) and fosters deeper learning (Cordova & Lepper 1996; Hapgood et al., 2005).

A mistake that is sometimes made with entertainment games is to try and make them over-realistic—at the expense of game play. For example racing games would become unplayable if they required the player to have the skills of a real racing driver, but are toned down to make them fun to play (Dormans, 2008). There is a balance to be struck between the amount of realism necessary for a game to be acceptable and for the learning from the game to transfer into real life (this will, of course, depend upon the type of game used and whether the skills are actual or abstract).

4. Work with Developers Who Share Your Conceptual and Cultural Frameworks

When designing games for learning, it is important not to lose sight of what is trying to be achieved in terms of learning and in what contexts the game will eventually be used. Games designers typically work from a clearly-defined conceptual brief, often driven by mechanics and narrative, while educational designers work on learning outcomes and assessment criteria. Game-based learning products must be a synthesis of these, so an understanding of the two cultures – and where they might clash—is essential. Working with a team that share the same vision, goals and cultural norms is key in any game development, but crucial in the field of educational games, where there is a potential clash of expectations and practices. It is important that each takes time to listen to and respect the skills of the other in the development of educational games. The results of

not doing so can be graphically stunning games that are pedagogically trivial or educationally-sound games that are so complex and boring that they are hardly games at all.

It is important to recognise that educational computer games require a range of hybrid and cross-disciplinary skills in order to great engaging games that are appropriate for learning. Where this skill mix cannot be achieved within an existing team it may be necessary to build partnership or relationships with others. While different views and opinions among team members can lead to healthy critical debate and overall a better product, problems can occur when individuals do not share an underpinning ethos. There is a potential tension between designing games for fun and designing games for learning and it is crucial to make sure that the people designing educational games want to be doing that and have a real passion for learning, and not people who really want to be designing shoot-em-ups.

5. Trust the Intuitive Creatives

The design of effective and engaging games contains an element of "art" and "craft" as well as "science." Commercial games are invariably the concept of one person's intuition, the lead designer, or a small group of individuals, for example Peter Molyneux's Black and White or Shigeru Myamoto's Mario games.

There is no reason why this principle should not apply to educational games too. Designing games in large groups or with multi perspectives, objectives or desired outcomes is problematic so it is crucial to have a single person who leads the project and holds the vision of the game (Blenkharn et al., 2006). The process of developing a game design concept is not necessarily a collaborative one and it is crucial to trust the people whose job it is to do it. Games should not be designed by committee.

6. But... Make Sure that Risk-Taking is Measured

Having said that it is important to trust the intuitive creatives, it is also important to appreciate that education is not the appropriate arena for extreme risk-taking. At one end of the spectrum, games for learning, particularly for younger age groups, are typically designed around a structure of levels and rewards, sticking to the principles of behaviourist approaches to game design. In terms of game design this type of framework is tried-and-tested, relatively easy and cheap to implement and re-usable in different contexts because the learning is divorced from the game dynamic. However, it may not be the best pedagogic approach to adopt as it is difficult to support deep learning without a close integration between the goals of the game and the learning goals.

At the other end of the scale, entertainment game developers are pushing the boundaries of what is possible in terms of graphic design, interaction methods, and game mechanics. These innovations can be extremely innovative but also involve a high level of expense and risk. In terms of games for learning, there are challenges, related to implementation, of accommodating diverse pedagogic approaches. For example with a constructivist pedagogy, to create games that support collaboration, problem-solving, learning through experience, and reflection or the process by which knowledge is constructed by the mental activity of Learners (Driver et al., 1994), before innovation in game design is even considered. There need to be established paradigms for the effective design, development and implementation of constructivist games first, and more research is needed before their use can be seen as mainstream or good practice can be established.

While it is not necessary to always conform to game development conventions of frameworks, and educational game designers should not be afraid to innovate, game-based learning is a field in which extreme risk taking or technical innovation may not be appropriate.

7. And... Say No to Feature Creep

Again, this may seem to go against the point about trusting intuitive creatives, but there must be a balance between initial flexibility and creativity and the ability to effectively plan and manage a project over its life cycle. Feature creep, where additional functionality keeps being added over-and-above the initial agreed specification, has prompted the premature burial of many a great game. It is always tempting to add additional functionality to a specification while a game is in development, which is why it is essential that it is tightly specified at the start. Both those commissioning games, and those developing them, need to keep their personal urges in check.

The author, from personal experience, sites two examples of this: Black and White on the Playstation console (over two and a half years in development to a point where console technology development superseded development of the game) and an Isle of Mann TT simulation in development for nearly five years (mapping and accurately simulating all 36.2 miles of the course proved time-consuming and prohibitive).

Remember that what is cool may not be educational and there is a need to balance motivational and educational values—what the developer or commissioner believes to be cool may be very different from the perceptions of the target audience. Thorough and detained planning, specification and documentation is essential to ensure that the game originally envisaged, meeting the learning outcomes intended, is developed without getting sidetracked down routes influenced by the personal interests or perspectives of teachers or developers.

8. Know the Audience

The entertainment games industry is notorious for lack of engagement by users in the development process (in a sense, this point is a lesson from the games industry in how *not* to do things). A deep engagement with target audience is essential to ensure that a game developed is appropriate, acceptable and accessible.

It is easy to make assumptions about certain groups such as "digital natives" or the 'games generation' without really understanding their needs or preferences. This is particularly important because of some of the assumptions that surround the use of games-based learning regarding engagement and motivation. It is not the case that all learners will find something motivating simply because it is a game (Whitton, 2010). A clear understanding of the target learner group is essential for educational game design, particularly in post-compulsory education, because if it is not seen as an appropriate way to learn, many learners will simply not engage at all.

It is crucial not to take the audience for granted or rely on "targeted focus groups," which are groups representative of potential buyers of games who are provided with Beta versions to test usability and playability. This is problematic in that this small subset of users are often comfortable with game concepts, and accustomed to the interfaces and with the genre of game, which this can inhibit objective feedback. Diverse learner groups in education present a much greater challenge.

Involving learners in the game development process, through participative design, is a key way in which to meet higher-level learning objectives while creating a game that is tailored for its target audience. When collecting feedback from educational games it is crucial to make a distinction between people who liked the game and those who learned from it—as these can be very different.

9. Decide how Success will be Measured

The primary focus for measuring success in the entertainment games industry is sales of a game. However, this does not distinguish between those who bought the game and played it once and those who engaged deeply. While this single measure is perhaps unhelpful in the context of educational

games, what it does highlight is that there needs to be some objective way of evaluating whether any game created has achieved its goals or had an impact. It is important to this about how success will be measured at the start.

It is also crucial that impact is not judged solely on quantitative measures such as number of downloads or users, as this stifles creativity and innovation and does not give a full picture of the educational impact of the game. The use of qualitative evaluation techniques increases the engagement with users and moves beyond simply measuring how much a game is used to understanding the rich nature of learner engagement with it.

Curriculum imperatives, which are often politically driven, are often also the driver for educational game development, meaning that games may quickly become obsolete as emphases change. It is better to create something that is reliable and tested in terms of pedagogy, game design and technological platform than to simply be jumping from bandwagon to bandwagon.

10. Be Prepared for Failure

In the entertainment industry, it is accepted that not all games will be a success (in terms of sales). The experience of the authors suggest this figure to be in the region of eighty per cent – there are games that "burn brightly," games that are "slow burners," but mostly games that simply "burn out" (this rate may, of course, be related to the general failure to engage with the target audiences). It is questionable whether this would be seen as an acceptable failure rate for educational games. Commercial success may also not imply successful learning and it may be a difficult balancing act between creating a product that is commercially viable and one that meets its intended learning goals.

It is difficult to gauge failure rates in the same way in education as the "profitability" is simply not an issue—even in Higher Education institutions the costs and incomes of individual courses or modules is often not calculated. What is certain is that an 80% failure rate would simply not be acceptable in terms of the metrics that are used in education, such as student retention or learner attainment. Perhaps educationalists need to accept and examine failure more critically, as is done in the games industry, to learn from it rather than it being seen as something that is unacceptable—if there is not a climate where it is okay to make mistakes (and learn from them) then innovation and creativity simply will not happen

CONCLUSION

This paper has aimed to highlight ten areas in which those involved in developing or commissioning the development of educational games could learn from the commercial entertainment games industry. Although this is not intended to be a comprehensive list, it is intended to highlight that there are some lessons that can be learned from other sectors and that those involved with creating games for learning could avoid making many of the mistakes already made.

The development of any game is not an easy task, creating the right balance of game mechanic, aesthetics and brand appeal. This equation is further complicated by the addition of learning outcomes and the practicalities of embedding the game within a teaching context. As well as focussing on what can be learned from the design of entertainment games, there is also much that can be learned from the development process. Educational games are an expensive way to teach and developers need to focus on where they can add the most value to the learning process, be it in terms of motivation, engagement or pedagogic design.

In the future bespoke development may be in the means of more and more educationalists and smaller teams within or outside of institutions. It is important, therefore, that the games research community focus on what elements of games really add value to the learning experience, and

build on the large amounts of research (albeit typically "non-academic") that is continually being undertaken in the games development industry. A critical awareness of this (and other related) sector will allow educators to take account of lessons already learned and avoid making the same (often costly) mistakes.

ACKNOWLEDGMENT

The authors would like to express their grateful thanks to Keri Facer, Jason Rutter, Alex Moseley, Jostein Hassel and David Squire for their valuable comments and feedback.

REFERENCES

Blenkharn, L., Carlisle, P., Charlton, J., Hollins, P., Ranyard, R., & Williams, A. (2006). *Engagement and motivation in games development processes.* Retrieved from http://www.freewebs.com/pams-gamelearning/BECTA-games.pdf

Cordova, D., & Lepper, M. R. (1996). Intrinsic motivation and the process of learning: Beneficial effects of contextualisation, personalisation and choice. *Journal of Educational Psychology*, *88*(4), 715–730. doi:10.1037/0022-0663.88.4.715

Crawford, C. (2003). *Chris Crawford on games design.* Indianapolis, IN: New Riders Publishing.

Dickey, M. (2007). Game design and learning: A conjectural analysis of how massively multiple online role-playing games (MMORPGs) foster intrinsic motivation. *Educational Technology Research and Development*, *55*(3), 253–273. doi:10.1007/s11423-006-9004-7

Dormans, J. (2008, July 22-27). Beyond iconic simulation. In *Proceedings of Gaming: Designing for Engaging Experience and Social Interaction*, Amsterdam, The Netherlands.

Driver, R., Mortimer, E., Asoko, H., Leach, J., & Scott, P. (1994). Constructing scientific knowledge in the classroom. *Educational Researcher, 23*(7), 5–12.

Ebner, M., & Holzinger, A. (2007). Successful implementation of user-centered game based learning in higher education: An example from civil engineering. *Computers & Education, 49*(3), 873–890. doi:10.1016/j.compedu.2005.11.026

Garris, R., Ahlers, R., & Driskell, J. E. (2002). Games, motivation, and learning: A research and practice model. *Simulation & Gaming, 33*(4), 441–467. doi:10.1177/1046878102238607

Habgood, M. P. J., Ainsworth, S. E., & Benford, S. (2005, July 5). Intrinsic fantasy: Motivation and affect in educational games made by children. In *Proceedings of the AIED Workshop on Motivation and Effect in Educational Software.*

Knowles, M. S., Holton, E. F., & Swanson, R. A. (1998). *The adult learner*. Oxford, UK: Gulf Professional Publishing.

Koster, R. (2004). *A theory of fun*. New York, NY: Parglyph Press.

Malone, T. W., & Lepper, M. R. (1987). Making learning fun: A taxonomy of intrinsic motivations for learning. In Snow, R. E., & Farr, M. J. (Eds.), *Aptitude, learning and instruction III: Conative and affective process analyses*. Mahwah, NJ: Erlbaum.

McFarlane, A., Sparrowhawk, A., & Heald, Y. (2002). *Report on the educational use of games*. Retrieved from http://www.teem.org.uk/resources/teem_gamesined_full.pdf

Oblinger, D. (2004). The next generation in educational engagement. *Journal of Interactive Media in Education, 8.*

Online Education. (2009). *Videogame statistics.* Retrieved from http://www.onlineeducation.net/videogame

Prensky, M. (2007). *Digital game-based learning.* St Paul, MN: Paragon House Publishers.

Robertson, J., & Howells, C. (2008). Computer game design: Opportunities for successful learning. *Computers & Education, 50*(2), 559–578. doi:10.1016/j.compedu.2007.09.020

Salen, K., & Zimmernam, E. (2004). *Rules of play: game design fundamentals.* Cambridge, MA: MIT Press.

Sandford, R., & Williamson, B. (2005). *Games and learning.* Bristol, UK: Nesta Futurelab.

Squire, K., & Barab, S. (2004). Replaying history: Engaging urban underserved students in learning world history through computer simulation games. In *Proceedings of the 6th international conference on Learning sciences*, Santa Monica, CA (pp. 505-512).

Wallop, H. (2009). Video games bigger than film. Retrieved from http://www.telegraph.co.uk/technology/video-games/6852383/Video-games-bigger-than-film.html

Whitton, N. (2010). *Learning with digital games.* New York, NY: Routledge.

Whitton, N., & Hynes, N. (2006). Evaluating the effectiveness of an online simulation to teach business skills. *E-Journal of Instructional Science and Technology, 9*(1).

Wolfe, J., & Crookall, D. (1998). Developing a scientific knowledge of simulation/gaming. *Simulation & Gaming, 29*(1), 7–19. doi:10.1177/1046878198291002

This work was previously published in the International Journal of Virtual and Personal Learning Environments, Volume 2, Issue 2, edited by Michael Thomas, pp. 73-82, copyright 2011 by IGI Publishing (an imprint of IGI Global).

Section 2
Innovation

Chapter 8
Social Networking Sites and Language Learning

Billy Brick
Coventry University, UK

ABSTRACT

This article examines a study of seven learners who logged their experiences on the language leaning social networking site Livemocha over a period of three months. The features of the site are described and the likelihood of their future success is considered. The learners were introduced to the Social Networking Site (SNS) and asked to learn a language on the site. They were positive about two aspects of the site: the immediate peer-feedback available and the ability to converse synchronously and asynchronously with native speakers of their target language. However, there was universal criticism of the "word-list" based language learning materials and several participants complained about the regular cyber-flirting they encountered. Other aspects of the site including accessibility, ease of use, syllabus, activities, and relationships with other members are also considered. The potential for integrating some of the features of SNSs for language learning into the Higher Education (HE) curriculum and the implications of this for educators are also discussed.

INTRODUCTION

In language teaching here has been a long tradition of encouraging learners to use the target language to communicate with others, in their own time. Sociocultural theory (Vygotsky, 1978) supports this approach, by emphasising the interdependence of individuals and the importance of group processes in the co-construction of knowledge.

Originally one of the ways that teachers advocated collaborative language learning was through penpalling, and then, with the advent of the internet, through keypalling (Choi & Nesi, 1999). Most recently social networking sites (SNSs) such as Livemocha have sprung up, offering learners the opportunity to practise the target language with other members of the online community. In order for foreign language educators to evaluate

DOI: 10.4018/978-1-4666-2467-2.ch008

and harness the potential of these sites it would be useful for them to know more about how they work.

Integrating SNSs into the classroom faces some practical obstacles including the lack of control that many tutors have over the curricula and the fact that language courses are often taught by a number of tutors who do not necessarily coordinate their efforts to ensure a degree of consistency. In addition to this there are wider questions which create tensions (JISC, 2009) including the lack of clear policies if a site that a course is reliant on ceases to operate, the lack of experienced learning technologists who have an understanding of Web 2.0 technologies, and the technical difficulties that face those with institutional support responsibilities to integrate tools which have been developed and maintained externally (Conole & Alevizou 2010). A further obstacle is the fact that the majority of language classes are introductory, and although SNS messages might sometimes seem superficial, they require advanced pragmatic knowledge that beginners are likely to lack (Furman et al., 2007).

McLaughlin and Lee (2008) propose a dynamic student-led "Pedagogy 2.0" curriculum, but institutional constraints make such flexibility problematic. Pedagogy 2.0 has emerged from the Web 2.0 movement and its innovative use of social software tools which offer opportunities for people to connect, share and discuss ideas (Conole & Alevizou) and to challenge previous centralized models of learning. McLaughlin and Lee (2008) define Pedagogy 2.0 as integrating "Web 2.0 tools that support knowledge sharing, peer-to-peer networking, and access to a global audience with socioconstructivist learning approaches to facilitate greater learner autonomy, agency, and personalization". The approach leads to individual learner empowerment (Rogers et al., 2007; Sims, 2006; Sheely, 2006) and the development of learners' Personal Learning Environments (PLEs).

Godwin-Jones (2005) has referred to SNSs as 'disruptive technologies' in that they allow for new

and different ways of doing familiar tasks". They have the potential to transform language learning by offering synchronous and asynchronous interaction, and speaking, writing, reading and listening activities at a time and place of learners' own choosing (McBride, 2009). Although SNS contact is not face-to-face it is authentic communication with native speakers, something which was previously difficult to replicate in the language classroom. The peer-review features and the oral practice opportunities afforded by SNSs have been praised by users such as the bloggers, Street-Smart Language Learning (2010) and Fluent in 3 months (2010)

A recent report (Johnson et al., 2010) identified the following three trends as key drivers of technology adoption in HE between 2010 and 2015:

- The abundance of online resources and relationships, inviting a rethink of the educators' role.
- An increased emphasis on ubiquitous, just-in-time, augmented, personalised and informal learning.
- Greater collaboration between students.

These predictions map across to features of SNSs for language learning, as can be seen from the overview of Livemocha.com provided below, and this suggests that more widespread adoption of SNSs for language learning is about to take place.

The Affordances of SNSs for Language Learning

Attitudes towards the use of SNSs for learning in HE in the UK can be summarised by the findings of a recent report (JISC, 2009):

Yet technology-enhanced learning remains a source of concern for institutions. This finding may reflect the extent to which supporting such practice makes demands on institutional resources... Access, especially to the internet and social software, may have increased, but this does not mean that technology is always used to its best advantage, either by teachers or learners.

This cautious approach contrasts sharply with the emergence of PLEs and "Pedagogy 2.0" curriculum referred to in the introduction.

Boyd and Ellison describe SNSs as "web-based services that allow individuals to:

1. Construct a public or semi-public profile within a bounded system.
2. Articulate a list of other users with whom they share a connection.
3. View and traverse their list of connections and those made by others within the system." (Social Network Sites: A definition, 2007).

SNS technology can be utilised in two different ways, affording learners greater or lesser control over their own learning process. On the one hand tutors can encourage learner interaction in an institutional Virtual Learning Environment (VLE) incorporating videoconferencing software such as Skype. This approach allows tutors to maintain control over the membership of the group and to provide a structured learning environment, based on the principles of tandem learning. The effects of Skype-based tandem language learning have recently been investigated in a study by Mullen, Appel and Shanklin (2009), who replicated some of the features of SNSs with classes of students in Japan and the US, using a Moodle site they had constructed themselves. The feedback from participants was positive and the project has proved to be sustainable with criticism restricted to complaints about the time difference. Practical suggestions were made to address this, such as setting up a fixed time when all students were available. Alternatively tutors can encourage students to register on a commercial site which allows them complete freedom to interact with any other site member. Most commercial language

learning SNSs offer some free content alongside a premium feature for which registration and payment is required. The sites often include a peer review facility where students can provide feedback to learners of their own first language, and some sites incorporate an award system in the form of "Mochapoints" and "medals" (www.livemocha.com) or "berries" (www.busuu.com). This serves to motivate participants by rewarding them for their progress and for their peer review activities.

Livemocha as a platform for ethnographic research into relationship building and mediation has recently been investigated by Harrison and Thomas (2009, p.121). Their study found that sites such as live Livemocha "offer to transform language learning, by providing environments that allow new modes of active learning" and that SNSs present opportunities to examine existing learning theories in the age of digital literacies.

Livemocha.com: An Overview

The Livemocha site was the first of its kind and remains the most popular, with over 5 million members worldwide, mostly in the 18-35 age group (Livemocha, 2009). Livemocha members can take courses free of charge in 35 different languages, with the option to pay for premium content in some of these. Livemocha make no mention of tandem learning on their web site, but they do refer to their pedagogical principles:

If you are looking to translate a 1,000 page dissertation or write text in an ancient language, then Livemocha is not for you. But, if you are looking to gain practical, real-life language skills, Livemocha is your ticket. Livemocha courses are focused on building practical conversation skills - every lesson includes speaking and writing exercises that are reviewed by native speakers. Livemocha helps you build the confidence you need to speak a new language (Livemocha, 2010).

Figure 1. Log in screen (© 2010, Livemocha: Used with permission)

The site is divided into four parts: Home, Learn, Share and Teach. In the Home section (Figure 1) learners can keep track of their progress, view their reward points, monitor their recent activity, view the work they have submitted for peer review and access requests from other community members to review their work.

The Learn section (Figure 2) provides a list of the courses the learner is currently taking, a section which creates flashcards based on what the student has learnt, and further sections to view work submitted for review and for further practice. There are seven activities (Jee & Park, 2009):

1. **Learn:** Learners listen and click the right picture for vocabulary learning.
2. **Reading:** Learners read the sentence and click the right picture.
3. **Listening:** Learners listen and click the right picture.
4. **Magnet:** Learners listen and arrange words in a correct sentence.
5. **Writing:** Learners read the prompt, write an essay, and submit it to receive feedback

from other anonymous users or their invited friends.

6. **Speaking:** Learners record a paragraph length discourse sample and submit it for peer review.
7. **Dialogue:** Learners practice a paragraph-length given dialogue with a partner of their choice.

Jee and Park (2009) criticised the quality of the learning materials available on the site: "The instructional content in the system could benefit from guidance from second language acquisition (SLA) practitioners to improve its pedagogical design and offer a more systematic approach to effective learning" (n.p.). However, they acknowledged that Livemocha learners would benefit from the authentic communicative experience with native speakers, even without the presence of a tutor. Since Jee and Park's (2009) publication, the English language learning section of Livemocha has become part of a new collaboration with Pearson Publishing, leading to the addition of

Figure 2. Learn screen (© 2010, Livemocha: Used with permission)

premium content called "Study English" (Livemocha, 2010).

The share section (Figure 3) allows users to review submissions by other users and to provide feedback. It is in this section that learners are able to contribute to the community and in doing so earn Mochapoints and, eventually "medals".

The Teach tab (Figure 4) encourages users to complete their profile in anticipation of the increased functionality that will be added to the site in the near future. Few details have so far been provided, but it is suggested that those users with high Mochapoints ratings are likely to benefit through having the option to teach on the site in exchange for money or Livemocha points.

Learners are encouraged to search for other learners on the site and to make friends in much the same way as they would on other SNSs such as Facebook. This friendship is supposed to offer mutual benefits to both parties as they can provide feedback for each other's oral or written work and communicate asynchronously, via an in-built texting tool, or synchronously, via a Voice over Internet Protocol (VoIP) tool. There is also the possibility to use built-in video-conferencing software to communicate with friends within the site. Peer review is at the centre of the design of the site, and "Mochapoints" are awarded to members who choose to review the written or oral submissions of other site members. "Fluent in 3 months", a blogger who has used Livemocha, is positive about the peer review system:

The best thing would be to get to know other users and to come to a mutual agreement about helping one another.... The fact that you can find such people eager to help you within the system is a huge plus (2010).

The Livemocha site continues to evolve and has already changed substantially since Jee and Park (2009) wrote their initial review. The company now claims to have over 6 million users worldwide with members in over 200 countries. However, there are no statistics available to indicate how many of these users are active on the site on a regular basis. One of the founders of Livemocha, Krishnan Seshadrinathan, claims that the company

Figure 3. Share screen (© 2010, Livemocha: Used with permission)

will be able to expand substantially and support a range of new services over the next five years, due to growth in the market for language learning as a result of globalization, immigration and travel, According to Seshadrinathan, Livemocha will become available on a variety of electronic devices, will offer 100 different languages, and will have between 30 and 50 million users (Maclure, 2009).

Figure 4. Teach screen (© 2010, Livemocha: Used with permission)

Research Questions

Whether Seshadrinathan's predictions are correct or not, the sheer number of people currently registered on Livemocha and numerous other SNSs for language learning suggests that they will play an important role in foreign language learning in the future. This raises a number of general questions for HE practitioners, the answers to which are likely to be clearer over the next few years. Should we attempt to integrate such sites into the curriculum? If the answer to this question is yes, then which site should we select and what sort of guidance should we provide for learners? If the answer is no, then should we attempt to recreate some of the features of these sites in a more controlled environment such as that described by Mullen et al. (2009)? If we choose to eschew SNSs in favour of more traditional methods, and then do we run the risk of learners learning languages in forums we are unfamiliar with and which we are unable to offer appropriate advice about?

The following section reports on the experiences of a sample of UK HE students who accessed Livemocha over a period of three months. By observing these students and gathering reports of their experiences using Livemocha I was able to explore the potential of SNSs as a means of providing language instruction, language support and collaborative learning opportunities within the context of a university level language programme.

The specific questions this paper seeks to answer are as follows:

How easy is the site to access and use? What are the strengths and weaknesses of the syllabus and activities available on the site? What were the reactions of the participants to the social networking element of the site?

THE STUDY

Methods

The participants were seven undergraduate learners from various L1 backgrounds who were either taking, or had taken, courses in Polish, Portuguese, Spanish. For the purposes of the study they were allowed to learn whichever language they wished. The study followed their interactions in the Livemocha language learning SNS, adopting a repeated measures design and eliciting multiple samples from the same learners over a three month period from January to March 2010. The data was collected via log sheets (Appendix) and meetings in which common issues were discussed.

The participants were required to fill in a log sheet each time they visited the site and were also required to attend four scheduled meetings and

Table 1. Log in sheet template

	Date:	
Session no:	Logged in at:	Logged out at:
I studied:		
I learned (can refer to 'anything', not just the language you are studying):		
I communicated with …. (name of language partner) by …. (message, text chat, voice chat, other?):		
I made mistakes with:		
I was pleased with:		
I wasn't pleased with:		
My difficulties are:		
I would like to know:		
My learning and practising plans for next time are:		

notes were taken as they discussed their experiences. Watts and Ebbutt (1987) have considered the advantages of group interviewing as a means of collecting data: it allows for discussions to develop, thus yielding a wider range of responses and causes minimum disruption. As recommended by Arksey and Knight (1999), there were always two interviewers present as a means of cross-checking and producing a more complete record. The research was confined to the free content on Livemocha rather than including the premium services, and participants were simply asked to use the site, and did not receive specific instructions to concentrate on particular features or languages. In order to familiarize students with the various functions Livemocha offers, an introductory session was held in which the various features were demonstrated and the aims of the study were explained.

The following section is a summary of the comments and evaluations collected from the participants. The combination of regular log sheets, completed immediately after they had visited Livemocha and discussions during the scheduled meetings, provided a rich variety of data covering a wide range of opinions about the site.

RESULTS

Accessibility and Ease of Use

The initial reaction to using the site was a positive one; all participants were able to set up an account and make a few friends, although Participant 1 reported difficulties in trying to work out how to remove somebody from her list of 'friends'. There were no complaints regarding access to the site. The pages were found to load quickly and the site was considered intuitive to use.

One of the participants (#3) reported that she had managed to access some of the premium content (a crash course in French for travellers, offered as a reward for recommending new members) by convincing three of her friends to sign up for the site.

Syllabus

All the participants complained about the quality of the language learning materials on the site. Participants 1, 3 and 7 complained that the Spanish materials were geared towards Latin American Spanish, which differs considerably from the Castilian Spanish which they were more familiar with. Participant 1 discovered incorrect translations in the Spanish learning materials and participant 3 criticised the syllabus, which consisted largely of the names of people and objects, rather than the common language functions normally associated with beginners' courses, for example greetings, requests and directions. This "word list" approach is followed across all of the languages on offer. Towards the end of the evaluation period a common complaint from all of the participants was the lack of grammar learning opportunities. None of the freely available learning activities explicitly focus on the grammar of the target language.

Activities

Four of the participants (1, 3, 4 and 7) chose to learn more than one language because this was free of charge, they did not need to invest in a text book, and they could receive almost instantaneous feedback from native speakers in the Livemocha community. However, the peer review feature also received some negative feedback; learners liked the immediacy of the responses to written and spoken submissions, but at the same time were critical of the value of corrections offered by community members All of the participants believed that it was possible to build up a network of reliable friends to provide feedback on the site, but that this took time to achieve. The only way this is possible is by trial and error. Members need to submit written texts for review and slowly build up a network of friends whose feedback they judge to be of a high quality.

One of the key principles of tandem learning is reciprocity (Little, 2003) which means that each partner should benefit from the experience equally. This was often deemed not to be the case and participants 1, 3, and 7 speculated that the reason for this was that some members of the Livemocha community are keen to learn English from native speakers rather than developing a relationship based on the principles of tandem learning, and that the number of learners wanting to learn English far outweighs the number of English native speakers wanting to learn a foreign language.

There is as yet no facility to enable learners studying the same material to communicate with each other; Participant 3 suggested that this would be a useful addition to the site.

Throughout the survey none of the participants took advantage of the built in video-conferencing feature although several participants commented on requests they had received to continue communicating with partners using other software such as MSN or Skype. The only reason provided to explain this was lack of familiarity with Livemocha's in-house communications software.

Participants 2, 3 and 5 also commented on how they liked the translator tool which is available within the text chat feature. This enabled them to quickly translate phrases whilst chatting to language partners in their target language.

Relationships with Other Participants

Participant 1 was the only participant who registered to improve her knowledge of a language she knew already (Spanish). She reported that she had met a learning partner on Livemocha but had then gone on to build a tandem-learning relationship with him using Skype rather than the tools available within Livemocha. She also reported that both her and her Spanish partner had become less inhibited as they got to know each other better and revealed that they were able to "laugh at each other's mistakes and attempt more challenging tasks".

However although this student had a good relationship with her learning partner, throughout the duration of the study one recurring criticism was the numerous inappropriate advances made towards the participants by community members. Participant 1, for example, reported experiencing inappropriate behaviour on her second visit to the site. This type of behaviour is known as cyber-flirting (Whitty & Gavin, 2001; Vie 2007). Apart from inquiries into their marital status and whether they had a boyfriend or not, the approaches included requests to become Facebook friends or to meet elsewhere on-line outside the parameters of the site (participant 5). None of these advances were deemed serious enough to warrant making a complaint. All participants chose to register on Livemocha using their real identity rather than a pseudonym, and four of the seven (participants 2, 4, 6 and 7) chose to upload a profile picture. These four reported a greater incidence of cyber-flirting than those who chose not to post a photograph to their profiles. It should be noted that this type of behaviour is common on SNSs generally, as Ibrahim (2008) points out.

DISCUSSION

The participants reported both negative and positive reactions to using Livemocha on a regular basis over the three month period. The most common criticism concerned the quality and relevance of the free learning materials, which were always based around a series of pictures. Some of the participants also complained about the complete lack of explicit grammar teaching on the site. Although the learning materials seem to be quite poor, it is easy to understand why both of the market leaders, Livemocha and Busuu, have taken this approach. Materials based on "word lists" are particularly cheap to produce because the approach can be applied to all languages using the same prompts. The complete lack of grammar on the site is also one of the main criticisms made by the blogger Street Smart Language Learning (2010), who reported his unsuccessful attempt to study the German case system using Livemocha, and his eventual decision to abandon Livemocha in favour of other non-SNS language learning web sites and books. Street Smart Language Learning (2010) also goes on to mention that he had learnt German in the past and had hoped to review the grammar rules he had previously learnt. This proved to be impossible via Livemocha. A beginner would undoubtedly find learning grammar from Livemocha even more difficult.

Livemocha has not yet addressed the perceived weakness in the teaching of grammar on their site but their European competitor Busuu, have recently launched additional premium grammar content in collaboration with Collins publishing. The grammar guides provide explicit grammatical explanations which integrate with the learning units.

Livemocha offers "premium content" in conjunction with a publishing house for a monthly fee, but although one of the premium packages includes the services of a tutor, it is unclear how much weekly contact time is provided, or what the tutor's teaching qualifications may be

The cyber flirting (Whitty & Gavin, 2001; Vie, 2007) referred to by several of the participants is obviously a concern for practitioners but it is by no means certain whether we should advise against registering for SNSs on this account. When students undertake a study year abroad we do not advise them to communicate only with students from their host university, and to avoid communicating with members of the wider community, for fear that they may encounter unsavoury characters

with questionable motives. On the contrary, we encourage them to experience as much of the local culture as possible and expect them to use their common sense to avoid placing themselves in potentially dangerous situations. Perhaps the same philosophy should be adopted with regard to SNSs.

The comments of the two bloggers Street-Smart Language Learning (2010) and Fluent in 3 months (2010) concur with the findings of this study. They are both extremely critical of the free learning materials (neither comment on the premium content) but they both agree that the site offers a unique opportunity for learners to practise their oral skills with native speakers and that they facilitate almost immediate feedback. Neither of the two (male) bloggers made any reference to the cyber flirting, suggesting that this type of behaviour tends to be directed at women by men.

According to Harpercollins, (2010) 375 million people worldwide want to learn a language and the market is currently estimated to be over $80 billion. If this is true, the likelihood is that the number of people choosing to learn languages in this way will increase. We should also expect increased functionality, options to study a wider variety of languages and the availability of services on a wider range of electronic devices. One student reported that she managed to access Livemocha via her iPhone. A recent blog (Winkler, 2010) suggests that it is this market sector (iPhone, iPad and Android devices) which the company intends to target next to increase its market share. There is certainly potential for SNSs for language learning to become embedded as part of language learners' PLEs once these technologies become widely accessible. Over the coming years we are likely to see an expansion in the various offers made by language learning SNSs including models that offer tutor support and the introduction of platforms aimed specifically at HE in direct competition with e-learning software providers such as Rosetta Stone and Auralog.

Harrison and Thomas (2009, p.118) reported that learners "felt a certain amount of unease... and chose to use pseudonyms rather than their real names". The opposite was true with the learners who took part in the project: all of them chose to use their own names rather than pseudonyms. Further research needs to be carried out in this area to establish which behaviour is typical and to investigate whether cultural factors play a role in how students choose to compose their profiles.

As mentioned previously, Mullen et al. (2009) have described another approach to creating opportunities for language learners in HE to communicate in their target languages. On the one hand this approach allowed tutors to more carefully monitor the interactions between learners and have some control over matching ability levels. They also had a degree of insurance that the learners were able to offer constructive feedback as they were university students with some experience of language learning. There are also disadvantages to this approach, however, not least the small numbers of learners involved compared to those found on www.livemocha or www.busuu.com. The critical mass of learners available on-line across the globe on these two sites and numerous others ensures that there are always language learners available for members to interact with, meaning that time differences are of no consequence. On the other hand, Mullen et al.'s (2009) model relies on learners being available at specific times of mutual convenience.

Hybrid sites are likely to emerge combining some of the functionality of commercial SNSs with the principles of tandem learning. In response to the positive feedback from participants in the study, one such site is currently being developed at Coventry University which aims to facilitate both face-to-face and online language exchange via a Moodle web open to both Coventry University students and students from other partner universities. Learners are able to construct a profile including their Skype address and can then search within discussion forums, which are threaded according

to target language, for language exchange partners. Once a learner has found a partner, they can arrange to meet up face-to-face or over the internet via Skype. Links to suitable language exchange learning materials, created at Bochum University for the eTandem project (2001), are also provided on the site along with the a link to the Common European Framework (CEF) which serves as a point of reference for learners to estimate their levels. If learners are unable to locate a partner within the site, they are directed towards SNSs.

Similar developments are likely to follow from language learning software companies. Indeed, Rosetta Stone, the US-based language learning software company, has recently launched a new platform which provides opportunities to practise speaking with native speakers (Overly, 2010).

The fact that none of the participants chose to use the web conferencing feature available within the site but chose instead to migrate to more familiar platforms cannot be easily explained. Perhaps their familiarity with tools such as Skype and MSN instant messenger prompted this, rather than a lack of confidence in the in-house product.

Stevick (1971) and Guo (2010) have both argued the importance of building motivation concepts such as immediacy and authenticity into language learning materials. SNSs offer both of these and according to Guo (2010, p. E14), "The educational language website or computer application based on motivation is a true step forward as compared with inventions of printing, computer, the Internet and their applications to human language learning". However, it should be noted that participants reported varied experiences with regard to peer review feedback, depending on who was providing it and their level of expertise. It was also suggested that it may take time to develop a network of trusted partners within the site and that this can only be built up on a trial and error basis. Street Smart Language Learning (2010) supports the idea that you have to develop a network of friends in whom you have confidence:

I now have a core group of tutors to whom I consistently submit such assignments to, and their feedback is phenomenal. They drill into my work to find even subtle mistakes and offer excellent explanations of what I'm doing wrong. So, while initially you may find that the feedback you get is not all that great, as you separate the wheat from the chaff you'll eventually end up with excellent tutors.

The blogger goes on to describe Livemocha as "ingenious social engineering" because members are presented with work to correct immediately after they have had a piece of work corrected themselves. They then feel eager to reciprocate by providing good feedback for someone who has done the same for themselves.

Since UK National Student Surveys (NSS) were initiated in 2005 there has been a consistently negative response regarding feedback; according to the Higher Education Funding Council for England (2009) only 57% of students considered it to be prompt and useful. Perhaps the quality of the feedback on SNSs for language learning is variable, depending on your network of friends, but it is certainly fast, often taking only a few minutes to arrive. This compares favourably with HE institutions where the turnaround time can be several weeks.

CONCLUSION

SNSs for language learning provide the opportunity, previously unavailable, for learners to practise oral skills with native speakers and to receive immediate feedback, thus justifying their designation as "disruptive technologies" (Godwin Jones, 2005). These two features are the ones which received the highest praise from the participants, as opposed to the learning materials which received universal criticism. The number of

sites and the number of people joining these sites is likely to continue in the foreseeable future, even more premium content is likely to be offered and opportunities for learners to access the sites on various mobile platforms are likely to increase. In the face of ongoing cuts in HE (Atwood, 2010) and the concomitant pressures to teach more and more students with decreasing levels of resource, educators cannot afford to ignore SNSs for language learning. Tutors will also need to be made aware of SNSs, and to be trained in their use (Elliott, 2009). Further research in this rapidly developing area is essential to enable practitioners to make informed choices with regard to their role in the curriculum.

REFERENCES

Arskey, H., & Knight, P. (1999). *Interviewing for social scientists*. London, UK: Sage.

Attwood, R. (2010). *Changed utterly: Cuts expected to transform the teaching landscape.* Retrieved from http://www.timeshighereducation.co.uk/story.asp?sectioncode=26&storycode=414005

Boyd, D. M., & Ellison, N. B. (2007). Social networks: Definition, history, and scholarship. *Journal of Computer-Mediated Communication, 13*(1). doi:10.1111/j.1083-6101.2007.00393.x

Busuu. (2010). *busuu.com enters into strategic partnership with leading language learning publisher Collins.* Retrieved from http://blog.busuu.com/busuu-com-enters-into-strategic-partnership-with-leading-language-learning-publisher-collins/

Choi, J., & Nesi, H. (1999). *An account of a keypal project for Korean children.* The Internet TESL Journal.

Conole, G., & Alevizou, P. (2010). *A literature review of the use of Web 2.0 tools in Higher Education.* Retrieved from http://www.heacademy.ac.uk/assets/EvidenceNet/Conole_Alevizou_2010.pdf

Elliott, D. (2009). Internet technologies and language teacher education. In Thomas, M. (Ed.), *Handbook of research on Web 2.0 and second language learning* (pp. 432–450). Hershey, PA: IGI Global. doi:10.4018/978-1-60566-190-2.ch023

eTandem. (2001). *Brammerts Ruhr-Universität Bochum.* Retrieved from http://www.telecom-paristech.fr/

Fluent in 3 months. (2010). *Busuu & LiveMocha: review of pros and cons.* Retrieved from http://www.fluentin3months.com/busuu-livemocha-review/

Furman, N., Goldberg, D., & Lusin, N. (2007). *Enrollments in languages other than English in United States institutions of higher education, Fall 2006.* Retrieved from http://www.mla.org/pdf/06enrollmentsurvey_final.pdf

Godwin-Jones, B. (2005). Emerging technologies: Skype and Podcasting: Disruptive technologies for language learning. *Language Learning & Technology, 9*(3), 9–12.

Guo, S. (2010). From printing to Internet, are we advancing in technological application to language learning? *British Journal of Educational Technology, 41*(2), 10–16. doi:10.1111/j.1467-8535.2008.00867.x

Harpercollins. (2010). *Collins language and Livemocha sign multi-language online learning agreement.* Retrieved from http://www.harpercollins.co.uk/News_and_Events/News/Pages/Collins-Language-and-Livemocha-Sign-Multi-Language-Online-Learning-Agreement.aspx

Harrison, R., & Thomas, M. (2009). Identity in online communities: Social networking sites and language learning. *International Journal of Emerging Technologies & Society, 7*(2), pp, 109-124.

HEFCE. (2009). *The national student survey.* Retrieved from http://www.hefce.ac.uk/learning/nss/data/2009/

Ibrahim, J. (2008). The new risk communities: Social networking sites and risk. *International Journal of Media and Cultural Politics, 4*(2), 245–253. doi:10.1386/macp.4.2.245_3

Jee, M. J., & Park, M. J. (2009). *Livemocha as an online language-learning community, Calico software reviews.* Retrieved from https://calico.org/p-416-livemocha%20as%20an%20online%20language-learning%20community%20%28012009%29.html

JISC. (2009). *Effective practice in a digital age: A guide to technology-enhanced learning and teaching.* Bristol, UK: JISC.

Johnson, L. F., Levine, A., & Smith, R. S. (2009). *Horizon report.* Austin, TX: The New Media Consortium.

Kelly, L. G. (1969). *25 centuries of language teaching.* Rowley, MA: Newbury House.

Little, D. (2003). Tandem language learning and learning autonomy. In Lewis, T., & Walker, L. (Eds.), *Autonomous language learning in tandem.* Sheffield, UK: Academy Electronic Publications.

Livemocha. (2009). *Livemocha and Pearson announce partnership for online language learning.* Retrieved from http://www.livemocha.com/pages/pr/03102009

Livemocha. (2010). *What makes Livemocha so popular?* Retrieved from http://www.livemocha.com/language-learning-method

Long, M. H. (2000). Second language acquisition theories. In Byram, M. (Ed.), *Encyclopedia of language teaching* (pp. 527–534). London, UK: Routledge.

Maclure, M. (2009). Livemocha creates an online language learning platform. *Information Today*, 10.

McBride, K. (2009). Social-networking sites in foreign language classrooms. In Lomicka, L., & Lord, G. (Eds.), *The next generation: Social networking and online collaboration in foreign language learning*. San Marcos, TX: CALICO Book Series.

McLoughlin, C., & Lee, M. J. W. (2008). Future learning landscapes: Transforming pedagogy through social software. *Innovate, 4*(5).

Mullen, T., Appel, C., & Shanklin, T. (2009). Sky-pebased tandem language learning and web 2.0. In Thomas, M. (Ed.), *Handbook of research on Web 2.0 and second language learning* (pp. 101–118). Hershey, PA: IGI Global. doi:10.4018/978-1-60566-190-2.ch006

Overly, S. (2010). *Q&A with Rosetta Stone chief: In using social media for education, it needs to serve learning goals, not just be a "time sink"*. Retrieved from http://www.washingtonpost.com/wp-dyn/content/article/2010/09/24/AR2010092405995.html

Rogers, P. C., Liddle, S. W., Chan, P., Doxey, A., & Isom, B. (2007). A Web 2.0 learning platform: Harnessing collective intelligence. *Turkish Online Journal of Distance Education, 8*(3), 16–33.

Sheely, S. (2006). Persistent technologies: Why can't we stop lecturing online? In *Proceedings of the 23rd ASCILITE Conference on Who's Learning? Whose Technology?* Sydney, Australia (pp. 769-774).

Sims, R. (2006). Online distance education: New ways of learning, new modes of teaching? *Distance Education, 27*(2), 3–5.

Stevick, E. (1971). Evaluating and adapting language materials. In Allen, H., & Campbell, R. (Eds.), *Teaching English as a second language* (pp. 102–107). New York, NY: McGraw-Hill.

Street-Smart Language Learning. (2010). *Livemocha review: Love the native speakers, the method not so much*. Retrieved from http://www.streetsmartlanguagelearning.com/2009/01/livemocha-review-love-native-speakers.html

Vie, S. (2007). *Engaging others in online social networking sites: Rhetorical practices in MySpace and Facebook*. Unpublished doctoral dissertation, University of Arizona, Tucson, AZ.

Vygotsky, L. (1978). *Mind in society: The development of bigger psychological processes*. Boston, MA: Harvard University Press.

Warriner-Burke, H. P. (1990). Distance learning: "What we don't know can't hurt us. *Foreign Language Annals, 23*(2), 131. doi:10.1111/j.1944-9720.1990.tb00351.x

Watts, M., & Ebbutt, D. (1987). More than the sum of the parts: Research methods in group interviewing. *British Educational Research Journal, 13*(1), 25–34. doi:10.1080/0141192870130103

Whitty, M., & Gavin, J. (2001). Age/sex/location: Uncovering the social cues in the development of online relationships. *Cyberpsychology & Behavior, 4*, 623–630. doi:10.1089/109493101753235223

Winkler, K. (2010). *The new CEO of Livemocha goes mobile and looks out for the best customer*. Retrieved from.http://www.kirstenwinkler.com/the-new-ceo-of-livemocha-goes-mobile-and-looks-out-for-the-best-customer/

This work was previously published in the International Journal of Virtual and Personal Learning Environments, Volume 2, Issue 3, edited by Michael Thomas, pp. 18-31, copyright 2011 by IGI Publishing (an imprint of IGI Global).

Chapter 9
Using Learning Platforms to Support Communication and Effective Learning

Johanna M. Armitage
London Borough of Hounslow, UK

ABSTRACT

This paper describes the development of resources for a unit of work for the English National Diploma in Information Technology. These on-line resources are designed to support a personalised learning environment that maximises opportunities for students to achieve greater control of their own learning and progression. The resources are designed to promote metacognition, with the intention of encouraging students to think about how they learn and how they can progress most effectively. The resources were developed to explore ways forward in developing personalised learning environments and implications for research on wider implementation across all National Diplomas.

INTRODUCTION

Personalised learning is a key national aspiration for secondary education in the UK. The government report, *2020 Vision for Teaching and Learning* DfES (2006, p. 6) describes personalised learning and teaching as "taking a highly structured and responsive approach to each child's and young person's learning, in order that all are able to progress, achieve and participate." Becta (2008, p.

2), as the government agency leading the national drive to ensure the use of effective and innovative use of technology, describes learning platforms as critical to these aspirations, with the ability to integrate learning and school management systems and the potential to provide exciting teaching and learning opportunities. Learning platform is the term used by the UK government in the context of school education and is the term used through out this paper. A learning platform can also be referred

DOI: 10.4018/978-1-4666-2467-2.ch009

to as a virtual learning environment (VLE) or learning management system (LMS). The learning platforms in Hounslow offer integration with the school data management systems, e-portfolio management, communication tools and tools to create and deliver on-line teaching and learning resources. The government wants every school in the UK to make full use of learning platforms by 2010, but learning platforms are in danger of becoming little more than administrative tools. Weller (2009, p. 2) warns that such systems offer acceptance of an e-learning approach and acknowledgement of tools already used by students, but a more decentralised model, that acknowledges the proliferation of free tools and services, will offer greater flexibility, although less control for the education provider. Four Hounslow schools have come together to form a consortium to deliver the Level 2 Higher Diploma in Information Technology. This presents an opportunity to investigate how a learning platform can enhance learning if linked to tools that can provide a powerful personal learning space that encourages collaboration, team work, and effective learning strategies.

Research by Ireson, Hallam and Lewis (2001, p. 213) describes motivation and engagement as dependant on metacognition, self-esteem and self-regulation, this suggests that to develop an inclusive learning environment that supports personalisation, we should consider opportunities to meet diverse needs by developing thinking skills and confident, independent learners with effective learning strategies. The following section considers literature that offers advice on planning for personalised on-line learning and use of digital technologies to promote inclusive practice in education.

Visual tools based on classroom research on teaching problem solving skills (Wallace, Maker, Cave & Chandler, 2004) and visual mapping tools to support metacognition (Cavaglioli & Harris, 2004) are also discussed and inform the lesson plans and development of tools for self-assessment, and for mapping personal learning,

thinking skills and functional skills in order to track progress and skilled thinking. The development of resources for a personalised learning environment is then described, as well as the delivery of lessons designed to help students make use of a personalised learning environment to their greatest advantage. The final section concludes that understanding pedagogical implications for on-line teaching and learning is crucial to success, supported by resources designed to help students to understand and reflect on the learning process. Teachers who used the visual tools when teaching the Diploma in Information Technology, concluded that such tools were valuable, but appropriate pedagogies to support use of personalised on-line learning spaces, within and beyond the classroom, need considering as part of professional development. The functionality of a centralised learning platform was acknowledged as lacking flexibility as implied by Weller (2009). Teachers found the learning platform a useful administrative tool, but restrictive for sharing resources. Students were not as attracted to the tools provided, as they were to those freely available on the Internet.

PLANNING FOR PERSONALISED ON-LINE LEARNING

Many students are not confident learners, particularly those with learning difficulties, which can affect motivation as described by Ireson, Hallam and Lewis (2001, p. 213). This must be addressed, like any other learning difficulty, with appropriate pedagogic practice. Claxton (2002, p. 41) supports this view by suggesting that good learners have the resilience to "lock-on to learning, to pay attention to what is going on around them in a number of ways … (they) use a varied toolkit of learning methods and attitudes to make them resourceful."

Programmes that develop thinking skills can contribute to this intention. The aim is to help students understand and take control of their own learning and attitude to learning, thus improving self-esteem and raising self-worth, which will result in improved motivation, performance, self-regulation and behaviour. Motivation requires learners to take control of their own learning and demands metacognition, self-regulation, and a belief in an ability to succeed. These are important aspects of programmes to develop thinking skills. However, Ireson et al. warn that there is mixed evidence from secondary education to support programmes designed to promote meta-cognition, if metacognitive skills are "added on" and not embedded into the curriculum. If programmes to develop thinking are not embedded, skills will not become transferable habits of good learning. However, Margerison (1996, 179) offers encouragement by suggesting that all students will find self-enhancement activities valuable and beneficial as they will, "enrich the educational experience of all children and the teacher".

Futurelab (2009, p. 13) suggest there is a growing body of evidence that the impact of ICT, "on intermediate learning outcomes – such as motivation, engagement and independence in learning – can be significant."

Technology is perceived as the key to personalised learning to engage learners, foster collaboration, encourage communication and to provide a myriad of digital resources. Futurelab (2009, p. 45) also describe learning platforms as providing all of these aspects, but as part of a wider range of technologies such as wikis, on-line games, blogs, podcasts, mobile technologies and on-line communities.

The move towards personalising learning is described by Becta (2008, p. 2) as creating a means to "understand and support the learning needs of every student, monitoring his or her progress closely. It requires the development of learning paths that best suit particular aptitudes." This includes anytime and anywhere access to learning resources, communication tools to enable dialogue between students and teachers and management tools to monitor progress. In addition, the student

should also be able to work at their own pace. For the IT Diploma, students and teachers from different schools need to be able to share resources and to collaborate and communicate with each other. Teachers also need to be able to moderate and assesses student work across the different schools as well as to manage data.

This review of literature suggests that learning platforms are intended to be part of a system that provides technology-related learner entitlement, whilst encouraging effective learning, summarised by Becta as:

- Giving learners the choice to learn at a pace and time to suit their needs.
- Improving the range of teaching approaches.
- Extending the choices available to learners.
- Offering a wide range of engaging learning experiences.
- Enabling learners to tackle a wider range of subjects, in greater depth.
- Supporting learners to create their own learning pathways (Becta, 2009, p.14).

Visual tools, linked to research on inclusion and motivation, should also be considered. Wallace, Maker, Cave and Chandler (2004, p. 75) describe the use of a graphic representation to depict the problem solving process as raising motivation and achievement across a full range of abilities. The process is represented by the Thinking Actively in a Social Context (TASC) Wheel (Wallace et al., 2004).

The TASC Wheel (see Figure 1) guides pupils through stages of the learning process: gathering and organising information; identifying criteria for success and what further information is required; generating ideas; deciding which are the best ideas to pursue; planning and implementing a task; evaluating against the success criteria; communicating and applying new knowledge; and learning from experience.

Figure 1. Thinking Actively in a Social Context (TASC) Wheel, Wallace, B. (2002) TeachingThinking Skills Across the Middle Years, London, David Fulton Publishers (with permission from author)

Cavaglioli and Harris (2004, p. 13) provide visual mapping tools, which they described as supporting metacognition by enabling the student to notice and monitor what they are thinking and how they are disposed to thinking. By examining these habits the student can learn to regulate their thinking in order to improve it.

A mixed-method doctoral research study Armitage (2003) indicated the importance of helping students to think well and to develop effective learning strategies as a way of supporting an inclusive learning environment. This research has provided a model for good practice, including asynchronous and synchronous learning environments, resource development and work on personalising learning. The research suggested that teaching specific skills for thinking, including monitoring one's own state of knowledge (metacognition), can produce an immediate gain in performance. However, pupils still do not necessarily transfer the cognitive techniques they have been taught to other lessons, or even different situations in the same lesson. This suggests

learning should become an apprenticeship with thinking skills modelled and analysed, mentored and coached, and supported by self-monitoring and evaluation strategies. Teaching that makes the problem-solving process clear, as described by Armitage and Scott-Saunders (2007), suggests that TASC is a valuable tool for making effective learning strategies explicit to students, for guiding lesson planning and as a tool to guide the pupils to think about their own thinking.

Conclusions from two classroom based research projects, Armitage and Scott-Saunders (2007), described the TASC Wheel as a fundamental tool for structuring projects and lesson planning, as well as vital support for developing effective learning strategies. The TASC model also recognises learning as active and social. This model therefore leant itself well to the IT Diplomas with objectives that emphasise team work and personal learning and thinking skills

My development of the Personal Learning and Thinking Skills (PLTS) Wheel, the visual tools for thinking and the self-monitoring guides for the IT Diploma, are based on the TASC Wheel, plus visual organisers influenced by the work of Harris and Caliglioli (2004) and the Personal Learning and Thinking Skills (PLTS) framework QCA (2008).

All diplomas require attention to personal learning and thinking skills (PLTS). These are described by the Qualifications and Curriculum Authority (QCA, 2008) as essential to achieving the aims of any of the Diplomas by "supporting successful learners, confident individuals and responsible citizens." The PLTS framework is comprised of six areas of focus: independent thinkers; creative thinkers; reflective learners; team workers; self-managers and effective participants, which informed the PLTS Wheel developed for this project (see Figure 2).

The common language enables the resources to be used to support effective learning strategies across all diplomas in order to help students to take greater control of their own learning whilst

Figure 2. Personal learning and thinking skills model styled on TASC (Thinking Actively in a Social Context)

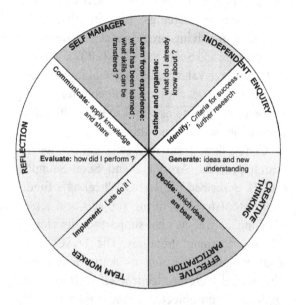

becoming more effective learners. Web 2.0 resources were used to support the development of team skills and co-operative learning as part of the lesson plans for Unit 3: Effective Communication of the Level 2 Higher Diploma in Information Technology, as discussed in the following section.

DEVELOPING A PERSONALISED ON-LINE LEARNING ENVIRONMENT

The Information Technology (IT) Diploma teaches young people about IT in business, they also have to demonstrate functional skills in English, maths and information and communication technology, as well as personal skills such as the ability to communicate and work in teams. Four schools formed a consortium to plan lessons and to develop resources for the seven units of work for access through the learning platform. Twenty seven students took part in the first year of presentation and were located at two different schools. They were

entering Key Stage 4 and were aged between 14 and 15 years old. They were studying the Diploma as an alternative to GCSEs and as a vocational learning pathway. This section is a description of the thinking behind the development of on-line teaching materials to support the personalised learning of the students.

Development of on-line teaching materials for Unit 3: Effective Communication, was an opportunity to investigate how a learning platform might provide a powerful anytime, anywhere personal learning space, if linked to tools that encouraged effective learning strategies and maximised opportunities for students to achieve greater control of their own learning and goal setting. It was also an opportunity to exploit Web 2.0 facilities in order to support on-line collaboration and team work that reflected a business-like working environment. This would provide an on-line exemplar to inform the development of other diploma units. Finally, visual tools for self-assessment and to map thinking skills and functional skills in order to track progress and skilled thinking were essential to support literature that describes motivation and engagement as dependant on metacognition, and ability to think about effective learning strategies.

PLTS became a core element of the course design. The teaching and learning aims were defined as follows:

- To develop on-line learning materials within a fully interactive and media–rich learning platform supporting anytime-anywhere learning.
- To make PLTS explicit throughout the unit and to foster thinking and problem solving in a social context.
- To scaffold the development of Functional Skills, (QCA, 2009) throughout the unit with self- monitoring guides. The QCA describe functional skills as essential for life, learning and work.

- To use mobile learning, Web 2.0 technologies and appropriate pedagogies to extend use of on-line learning within and beyond the classroom.
- To identify barriers to successful outcomes and seek, by appropriate interventions, to remove them and ensure positive outcomes and whole system change.
- To identify strategies and solutions relating to the development of new personalised learning environments and pedagogies.

The opening welcome page has standard links to learning objectives, resources to support the course and on-line guides for using various software, web 2.0 resources and tips for presenting work. From the welcome page, there are links to three episodes: Episode 1: Gathering information on the course and working in a team; team; Episode 2: Communication media and effective teamwork; Episode 3: Individual and group tasks.

The introduction to Episode 1 makes it clear that studying this part of the module will help students to gather and organise information about the course, to understand the learning objectives and assessment methods and how to work effectively in a team. A PLTS icon indicates that the Episode will cover gathering and organising of informa-

tion as part of an exploratory task on effective communication and team work. Each activity is flagged with an icon throughout the course with a description of the stages in the learning process (see Figure 3).

Episode 2 supports independent enquiry through an investigative team task to identify what further information needs to be gathered to succeed, what questions need to be asked and the criteria for success. Identifying criteria for success is important as it will support evaluation at a later stage. Students consider criteria for success for each learning objective, which they will then self-assess at each stage, giving them an opportunity to work towards higher marking bands with explicit direction.

By the end of the first two episodes the students should be aware of all the learning objectives for the course and criteria for success, they will have thought carefully about how to work successfully in a team and will have an understanding of the learning process. They will have gathered evidence to demonstrate research skills and identified targets for progression.

Reflection on the learning process is supported by a graphic organiser depicting the PLTS Wheel with guidelines for each of the sections.

Figure 3. Icons used alongside activities to help student reflect on the learning process

⊕	**Independent Enquiry** Gather and organise information	⊕	**Creative Thinking** Generate ideas
⊕	**Identify** Criteria for success and further research needs		
⊕	**Effective Participation** Decide on the best ideas	⊕	**Team Work** Implement the ideas
⊕	**Reflect** Evaluate against success criteria	⊕	**Communicate** Apply the ideas
⊕	**Self Manage** Learn from experience		

Episode 3 requires preliminary independent research, which leads into team planning for an advertising campaign. A learning diary contributes to evidence that learning objectives have been met and the learning process is tracked using the PLTS Wheel as a reflection tool, enabling the diary to become a metacognitive exercise that informs future and transferable learning experiences.

Evidence of effective team work is secured through on-line work intended to simulate business practice in the real world. The students use functionality within Adobe Connect to work on shared documents and to participate in meetings through web conferences. These are recorded and provide on-line evidence of team work and course work. Students take turns to minute and type up the content of each team meeting, accurately and concisely, and circulate these minutes through email or Adobe Buzzword. Students can only gain marks based on their own contributions to the team work during a specific window of time, this communication method provides clear evidence of contributions from each student even if working from outside school. On-line guidance for using Web 2.0 tools is available through links from Unit Three.

Students were offered three different scenarios based on the food industry, sports industry and retail industry. For example, for the food industry the students are asked to produce an advertising campaign based on Jamie Oliver's "Ministry of Food" television programme to promote good eating.

Research was required on the different types of communication media that could be used. Examples were given of how these were already being used by Jamie Oliver and other celebrity cooks in the form of printed media, audio facilities such as podcasts and radio, and digital media such as films and photo stories. See Figure 4 for an outline of the lesson plan.

The team work builds on the skills the students have already developed during the previous two episodes and the team task introduces Web 2.0 tools in a business scenario (see Figure 5)

As can be seen from the lesson plans, there are embedded links to graphic organisers for scaffolding the thinking process, for example, effective decision making or making comparisons. Functional skills relevant to each learning objective are also highlighted and supported at the beginning of each episode.

Figure 4. Individual task with explicit reference to PLTS and the learning process

Independent Enquiry	**Gather information** on the ways the food industry uses three different types of media to promote products and brand names, e.g. promotions, fliers, billboards, web pages etc. Use the Discoveries and Observations sheet to record and **organise** your observations
Independent Enquiry	**Identify** examples of three types of media. Identify their purpose for the business/ product they are promoting, e.g., appeal to wide audience, promote an image, value for money etc. Consider the benefits and limitations for each example. Use the Communication Media to Promote sheet and Communication Media Analysis sheet
Creative Thinking	**Generate** ideas for the group task. **Plan and create** a presentation to your team on three types of communication media, describing how they have been used in a business context and pointing out the benefits and limitations. You could present a Powerpoint with links to web sites and with embed photos and examples of adverts. Persuade your fellow team members that yours are good ideas. The Persuasion sheet may help. *Software Links*: Photoshop.com; Open Office; Prezentit *Video Links*: Tips for Public Speaking; What you need for good team work

Figure 5. Team task with explicit reference to PLTS and the learning process

 **Effective Participation**	**Decide** the best type of media to use to promote your product. Use a Fishbone Diagram to show the benefits and limitations. Use the Compare and Contrast sheet to compare the different media. **Justify** your choice and **organise** your ideas as a Bubble Diagram then present your reasons as a written report and upload it to your e-portfolio. **Decide** which team members will work on the different media you have chosen for your campaign **Plan** your campaign using the PLTS Wheel and PLTS Planning Grid, which can be part of your learning diary **Plan** a work schedule using a Flow Diagram. Put meeting dates and deadlines into your electronic diary.
 **Team Work**	**Implement** Follow your plan and implement your ideas Read each other's reports and comment on-line *Software Links:* Adobeconnect; Mindomo; OpenOffice; Buzzword Liaise with your team and organize meetings *Software Links:* Google calendar
 **Reflection**	**Evaluate** Evaluate how well your campaign met the criteria you identified for a successful campaign. Record this in your diary.
 **Communicate**	**Communicate** Publish your campaign Present to the other teams *Software Links:* Prezentit
 **Self Manage**	**Learn from Experience** Fill in your own PLTS Wheel and comment on how well you completed each section as an individual and as a team member

DELIVERY OF A PERSONAISED LEARNING ENVIRONMENT

Delivery of the diploma unit highlighted difficulties linking pupils working across different locations and learning platforms. We established Campus Hounslow on the main learning platform, to act as a portal for participating teachers and students. The virtual campus gives access to resources for each of the seventeen diplomas as well as access to virtual "rooms" for functional skills, PLTS and the visual mapping tools for thinking. Campus Hounslow, ideally, should offer seamless access wherever a student is located, or whatever their school's designated learning platform, but communication across different learning platforms

has proved difficult with administration and access rights inhibiting flexible use. One solution might be to place the virtual resources in a different location to the learning platform, such as a separate web-based solution or elearning cloud as described by Sclater (2010, p. 10) from which all resources and many tools could be accessed. Sclater suggests learning platforms can be restrictive and users often prefer tools freely available on the Internet. The teachers preferred the free web-based tools for creating the lessons and students preferred Web 2.0 tools for collaboration.

The unit design helped teachers to become aware of the liberating opportunities presented by new technologies to extend thinking and learning. The detail of the unit and links to visual tools in order to scaffold thinking has been perceived as impressive. However, concern has been expressed about how much time a classroom teacher has to develop other units along the same lines. The PLTS resource area within Campus Hounslow is now used by teachers to link to visual mapping tools from units they are developing themselves, thus saving time. The PLTS virtual room on the learning platform, provides the visual thinking tools to support self-direction and independent thinking and an opportunity for consistency of approach across all units and diplomas. The PLTS resources are also being used with younger students as part of learning to learn programmes and cross curricula project work.

Teachers working on a range of diplomas across the fourteen secondary schools in Hounslow studied the unit to establish guidelines for developing personalised, on-line learning environments. These included:

- To provide clear learning objectives.
- To provide a clear breakdown of criteria for success for the marking bands of each learning objective and grids for self assessment.
- To ensure that tasks provide evidence and meet criteria for all marking band levels.
- To ensure that tasks are not gender or culturally biased.
- To make the learning process explicit and build in review opportunities that enable students to understand their own thinking processes through mapping PLTS and functional skills.
- To provide each unit and learning objective with an introduction and lead in activity to establish base line knowledge, followed by a main and review activity.
- To use the PLTS framework as a guide for lesson planning and to support metacognition.

The first cohort of students has now completed Unit 3. They were of mixed ability and concerns were raised that some of the students would find elements of the course challenging. They were taught by teachers from the two schools. The lead teacher for Unit 3 was new to teaching and had limited experience of developing thinking skills, but fully appreciated the need to develop functional skills and was experienced in this area. She did this extremely well by integrating functional skills into the lessons and guiding her students on team work and presentation techniques based on the resources. The students used the visual mapping tools based on the PLTS wheel and this helped to make the thinking process explicit. However, at the start of the course, the teacher was concerned that the students did not fully appreciate the PLTS aspect of the course and that it would distract the more challenged and less motivated students. Motivation, as described by Ireson et al. (2001), is dependant on metacognition, self-esteem and self-regulation and evidence from my previous research demonstrated that such students need to feel in control of the learning process in order to engage and succeed. More experienced colleagues recognised the value of making the learning process explicit and building in opportunities for metacognition throughout the course. They advised the teacher to continue using the visual tools. The teacher persisted with the visual maps and the students did become more motivated. This highlights the importance of taking account of the pedagogical aspects of teaching and learning attached to learning platforms and the importance of training opportunities for teachers.

CONCLUSION

The exemplar on-line unit is now in place, designed to foster collaboration, team work and effective learning strategies within a personalised learning environment that supports anytime, anywhere learning. Visual mapping for a metacognitive approach to PLTS, functional skills and effective learning strategies, throughout the unit, are perceived by teachers as valuable, as are the tools for self-monitoring and assessment. On-line support for the use of Web.2.0 Tools is in place, but appropriate pedagogies to extend use of on-line learning within and beyond the classroom need developing. This will maximise opportunities for motivating and raising self-esteem by enabling students to achieve greater control of their own learning and goal setting. Strategies and solutions relating to the development of personalised learning environments and pedagogies, as well as a more flexible curriculum, are being developed by teachers, giving ownership to the continuing evolvement of Campus Hounslow, whether it remains within the learning platform or is located elsewhere.

Future implications include the development of a resource bank of visual tools to support thinking and learning, PLTS and Functional Skills within Levels 1, 2 and 3 of all the National Diplomas and continuing professional development for teachers on pedagogy and learning within virtual learning environments, leading to a research project with a larger number of students and wider range of diplomas. Teaching specific skills for thinking and monitoring one's own state of knowledge and progress was found to be beneficial, particularly for the students who were not confident learners and the visual maps provided substantial evidence that learning objectives had been met, thus ensuring a pass for all students. This suggests that developing specific skills for thinking and metacognition are important aspects to consider when providing for personalised, on-line learning environments. If students are to benefit from taking greater control of their own learning, anytime and anywhere, and are to use tools and information freely available on the Internet, they need to manage the information well and need to utilise the skills taught through the PLTS Wheel. In order for these skills to become embedded and transferable, teachers also need to understand and make these skills explicit through their teaching.

REFERENCES

Armitage, J. (2003). *An exploratory study on the benefits of a thinking skills programme, cognitive enrichment advantage, informed by the needs of pupils identified with special educational needs.* London: Institute of Education University of London.

Armitage, J., & Scott-Saunders, R. (2007). The primary mystery challenge. *Teaching Thinking and Creativity, 8*(24), 48–53.

Armitage, J., & Scott-Saunders, R. (2007). From questions to cartoons. *Teaching Thinking and Creativity, 8*(24), 54–57.

Becta. (2008). *Personalising learning in a connected world: A guide for school leaders.* Coventry, UK: Becta

Becta. (2009). *Enabling next generation learning: Enhancing learning through technology A guide for those who work with schools.* Coventry, UK: Becta

Cavaglioli, O., & Harris, I. (2004). *Reaching out to all thinkers.* Stafford: Network Educational Press Ltd.

Claxton, G. (2002). *Building learning power.* Bristol, UK: TLO Ltd.

Department for Education and Skills. (2006). 2020 *vision report of the teaching and learning in 2020 review Group.* Nottingham, UK: DfES Publications.

Futurelab. (2009). *Using digital technologies to promote Inclusive Practice in Education.* Bristol, UK: Futurelab.

Harris, I., & Caliglioli, O. (2004). *Reaching out to all thinkers*. Stafford: Network Educational Press Ltd.

Ireson, J., Hallam, S., & Plewis, I. (2001). Ability grouping in secondary schools: Effects on pupils' self-concepts. *The British Journal of Educational Psychology*, *71*(2), 315–326. doi:10.1348/000709901158541

Margerison, A. (1996). Self-esteem: Its effect on the development and learning of children with EBD. *Support for Learning*, *11*(4), 176–180. doi:10.1111/j.1467-9604.1996.tb00256.x

QCA. (2008). *Personal learning and thinking skills: Supporting successful learners, confident individuals and responsible citizens*. London: Qualifications and Curriculum Authority.

QCA. (2009). *Functional skills: Essential for life, learning and work*. London: Qualifications and Curriculum Authority.

Sclater, N. (2010). eLearning in the cloud. *International Journal of Virtual and Personal Learning Environments*, *1*(1), 10–19.

Wallace, B. (2002). *Teaching thinking skills across the middle years*. London: David Fulton.

Wallace, B., Maker, J., Cave, D., & Chandler, S. (2004). *Thinking skills and problem solving an inclusive approach*. London: David Fulton.

Weller, M. (2010). The centralisation dilemma in educational IT. *International Journal of Virtual and Personal Learning Environments*, *1*(1), 1–9.

This work was previously published in the International Journal of Virtual and Personal Learning Environments, Volume 2, Issue 1, edited by Michael Thomas, pp. 54-64, copyright 2011 by IGI Publishing (an imprint of IGI Global).

Chapter 10
Connected Learning in an Australian Technology Program:
A Case Study

Jane Louise Hunter
University of Western Sydney, Australia

ABSTRACT

Connected learning using video conferencing, the interactive whiteboard and Web 2.0 tools is possible in the new "interactive classroom" more than 2,240 New South Wales public schools will receive over the next four years. In Australia the New South Wales Department of Education and Training (NSWDET) is delivering $AUS 158 million of infrastructure and services to schools and technical and further education campuses for new technologies and applications to support teaching in the 21ˢᵗ century. The intention of the Connected Classrooms Program is to create a "large connected and collaborative learning community" of teachers, students and parents that can go online for information, resources and communication "anywhere, anytime" across a state that covers over 800,000 square kilometres. This paper describes the three projects in the program, the underpinning prior work and seven teacher professional learning platforms that reference anticipated learning outcomes and future directions. In its third year, this case study is a descriptive insiders snapshot. It provides an overview for project administrators and participants in other national and international education milieu who may be responsible for planning and implementing enhanced technology environments.

DOI: 10.4018/978-1-4666-2467-2.ch010

INTRODUCTION

The *Connected Classrooms Program* has a four-year timeframe (2007-11) to provide education sites with enhanced technologies and applications for teaching and learning. This approach sits in a broader Australian education policy context that seeks to improve infrastructure for information and communication technologies (ICT) in schools, as well as recognise that today's students like to learn digitally. Led by NSWDET this initiative is built on prior evidence from education research in schools, regional ICT strategies and local trials in technology (Schuck & Kearney, 2006; DET-Engaging Pedagogy, 2007; Groundwater-Smith, 2007).

THE AUSTRALIAN CONTEXT

In Australia significant reports published by the Ministerial Council on Employment, Education, Training and Youth Affairs Information and Communication Technologies in Schools Taskforce (2005, 2006, 2008) document technology integration in teaching and learning. Other key education guidelines (Kearns, 2002), in particular the *Education Goals for Young Australians,* cite reasons for schools to give priority to student learning with technology:

Successful learners have the essential skills in literacy and numeracy and are creative and productive users of technology, especially ICT, as a foundation of success in all leaning areas when students leave school they should be confident, creative and productive users of new technologies, particularly information and communication technologies, and understand the impact of those technologies on society (p.4).

Initiatives of the *Schools Taskforce* and the *National Goals* seek Australian or bi-lateral collaboration on digital content, systems and services, policy, standards and operational agreements. This action supports the development of a framework by which jurisdictions can evaluate and report their progress on the implementation of ICT priorities detailed in *Learning in an Online World* (2005).

Prior to the election of Prime Minister Kevin Rudd in 2007, the promise of a "digital education revolution" further positioned technology as a key political platform for effective learning for students in Australian schools. Commitment by the Federal government involves $AUS 1.2 billion over five years (2008-12) to "turn every secondary school in Australia into a digital school" (Ministerial Council on Employment, Education, Training and Youth Affairs, 2008, p. 5).

In July 2008, the Federal Minister for Education, Training and Industrial Relations, Julia Gillard, wrote to all teacher employers in Australia indicating that funds of up to $AUS 11.25 million will be directed to ICT- related school based professional development for teachers under the Australian Government Quality Teacher Program (AGQTP). Further funds for such programs are not available beyond 2009, and are being replaced by new funding arrangements for teacher professional learning using ICT.

NSW initially withdrew from the Council of Australian Governments (2008) agreement in September 2008 arguing that the initial $AUS 1.2 billion was insufficient to cover the delivery, installation and ongoing maintenance of wireless learning devices for each student. By December, the Commonwealth had agreed to provide an additional 807 million to meet further costs incurred by the States in implementing the *National Secondary School Computer Fund*:

Each State will report on their progress toward reaching 1:1 student to computer ratio for Year 9 to 12; and to pass on the non-government sector their share of these funds (Council of Australian Governments, 2008).

In 2010 the Ministerial Council on Employment, Education, Training and Youth Affairs and the Australian ICT in Education Committee are developing a *Digital Education Revolution Road Map* that includes a *Teaching in the Digital Age Work Plan*. It focuses on the teacher professional development required to integrate ICT into pedagogical practice to connect learning, to meet students' needs and therefore harness the resources of the "digital education revolution."

NSWDET CONTEXT

Historically public schools and technical and further education (TAFE) colleges have implemented various strategic plans for ICT integration. Such plans have included large and small-scale technology reforms; technology oriented professional learning and training for teachers, as well as technical hardware and services for classrooms. This public education system has 2,243 schools and 10 TAFE institutes with 100 campuses taught by over 90,000 full-time teachers with more than 1.5 million enrolled students.

In the early 1980s computers were provided to all public schools. Hardware resources were accompanied by technology professional learning programs for teachers, for example *Technology Integration into Teaching and Learning*. Alongside developing the technology skills of teachers NSWDET sought to assess whether this was being translated into improved computing skills for students.

In 2006 the NSW Board of Studies trialled and implemented various computer skills assessment regimes, eventually authorizing a computer skills test for all Year 10 School Certificate students. This test assesses five computer skills in operations, word-processing, spreadsheet and database, graphics and multimedia, internet and email skills.

In March 2007, a State election commitment of $AUS 158 million was announced for NSWDET with *Connected Classrooms*, the largest State Treasury enhancement for an education technology program in Australian education history. This four year program seeks to increase bandwidth to education sites, provide an "connected classroom" for every school, and enable access to a range of new learning tools and Web 2.0 applications for teachers and students.

For reader ease the *Connected Classrooms Program* will be referred to as the "Program" for the remainder of the case study.

UNDERPINNING RATIONALE FOR THE PROGRAM

Alongside NSWDET technology reforms and various national initiatives (affecting the education landscape across Australia, are local projects, research and trials that have increased understanding of how, when and why teachers integrate technology into teaching and learning.

Key evidence for the development of the Program arose from five substantial reports containing:

- Research conducted by NSWDET in partnership with the University of Technology, Sydney which explored pedagogy using interactive whiteboards (Schuck & Kearney, 2006).
- Results of a micro trial in February 2007 in six schools of a learning management system tool to support teachers' meta-cognitive planning for learning.
- Outcomes from a quantitative study in May 2007 which examined how 300 teachers used online resources in student learning.
- Findings from another technology teacher professional learning project titled *Engaging Pedagogy*.
- Further research in a study (Groundwater-Smith, 2007) undertaken with 200 students to understand how they learn with digital technologies at home and at school.

Findings from these five data sets, including a year-long interactive whiteboard strategy in Western NSW Region, and a small-scale trial of 'connected classrooms' in Western Sydney Region informed direction of the Program.

TEACHING AND LEARNING AIMS AND OBJECTIVES OF THE PROGRAM

The vision of the Program is to create a "large connected and collaborative learning community," it also stems from the demands of teaching and learning in a digital age. As an initiative of the NSW state government its objective is:

to provide staff and students with new opportunities to connect with each other across enhanced facilities for sharing resources and data collaboration. (Program Flyer, 2008, p. 1)

The Program is governed by a Business Executive, a Program Control Group and a Business Executive for each project; there are three projects in the Program:

1. **Interactive Classrooms:** This project commands the largest capital input with over $AUS 66 million, it will equip every school with an 'interactive or connected classroom' and provides the necessary infrastructure to facilitate collegial support networks for teachers across the state. It consists of an interactive whiteboard, video conference facility and desktop sharing software.
2. **Network Enhancement:** The project will increase bandwidth capacity to 10Mbps to enhance interactive environments and the delivery of learning tools to all sites by providing greater bandwidth and speed. Valued at $AUS63 million, it will also enhance authenticated and filtered internet browsing services.

3. **Learning Tools:** The third component will deliver the latest Web 2.0 technologies (e.g. blogs and wikis) and provide a secure online workspace for staff and students to support the creation, storage, editing and delivery of digital content from collections and repositories across the NSWDET. Valued at $AUS29 million, the project includes upgraded email, access to student reports for parents and collaborative environments for the discovery and sharing of digital content.

Teacher professional learning to support the changing ICT context and deliver the 'connected' environment required by the Program is built upon seven significant platforms:

*   Program office support structure and the appointment of specialist education outcomes business change managers at a senior Program level.
*   Master training in the hardware and software applications at the system level.
*   Program bulletin, website and specialist learning activities.
*   NSWDET professional learning initiatives and models of practice.
*   Regional models, including accreditation, technology innovation centres and school based projects.
*   Teaching standards in ICT from the Professional Teaching Standards Framework developed by the NSW Institute of Teachers.
*   Technology user groups managed by vendors.

Each platform is described in the following sections.

1. Program office support structure and the appointment of specialist education outcomes business change managers at a senior Program level.

The Program has an office structure supported by a director, program co-ordinator, finance specialist, communications senior project officer and two education outcomes business change managers. There is often criticism that the world of technology does not respect the educational knowledge of teachers (Zhao, 2003). In the school context the issue of technology integration is often "somebody else's problem." The two domains of technology and pedagogy are ruled by different people; teachers are in charge of pedagogy and technicians are in charge of technology. One group views the other as 'luddites' and the other sees an ignorance of learning, education theory and the reality of schools and classrooms.

The governance structure of the Program recognized this divide and has sought to bring these "two worlds" together, the office structure is also a departure from previous public school reform models:

The organization (NSWDET) has finally recognized that in order to implement successful whole of system technology change to teachers' work requires the adoption of a business model of change (Comment from a senior officer, 2008).[1]

2. Master training at the system level in lesson creation software.

Enterprise lesson creation software for the 'interactive classroom' was purchased after a tender and procurement process. Such large-scale procurement of software necessitates teachers to be skilled in how to use the software application in an effective and time efficient manner.

The successful vendor provided two 'master trainers' from the United Kingdom to train 62 senior officers who would act as "master trainers" in the ten regions. This "train the trainer" model of teacher professional development in software use meant 'expert users' worked with teachers in schools as each "interactive classroom" was installed. Regions also provided additional training which is supported by teams from the Information Technology Directorate.

In March 2009 the "procured software" was expanded to include two applications. Teachers had demanded greater choice of software; this decision recognised that many were already highly experienced and adept in using a range of interactive whiteboard software. The second application is supported by a similar training and skills regime.

3. Program bulletin, website and specialist learning activities.

Communication to all stakeholders is a key activity of the Program. Each fortnight the *CCP Bulletin* is published and distributed across the intranet. At its core, this publication has a professional learning focus as providing updates to schools and TAFE about new developments including *Stories from the Field* (i.e., short case studies or examples of practice of teachers and students using the new connected technologies in the local context).

A virtual 3D model of a 21st century learning environment' is a feature of the Program website and is available at https://www.det.nsw.edu.au/strat_direction/schools/ccp/index.htm.

Principals use the model to support planning a suitable site for the new "interactive classroom" in their own context, the model is iterative and is added to as new components commence.

Various specialist learning activities have been supported by the Program to enhance teacher professional learning using digital technologies including conferences and workshops. For example, the Program held a *Dig for a Dinosaur* video conference to "model practice" for teachers in schools. Two palaeontologists from the Australian Museum spoke to 300 Stage 3 primary students in 10 schools. This simple concept reinforced to schools the notion of good planning, compelling content and engaging presenters, which, according to Martin *"needs creative and imaginative teachers to unlock the potential of video conference"* (2005, p. 404). The activity arose out of work with students when they were asked *"who they would like to talk to using video conference"* (Hunter, 2008, p. 3).

4. NSWDET professional learning initiatives and "models of practice."

Every public school has a budget for teacher professional learning. The funds enable teachers in each region to engage in professional initiatives on a regular basis. This learning might involve Curriculum K-12 Directorate consultants, Commonwealth education colleagues or academics in universities. For example, Curriculum K-12 Directorate has specialist curriculum consultants who develop units of work with teachers according to NSW Board of Studies (BoS) syllabus documents. These subject matter experts produce high quality resources, provide advice, host workshops and courses, and plan syllabus implementation in collaboration with teachers, professional associations and officers from the BoS:

Professional learning contributes to the professional growth of staff and improves learning in NSW public schools. The individual, the school, the state office and regions share responsibility for promoting, planning, implementing and evaluating professional learning in schools (NSW Public Schools, 2009, p. 3).

Teacher professional learning "models of practice" that embed digital technologies include:

*   Small and large–scale action learning projects.
*   Specialist education research on particular education issues, including practitioner research.
*   Evaluation studies.

*   Mentoring programs in the school context with beginning teachers based on the ICT components in the Professional Teaching Standards Framework.
*   The establishment of professional learning communities in the regional or school context. including side by side professional learning in the classroom.
*   Whole school change plans.

Martha School is an example of whole school change planning in ICT using "connected learning." This school for specific purposes (SSP) in Sydney Region has 70 students ranging in age from 4 to 18.[2] The principal described how the school embraced its move into an ICT enhanced context:

I wanted to find out how cabling and installation of IWBs and other new connected technologies in a school without any such resources might be prepared (Dina, 2009)

Central to its foray into "ICT readiness" were targeted classes who participated in an "ICT for the 21st Century" action research curriculum project support by their regional office. The project tracked the introduction of ICT over two terms in an "adopting school"| context and eventually mapped a three year plan for technology development.

5. Regional support models, including accreditation, technology innovation centres and school based projects.

The ten regions that manage 2,243 schools cover a geographical area of over 800,000 square kilometres. In physical geography terms, NSW is a large area where one region, Western NSW, crosses two time zones and is greater than the size of Germany. The sheer size of NSW and the nature of the Program implementation mean ICT consultants in each region have significant responsibility for supporting teacher professional learning using the new technologies in the local context.

One regional support model involves teams from the Information Technology Directorate certifying groups of teachers to be proficient in:

- The use the interactive whiteboard.
- The construction of learning sequences in the lesson creation software.
- The provision of "hands on" tuition in the use of video conference to single and multiple school sites.
- The use of an online booking system for schools for "virtual excursions" both in and beyond NSW.[3]

Certification gained from this two-day course is approved by the NSW Institute of Teachers and acts as 16 hours of professional accreditation for teachers at the level of Professional Accomplishment. In 2009-10 an ongoing regional support model for video conferencing was provisioned. This means technical support to schools from a regional office, as well as access to a centralised Helpdesk service.

Technology innovation centres like the Centre for Learning Innovation in NSWDET have a mandate to "the produce quality learning resources and provide leadership to staff in the use of technology in education and training." www.tale.edu.au is one example of the type of service this centre provides to teachers, parents and students in ICT.

Technology learning using school based project approaches led by specialist innovation centres affiliated with NSWDET. The Macquarie ICT Innovations Centre at Macquarie University is one such instance. At this centre, groups of teachers from schools attend workshops, conferences and presentations on a range of technology applications. To illustrate this point, the centre engages teachers in projects that involve animation software like *Marvin*, other have experimented with learning activity management systems like *LAMS* and *Moodle*.

In addition to projects led by technology innovation centres, more than 750 schools participate annually in large Commonwealth funded teacher professional development opportunities like the Australian Government Quality Teaching Programme. This activity uses an action learning framework, lesson study in the school context and in recent years, has required teachers to embed ICT into teaching and learning across all curriculum areas.[4]

6. Teaching standards that refer to ICT in the Professional Teaching Standards Framework from the NSW Institute of Teachers.

All graduate teachers are required to be registered with the NSW Institute of Teachers in order to teach in a public school. For early career teachers part of their undergraduate or postgraduate study at university has mandated components of technology learning. At the Graduate Teacher level in Element 1 for example, *Teachers Know their Subject and How to Teach that Content to their Students,* the aspect of "Knowledge of Information and Communication Technology" states teachers must demonstrate:

Current knowledge and proficiency in the use of the following: basic operational skills, information technology skills, software evaluation skills, effective use of the internet, pedagogical skills for classroom management (NSWIT Handbook, 2006, p. 4)

Element 4 is another ICT standard, *Teachers communicate effectively with their students,* the aspect of "Teaching Strategies" states teachers must:

Use a range of teaching and learning strategies and resources including ICT and other technologies to foster interest and support learning (NSWIT Handbook, 2006, p. 9)

In order to be deemed professionally competent and pass their probationary year, early career teachers need to move from Graduate Teacher level to that of Professional Competence where they are required to demonstrate application, creation, selection and use of ICT in teaching and learning.

7.   Technology user groups.

Vendor driven technology user groups have arisen from the needs of teachers in the school context. Recognition of this need by business has enabled another source of teacher technology learning to flourish. When bureaucracies procure technical resources centrally one of the criteria considered is the vendor's ability to also provide technical skills based education and after sales service. For example, SMART Technologies have established user groups in most regions. Teachers in these groups meet regularly in their own time to build technology skills and share resources.

All seven teacher professional learning platforms form a tapestry of available ICT support designed to weave the "large connected and collaborative learning community."[5]

TECHNOLOGY INFRASTRUCTURE

Technology infrastructure for the Program targets greater bandwidth capacity and reliability, authenticated and filtered internet browsing services and faster internet speed:

The vast majority of our schools today are on two megabits [bandwidth speed] and we would hope that we would be able to increase their speed to 10 megabits or more [by 2011]. Instead of storing files on either the school's local area network or on thumb drives ... teachers will be able to store files in a secure environment and access it where they want and when they want (Wilson, 2008, pp. 13-14)

In 2009 the major procurement activity allowed for the expansion of the core network. This development enabled blogED to be released in March 2010. The new blogging tool allows teachers who want to use it to create "private" and "public" blogs for teaching and learning. The current priority in the Learning Tools Project is the creation of an *e-backpack* for staff and students to access online storage and wikis.

LEARNING OUTCOMES AND FUTURE IMPLICATIONS OF THE PROGRAM

The Business Benefits Realisation Framework has been developed in consultation with various external bodies to examine the educational outcomes agreed to by NSW Treasury for the original *Connected Classrooms* business case. Following a model that uses the language of business, the key performance indicators (KPIs) for the Program sit within the State Plan. KPIs target being able to measure increased student learning, student retention and expanded curriculum offerings as a result of the $AUS158 million investment. The evaluation framework includes metrics of usage and case studies of practice using the "connected technologies" in the Program. Planned research on the Program as it was being implemented did not occur. Future implications from the Program for technology focussed professional learning for teaching may well be considerable. There is intense interest in the Program's experience to date, and keen consideration of the final report on how *Connected Classrooms* were implemented is awaited.

Early evaluation of the experience of 200 school principals in the "first phase of the Program" in 2008 resulted in changes to initial installation processes, software procurement and policy direction. The Program was flexible enough to respond to the changing demands of the deployed technologies, or any global pricing fluctuations, as well as respond to the needs of principals, teachers and students in public schools and TAFE colleges. Almost at the end of its third year, it is timely to describe what has occurred in this government commitment, and try to predict what observers might see when the Program is completed in 2011 when it's 'business as usual' in the NSWDET.

ACKNOWLEDGMENT

The author wishes to acknowledge Claire Hunter who read and edited various drafts of the case study.

REFERENCES

Council of Australian Governments. (2008). *Council of Australian Governments' Meeting.* Retrieved March 10, 2009, from http://www.coag.gov.au/coag_meeting_outcomes/2008-11-29/attachments.cfm

DEST. (2009). *National Goals of Schooling in the 21st Century.* Retrieved March 25, 2009, from http://www.dest.gov.au/sectors/school_education/policy_initiatives_reviews/national_goals_for_schooling_in_the_twenty_first_century.htm#Goals

Groundwater-Smith, S. (2007). *Supporting Student Learning in a Digital Age.* Sydney, Australia: NSWDET.

Hunter, J. (2007). Fresh equation: quality digital resources + interactive whiteboards + collaborative tools = engaging pedagogy for the classroom. *Learning, Media and Technology, 32*(3), 245–260.

Hunter, J. (2008). *Video conferencing and students: Listening to State Student Representative Council voices in NSW.* Sydney, Australia: NSWDET.

Kearns, P. (2002). *Towards a connected learning society.* Canberra, Australia: Global Services.

Martin, M. (2005). Seeing is believing: the role of video conferencing in distance learning. *British Journal of Educational Technology, 36*(3), 397–405. doi:10.1111/j.1467-8535.2005.00471.x

Ministerial Council on Education and Employment Training and Youth Affairs. (2005). *Learning in an online world.* Canberra, Australia: DEST.

Ministerial Council on Education and Employment Training and Youth Affairs. (2006). *Report of the ICT in schools taskforce.* Canberra, Australia: DEST.

Ministerial Council on Education and Employment Training and Youth Affairs. (2008). *Digital Education: Making Change Happen.* Canberra, Australia: DEWAR.

New South Wales Government. (2009). Connected Classrooms Program. Retrieved March 25, 2009 from https://www.det.nsw.edu.au/strat_direction/schools/ccp/index.htm

New South Wales Institute of Teachers. (2006). *Handbook of professional teaching standards.* Sydney, Australia: NSWDET.

NSW Department of Education and Training. (2005). *Micro trial of LAMS report.* Sydney: Centre for Learning Innovation.

NSW Department of Education and Training. (2007). *Report on how DET teachers discover, access and use online learning resources in their practice.* Sydney, Australia: Centre for Learning Innovation.

NSW Department of Education and Training. (2007). *Engaging pedagogy: Teachers in the field.* Sydney, Australia: Centre for Learning Innovation.

NSW Public Schools. (2009). *Home.* Retrieved March 24, 2009, from http://www.schools.nsw.edu.au/

Schuck, S., & Kearney, M. (2006). *Exploring pedagogy with interactive whiteboards: A case study of six schools*. Sydney, Australia: UTS Press.

Wilson, S. (2008). Address to the Connected Learning Conference. In *Side by Side*. Sydney, Australia: DET School Newspaper Pty Ltd.

Zhao, Y. (2003). *What teachers should know about technology: Perspectives and practices*. Greenwich, CT: Information Age Publishing.

ENDNOTES

1. The Program uses Prince2, a process-driven project management methodology.
2. Martha School and the principal's names are pseudonyms. The students needs reflect challenging levels of behaviour, difficulties with engagement due to autism, obsessive compulsive disorders and cognitive impairments that impact on their academic capabilities.
3. For example, schools use video conference for debates, master classes, specialist assessments, learning tournaments, teacher professional learning and trips to NASA and the Great Barrier Reef.
4. In 2009, the government mandated that 25% of all school professional learning projects need an ICT component.
5. The Program engages in regular consultation with the teachers union in NSW, parent associations and school principals to ensure any potential concerns regarding the amount and timing of teacher professional learning in technology are addressed.

This work was previously published in the International Journal of Virtual and Personal Learning Environments, Volume 2, Issue 1, edited by Michael Thomas, pp. 65-73, copyright 2011 by IGI Publishing (an imprint of IGI Global).

Chapter 11
Motivation, Engagement and Learning through Digital Games

Ioanna Iacovides
The Open University, UK

Eileen Scanlon
The Open University, UK

James Aczel
The Open University, UK

Josie Taylor
The Open University, UK

Will Woods
The Open University, UK

ABSTRACT

Digital games can be powerful learning environments because they encourage active learning and participation within "affinity groups" (Gee, 2004). However, the use of games in formal educational environments is not always successful (O'Neil et al., 2005). There is a need to update existing theories of motivation and engagement in order to take recent game-related developments into account. Understanding the links between why people play games, what keeps them engaged in this process, and what they learn as a result could have a significant impact on how people value and use games for learning. This paper examines key research that relates to motivation, engagement, and informal learning through digital games, in order to highlight the need for empirical studies which examine the activities that occur in and around everyday gaming practice.

INTRODUCTION

"Press Start," the familiar command appearing to players before they can begin to play almost any game. If faced with this screen, the choice to play has already been made, so can this really be the start of the game-play experience? Why this game? Why now? Why keep playing and what does all this have to do with learning? This paper raises the concern that there is much about the player experience yet to be understood and seeks to further explore the questions just raised by discussing motivation and engagement in relation to the informal learning that occurs through playing digital games.

The paper begins by considering research relating to games and learning, and argues for an empirical examination of the context and socio-

DOI: 10.4018/978-1-4666-2467-2.ch011

cultural factors around every-day game-playing, in order to provide greater insight into the effectiveness of learning through games. The concepts of gaming capital and paratexts (Consalvo, 2007) are highlighted as being of potential use in such analysis. The paper goes on to look at traditional conceptualisations of motivation and engagement in the research literature, in the light of new kinds of games, interfaces, online interactions and new audiences of players. It is suggested that work by Calleja (2007a, 2007b) on involvement offers the potential for a fuller account of how contextual aspects relate to the gaming experience. Consideration is also given to the suggestion of Boyle and Connolly (2008) that reversal theory can be helpful in understanding certain emotional flips that people can experience whilst playing games.

A number of methodological challenges are raised, and it is suggested that a multi-method case study research approach—including interviews, surveys, game-play recordings and physiological measures—could help address some methodological limitations of previous research. The paper concludes with an illustration of the kind of research that could be useful.

GAMES: FORMAL AND INFORMAL LEARNING

Academic interest in gaming and learning seems to stem from the fact that digital games are considered to be effective motivational tools and learning environments (Kirriemuir & McFarlane, 2004; Mitchell & Savill-Smith, 2004; de Freitas, 2006). Games can promote "active" and "critical learning" both within the game and the "affinity groups" of players that surround specific titles and genres (Gee, 2004). However, the literature often fails to explore the potential links between what motivates players to play a game (motivation), what keeps them engaged in the game (engagement) and the learning that occurs as a result of game-play and participation in gaming practices

(informal learning). This is important because when games are used within formal educational environments, the links can break down. For instance, de Castell and Jenson (2003) argue that educational games have "not been hugely successful at taking up and exploiting the resources digital technologies make available for learning" (p. 656) since there is often only a tenuous connection between the game-play and the learning tasks within the game. Furthermore, learners do not all agree that they find games intrinsically motivating within an educational context (Whitton, 2007) and it has also been found that when commercial games are used to support learning in educational environments, the games used do not always appeal to all students (Squire, 2005).

In the area of games and learning, a distinction is often made between formal and informal learning. This distinction usually refers to the context in which the learning takes place, as opposed to whether the game in question has been explicitly designed for educational purposes. There are several different ways to classify informal learning but Vavoula (2005) presents a typology which focuses on defining formal and informal learning in terms of control over the processes and goals of learning, and also with respect to the intentionality of the learner. For instance, when using a commercial game in the classroom, the teacher would have explicitly prescribed both the process and goals, while the student is there for the purpose of learning; so this can be seen as an example of intentional, formal learning. However, when the focus of research is on the learning that occurs whilst someone plays a game in their spare time at home during game-play—usually a voluntary, leisure time activity—this could be classified as focusing on unintentional, informal learning.

In relation to the use of games for formal learning purposes, O'Neil et al. (2005) reviewed the literature and found a total of 19 studies that met their criteria for review. The studies included had to be peer-reviewed published journal articles which used adult participants and also contained some quantitative or qualitative information about the effectiveness of the games used. O'Neil and colleagues concluded that "the evidence of potential is striking, but the empirical evidence for effectiveness of games as learning environments is scant" (O'Neil et al., 2005, p. 468). However, the authors note that learning outcomes seem to depend on how instructional strategies around the game are employed. Similarly, Pivec (2009) in a report commissioned by BECTA, agrees that the evidence for the effectiveness of game-based learning is mixed, suggesting that it is not just the game but how it is used within a specific environment (what he terms the "meta-game") which helps lead to effective learning.

It seems likely, then, that at least some of the issues that affect formal game-based learning are due to the context in which the game-play occurs. Further, it is also possible the lack of empirical support in the area "may indicate that learning through immersive worlds involves a more complex understanding of learning, one that is not so easy to tie to specified learning outcomes" (de Frietas, 2006, p. 18). This suggests that there is a need to further our understanding of what occurs during everyday game-play practices in order to examine how and what players learn when playing games during leisure time. By taking the context and socio-cultural factors around the game into account, as researchers such as de Castell and Jenson (2003), Squire (2005), Pelletier and Oliver (2006) suggest, we can identify how successful commercial games support learning within and around game-play and start to think more about how to support learning in more formal contexts.

An account of informal learning that attempts to consider the context around game-play in more depth is provided by Gee (2004) in his book '*What video games have to teach us about learning and literacy.*' Gee (2004) describes how people learn to play games from their individual efforts to master the progressive challenges provided by the game to their participation in "semiotic domains" and "affinity groups." This could be described as an

account of how people learn informally, through games, since Gee (2004) is discussing game-play in terms of people playing commercial games outside of educational environments. Egenfeldt-Nielsen, Smith, and Tosca (2008) describe Gee's (2004) approach to the analysis of game-play activity as socio-cultural since digital games are viewed as "tools for constructing viable learning experiences" that "mediate discussion, reflection and analysis" (p. 216). Gee (2004) argues that "critical learning" occurs when people learn to play new video games as they are actually learning a new literacy. This literacy includes multi-modal texts and graphical representations. Through gaming, players learn to participate in "semiotic domains" made up of words, pictures, and/or anything that is used to communicate different types of meaning. These domains are associated with specific "affinity groups" of players whose knowledge, skills, tools and resources contribute to form complex systems of distributed parts. These essentially make up a community of practice (Lave & Wegner, 1991; Wegner, 1998) where players can gain resources from fellow members to help them to solve problems within, and sometimes outside of, the specific domain. Gee (2004) sees this as evidence of "critical learning" which occurs when a player thinks about "the domain at a meta-level as a complex system of interrelated parts" (p. 23).

Further, Gee (2004) points out that his ideas fit in well with the view that "learning is a change not just in practice, but in identity" (p. 190), as researchers such as Lave and Wegner (1991) suggest. With respect to games, Gee (2004) talks about learning that occurs from the adoption of and experimentation with different identities, as well as being able to reflect upon the relationship between old and new identities. While Gee (2004) argues that all deep learning is tied in with the notion of identity, "critical learning" will only occur when the player is willing to see him or herself as someone who can learn, use and value the new semiotic domain. This can only happen in the space where the learner can "transcend the limitations both of the virtual identity and the learner's own real world identity" (p. 66) resulting in a more powerful learning experience.

However, Gee's (2004) writing is based mostly on his own experiences and observations, so there is a need for further empirical research to substantiate his account. It is not clear whether everyone who plays games engages with them in the same sort of way and whether they would all get the same benefits from doing so. It can be argued that further studies are needed to examine the different ways in which games are played in practice. In addition to finding out more about why players choose to play different games and what happens when they do, it would also be useful to explore what motivates players to put more effort into their game-playing experiences.

Gaming Capital and Paratexts

In understanding the socio-cultural aspects associated with games, the concept of "gaming capital" may be a useful one, not just in relation to game-play but also in relation to the activities that occur around it. Consalvo (2007) developed this concept from Bourdieu's (1984) notion of "cultural capital" in order to:

capture how being a member of game culture is about more than playing games or even playing them well. It's being knowledgeable about game releases and secrets, and passing that information on to others. It's having opinions about which game magazines are better and the best sites for walkthroughs on the Internet. (Consalvo, 2007, p. 18)

Consalvo (2007) discusses how "paratexts" can help players to acquire gaming capital. Paratexts are external resources that can "surround, shape, support, and provide context for texts" (p. 182). With respect to gaming, games themselves can be considered to be the primary texts, whereas some examples of paratexts include walkthroughs, previews, YouTube videos, blogs, reviews, magazines etc that relate to games. Players can thus increase their knowledge about games and game-play practices by using different forms of paratext. Some of this knowledge may also translate to greater competence within specific games. Both the concept of gaming capital and the idea of paratexts could be helpful for considering motivation and informal learning in relation to community membership. They could also be useful for discussing game-related activities that occur outside the experience of play e.g., consulting a game guide.

MOTIVATION AND ENGAGEMENT

It has been suggested above that there is a need for empirical examination of the context and socio-cultural factors around everyday games-playing, in order to provide further insight into the effectiveness of games used for learning e.g., Squire (2005). It can also be argued that socio-cultural factors are important in relation to research into aspects of motivation and engagement associated with games.

In terms of theories about what makes games motivating, the most influential work comes from Malone and colleagues. Malone proposed a theory of intrinsic motivation in games, based on experimental manipulations of different games, which suggested that games are rewarding due to a combination of fantasy, challenge and curiosity (Malone, 1981). "Fantasy" refers to the way players can imagine themselves in contexts using vivid realistic images provided by the game. A distinction is made between extrinsic or exogenous fantasy (where the fantasy depends on the skill) and intrinsic or endogenous fantasy (where the skill and fantasy depend on each other). "Challenge" depends on the degree of difficulty and level of uncertainty to drive players. The four attributes of challenge are goals, uncertain outcome, self-esteem and toys vs. tools (where toys are used for their own sake with no external goal and tools are used to achieve an external goal). In order for the challenge to be an effective motivator, a balance must be struck with the game being neither too difficult nor too hard. Finally, "curiosity" refers to the way players continue to play a game in order to find out what will occur after certain actions are taken. A further distinction is made between sensory curiosity (attention-attracting changes that involve our senses) and cognitive curiosity (driven by a desire to bring coherence to our knowledge structures).

In order to take into account the impact that social factors have on motivation, later work added the element of control, and three interpersonal motivators; recognition, competition and cooperation (Malone & Lepper, 1987). Games can give players a powerful sense of control though it is worth noting that it is the player's perceived control that can increase motivation, as opposed to the level of control they actually have. To increase a sense of control the game needs to be contingent on the player's responses, provide the player with a number of choices, and enable the player's actions to have "powerful effects," where the difference in outcomes between choices is obvious. The three interpersonal motivations (cooperation, competition and recognition of our efforts by others) help motivate players by increasing their sense of satisfaction through helping others, comparing themselves favourably to others, and/or having their efforts recognised by others. Malone and Lepper (1987) do note that these can be decomposed into individual motivations (e.g., competition can be used to increase a sense of challenge) and that they can sometimes be considered extrinsic (e.g., recognition). However, they also point out "these interpersonal factors do provide intrinsic motivations that would not be present in the absence of other people" (p. 242).

Empirical research carried out by Malone and Lepper (1987) has provided support for this theory of intrinsic motivation in games (Malone & Lepper, 1987; Cordova & Lepper, 1996). However, Habgood, Ainsworth, and Benford (2005) question the claim that intrinsic fantasies are "more instructional than extrinsic fantasies" (Malone, 1981, p. 361), regarding this as an untested hypothesis, noting Malone (1981) did not measure any learning outcomes in his original study. Moreover, Habgood et al. (2005), question the usefulness of the concept of endogenous fantasy for understanding the differences between games in relation to learning. As an alternative to intrinsic fantasy, Habgood et al., suggest that the experience of flow (Csikszentmihalyi, 1988), how the information is represented and how players make meaningful decisions within the game, are factors more likely influence the integration of motivating factors and learning content within educational games.

Egenfeldt-Neilsen et al. (2008) also argue that despite the later inclusion of interpersonal motivators, in Malone's (1981) work, there is too narrow a focus on the structure of the game itself, without sufficient attention being paid to the social dynamics and context that occur around it. For instance, the theory would have trouble explaining any data substantiating the claim that video games "are surrounded by strong social networks, which facilitate the learning experience" (Engenfeldt-Nielsen et al., 2008, p. 216). The theory would also have difficulty considering the role paratexts and gaming capital might play in creating and sustaining motivation to play different games. Further, Egenfeldt-Nielsen (2006) points out that Malone's (1981) theory resulted from his research on how children responded to manipulations of drill and practice type games, which arguably look very different to the commercially available titles available today, especially in terms of graphics. In addition, as Jenson and de Castell (2008) note, the recent introduction of new games controllers such as dancemats, motion sensitive controllers and guitar shaped peripherals, have led to very different forms of game-play. Arguably, such improvements in graphical realism and the new interaction techniques could result in different experiences of engagement and learning that have yet to be determined.

In addition, gaming is now seen as "normal" activity, one that is culturally acceptable on a large scale, since more people are playing them (Juul, 2009). Juul argues that part of this is due to the rise of casual games that require less of a time and energy commitment from games players. Many of these games are easy to access on PCs or mobile phones (e.g., downloadable casual games such as Bejewelled) and others use mimetic interfaces (such as the guitar shaped controllers mentioned earlier for Guitar Hero) which are easier to learn how to use since players are already familiar with how the controllers are supposed to work, thus lowering the barriers of access. Juul highlights the fact that many games that are played casually tend to include a social component, which also seems to have broadened the general appeal of games. It is also interesting to note that companies such as Nintendo have purposefully aimed to broaden their market by finding ways to make games more mainstream. For instance, in his keynote address during Nintendo's 2008 fall conference, company president Satoru Iwata refers to Nintendo's basic mission to expand the gaming population by making games that everyone can enjoy (regardless of age, gender and experience) (Iwata, 2008)

One model of motivation and engagement that allows for greater emphasis to be placed on how the social aspects influence the gaming experience is presented by Calleja (2007a, 2007b). In seeking to explain player involvement within Massively Multiplayer Online Games (MMOGs), Calleja (2007a, 2007b) notes that two meanings of the term "immersion" are often conflated: sometimes labelling an experience of intense engagement or deep absorption, and sometimes labelling a powerful sensation of being located within a virtual environment (often called "presence"). Instead of "immersion," Calleja (2007a, 2007b) drew on ethnographic research involving participant observation and interviews to propose

a Digital Game Experience Model (DGEM). The DGEM portrays players' "involvement" with reference to six "frames"; where "each frame represents a modality of meaning through which the role-playing experience is interpreted and performed" (pp. 236-237). The player experience can be described with reference to how the tactical, performative, affective, shared, narrative and spatial frames come together in different ways during instances of play. A brief description of each frame is provided below:

1. Tactical involvement refers to any form of decision-making and strategy formation within the game that relate to how the player interacts with the rules, the game environment and other players.

2. Performative involvement depends on how the player exerts agency within the game world and it is in this frame where the player actualises the strategies they have formed within the tactical phase. This relates to game piece control and movement within the game, the player's view of the world and mastering the controls.

3. Affective involvement deals with the way the game affects the player's moods and emotional states through a cognitive, emotional and kinaesthetic feedback loop. The mode of representation is often important in this e.g., audio, visual.

4. Shared involvement relates to how a player interacts with other agents within the game-world (either AI controlled or human in multiplayer games).

5. Narrative involvement helps to provide the other frames with a sense of context. A growing personal narrative can still heighten affective aspects of the game even if there is a lack of engagement with the designed narrative, by making the game personally meaningful.

6. Spatial involvement relates to how the player is able to locate themselves within the game

world. A growing sense of familiarity here leads to feelings of comfort and belonging which can make the player feel more involved.

Each of the frames describes experiences that range on a continuum from conscious attention to internalized knowledge, which will eventually lead to "incorporation" as the player internalises each of the frames. This is described as "the subjective experience of inhabiting a virtual environment facilitated by the potential to act meaningfully within it while being present to others" (Calleja, 2007a, p. 257). Calleja (2007a) states his focus was on the "various forms of engagement with digital games, ranging from their general motivations and attractions to a detailed analysis of moment by moment involvement in game-play" (p. 6) using the terms "macro involvement" to refer to player's "general motivations for engaging with games" and "micro involvement" to refer to "the moment by moment instance of game play" (p. 9).

The DGEM is primarily a descriptive framework that allows for qualitative comparisons between different instances of play and can be used to discuss long term motivations as well as episodes of engagement. Further, the description of how a player incorporates the different frames is especially interesting from a learning perspective as it gives researchers a way of understanding how the relationship between the learning and involvement is experienced by game players. It also has the potential to distinguish between involvement that occurs on both a micro and macro scale. This could allow for a discussion of specific game-play episodes but also about how activities outside of the moment of game play, such as looking at a walkthrough or discussing a game with friends, might affect longer term motivations to play games.

However, the DGEM was based on the study of massively multiplayer online games (MMOGs) so it would be interesting to see how it can deal with instances of single and co-located play. For instance, Iacovides (2009) applied the DGEM in order to explore the informal learning that occurs within game play and how this learning relates to the experience of player involvement during episodes of play. A qualitative case-study approach was adopted where participants were first observed playing a game of their choice and then interviewed about their experiences using a recording of the game-play as a cue. Five case studies were carried out with four male participants and one female participant (age range 24 to 52 years). In usability testing, critical instances are defined as "an event that has a significant effect, either positive or negative, on user task performance or user satisfaction with the interface" (Gabbard et. al, 1999, p. 54) and this definition was adopted as a guideline for selecting which game play instances or themes should be analysed further. The DGEM was then used to analyse these instances and themes in terms of what was being learnt and what kinds of involvement were being experienced, through describing the process of internalising the relevant frames. It was concluded that the DGEM did prove useful for identifying how deeper levels of involvement actually depend on internalisation (i.e., learning) as incorporation can only take place once the relevant frames have been internalised successfully.

It is worth noting that this was a short term study with only five participants and the game-play took place inside a lab as opposed to a more natural game-play environment. In addition, further work is required to explore whether the metaphor of incorporation is relevant to all forms of digital game play. Iacovides (ibid) was also focusing on micro involvement, so there is also need to consider how the DGEM might be used to account for longer terms motivations for game-play.

Work and Play

Research in the area of games and learning often reveals a potential tension between being motivated to play a game and being motivated to learn

(Whitton, 2007). This seems similar to the idea that work and play are mutually exclusive activities, with Calleja (2007a) arguing that "pinning motivation for game-playing on the notion of fun risks missing important dimensions of the game experience" (p. 136). As Yee (2006) points out, players often engage in activities that feel a lot like work because of the time and energy they have invested in them, as part of their routine game-playing experiences. It seems that the relationship between work and play is more complex than is often assumed.

While it has not been applied extensively to the study of motivation in games, Boyle and Connolly (2008) suggest that Apter's reversal theory may have particular relevance when it comes to explaining the blurred distinction between work and play. Reversal theory discusses motivation and emotion with reference to eight pairs of opposing states which occur within four different domains of experience: telic/paratelic, conformist/negativistic, master/sympathy and autic/alloic (Apter, 2007). The telic and paratelic states occur within the means-end domain and refer to the serious minded and playful states respectively. Within the domain of rules, the conformist and negativistic states relate to our desire to conform or rebel. The mastery and sympathy states occur within the transaction domain, and where the former refers to power, and the latter to likeability. Finally, within the relationship domain, the autic or alloic states are experienced, where the person is either concerned with themselves or with others. Though they are mutually exclusive, people can and often do "reverse" between the states, sometimes quite rapidly.

Instead of presenting a u-shaped curve for the relationship between performance and arousal, Apter (2007) proposes that the y-axis should represent hedonic tone (or valence i.e. how pleasant or unpleasant something is experienced as being) instead of performance and that two curves be used to represent the opposing states, such as telic and paratelic. The theory can thus account for high levels of arousal which are experienced as being pleasurable, and for low levels of arousal which are experienced as being unpleasant. It also helps explain how people switch between these different states within the same activity depending on whether they are in arousal seeking, or arousal avoidance mode.

Boyle and Connolly (2008) suggest the theory, and the telic/paratelic states specifically, can account for the emotional flips that people experience whilst playing games. In telic mode, the player is serious and forward looking, with a focus on achieving goals. Paratelic mode is the playful mode where the focus in on the activity itself. Excitement is supposed to occur in the telic state, whilst relaxation occurs in the paratelic. Whilst the modes do not occur at the same time, one will be in the focus while the other is in the background. This would suggest that different game-play activities could be experienced as either fun or serious depending on whether the player is within telic or paratelic mode. This switching between states may help explain why different parts of the game-play experience can be considered as either work or play.

METHODOLOGICAL ISSUES

Some key research relating to motivation, engagement and informal learning through digital games has been outlined, and it was suggested that there is a need for empirical studies examining the kinds of learning that occur in and around everyday gaming practice. However, it is worth noting some of the methodological challenges for such studies by first outlining some of the different methods that have been used to examine different aspects of the game play experience.

In terms of eliciting the different reasons why people play games and their conceptions of game play, interviews are often used while the data collected is then used to develop a questionnaire that can be used to survey larger populations (Yee, 2007; Whitton, 2007). Meanwhile, analysis of paratexts (Consalvo, 2007) offers the potential to identify the development of gaming capital and community values, and thus gain insight into why certain games are chosen, why hardcore gamers might play them differently to casual games, and into the informal learning processes that occur both inside and outside of game-play.

In terms of analysing experiences during game-play, there has been a recent move within Human Computer Interaction (HCI) research towards evaluating the user experience as a whole, rather than purely focusing on performance outcomes (Mandryk & Atkins, 2007). This parallels recent interest in considering affective issues (including motivation) in relation to the use of technologies for learning (Jones & Issroff, 2005).

For instance, Pelletier and Oliver (2006) focus on the learning process that occurs during game play itself and without looking for specific learning outcomes. They developed a method based on Activity Theory (AT) which focused on the influence that "contradictions" (i.e., breakdowns) have on learning within instances of observed play. An example from a gaming context would be making the same mistake more than once due to misunderstanding how an object within the game works. Pelletier and Oliver were specifically interested exploring how these breakdowns influence learning within instances of observed play and used Kuuti's (1996) further refinement of AT to analyse these instances. The three levels of analyses proposed by Kuuti (1996) are:

- Activities (high-level plans e.g., building a house).
- Actions that contribute to the activity (e.g., building a wall).
- Operations that contribute to each action (e.g., laying a brick), which are routine or automatic unless something goes wrong (a contradiction arises).

The method consisted of analysing video recordings of game-play in conjunction with a table used to record player activities, where the activities were broken down into actions and operations. The table was also used to keep track of any contradictions and any evidence of learning. Three case studies (with three players playing one of two games) were carried out in order to test this. Players were observed and recorded playing either Harry Potter and the Chamber of Secrets or Deus Ex for a time period of 25 minutes to two hours (depending on the participant). While the authors suggest a general description of the game-play session is useful, they were particularly interested in any failures or mistakes that occurred and any evidence they could find of the player having resolved these contradictions e.g., being successful after trying a different strategy.

Pelletier and Oliver (2006) do note however, that while the method allowed them to document the learning that occurred, they needed to make inferences about the reasons behind the operations carried out. As a result, they attempted to come up with a set of rules based on these proposed explanations of player behaviour that can be viewed as a set of strategies the player turns to when learning a new game e.g., "spot unusual objects and click on them" (p. 335). The authors conclude the method helped them to analyse the process by which players learn game strategies, while they see the method developed as being useful for helping educators consider which specific game might be useful to use under different circumstances. However, it could be argued that by not taking the player's perspective into account, it is not clear how far the inferences made actually govern player behaviour.

Using a very different approach, Mandryk and Inkpen (2004) decided to test the efficacy of physiological measures as a way of evaluating player engagement with collaborative entertainment technologies. The authors give an overview of various physiological measures e.g., galvanic skin response (GSR), electromyography (EMG) and carried out an experiment to test whether these sorts of measures could be used to provide an objective account of the player experience. Five pairs of players were observed and recorder playing a computer game either with another co-located player or against the computer for a period of five minutes. The authors conclude that the method did reveal that there is a physiological difference between playing a friend or a computer (as indicated by GSR), where playing with a friend is more enjoyable than with a computer, but that further improvements to their methodology were required and further testing in order to validate their findings.

There are some difficulties when gathering physiological data that should be pointed out. For instance, measures such as GSR are not consistent across experimental sessions and subject to other physiological happenings (e.g., digesting) which can make it difficult to make between groups comparisons (Mandryk & Inkpen, 2004). It is also worth noting that EMG measurements can also be disrupted by talking or laughing (Mandryk & Atkins, 2007). While physiological data could allow for concrete comparisons to be made between different cases, the collection and analyses of such data requires an in-depth and complex approach. This is in part due to the fact that it is not always clear what emotions are being measured through such readings (Mandryk & Atkins, 2007). Further, while the method did pick up differences between conditions, it is not clear whether a play period of only five minutes is really long enough for the players to become truly immersed in an activity. However, Mandryk and Atkins (2007) do suggest that the data might also be useful when used in combination with video data to identify incidents when a change in emotion occurs.

It could be argued that in order to fully understand what is really occurring during an episode of game-play, a multi-method case-study approach needs to be adopted. Barr (2007) for instance, used a collective case study approach (with five people, who each played the same set of five games) to examine the relationship between the interface and the "values" expressed during play. Values are defined as "a sustained belief that one mode of conduct is preferable to other potential modes of conduct" (p. 3). Barr (2007) used a variety of data collection methods to do so including the researcher gaining prior knowledge of the games (gained by playing each game for at least 20 hours and taking notes on it), taped observation and concurrent think aloud during game-play, DVD capture of game play, semi-structured post-play interviews and analysis of game documents. Activity Theory was used to analyse instances of game play, especially in terms of contradictions, while grounded theory was used to uncover the values expressed during play. Barr wanted to maximise differences between cases in order to get the most generalisable results while also emphasising the importance of the researcher having first-hand knowledge of the games when using a case study approach.

There are a number of disadvantages of such an exploratory approach. Firstly, a great deal of time is required to collect and analyse all the data. Secondly, it may be difficult to make larger scale generalisations on the basis of a small number of case studies. Thirdly, most of the data was gathered from a lab environment, with little attention being paid to activities occurring outside the episode of game-play. Nevertheless, the approach offers the opportunity to gain a richer understanding of what occurs during the game-play, while allowing for the generation of hypotheses that could be tested by subsequent studies. As Yin (2009) points out, while case studies do not allow for statistical generalisations they can be used for analytic generalisations in terms of helping to develop and provide support for theories. Though Barr (2007) was not interested in explicitly identifying learning, it would be interesting to see whether similar techniques could be used to establish what and how people learn from games and whether this has any relationship to their experiences of motivation and engagement.

DISCUSSION

It seems then that there is mixed evidence concerning the successful implementation of games within educational contexts. Factors might include the environments within which games are played; differences in design between games designed for leisure and games designed for learning; difficulties inherent in tying game-play to required learning outcomes; aspects of choice, control, intention and mood of individual players; and the social dynamics associated with playing games.

So while the work of Malone and Lepper (1987) has been hugely influential in the area, there is a need to update our ideas in order to really understand why people play different games and what they get out of the experience. The literature indicates that there are different motivations behind various forms of game play, and that engagement can be affected by factors such as the player, the game itself, how the player interacts with the game and the context in which the game is played; all of which will also affect the process of informal learning occurring within and around periods of game-play. There are also a variety of methods that can be used to examine aspects of game-play so some thought needs to be given to which methods would be most suitable to answer a specific set of research questions.

What the area would benefit from is a greater understanding of the relationship between motivation, engagement and learning within different game-play contexts as there is very little research that tries to explain how these processes relate to each other. In fact, the relationship is often seen as implicit and rarely questioned by those that refer to theories of motivation (Whitton, 2007). First we need to develop methods that can capture the complexity of what occurs within and around episodes of game-play. This will help further our understanding of how learning occurs and what is learnt when people engage in gaming and gaming-related activities within a leisure context (i.e., within contexts that are genuinely intrinsically motivating). This will help us to further appreciate the value that these activities offer and will also be useful for considering how to support game-based learning in more formal contexts.

DIRECTIONS FOR FURTHER RESEARCH

Current research being carried out at the Institute of Educational Technology, Open University, UK, has been using the following methodology to investigate games based learning. The aim of the research is to address some of the issues highlighted in the paper by first finding out more about the game-playing and game-related activities that different people engage in during their leisure time. This was achieved through carrying out a series of email interviews with different game-players. The DGEM and a thematic analysis are being used to analyse the data. By finding out more about the everyday activities different players engage in, we can start to build a picture of how motivation, engagement and informal learning come together in practice. The findings will then feed into subsequent research that aims to explore these processes in more depth through using a combination of methods such as gaming diaries, interviews, and observational data including the use of physiological data.

The interview study currently being analysed is examining what motivates people to play games, what factors affect engagement during play, and how players describe learning within the context of gaming. Thirty participants, aged 22-58, were interviewed. The asynchronous nature of using email meant participants were able to answer in their own time and to be more reflective about their answers (Bampton & Cowton, 2002). The DGEM used as an overarching framework for analyses, in which motivation and engagement are re-conceptualised as macro and micro involvement respectively.

Thematic analysis indicates that there are varying levels of participation within the types of communities Gee (2004) describes and that these levels may be dependent on how much the player identifies him or herself as a "gamer." Consalvo's (2007) work on gaming capital and paratexts has also proved useful in terms of considering the relationship between informal learning and identity.

In order to illustrate how players can differ in terms of their game-play activities and experiences, two player profiles are provided below:

The Casual Player

Rosie is a 29-year old Ph.D. student who mainly plays games socially. She does not own a games console but does play on consoles at her friends' houses or in the shared space at the campus library. Her stated reasons for playing games are "mainly because my group of friends would be playing, but I think essentially they're fun." Graphics can grab her attention but the feeling of progress and competition tend to keep her playing. The games she plays tend to depend on whatever her friends are playing, with recent titles including Big Brain Academy, Wii Sports, Lego Indiana Jones and Halo. She does not play games very often (less than once a month) and usually for about a couple of hours each time, but in the past she has spent a lot of time playing them. She prefers to learn how to play from observing and watching others around her but while she can see how games might help hand-to-eye coordination and problem solving skills, she does not think she has personally learnt much from playing them, apart from perhaps "learning to progress."

The Gamer

Marco is a 28-year old Assistant Portal Manager who works in the games industry. He uses a variety of gaming platforms (though the Xbox 360 is his platform of choice) and plays a wide variety

of games on a daily basis. Some games he has recently played are: Modern Warfare 2, Counter Strike, Streetfighter IV, Final Fantasy, Left 4 Dead and Fat Princess. His main reasons for playing are "general escapism, sometimes just to relax and de-stress after a hard day." He plays different games for different reasons, for instance he enjoys the stories in role-playing games (RPGs), and the release of frustration he experiences when playing action titles. He often plays with other people, including going to the arcade with colleagues during lunch time and playing first-person shooters (FPS) online. While he jokes about the issue of violence in games he does think that games keep his mind "sharp" and that they have helped him learn how to work in a team and how to be a good person. He sees helping others as part of being a "good gamer" and has opinions about debates within the gaming community.

The preliminary analyses suggest that one of the main differences between Rosie and Marco is in terms how they identify themselves. Though Rosie does say she used to play games more regularly, it seems to be an activity she has moved away from due to "priorities changing and energy" as well "access to games" being easier when she was a child (as her parents would pay for games consoles). Now it's just an activity she shares occasionally with her friends. In contrast, gaming is something Marco engages in every day, for long periods, and he considers it a main social activity. While Rosie is put off by other players being better than her, Marco is good enough at games to help others improve. Marco does refer to paratexts in relation to how the reviews of new games affect his expectations, while he also expressed his concerns about the effect of political correctness within the games industry. For instance, his interview response also contained a link to an article about a song being removed from Little Big Planet for containing a verse from the Quran (thus postponing the game's release date). So while he uses paratexts as a way of gaining knowledge about games, this use also indicates how involved he is within debates that are relevant to a wider gaming community.

It would seem then that identity and community are both important themes, as are knowledge of games and being competent, and these all seem to relate to the concept of gaming capital and how it might be established. While shared involvement is important to both players, it is clear that Marco pursues gaming and the activities around it as an active hobby, while Rosie sees it as a social activity which happens occasionally with friends. The issues of identity and community may help explain why Marco is willing to engage in activities and debates around gaming and Rosie is not; engaging in these practices (and potentially a community of practice) is part of what it means to be a gamer and part of the gamer community. All these factors seem to indicate that Marco is a hardcore gamer while Rosie is a more casual player. Further, while Marco's experience seems to fit in well with Gee's (2004) description of how people learn through games, it is less clear how well Rosie fits into this account of learning and whether she would benefit from games to the same extent. It would be interesting to investigate these differences and communities further, especially in relation to considering the implications they might for have the design and use of educational games.

Building and comparing profiles of players in this way is has useful for considering the reasons people have for playing games and the ways in which they engage in the activity, thus helping us to understand more about how motivation, engagement and informal learning come together in different ways. The DGEM can help researchers describe how these processes occur, while the concept of gaming capital indicates that the notions of community and identity are important ones to consider as they may have an impact on both learning and involvement in this context. However, a limitation of this interview study is that it relies on participants' retrospective accounts

of their experiences. So it would be interesting to see whether similar findings result from observations of player behaviour.

While Iacovides (2009) used a case based approach to observe participants playing a game of their choice and interviewed them about their game-play experience afterwards, the participants only came into the lab on one occasion and it could be argued that the lab was not set up to be a natural game-play environment. Further work is needed in which players are observed playing games in as natural a context as possible over a sustained period of time, in order to tap into what actually happens when people play games during their leisure time. In addition, it would also be useful to explore methods for keeping track of what happens outside instances of game-play in order to consider the influence of different game-related activities that players take part in.

Physiological measures may be able to provide an objective measure for evaluating the game play experience as Mandryk and Inkpen (2004) suggest but further work is needed to identify what emotions are being experienced during play. Another way to use these measures would be during real-time observation to indicate when significant events have occurred, as suggested by Hazlett (2008), or in conjunction with video data post-play, as suggested by Mandryk and Inkpen (2004). While some work is being carried out to explore how physiological measures can be used to identify different forms of engagement (Mandryk & Atkins, 2007; Lindley, Nacke, & Sennersten, 2008), there is little research that considers whether these measures would be useful for considering the learning that occurs in this context.

CONCLUSION

This paper highlights some of the issues concerning motivation, engagement and informal learning in relation to playing digital games. It is clear that the links between these concepts are not well understood and there is a need for further empirical studies to assess how they relate to each other. There is also a need for studies that do not look at people playing games in isolation but as part of a larger socio-cultural activity (de Castell & Jenson, 2003; Squire, 2005; Pelletier & Oliver, 2006) to fully understand how players participate within affinity groups and semiotic domains. Further, methods and frameworks need to be developed to aid researchers in exploring these issues.

If educators want to try and replicate people's enthusiasm for games within a formal educational context, then there is a need to first understand how this enthusiasm occurs in everyday gaming practices. This will not only lead to a greater understanding of how to design more involving commercial games but will also have implications for the design of educational games. By exploring how this process varies across individuals, we can also consider the implications for how educational games should be designed and used within different contexts.

It is possible that educational games may never be as motivating as ones played for leisure purposes, since making the activity compulsory reduces the voluntary aspect of play (de Castell & Jenson, 2003), but there is still much we can learn from gaming about how motivation to play and improve is created and sustained. Further research is needed to explore how this occurs, what factors influence the process and how this knowledge can be used to design more effective and enjoyable learning environments.

REFERENCES

Apter, M. J. (2007). *Reversal theory: The dynamics of motivation, emotion and personality.* Oxford, UK: Oneworld Publications.

Bampton, R., & Cowton, C. J. (2002). The e-interview. *FQS Forum: Qualitative. Social Research, 3*(2).

Barr, P. (2007). *Video game values: Play as human computer interaction.* Unpublished doctoral dissertation, Victoria University, Wellington, New Zealand.

Bourdieu, P. (1984). *Distinction: A social critique of the judgment of taste.* Cambridge, MA: Harvard University Press.

Boyle, E., & Connolly, T. (2008, October 16-17). A review of theories of player enjoyment in playing computer games. In *Proceedings of the 2nd European Conference on Games-Based Learning,* Barcelona, Spain (pp.59-67).

Calleja, G. (2007a). *Digital games as designed experience: Reframing the concept of immersion.* Unpublished doctoral dissertation, Victoria University, Wellington, New Zealand.

Calleja, G. (2007b). Digital game involvement: A conceptual model. *Games and Culture, 2,* 236–260. doi:10.1177/1555412007306206

Consalvo, M. (2007). *Cheating: Gaining advantage in videogames.* Cambridge, MA: MIT Press.

Cordova, D. I., & Lepper, M. R. (1996). Intrinsic motivation and the process of learning: Beneficial effects of contextualization, personalization, and choice. *Journal of Educational Psychology, 88,* 715–730. doi:10.1037/0022-0663.88.4.715

Csikszentmihalyi, M. (1988). The flow experience and human psychology. In Csikszentmihalyi, M., & Csikszentmihalyi, I. S. (Eds.), *Optimal experience* (pp. 15–35). Cambridge, UK: Cambridge University Press.

De Castell, S., & Jenson, J. (2003). Serious play. *Journal of Curriculum Studies, 35*(6), 649–665. doi:10.1080/0022027032000145552

De Freitas, S. (2006). *Learning in immersive Worlds: A review of game-based learning.* Retrieved from http://www.jisc.ac.uk/media/documents/programmes/elearninginnovation/gamingreport_v3.pdf

Egenfeldt-Nielsen, S. (2006). Overview of the research on the educational use of video games. *Digital Kompetanse, 1,* 184–213.

Egenfeldt-Nielsen, S., Smith, J. H., & Tosca, S. P. (2008). *Understanding video games: The essential introduction.* London, UK: Routledge.

Gabbard, J. L., Hix, D., & Swan, J. E. (1999). User-centered design and evaluation of virtual environments. *IEEE Computer Graphics and Applications, 19*(6), 51–59. doi:10.1109/38.799740

Gee, J. P. (2004). *What video games have to teach us about learning and literacy.* New York, NY: Palgrave Macmillan.

Habgood, M. P. J., Ainsworth, S. E., & Benford, S. (2005). Endogenous fantasy and learning in digital games. *Simulation & Gaming, 36,* 483–498. doi:10.1177/1046878105282276

Hazlett, R. L. (2008). Using biometric measurement to create emotionally compelling games. In Isbister, K., & Schaffer, N. (Eds.), *Game usability: Advice from the experts for advancing the player experience* (pp. 187–206). San Francisco, CA: Morgan Kauffman.

Iacovides, I. (2009, September 1-5). Exploring the link between player involvement and learning within digital games. In *Proceedings of the 23rd Conference on Human Computer Interaction,* Cambridge, UK (pp.29-34).

Iwata, S. (2008). *Keynote address: Nintendo Fall Conference.* Retrieved from http://www.nintendo.co.jp/n10/conference2008fall/presen/e/index.html

Jenson, J., & de Castell, S. (2008, October 16-17). From simulation to imitation: New controllers, new forms of play. In *Proceedings of the 2nd European Conference on Games-Based Learning,* Barcelona, Spain (pp. 213-218).

Jones, A., & Issroff, K. (2005). Learning technologies: Affective and social issues in computer supported collaborative learning. *Computers & Education, 44*(4), 395–408. doi:10.1016/j.compedu.2004.04.004

Juul, J. (2009). *A casual revolution: Reinventing video games and their players.* Cambridge, MA: MIT Press.

Kirriemuir, J., & McFarlane, A. (2004). *Literature review in games and learning.* Retrieved from http://www.futurelab.org.uk/resources/documents/lit_reviews/Games_Review.pdf

Kuutti, K. (1996). Activity theory as a potential framework for human computer interaction research. In Nardi, B. A. (Ed.), *Context and consciousness: Activity theory and human-computer interaction* (pp. 17–44). Cambridge, MA: MIT Press.

Lave, J., & Wegner, E. (1991). *Situated learning: Legitimate peripheral participation.* Cambridge, UK: Cambridge University Press.

Lindley, C. A., Nacke, L., & Sennersten, C. C. (2008, November 3-5). Dissecting play: Investigating the cognitive and emotional motivations and affects of computer gameplay. In *Proceedings of the CGAMES,* Wolverhampton, UK (pp. 9-16).

Malone, T. W. (1981). Toward a theory of intrinsically motivating instruction. *Cognitive Science: A Multidisciplinary Journal, 5,* 333-369.

Malone, T. W., & Lepper, M. R. (1987). Making learning fun: A taxonomy of intrinsic motivations for learning. *Aptitude. Learning and Instruction, 3,* 223–253.

Mandryk, R. L., & Atkins, M. S. (2007). A fuzzy physiological approach for continuously modeling emotion during interaction with play environments. *International Journal of Human-Computer Studies, 6*(4), 329–347. doi:10.1016/j.ijhcs.2006.11.011

Mandryk, R. L., & Inkpen, K. M. (2004). Physiological indicators for the evaluation of co-located collaborative play. In *Proceedings of the ACM Conference on Computer Supported Cooperative Work*, Chicago, IL (pp. 102-111).

O'Neil, H. F., Wainess, R., & Baker, E. L. (2005). Classification of learning outcomes: Evidence from the computer games literature. *Curriculum Journal, 16*(4), 455–474. doi:10.1080/09585170500384529

Pelletier, C., & Oliver, M. (2006). Learning to play in digital games. *Learning, Media and Technology, 31*, 329–342. doi:10.1080/17439880601021942

Pivec, P. (2009). *Game-based learning or game-based teaching?* Retrieved from: http://emerging-technologies.becta.org.uk/upload-dir/downloads/page_documents/research/emerging_technologies/game_based_learning.pdf

Squire, K. (2005). Changing the game: What happens when video games enter the classroom? *Innovate: Journal of Online Education, 1*(6).

Vavoula, G., Scanlon, E., Lonsdale, P., Sharples, M., & Jones, A. (2005). *Report on empirical work with mobile learning and literature on mobile learning in science (Tech. Rep. No. IST 507838)*. Brussels, Belgium: The European Commission.

Wegner, E. (1998). *Communities of practice: Learning, meaning and identity.* Cambridge, UK: Cambridge University Press.

Whitton, N. (2007). *An investigation into the potential of collaborative computer game-based learning in higher education.* Unpublished doctoral dissertation, Napier University, Edinburgh, UK.

Yee, N. (2006). The labor of fun: How video games blur the boundaries of work and play. *Games and Culture, 1*, 68–71. doi:10.1177/1555412005281819

Yin, R. K. (2008). *Case study research: Design and methods.* Thousand Oaks, CA: Sage.

This work was previously published in the International Journal of Virtual and Personal Learning Environments, Volume 2, Issue 2, edited by Michael Thomas, pp. 1-16, copyright 2011 by IGI Publishing (an imprint of IGI Global).

Chapter 12
An Evaluation of Neurogames®:
A Collection of Computer Games Designed to Improve Literacy and Numeracy

Misbah Mahmood Khan
University of Hertfordshire, UK

Jonathan Reed
Neurogames, UK

ABSTRACT

Games Based Learning needs to be linked to good learning theory to become an important educational intervention. This study examines the effectiveness of a collection of computer games called Neurogames®. Neurogames are a group of computer games aimed at improving reading and basic maths and are designed using neuropsychological theory. The effectiveness of Neurogames was assessed using a matched pairs experimental design. Short exposure to Neurogames resulted in a significant increase in mathematical ability compared to control. The games resulted in a significant increase in reading ability. The study shows that brief exposure to computer games can result in significant changes to academic development. The implications for education and further research are discussed.

INTRODUCTION

In order for Games Based Learning to develop as an important educational intervention it needs to be tied to good theories of learning and shown to be empirically effective. There is increasing interest in the use of computer games in education, known as Games Based Learning (Gee, 2003; Howard-Jones, 2009; Mitchell & Savill-Smith, 2004). This is because many children use computer games in their everyday life and are used to computer-based interfaces. Interest in computer games in education is also occurring because computer games are believed to be motivating (Whitton, 2007;

DOI: 10.4018/978-1-4666-2467-2.ch012

Howard-Jones, 2009). Many children do not find education intrinsically motivating and therefore using computer games may help to motivate. Active participation, intrinsic and prompt feedback, challenging but achievable goals and a mix of uncertainty and open-endedness all contribute to the motivational dimension of these games (Mitchell & Savill-Smith, 2004). Computer games are typically fast and responsive, and provide a rich variety of graphic representations to generate a wide range of options and scenarios not possible with non-computer games (Prensky, 2001). In addition to these psychological motivating factors, playing video games has been shown to result in increased release of the neurotransmitter Dopamine, which is associated with reward and pleasure (Koepp et al., 1988). However not everyone who plays games finds them motivating (Whitton, 2007). Therefore it is important to build in explicit reward features to try and enhance motivation when designing educational based computer games.

Another potential benefit of computer game based learning is that it has the potential to provide a standardised, reliable and effective intervention. It should be possible to build in learning features to computer games so that they are delivered in an effective, reliable way. Unlike human teachers computer games provide the same responses, choices, and rewards each time they are played. This standardisation means that games should be capable of being scientifically evaluated. Through manipulation it should be possible to find the elements of teaching that are effective and build on these to increase efficiency. However despite this potential, so far there has been limited scientific evaluation of games on learning. For games based learning to develop effective intervention it needs to be tied to proven theories of learning (Gee, 2003).

The last ten years have seen an explosion of knowledge and research in the area of child neuropsychology, which is the study of children's brain, cognitive and psychological development (Reed & Warner Rogers, 2008). This is providing

the basis for robust models of learning involving both neurological and psychological development. In particular very thorough theories of the development of reading and maths have been built (Goswami, 2008; Butterworth, 2005). Educational computer games could be designed to incorporate this knowledge.

In terms of reading there is strong evidence that the development of phonological understanding is important for the development of reading. When learning to read, it is necessary to phonologically decode words i.e., to work out (decode) the link between symbols (letters) and sounds (phonemes) (Goswami, 2008). Phonological decoding is based on phonological awareness. The onset of phonological awareness has been found to be a strong predictor of later reading in longitudinal studies (Bradley & Bryant, 1983). Training in phonological awareness results in higher levels of reading longitudinally, suggesting a causal relationship between phonological awareness and reading (Bradley & Bryant, 1983). The phonological structure of a language also seems to be important to reading acquisition. Differences in phonological structure account for differences in acquisition of reading across cultures (Ziegler & Goswami, 2005). In languages with simple consonant vowel phonological structure such as Italian, children in the first year at school were assessed to be 95% accurate in their Grapheme-Phoneme decoding skills. This contrasts with accuracy rates of 34% of children in Scottish schools learning to read the more phonologically complex English language (Seymore, Aro, & Erskine, 2003).

The importance of phonological awareness in the development of reading can also be at the brain level in the neuroimaging research literature. Phonological understanding develops in the left sided parieto-temporal region in the brain (Shawitz, 2003). Children with difficulties in phonological decoding (i.e., developmental dyslexia) seem to process reading on the opposite (right) side of the brain (Goswami, 2008). However it has been shown that with phonological training, children with reading difficulties can improve reading and restore function to the left side of the brain as seen on neuroimaging (Meyler et al., 2008).

Research into early years reading suggests that there is a sizable minority of children who continue to be below the expected standard in their development of reading. The Independent Review of the Teaching of Early Reading for the UK Government Department of Educational and Skills (Rose, 2006) reported that 19% of boys were not at the expected standard in terms of reading at stage 2 of the national curriculum. In line with the research literature reviewed here the report recommended that a more widespread phonics approach be implemented nationally. It concluded after a review of research and practice that " *'synthetic' phonics, offers the vast majority of young children the best and most direct route to becoming skilled readers and writers.* " The report also highlighted the difficulties of implementing such practice *"Despite the content of phonic work being a statutory component of the National Curriculum over that time, reports from Her Majesty's Inspectors show that it was often a neglected or a weak feature of the teaching"* (Rose, 2006). The research base therefore suggests that computer games designed to help reading should incorporate knowledge about phonological awareness if they are to be effective. Using computer games based on phonics and synthetic phonics (blending phonics together) may help the more widespread dissemination of this approach.

The development of numeracy has also been described in detail. There is a basic developmental sequence that children need to learn in order to grasp mathematics. Children need to learn that number words follow a set order, that each number is linked to only one object and that the total number of objects is determined by the last number word (Gelman & Gallistel, 1978). One of the core developmental features in learning maths is the ability to understand numerosities (Butterworth, 2008). Understanding numerosities involves the ability to automatically recognise the

number of objects in a set. This ability is thought to develop very early and has been demonstrated in very young infants (Xu & Spelke, 2000). Understanding Numerosities is associated with the intraparietal sulcus area of the brain (Butterworth, 2008). The ability to understand neumerosities is thought to underpin normal development of mathematical thinking. Children with difficulties in maths development, namely developmental dyscalculia, are thought to have a deficit in understanding numerosities (Butterworth, 2008). Following developing understanding of the basic principles of mathematical concepts, children learn to add on numbers and subtract. Initially they use objects or digits to do this but over time they are able to hold the numbers in their mind. Holding numbers in mind requires adequate working memory. Children later learn to store important number bonds and multiplication facts in semantic long term memory. Neuroimaging studies have shown that training maths ability causes a shift from the intraparietal sulcus to the left angular gyrus, which suggests a shift from quantity based processing to more automatic retrieval (Delazer et al., 2003). Automatic retrieval is more efficient by allowing more processing resources to undertake other aspects of calculation. Intervention to help develop numeracy should therefore be based on what is known in terms of neuropsychological development; however, as yet there is no body of literature showing this.

Early educational research also suggests that a significant proportion of children in the UK continue to have difficulties with maths development. The Independent Review of Mathematics Teaching in Early Years Settings and Primary Schools for the Department of Children, Schools and Families (Williams, 2008) reported that around 6% of children in the UK did not reach level 3 of the national curriculum when they were expected to (around 30,000 to 35,000 children in the UK). At present there is not the same consensus as there is with literacy intervention regarding the most effective intervention programmes for maths. A recent review of interventions for early years numeracy concluded that although children made gains using three different interventions (Mathematics Recovery, Numeracy Recovery and Numicon) there was a lack of evidence for any of the programmes being more effective than the others (Dowker, 2009).

Therefore there is a strong need to develop interventions for numeracy that are shown to be effective. Developing computer game based interventions based on a neuropsychological model of maths development may be helpful in this regard.

As well as directly understanding the development of specific abilities involved in reading and maths there are other more general neuropsychological concepts that are important for learning. Working memory in particular is important. Working memory is the ability to hold information in mind. It consists of several interacting subsystems including specialised stores for verbal and visuo-spatial material and an attention component that controls activity within working memory (Baddeley, 2000). Working memory is associated with the front part of the brain and with the neurotransmitter dopamine (McNab et al., 2009). The majority of children with poor working memory are slow to learn in the areas of reading, maths and science, across both primary and secondary school years (Gathercole & Alloway, 2008; Gathercole et al., 2004; Jarvis & Gathercole, 2003). Games for education should take into account the game demand in terms of working memory.

Most computer games involve an element of trial and error. However children who find learning difficult and particularly children with executive function difficulties typically seen in neurodevelopmental difficulties and acquired brain injury often have problems with trial and error learning (Ylvisaker et al., 2005). Trial and error learning is associated with executive functioning in the front part of the brain and is linked with working memory. Younger children with earlier stages of

brain development and children who find learning difficult can find it frustrating to keep getting the wrong answer and tend to give up easily. Children with working memory difficulties find it hard to keep information in mind in order to try different solutions. Therefore it is helpful to consider alternatives to trial and error approaches when designing educational games for such children.

This current study examines the effectiveness of a new set of computer games called Neurogames®. These games were developed specifically to improve reading and maths using a computer game format. They were designed to help younger children at the early stages of literacy and numeracy development and to help children who find learning difficult. There are two games looking at reading. The Letter Lilies game teaches phonological understanding of the 44 phonemes in the English language. The Word Patch game teaches blending of the phonemes to make words (synthetic phonics) and also automatic word recognition. The reading games were specifically designed to teach phonological awareness in line with the research literature on reading development. There are two games looking at numeracy. The Tomato Tumble game addresses the development of numerosities and early basic mathematical concepts. It teaches counting, associating numbers with quantity and numbers with objects. The Nutty Numbers game addresses automatic number bond learning. The first numeracy game is based on the theory of developing basic number understanding including numerosities. The second game is based on developing automatic number learning and taking the load off working memory.

The games address working memory by using a visually based error free learning paradigm. This means that the information is always visually available and in a multiple choice format thus cutting down on memory retrieval demands. The games also reveal the right answer when a child makes a mistake, thus using an error free learning paradigm. Each time a child gets an answer right they receive a verbal reward and a visual reward. The visual rewards in the form of cartoon seeds build to a final end of game reward of growing a garden, which can be printed. The game is designed to provide a repetitive yet rewarding way of learning. The challenge comes from getting the answers right first time and moving onto harder levels which, result in different rewards. The games are visually based and they are designed to gain young children's attention. They include an animated character, which is in line with other forms of children's media.

The following study looked at the effectiveness of Neurogames by assessing the impact of short-term exposure on the development of numeracy and literacy with normally developing children.

METHODS

A matched pairs experimental design was implemented. All the children were paired according to initial ability scores and one child from each pair was put in experimental group and the other in the control group. This ensured that the experimental and control groups formed would be comparable and that any potential changes as a result of the Neurogames intervention were not due to pre intervention ability levels. The dependent variable was the post-test independent assessment of mathematical reasoning scores as an indicator of numeracy skills and post-test independent assessment of reading scores. The independent variable was exposure to the intervention programme Neurogames.

Participants

All the subjects were students at an inner city state run infant school. All the children were in the average to above average range in terms of intellectual development (92-121). The children's

pre-test reading scores ranged from low average to above average (84-129). Their maths scores ranged from low average to above average (83-127). Following the pre-test session, children were paired according to similar reading, mathematic and IQ subtest scores. One child from each pair was allocated to the experimental group and the other to the control group, to ensure the groups were comparable. The experimental group consisted of 10 children, 5 females and 5 males aged 4-7yrs., with a mean age of 5.7yrs. The control group had 10 children, 5 males and 5 females aged 4-7yrs, with a mean age of 5.9yrs.

Material

In normal development reading and intellectual ability are dynamically linked (Ferrer et al., 2010). For this present study intellectual ability (IQ) was assessed in order to match the control group with the experimental group to ensure that IQ differences were not the factor influencing the changes gained from the Neurogames intervention. Initially 4 subtests of the Wechsler Preschool and Primary Scale of Intelligence (WPPSI) (Wechsler, 1967) were used to indicate IQ. These included 2 non-verbal measures. The first was Picture Completion, which involved a series of incomplete pictures and children had to identify the missing aspect or part. The second test, Animal House, was in the form of a wooden puzzle, at the top there was a row of colour coordinated animals as indicators of house colour for a specific animal, the task involved puzzling the correct coloured houses to each animal presented in a series of rows according to the key. Two verbal measures included Information in which a series of general knowledge questions were asked for example "what are the four seasons" and "point to your nose" and vocabulary in which words were read out and subjects had to explain the meaning.

For measures of Literacy and Mathematics ability sub tests of the Wechsler Individual Achievement Test (WIAT) (Wechsler, 1992) were used. The Mathematical Reasoning test involved basic numerical questions. The Reading test involved pointing to the word describing a picture, pointing to words starting and ending with specific sounds and reading out a series of words.

Two laptops set up with headphones were used to carry out the intervention and play the Neurogames. Four different Neurogames were used, two based on mathematic skills and two based on reading skills. Nutty Numbers involved mainly simple addition, subtraction and multiplication; Tomato Tumble involved identifying and selecting a larger or smaller group of tomatoes, the group of tomatoes corresponding to a specific number and selecting specific numbers. Letter Lilies involved selecting letters corresponding to specific sounds and Word Patch involved selecting words corresponding to specific sounds.

All the games were very colourful and well animated. For each incorrect response, the correct answer was shown and the child was asked to try again. For each correct response one colourful petal for a flower appeared, each flower had five petals and the number of flowers, which had to be filled with colourful petals, varied according to the level. Once all the flowers were filled with coloured petals, the participant was taken to the flower garden where they watched the flowers being planted before returning to the main screen and selecting the next level.

Procedure

The documents sent to parents included a letter with general information, a consent form and an information sheet, in which parents were informed of freedom to withdraw their child along with any data gained from their child at any stage without any reason and with full confidentiality. The school collected the signed consent forms. Children were selected in accordance with the criteria of half being males and half being females for the study. The

outline of the study was explained, confidentiality was assured and the children were told prior to testing and throughout the test sessions that they had the freedom to withdraw at any stage. The children were then individually tested, on four sub tests of the WPPSI; these were "Animal House," "Picture Completion," "Vocabulary" and "Information" with the option of breaking at any point. The children were then given the WIAT Reading and Mathematical Reasoning tests as pre test measures of reading and mathematics ability. For all tests the procedure was explained and children were allowed to ask any questions at any time if they did not understand. The WPPSI tests and the WIAT tests were scored and children were matched in to pairs as much as possible. Although exact matches were not found, it was ensured that children with low IQ subtest scores, reading ability and mathematics ability scores were not paired with someone at the top end of the scale. This was also done to ensure the distribution of abilities was even in the experimental and control groups. One individual was selected from each pair randomly to be in the experimental group ensuring 50% were female and 50% male for both control and experimental groups.

The participants then attended a trial session in pairs. This was set in a room within school that was familiar to all the children and considered a comfortable setting. In this session the children were talked through the games and given a chance to play the games so they understood the procedure.

Following this each child attended sessions to play the games twice a week over a period of six weeks, one reading and one mathematics game was played in each session. Although children attended the sessions in pairs the games were played individually. The children were seated away from one another, so they could not see each other's screens and headphones were used to help the children concentrate. Attending sessions in pairs made it less formal and more fun for the children. A manual tally was kept of the correct and incorrect responses. The sessions varied in time length ranging from 15 to 45 minutes depending on the child's age and school timetable. All children went at their own pace so the number of questions or levels attempted varied. For the first three weeks, the "letter lilies" and "Tomato Tumble" were played as these target basic level processes in reading and numeracy. For the final three weeks the "Word Patch" and "Nutty Numbers" games were played as these are aimed at higher-level reading and numeracy abilities.

After six weeks, all the children from both the experimental and control groups were re-tested on the WIAT Reading and WIAT Mathematical Reasoning tests. The children were thanked for their support and hard work. A debrief sheet was then sent via the school to parents of all the children who participated in the study, explaining what was done.

RESULTS

A Comparable Experimental and Control Sample

In order to ensure the two groups formed were comparable the initial ability scores were compared.

Table 1 shows that the maximum, minimum and mean scores for mathematics and IQ were very similar for the experimental and control groups. In the case of reading the mean and maximum score was slightly higher in the control group, the range of scores was still very similar, which would indicate a comparable sample.

A series of independent sample t-tests were conducted for Mathematics, reading and IQ subtest scores between the experimental and control groups prior to any intervention.

Table 1. Table to show initial mathematics, reading and IQ subtest scores for the experimental and control groups

Pre-test scores	Experimental Group Exposed to Neurogames	Control Group Not exposed to Neurogames	Statistical Result
Mathematics Maximum score	124	127	
Mathematics Minimum score	87	83	
Mean Mathematics Score **SD**	**102.20** **12.506**	**103.60** **14.037**	p=0.817 Not significantly different
Reading Maximum score	124	129	
Reading Minimum score	86	84	
Mean Reading score **SD**	**101.70** **11.719**	**106.40** **15.204**	p=0.449 Not significantly different
IQ Maximum score	121	118	
IQ minimum score	100	92	
Mean IQ subtest score **SD**	**108** **7.056**	**109.20** **8.56**	p=0.614 Not significantly different

Table 2. Table to show the mean mathematics score and mean reading score before and after exposure to the Neurogames

	Pre-test	Post-test	Statistical results
N	10	10	
Mean Mathematics Score	**102.20**	**123.70**	p=0.000 Significant difference
SD	12.506	11.441	
Mean Reading Score	**101.70**	**114.19**	p=0.000 Significant difference
SD	11.719	16.901	

There was no significant difference in pre-test mathematics scores between the experimental group (M=102.20, SD=12.506) and control group (M=103.60, SD=14.073), t (18)=-.235,p=0.817.

There was no significant difference in pre-test reading scores between the experimental group (M=101.70, SD=11.719) and control group (M=106.40, SD=15.204), t (18)=-.774,p=0.449.

There was no significant difference in pre-test IQ subtest scores between the experimental group (M=108, SD=7.056) and control group (M=109.20, SD=8.56), t(18)=-.513,p=0.614.

Attaining two groups of children with exactly the same mathematic, reading and IQ subtest scores was not possible; however from the above it is clear scores on all three measures did not differ significantly between the two groups.

Was There a Significant Improvement in Mathematical and Reading Ability After Playing the Neurogames?

Table 2 shows the mean mathematics and mean reading scores attained by the children were higher after playing the neurogames compared to scores before playing the neurogames.

Paired sample t-tests were conducted to compare mathematics scores and reading scores before

and after the intervention, exposure to the neurogames.

The post-test mathematic scores were significantly higher (M=123.70, SD=11.441) than the pre test mathematic scores (M= 102.20, SD=12.506), t(9)=-11.650, p=0.000. This suggests mathematics scores significantly improved following exposure to the Neurogames.

The post-test reading scores were significantly higher (M=114.19,SD=16.901) than pre-test reading scores (M=101.70, SD=11.719), t(9)=-6.128, p=0.000. This suggests reading scores significantly improved following exposure to the Neurogames.

Was the Post-Test Mathematics and Reading Ability Significantly Better Within the Experimental Group Than the Control Group?

Table 3 shows that both mathematics and reading mean post-test scores were higher in the experimental group than the control group; the difference in mathematic scores was greater than that of reading scores.

In order to see if these differences were significant independent sample t-tests were conducted to compare post-test mathematic and post-test reading scores between the experimental and control groups.

Table 3. Table to show mean post-test mathematic and reading scores for the group exposed to Neurogames and the group not exposed to Neurogames

	Experimental Group Exposed to Neurogames	Control Group Not exposed to Neurogames	Statistical result
N	10	10	
Mean post-test Mathematic score	**123.70**	**109.90**	p=0.023 Significant difference
SD	11.441	13.287	
Mean post-test Reading score	**114.90**	**109.10**	p=0.439 Not significantly different
SD	16.901	15.878	

The post-test mathematic scores were significantly higher for the group exposed to Neurogames (M=123.70, SD=11.441) than the group not exposed to Neurogames (M=109.90, SD=13.287), t(18)=2.489, p=0.023. Individuals playing the Neurogames showed significantly better post-test mathematics scores than those individuals who did not play the neurogames.

The post-test reading scores were higher for the group exposed to neurogames (M=114.90, SD=16.901) than the group not exposed to neurogames (M=109.10, SD=15.878), however this difference was not significant t(18)=0.791, p=0.439. The post-test reading scores in the group exposed to neurogames were not significantly better than the group not exposed to neurogames.

Were the Neurogames More Influential on a Specific Sex?

An independent sample t-test was conducted to compare the mean change in mathematics scores between males and females. There was no significant difference in changed scores between males (M=22.60, SD=7.335) and females (M=20.40, SD=4.450), t(8)=0.573, p=0.582.

An independent samples t-test was conducted to compare the mean change in reading scores between males and females. There was no significant difference in changed scores between males (M=14.00, SD=9.566) and female (M=12.40, SD=3.362), t(4.973)=0.353, p=0.739.

Table 4. Differences between male and female scores on reading and Mathematics

	Males	Females	Statistical result
N	10	10	
Mean Mathematic score change	**22.60**	**20.40**	p=0.582 Not significantly different
SD	7.335	4.450	
Mean Reading score change	**14**	**12.40**	p=0.739 Not significantly different
SD	9.566	3.362	

Table 5. Correlations between improvement in maths and reading and IQ

	IQ	Statistical result
N	10	
Level of improvement in maths	r=-.227	p=0.529 Not a significant relationship
Level of improvement in reading	R=-.092	p=0.799 Not a significant relationship

Was There a Relation Between IQ Subtest Score and Level of Improvement in Mathematics and Reading After Playing the Neurogames?

A Pearson's correlation was computed to find out whether initial IQ subtest score and the level of improvement in mathematics (Table 4) following the intervention of exposure to the neurogames was correlated. This showed the two variables had a very weak negative correlation which was not significant, r = -.227, n = 10, p = 0.529.

A Pearson's correlation was computed to find out whether initial IQ subtest score and the level of improvement in reading following the intervention of exposure to the neurogames was correlated. This showed the two variables had a even weaker negative correlation which was not significant, r = -.092, n = 10, p = 0.799.

These findings (Table 5) indicate within the group of children playing the Neurogames, that the initial IQ subtest score did not significantly correlate with either level of improved reading or mathematics scores.

Summary of Results

Table 6 contains a summary of the research questions and findings.

CONCLUSION

This study has shown that the computer games, called Neurogames, are effective in improving Maths and Reading after a short exposure. The findings show that mathematic scores improved significantly following exposure to the Neurogames within the experimental group. Mathematical scores were significantly higher in the experimental group in comparison with the control group not exposed to the Neurogames.

Table 6. Summary of research questions and results

Research Question	Answer
Did reading improve following exposure to Neurogames?	Yes- statistically significant improvement
Did mathematical ability improve following exposure to Neurogames?	Yes- statistically significant improvement
Did reading improve more than the control group not exposed to Neurogames?	Yes- but not a significant statistical improvement
Did mathematical ability improve more than the control group not exposed to Neurogames?	Yes- statistically significant improvement

In terms of reading the findings showed there was a significant improvement in reading scores following exposure to the Neurogames within the experimental group, however the post-test reading scores were not significantly higher in the experimental group compared with the control group not exposed to the Neurogames. It should be noted that the reading control group started at a slightly higher base rate compared to the experimental group, which may explain the lack of a significant difference between the experimental and control group.

The results showed that the improvement in scores was not due to IQ differences or to gender differences.

These findings suggest that developing educational computer games based on established neuropsychology learning theory can be an effective strategy in improving literacy and numeracy development. Previous work has shown that training using phonological methods is an effective strategy for improving reading. This study suggests that training using a phonological approach can be embedded within a computer game and can also result in improvements in reading. There is not a body of existing literature regarding improving numeracy based on neuropsychological theory. This present study suggests that neuropsychological theory can be used to design a computer game and can result in improved numerical development. The study also suggests that including features to address working memory and trial and error learning can be effective in computer based learning games. It is not possible at present to determine the most effective components of Neurogames (the phonology aspect or the error free learning elements). It may be that different factors are important in different populations. Research that tries to isolate the relative impact of the different components would be needed.

There were limitations to the study. The exposure to the games was relatively brief i.e., 12 teaching sessions. Previous research has used a much higher number of teaching sessions, for example

in terms of phonological intervention, Meyler et al. (2008), used a 100 sessions to produce lasting change. It would be helpful to research the effects of longer exposure using Neurogames.

The best intervention studies use cognitive data combined with neuroimaging data to shown consistent outcome across domains. It would be helpful to measure the outcome for Neurogames using a combination of outcome data to see how robust any changes were.

The groups in this study were relatively small with 10 participants in each group. A larger study would be needed to test whether the findings can be replicated on a wider population. This present study demonstrated the effectiveness of Neurogames on a group of young normally developing children. It would also be helpful to test the games on children who find learning difficult. These groups of children would include those with significant reading and maths delay (for example dyslexia and dyscalculia), those with executive based difficulties including poor working memory, Attention Deficit Hyperactivity Disorder (ADHD) or Traumatic Brain Injury. It would also be helpful to test the games with children with general cognitive delay (learning disabilities). Existing educational services for these groups of children are patchy. If it is proved effective with these populations Neurogames may provide a cost effective intervention for raising literacy and numeracy skills for children who find learning difficult.

The group of games in Neurogames are aimed at younger children and therefore incorporate factors such as repetitive learning, simple visual rewards and help when mistakes are made. Much of the current Games Based Learning approach is a top down extension of existing gaming principles, i.e., immersive challenging environments requiring trial and error to master the game. Whilst this may be a good approach for older children and adolescents it may not be the best approach for younger children or children who find learning difficult. This study suggests that there may need to be different gaming approaches for different groups of children. The children in this study enjoyed playing the games and engaged with them well. The study shows that it is possible to design effective games for a younger audience.

The findings from this study have significant potential implications for future educational practice. There is an increasing body of knowledge about child and educational development at the psychological and neurological levels. Despite this knowledge recent UK government reviews of early learning have shown a significant number of children failing to reach expected levels at primary school. Despite national guidance there is continued concern about use of best practice. By incorporating child neuropsychology learning theory into computer games there is the possibility of wider dissemination of this knowledge. This study has shown that computer games incorporating learning theory can be effective in improving educational outcome even after brief exposure. Children enjoy playing games and this may be a particularly effective way to learn. It will be important in the future for schools to embrace technology in everyday classroom situations. Children are very used to computer-based interfaces in their everyday life. As well as being an appealing interface for children's learning this study also suggests that computer game-based learning can improve educational outcome. In terms of future developments games designers need to work alongside educational professionals and neuropsychologists to develop games that are based on the latest research into child neuropsychological development, as well as using appealing, motivating games design. Together these disciplines could bring a revolutionary approach to education and improve educational outcomes significantly.

REFERENCES

Badderley, A. D. (2000). The episodic buffer: A new component of working memory? *Trends in Cognitive Sciences*, *4*, 417–423. doi:10.1016/S1364-6613(00)01538-2

Bradley, L., & Bryant, P. E. (1983). Categorising sounds and learning to read: A causal connection. *Nature*, *310*, 419–421. doi:10.1038/301419a0

Bryant, P. E., MacLean, M., Bradley, L. L., & Crosssland, J. (1990). Rhyme and alliteration, phoneme detection, and learning to read. *Developmental Psychology*, *26*, 429–438. doi:10.1037/0012-1649.26.3.429

Butterworth, B. (2005). The development of arithmetical abilities. *Journal of Child Psychology and Psychiatry, and Allied Disciplines*, *46*(1), 3–18. doi:10.1111/j.1469-7610.2004.00374.x

Butterworth, B. (2008). Developmental Dyslexia. In Reed, J., & Warner-Rogers, J. (Eds.), *Child neuropsychology concepts: Theory and practice*. West Sussex, UK: Wiley-Blackwell.

Delazer, M., Domahs, F., Bartha, L., Brenneis, C., Lochy, A., & Trieb, T. (2003). Learning complex arithmetic- an fMRI study. *Brain Research. Cognitive Brain Research*, *18*, 76–88. doi:10.1016/j.cogbrainres.2003.09.005

Dowker, A. (2009). *What works for children with mathematical difficulties?* Retrieved from http://jumpmath.org/00086-2009BKT-EN.pdf

Ferrer, E., Shaywitz, B. A., Holahan, J. M., Marchione, K., & Shaywitz, S. E. (2010). Uncoupling of reading and IQ over time: empirical evidence for a definition of dyslexia. *Psychological Science*, *21*(1), 93–101. doi:10.1177/0956797609354084

Gathercole, S. E., & Alloway, T. P. (2008). *Working memory and learning: A practical guide for teachers*. London, UK: Sage.

Gathercole, S. E., Pickering, S. J., Knight, C., & Stegmann, Z. (2004). Working memory skills and educational attainment: Evidence from National curriculum assessments at 7 and 14 years of age. *Applied Cognitive Psychology, 40*, 1–16. doi:10.1002/acp.934

Gee, J. P. (2003). *What video games teach us about learning and literacy*. New York, NY: Palgrave Macmillan.

Gelman, R., & Gallistel, C. R. (1978). *The child's understanding of number*. Cambridge, MA: Havard University Press.

Goswami, U. (2008). Reading. In Reed, J., & Warner-Rogers, J. (Eds.), *Child neuropsychology concepts, theory, and practice*. West Sussex, UK: Wiley-Blackwell.

Howard-Jones, P. A. (2009). *Neuroscience, learning and technology (14-19)*. Cheshire, UK: Becta.

Javis, H. L., & Gathercole, S. E. (2003). Verbal and non-verbal working memory and achievements on national curriculum tests at 11 and 14 years of age. *Educational and Child Psychology, 20*, 123–140.

Koepp, M. J., Gunn, R. N., Lawrence, A. D., Cunningham, V. J., Dagher, A., & Jonnes, T. (1988). Evidence for striatal dopamine release during a video game. *Nature, 392*, 266–268.

McNab, F., Varrone, A., Farde, A., Jucaite, A., Bystitsky, P., & Frossberg, H. (2009). Changes in cortical dopamine D1 receptor binding associated with cognitive Training. *Science, 323*, 800–802. doi:10.1126/science.1166102

Meyler, A., Keller, T. A., Cherkassky, V. L., Gabrieli, J. D. E., & Just, M. A. (2008). Modifying the brain activation of poor readers during sentence comprehension with extended remedial instruction: A longitudinal study of neuroplasticity. *Neuropsychologia, 46*(10), 2580–2592. doi:10.1016/j.neuropsychologia.2008.03.012

Mitchell, A., & Savill-Smith, C. (2004). *The use of computer and video games for learning: A review of the literature*. Retrieved from http://www.m-learning.org/archive/docs/The%20use%20of%20computer%20and%20video%20games%20for%20learning.pdf

Prensky, M. (2001). *Digital game-based learning*. New York, NY: McGraw Hill.

Reed, J., & Warner-Rogers, J. (2008). *Child neuropsychology concepts, theory, and practice*. West Sussex, UK: Wiley-Blackwell.

Rose, J. (2006). *Independent review of the teaching of reading*. Retrieved from http://media.education.gov.uk/assets/files/pdf/i/independent%20review.pdf

Seymore, P. H. K., Aro, M., & Erskine, J. M. (2003). Foundation literacy acquisition in European orthogphies. *The British Journal of Psychology, 94*, 143–174. doi:10.1348/000712603321661859

Shawitz, S. (2003). *Overcoming dyslexia*. New York, NY: Vintage.

Wechsler, D. (1967). *Wechsler preschool and primary scale of intelligence*. San Antonio, TX: The Psychological Corporation.

Wechsler, D. (1992). *Wechsler Individual Achievement Test*. San Antonio, TX: Harcourt Assessments.

Whitton, N. (2007, December 2-5). *Motivation and computer game based learning.* Paper presented at the Ascilite Workshop on Providing Choices for Learners and Learning, Singapore.

Williams, P. (2008). *Independent review of mathematics teaching in early years settings and primary schools.* Retrieved from http://www.education.gov.uk/publications//eOrderingDownload/Williams%20Mathematics.pdf

Xu, F., & Spelke, E. S. (2000). Large number discrimination in 6-month-old infants. *Cognition, 74,* 1–11. doi:10.1016/S0010-0277(99)00066-9

Ylvisaker, M., Adelson, D., Braga, L. W., Burnett, M., Glang, A., & Feeney, T. (2005). Rehabilitation and ongoing support after pediatric TBI: Twenty years of progress. *The Journal of Head Trauma Rehabilitation, 20,* 95–109. doi:10.1097/00001199-200501000-00009

Ziegler, J. C., & Goswami, U. C. (2005). Reading acquisition, developmental dyslexia and skilled reading across languages: A psycholinguistic grain size theory. *Psychological Bulletin, 131*(1), 3–29. doi:10.1037/0033-2909.131.1.3

This work was previously published in the International Journal of Virtual and Personal Learning Environments, Volume 2, Issue 2, edited by Michael Thomas, pp. 17-29, copyright 2011 by IGI Publishing (an imprint of IGI Global).

Chapter 13
Personal Smartphones in Primary School:
Devices for a PLE?

Beat Döbeli Honegger
University of Teacher Education Central Switzerland, Switzerland

Christian Neff
Primary School Goldau, Switzerland

ABSTRACT

This paper describes the goals and first results of an ongoing two year case study in a European primary school (5th primary class) where the teacher and all students were equipped with a personal smartphone. Students are allowed to use phone and internet services at no charge and to take home their smartphones after school. In this project the students have access to an internet connected computing device which can be used for reading, writing, calculating, drawing, taking photos, listening or recording audio, and communicating. Does this setting help to achieve the goals of the official school curriculum? How do personal smartphones in primary school influence teaching and learning, especially weekly planning ("Wochenplanunterricht") and learning outside school? The paper describes the planning and introduction phase of the project as well as first best practice examples of using personal smartphones in and out of school after five months of use. The authors provide qualitative data from questionnaires with students and parents and quantitative data of phone and internet use. To date the results help to formulate specific research questions for further research and they encourage enlarging the case study to several classes in the near future.

DOI: 10.4018/978-1-4666-2467-2.ch013

INTRODUCTION

Switzerland is on its way into the information society. In recent years Switzerland was number one worldwide regarding per capita expenditure for ICT (IDA IG, 2008) and in 2009 it was ranked 8th worldwide in the ICT development index of the International Telecommunication Union (ITU, 2009). This high ICT saturation also applies to mobile phones and especially to teenagers and mobile phones. In Switzerland teenage ownership of mobile phones is comparable to its neighbouring country Germany, where 86% of 12/13 year old teenagers own a mobile phone (MPFS, 2008). As in other countries (OECD, 2005) this high overall ICT saturation contrasts with a relatively low use of ICT in Swiss schools. Swiss School ICT administrators mention four main reasons why Swiss teachers do not use ICT in class more often (Barras & Petko, 2007):

- 70.5% mention a lack of competences among teachers to use ICT in class.
- 63.8% say that there are not enough devices available in class for learners.
- 59.3% mention lack of time among teachers to prepare lessons with ICT or exploring the possibilities of the internet for school use.
- 57.5% see a motivational problem among teachers to integrate ICT in class.

So in spite of a high overall ICT saturation in Switzerland the second most mentioned reason for not using ICT in class more often is lack of hardware among learners. This leads to a paradoxical situation: More and more learners in Switzerland own mobile internet-capable multimedia devices, but are not allowed to bring them to class. In the past two years several Swiss school districts have banned mobile phones from school or are planning to do so.

Because the technological development continues, one can assume that in five years from now 90% of the 12/13-year olds will own smartphones. The pilot project described in this paper has been started to show that there is another way of dealing with smartphones than banning them from school and to gain experience with the learners' personal mobile internet.

THE IDEA BEHIND THE GOLDAU IPHONE PROJECT

In a two year pilot project all 17 students of a 5th grade class in Goldau received a personal smartphone (Apple iPhone 3G) in fall 2009, which they could take home and use outside of school after an introductionary eight week phase. The students are allowed to use phone and internet services free of charge. For at least two years the students have anytime and anywhere a device at their disposal for reading, writing, calculating, drawing, taking pictures, listening to music, recording sound, making phone calls as well as browsing the internet and communication via various channels. While using the device in and out of school, the students shall learn to use the smartphone as part of their personal learning environment. The students have to learn to deal with ubiquitous computing and internet in an emancipated manner.

The project has been initiated by the Institute for Media and School (IMS) at the University of Teacher Education Central Switzerland (PHZ). Devices and communication costs are sponsored by Swisscom, the largest Swiss telecommunication company. It is assured that neither the local school nor parents or students have to pay anything during the two year project period.

Up to now this project seems to be the first long term smartphone project in Europe, where the learners are allowed to take the devices home. The project can be seen in the perspective of Alan Kay as an implementation of his dynabook vision of 1972 (Kay, 1972), where he proposed personal internetworked computers for "children of all ages". The project combines aspects of one-to-one learning (Sharples et al., 2005; Chan et al., 2006), handhelds in education (Soloway et al., 2001; Norris & Soloway, 2004) and mobile learning (Sharples, 2005; Pachler & Bachmair, 2010).

PREPARATION PHASE

Before distributing the smartphones to the students in August 2009 there was a longer preparation phase. After finding a sponsor for the project without obligations for the school, the teacher or the students it was necessary to gain the confidence of the school authorities and the parents involved. The first parent-teacher conference was rather unusual as the class did not yet exist when the conference took place. After the parent-teacher conference the parents were given one week of respite before all the parents agreed with the project. The parents' main concern was envy of siblings and students outside the project. There was not much project-specific teacher preparation as the involved teacher is the local school ICT manager and has worked with the University of Teacher Education Central Switzerland in pedagogical ICT projects for several years. There wasn't much technical preparation either. No special deployment software or internet filtering was installed. The smartphones were set up nearly identical as a private user would initialise them.

INTRODUCTION PHASE

The smartphones were distributed in the first week of 5th grade in August 2009. In the first weeks the students were not allowed to take home the smartphones. In the introduction phase emphasis was not on technology but on prevention. The students learned about dangers and behavior on the internet both from their teacher and external experts. The students developed a written agreement with rules for the use of their smartphones in and out of school (Neff, 2009c). Previous experience shows

that students are more rigorous when they have to write their own rules and that compliance is higher compared to teacher-given rules. Before they were allowed to take home the smartphone the students and their parents had to sign the agreement. In the first nine month of the project the compliance to the agreement was very good. After more than six month the students were even able to recall all the points of the agreement by heart. Before letting the students take the smartphones out of school there was another project-specific parent-teacher conference where the parents learned how to use their child's smartphone and how to control the programs installed and the websites visited.

EXPERIENCES IN THE FIRST NINE MONTHS

Explicit Use

The smartphones have been used in various ways in the first nine months of the project. The teacher did not change the timetable, there was no such thing as a school subject "iPhone". But on several occasions the teacher told the students to use the smartphone in class. In most cases the students used the generic, not school-specific applications already preinstalled by Apple (called apps on the iPhone). Important usages in the first nine months were:

- Search for information on the web, using the web browser or the Wikipedia app.
- Learning words in a foreign language (English, French) with a dedicated app (Neff, 2009a).
- Mental arithmetic training with a dedicated app (Neff, 2009b).
- Look up spelling with a dedicated app.
- Listening comprehension and pronunciation practice in foreign language learning (English, French) with sound files from the

official teaching material provided as podcasts by the teacher

- Dictation practice and assessment with sound files recorded by the teacher enhancing equal practice opportunities for students with non German speaking parents (Neff, 2010a)

The smartphone is also used as a personal information manager (PIM):

- Use of a class calendar for birthdays, excursions, assessments etc. The calendar is fed by the teacher and automatically synchronized to all smartphones (Neff, 2009e).
- The smartphone is used as an email client for the official email account all students have.

Besides these common tasks where the teacher encouraged the students to use their smartphone there were also some special projects using the smartphones:

- Plan and produce stop motion films with the integrated camera (Neff, 2009d).
- Document the school trip.
- Visit at the local art gallery where the students had to take photos of an interesting picture and highlight certain details with an imaging app on the smartphone (Neff, 2010b).
- Explaining how to use the iPhone to university lecturers and therefore reversing the teacher student role (Döbeli Honegger, 2010b).

Implicit Use

In addition to the teacher initiated uses of the smartphones the students themselves found ways to use the devices for learning purposes in and out of school:

- The integrated camera has turned out to be very important for note taking. Students often take photos of information they need for their work or they have to remember.
- Students found out that they can prove the completion of some tasks by sending a screenshot of the app they used to the teacher.

Phone Calls

From a technological perspective GSM and UMTS connectivity for voice calls and internet is the main new functionality of this smartphone project compared to earlier one-to-one handheld and notebook projects. So an interesting question is how this anytime and anywhere connectivity would be used by the students. Overuse of the phone call functionality resulting in high (virtual) phone bills and escapism was a main concern of opponents of the project. Intermediate results after nine month show that phone calls are not as important as widely assumed. Figure 1 shows the total duration of outgoing phone calls per student in the first seven month of the project and Figure 2 shows the average of the total duration of outgoing phone calls over all 17 students. In the first seven month of the projects students made calls for about 20 minutes per month on average.

One fear of critics of the project was phone calls during class. The disturbance from phones ringing during class and students trying to take the phone call or silence the smartphone would distract from learning. The teacher and the students said after the first two months of the project that there were no phone calls during class. Figure 3 proves them right. It shows all 245 outgoing phone calls in October 2009. Each phone call is represented by a circle positioned at the starting time and day of the call (enlarged by factor 10 compared to the time axis). Only one phone call took place during class: 37 seconds on a Friday. The teacher

Figure 1. Duration of outgoing phone calls per student and month between September 2009 and March 2010

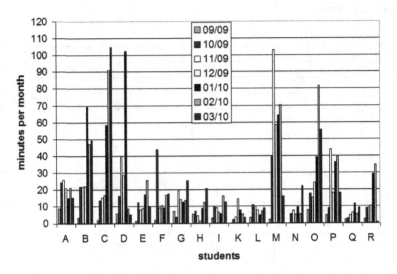

could explain this call: A student got sick and was told to call his parents if somebody was home.

An interesting question is who the students call. Figure 4 shows the total duration of outgoing calls between September 2009 and March 2010 and the amount of time used to call other students inside the same class, the teacher and other people. On average the students used 33% of their talking time on the phone to call other students inside the same class. Up to now we do not know

which amount of this time is used to discuss school subjects.

While phone calls are not as important as expected, the mobile internet is heavily used (Figure 5). Although there is WLAN available inside the school building and 7 out of 17 students have WLAN at home, the amount of data transmitted per student over UMTS is about 300 Mbytes per month. Up to now we have no data *where* mobile internet is used and what kind of data is transmitted.

Figure 2. Average of the total duration of outgoing phone calls between September 2009 and March 2010

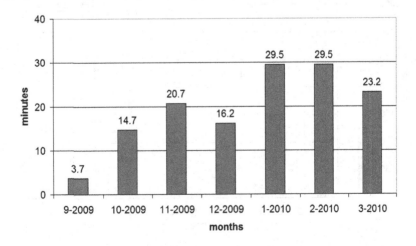

Figure 3. All 245 outgoing phone calls in October 2009 and class schedule plotted on a day/time dia-gram. For visibility reasons the duration of the phone calls (diameter of the circles) are enlarged by factor 10 compared to the time axis

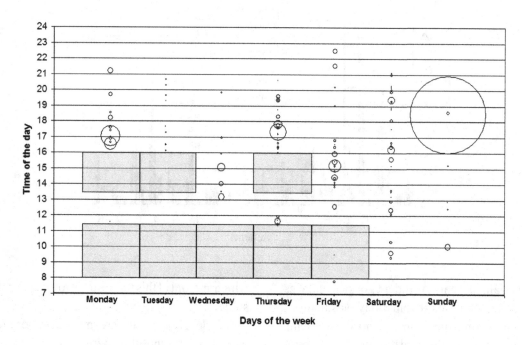

Figure 4. Duration of outgoing phone calls per student and month between September 2009 and March 2010 to other students, the teacher and third parties

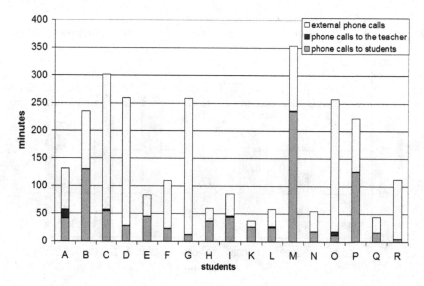

Figure 5. Mobile data traffic per student and month

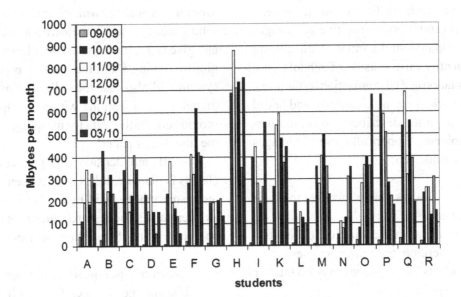

SMARTPHONES AS PART OF A PLE?

There are various definitions of the term Personal Learning Environment (PLE) (Figure 6) (Döbeli Honegger, 2010a). Some authors define a PLE as the collection of software tools someone uses for learning (Attwell, 2007) while others see a PLE as a combination of only web based social software tools. Schulmeister (2009) on the other hand provides a wide definition of a PLE including non digital artifacts and even non tangible aspects like the personal history and memory of the learner. Common to all definitions of the term PLE is the focus on the learner, his/her activity and the self regulation of the learning process. So the

Figure 6. The learning environment of the project class including digital and analogue tools and media

more general question is if personal smartphones support or even foster self-organized learning.

Anderson (2006) points out five advantages of PLEs compared to Learning Management Systems: identity (also outside of school), ease of use (installation and customization by the user), ownership, social presence, capacity and speed of innovation. In the described project the personal smartphones support all these advantages identified by Anderson:

- Students always have access to their smartphone.
- Students are always connected to the internet and therefore to their colleagues.
- The students' smartphones have no filter or limitations for content.
- Students are allowed to install their own applications on the device.
- Students personalize their smartphone with cases, stickers and personal content (music, pictures etc.)

On the one hand students have to learn when the use of the smartphone helps them with their learning; on the other hand students also have to learn how to deal with the possible distractions and the potential of addiction of such devices. First observations show that some students are able to find new ways of using the smartphone for learning purposes while other students only use the smartphone for tasks their teacher told them to do. Surprisingly, some students leave their smartphone in school over lunch time, overnight and in rare cases even over the weekend.

OUTLOOK

In Fall 2010 the students will start using an ePortfolio system called lerntagebuch.ch, (learninglog. org) developed by the Institute for School and Media (Moser & Petko, 2007). This consists of a personal weblog based on the blogging system Wordpress enhanced with school specific privacy settings and features for the teacher to ask questions and give tasks. Its aim is to foster learning strategies by writing about the learning process. This system will also ease the collection of students' thoughts about learning with a smartphone and provide qualitative data for the question posed in the title of this paper.

For 2011 an extension of the project with more classes is planned. It has not yet been decided if more smartphones will be used or if the iPad is an alternative. The research questions will focus on one or more of the following aspects:

- **Learner's perspective:** Do personal mobile internet devices foster self regulated learning?
- **Teacher's perspective:** What are best practices for integrating personal mobile internet devices into a teacher oriented education?
- **Media pedagogical perspective:** Is the integration of personal mobile internet devices in school an effective strategy to help students handle the dangerous aspects of ubiquitous computing?
- **Techno-societal perspective:** Is a closed system as the Apple iOS-ecosystem suitable for school?

REFERENCES

Anderson, T. (2006). *PLEs versus LMS: Are PLEs ready for prime time? Virtual Canuck – Teaching and Learning in a Net-Centric World.* Retrieved from http://terrya.edublogs.org/2006/01/09/ples-versus-lms-are-ples-ready-for-prime-time/

Attwell, G. (2007). Personal learning environments – The future of eLearning? *eLearning Papers, 2*(1).

Barras, J.-L., & Petko, D. (2007). *School and Internet in Switzerland: Overview and developments between 2001 and 2007.* Retrieved from http://doebe.li/t07870

Chan, T.-W., Roschelle, J., Hsi, S., Sharples, K. M., Brown, T., & Patton, C. (2006). One-to-one technology enhanced learning – An opportunity for global research collaboration. *Research and Practice in Technology Enhanced Learning, 1*(1), 3–29. doi:10.1142/S1793206806000032

Döbeli Honegger, B. (2009). *Wann wird telefoniert? Nicht im Unterricht!* Retrieved from http://www.projektschule-goldau.ch/permalink/757

Döbeli Honegger, B. (2010a). *Beats Biblionetz: Begriffe: Personal Learning Environment (PLE).* Retrieved from http://doebe.li/w01997

Döbeli Honegger, B. (2010b) *iPhone-Weiterbildung für PH-Dozierende.* Retrieved from http://www.projektschule-goldau.ch/permalink/869

Interdepartementaler Ausschuss Informationsgesellschaft (IDA IG). (2008). *Informationsgesellschaft Schweiz in Zahlen. In Bericht des Interdepartementalen Ausschusses Informationsgesellschaft für die Jahre 2006 - 2008 zur Umsetzung der Strategie des Bundesrates für eine Informationsgesellschaft in der Schweiz.* Retrieved from http://doebe.li/t09186

International Telecommunication Union (ITU). (2009). *Measuring the information society.* Retrieved from http://doebe.li/b04033

Kay, A. (1972, August). A personal computer for children of all ages. In *Proceedings of the Annual ACM National Conference*, Boston, MA (p. 1).

Medienpädagogischer Forschungsverbund Südwest (MPFS). (2008). *KIM-Studie 2008.* Retrieved from http://doebe.li/b03536

Moser, T., & Petko, D. (2007). Lerntagebuch.ch, Lernstrategien mit Weblogs fördern. *Unterricht Konkret 2007*(6), 44.

Neff, C. (2009a). *iMemento – Effektiv lernen mit Karteikarten.* Retrieved from http://www.projektschule-goldau.ch/permalink/314

Neff, C. (2009b). *Kopfrechnen – da wird geübt!* Retrieved from http://www.projektschule-goldau.ch/permalink/478

Neff, C. (2009c). *Vertrag – gemeinsam erarbeitet.* http://www.projektschule-goldau.ch/permalink/624

Neff, C. (2009e). *Kalender – Agenda für die ganze Klasse.* Retrieved from http://www.projektschule-goldau.ch/permalink/473

Neff, C. (2010a). *Diktat ohne stress.* Retrieved from http://www.projektschule-goldau.ch/permalink/857

Neff, G. (2009d). *iMotion – Trickfilme machen.* Retrieved from http://www.projektschule-goldau.ch/permalink/736

Neff, G. (2010b). *Kunst mit iPhone.* Retrieved from http://www.projektschule-goldau.ch/permalink/978

Norris, C., & Soloway, E. (2004). Envisioning the handheld-centric classroom. *Journal of Educational Computing Research, 30*(4), 281–294. doi:10.2190/MBPJ-L35D-C4K6-AQB8

OECD (Ed.). (2005). *Are students ready for a technology-rich world? – What PISA studies tell us* (p. 37). Paris, France: OECD.

Pachler, N., & Bachmair, B. (2010). *Mobile learning.* New York, NY: Springer. doi:10.1007/978-1-4419-0585-7

Schulmeister, R. (2009). *PLE zwischen Alltäglichem und Besonderem – Was konstituiert eigentlich eine LERNumgebung?* Paper presented at the Conference Personal Learning Environments in der Schule, Goldau.

Sharples, M. (2005). *Big issues in mobile learning.* Retrieved from http://mlearning.noe-kaleidoscope.org/repository/BigIssues.pdf

Sharples, M., Taylor, J., & Vavoula, G. (2005). Towards a theory of mobile learning. In *Proceedings of the Mobile Learning Conference,* Birmingham, AL.

Soloway, E., Becker, H. J., Norris, C., & Topp, N. (2001). Handheld devices are ready-at-hand. *Communications of the ACM, 44*(6), 15–20. doi:10.1145/376134.376140

Section 3
Change

Chapter 14

Personal Learning Environments:
Concept or Technology?

Sebastian H. D. Fiedler
Centre for Social Innovation, Austria & University of Turku, Finland

Terje Väljataga
Tallinn University, Estonia

ABSTRACT

This paper reviews and critiques how the notion of PLEs has been conceptualised and discussed in literature so far. It interprets the variability of its interpretations and conceptualisations as the expression of a fundamental contradiction between patterns of activity and digital instrumentation in formal education on one hand, and individual experimentation and experience within the digital realm on the other. It is suggested to place this contradiction in the larger socio-historic context of an ongoing media transformation. Thus, the paper argues against the prevalent tendency to base the conceptualisation of PLEs almost exclusively on Web 2.0 technologies that are currently available or emerging, while underlying patterns of control and responsibility often remain untouched. Instead, it proposes to scrutinise these patterns and to focus educational efforts on supporting adult learners to model their learning activities and potential (personal learning) environments while exploring the digital realm.

INTRODUCTION

It seems fair to say that in recent years the notion of "Personal Learning Environments" (PLEs) emerged mainly as a sort of counter-concept to the centralised provision of institutionally owned and controlled landscapes of tools and services in formal education. Fundamentally, it allowed its proponents to address and question the severe limitations of the mainstream approach to the mediation of teaching and studying activities with digital technologies. The emergence and growing

DOI: 10.4018/978-1-4666-2467-2.ch014

dissemination of loosely-coupled, networked tools and services and their surrounding practices in particular inspired some scholars to speculate about a transformation of the monolithic, centralised systems that dominated and are still dominating formal education. Downes (2005), for example wrote: "The e-learning application, therefore, begins to look very much like a blogging tool. It represents one node in a web of content, connected to other nodes and content creation services used by other students. It becomes ... a personal learning center, where content is reused and remixed according to the student's own needs and interests. It becomes, indeed, not a single application, but a collection of interoperating applications - an environment rather than a system" (section on "E-Learning 2.0).

Looking back two years later Downes (2007) reflected that "through 2005 and 2006, the concept of the Personal Learning Environment (PLE) slowly began to take form in the educational technology community, coalescing with a 'Future VLE' diagram released by CETIS's Scott Wilson" (p. 19).

Indeed, retrospectively it appears that the visual representation of Wilson's Future Virtual Learning Environment (VLE) (Wilson, 2005) served as a sort of anchor for the discourse on Personal Learning Environments for quite some time. According to Severance et al. (2008) the CETIS (Centre for Educational Technology & Interoperability Standards) group however, traces some of the ideas that drove the early stage of this discourse to an unpublished paper by Oliver and Liber (2001).

Be that as it may, Johnson et al. (2006) suggested that over the years the discourse gradually developed around a number of foci that can be interpreted as an expression of a desire for:

- Greater personal ownership of technology and data.
- More effective ways of managing technological tools and services.

- The integration of technologically mediated activities across all aspects of life.
- A removal of barriers to the use and combination of tools and services.
- Mediated collaboration and co-creation.

We will argue later in this paper that these "desires" actually occur in a specific socio-historic context and that they can also be read as an expression of a rising contradiction experienced in various activity systems and in formal education in particular.

A WIDE RANGE OF INTERPRETATIONS AND CONCEPTUALISATIONS

There are clear signs that over the years a wide range of conceptualisations and interpretations have surfaced in the ongoing debates and exchanges. Attwell (2007b), for example, reported his experience at a conference in the following terms: "there was no consensus on what a Personal Learning Environment (PLE) might be. The only thing most people seemed to agree on was that it was not a software application. Instead it was more of a new approach to using technologies for learning" (p. 1). Even this minimal consensus appears to be rather questionable after a thorough literature review on the topic. Kolas and Staupe (2007) also contested that "the variety of interpretation illustrates how diffuse the PLE concept still is" (p. 750). Johnson and Liber (2008) only recently asserted that "within this label, however, a number of practices and descriptions have emerged - not all of which are compatible, and discussions have raged as to the interpretation of the terms" (p. 3). This doesn't sound much different from what Johnson et al. (2006) had concluded already two years earlier: "This is a title that embraces a variety of different interpretations, and this essential ambiguity is reflected in the discourse that has emerged around it ... That such a variety of interpretation can emerge around the same terminology is indicative of a lack of clarity defining exactly what a PLE is" (p. 182). There is very little indication that this state of affairs has substantially improved or is currently improving.

PERSONAL LEARNING ENVIRONMENTS AS A CONCEPT OR APPROACH

Some authors clearly suggest treating the notion of Personal Learning Environments as a concept or approach. Attwell (2007a), for example, states explicitly that "it is critical that PLEs are being seen as not just a new application of educational technology, but rather as a concept. The development of Personal Learning Environments represents a significant shift in pedagogic approaches to how we support learning processes" (p. 59).

Downes (2007) seems to express a similar view when he writes: "The PLE is a recognition that the 'one size fits all' approach characteristic of the LMS (Learning Management System) will not be sufficient to meet the varied needs of students. It is, indeed not a software application per se, but is rather a characterisation of an approach to e-learning" (p. 20). He adds that "the key to understanding the PLE consists not in understanding a particular type of technology so much as in understanding the thinking that underlies the concept" (p. 20).

Johnson et al. (2006) also seemed to have a rather conceptual perspective in mind: "When examining current technologies, the PLE 'lens' affords us two key actions,... it allows us to critique current technologies, situating them in terms of what might be characterised as their 'PLE compliance'. Secondly, it generates a 'migration path' to move a current technology from a position of partial PLE-ness to full compliance" (p. 187).

Johnson and Liber (2008) on the other hand got a lot more specific when they suggested that "the Personal Learning Environment (PLE) concept

has emerged within the UK and abroad as a label associated with the application of the technologies of web 2.0 and Service Oriented Architecture to education" (p. 3). This particular view seems to be largely shared by Kerres (2007) who claimed that "for the user, this "personal learning environment" is not a separate space on the internet, it is an essential part of the users' workspace. It should be highly integrated with the user's framework of tools for his/her personal use of the internet" (p. 11). How this should be achieved remains rather obscure and Kerres seems to prefer a traditional distribution of roles. He envisions that "an instructional designer would arrange some of the materials and tools the learner will work on, but would also arrange the environment to be open to the vast sources and tools the internet provide, thus, providing a soft transition between the learning environment and the "other" internet" (p. 11). Nevertheless, he expects that "the learners themselves are gaining competencies to construct their personal environments where they select and sequence contents available on the internet" (p. 11).

Wilson et al. (2006) talked about a design pattern: "The critical design flaws inherent in today's learning systems can be addressed through adopting a new design pattern that shifts emphasis away from the isolated experience of the modular VLE. We characterize this new pattern a Personal Learning Environment, although unlike the VLE this is primarily a pattern concerned with the practices of users in learning with diverse technologies, rather than a category of software" (p. 4). Their vision leaves room for a broader (re-) instrumentation as it is evident in the following quote: "While we have discussed the PLE design as if it were a category of technology ... in fact we envisage situations where the PLE is not a single piece of software, but instead the collection of tools used by a user to meet their needs as part of their personal working and learning routine. So, the characteristics of the PLE design may be achieved using a combination of existing devices (laptops, mobile phones, portable media devices), applications (newsreaders, instant messaging clients, browsers, calendars) and services (social bookmarkservices, weblogs, wikis)" (p. 9).

PERSONAL LEARNING ENVIRONMENTS AS TECHNOLOGICAL SYSTEMS OR TOOL COLLECTIONS

Some authors like van Harmelen (2006) were even more explicit and suggested that "as such, a PLE is a single user's e-learning system that provides access to a variety of learning resources, and that may provide access to learners and teachers who use other PLEs and/or VLEs" (p. 815). This technological view is shared by Kolas and Staupe (2007) who state that "in order to meet the requirements of a PLE, a powerful computer architecture is needed, where it is easy to locate resources based on context and needs. There should also be a powerful search- and navigation system connected to the architecture. The architecture must ensure relevant, complete and consistent information" (p. 751).

Dron and Bhattacharya (2007) offered a rather tautological definition: "PLEs are a collection of interoperating applications that together form an individual's learning environment", while Milligan et al. (2006) seemed to envision a particular set of tools: "In a Personal Learning Environment (PLE), the learner would utilise a single set of tools, customised to their needs and preferences inside a single learning environment" (p. 507). They also suggest "a key technological component ... is the use of Web Services" (p. 508). They also emphasise a Service Oriented Approach (SOA) and the importance of the issue of interoperability. However, Milligan et al. (2006) also acknowledge that "what differentiates a Personal Learning Toolkit from any other type of tool is difficult to pin down in terms of features alone; the critical factors are primarily in how the system is used, by whom, and in the context of use" (p. 509). Nevertheless, these authors also suggested that one should have a look at a "wide range of tools and sites that exhibit what we felt were characteristics useful in a PLE context" (p. 509). In fact, they surveyed a number of ICT tools and identified 77 recurring patterns of use that they further categorised into nine distinct groups. They further identified a number of key services that recur in the patterns. Together, these use patterns and services make up their PLE Reference model. This reference model was used to create two PLE toolsets (a standalone desktop application and a portal based solution).

Chan et al. (2005) claim that foremost "the complexity of engaging with information and communication must be reduced" (p. 73). Their Interactive Logbook (IL) "is designed to address shortcomings of traditional VLEs through an integrated solution that allows learners to "access, piece together and manage the learning they do throughout their life, in a range of institutional, informal and work-based settings ... The PLE provides each student with a set of learning management tools to run on a wireless laptop or tablet computer" (p. 74). They seem to envision an all encompassing interface that "provides an integrated set of tools to support learning, including office, communications and web applications. Rather than replacing familiar packages such as Microsoft Office, IL presents documents, email, spreadsheets etc. within a single frame, with a set of tabs to switch between them" (p. 75).

Severance et al. (2008), for example, see personal learning environments married to the tools and services that are commonly labelled Web 2.0: "PLEs start with the current and expanding capabilities of the World Wide Web, especially those referred to often as 'Web 2.0' capabilities, those involving individual site customization of appearance, resource feeds, tools and tool placement, and increasingly group or social interactions, and add organizing mechanisms and tools focused on educational efforts to produce an environment that can be optimized for learning" (p. 48).

Johnson et al. (2006) emphasise the issue of interoperability: "The PLE reference model proposes a learning environment of interoperable services which may be accessed and organized through a variety of toolkits, where both tools and services may be selected by the learner without prejudice. To facilitate this, there are technical conditions to be met in terms of standards for interoperability and the eventual total separation of services from instruments" (p. 187). In addition, they claim that "the increasing integration of Web syndication into the functionality of the operating system represents a gradual evolution of the operating system into something which is more PLE-like" (p. 188).

This exemplary and somewhat impressionistic summary certainly serves to illustrate the overarching tendency to discuss personal learning environments either exclusively in relation to the current developments of Web technologies, or to even reduce it to a mere synonym for some sort to technological system or set of tools. If scrutinised, the claim of some authors that the term should be rather understood as a "concept" or "approach" and not as technology, often appears to be little more than lip service. Altogether, the current state of the literature on personal learning environments suffers from a wide range of, partially incommensurable, interpretations and conceptualisations.

IS THE VARIETY AN EXPRESSION OF PROFESSIONAL ORIENTATIONS OR MORE FUNDAMENTAL CONTRADICTIONS?

It seems obvious that part of the attested variability of interpretations and conceptualisations can be attributed to the various professional identities and orientations of the people who feel attracted to work on issues around the digital (re-) instrumentation of activities related to instruction and study.

Proponents of computer science, for example, are naturally more drawn to the computational (re-) engineering challenges in that area. Educational researchers and practitioners, on the other hand, tend to focus on the overall re-organization and re-instrumentation potentials for typical core activities in educational settings. It is not surprising, that the influence of these differing professional and disciplinary orientations is undeniably reflected in the current state of the discourse on personal learning environments.

However, some of the variability that we observe in the discourse can also be interpreted as an expression of a contradiction that is more fundamental and that is perceived and individually processed in rather different ways. We think that the emergence of "personal learning environment" as a counter-concept can also be understood as an expression of a growing conflict and tension that was, and still is, experienced by individual educational researchers and practitioners.

The situation could be described as the following: On one hand educational institutions have cultivated elaborate systems around a number of core activities (and their objects). These activity systems (Engeström, 1987) tend to absorb new instrumentation options (from the digital realm) while leaving the general patterns of control and responsibility (rules, division of labour, etc.) largely untouched (Fiedler & Pata, 2009). Central control and provision of instruments (for its core activities) has been a dominant pattern in these institutions for centuries. No wonder that the system tended to "process" emerging developmental offers in the digital realm accordingly. The result was the creation of Course Management Systems and a palette of digital instruments to be used in specific instructional activities.

On the other hand a growing number of individuals experience that the digital realm is penetrating or absorbing more and more activities in their life. They experience the digital instrumentation of all types of activities (in the workplace, in their social life with friends and family, related to hobbies and leisure, and so forth). Naturally, these individuals begin to experiment with the self-controlled, digital instrumentation also in relation to their learning activities (formal or non-formal). Within this self-directed instrumentation of activities particular patterns of control and responsibility, ownership, provision, and so forth, emerge. These compete with, contrast, and contradict the patterns that are still driving the institutional practices. From a historical perspective, the emergence of the term "personal learning environment" can be understood as an expression of this very contradiction and incompatibility experienced by educational researchers and practitioners already "living in" (not only with) the digital realm. The term that they created to express their tension, however, was and still is processed in fundamentally different ways within the wider research community.

PERSONAL LEARNING ENVIRONMENTS: WHAT IS IN THE TERM?

In principle there are two, fundamentally different, ways one can conceptually "slice" the term "personal learning environment". These two, fundamentally different, conceptions are reflected in the current state of the discourse and continuously surface in the literature on PLEs.

There is a large group of proponents who basically think and write about "(personal) learning environments". Their notion or understanding of the term focuses almost exclusively on issues of (re-)instrumentation of teaching and studying activity. They treat issues of personalization, selection, maybe adaptation, the separation of form and function, and so forth. All these issues tend to be discussed almost exclusively in relation to the existing (or emerging) state of the leading medium: Web standards, services, applications and so forth (for some recent examples see Godwin-

Jones, 2009; Taraghi, Ebner, Till, & Mühlburger, 2009; Zubrinic & Kalpic, 2008). In many cases, fundamental contradictions within the overall activity system are completely ignored or remain untouched.

In contrast to this former, rather technologically oriented, conceptualisation of the term it is equally possible to explore the notion of "(personal learning) environments", or to rephrase slightly, "environments for/of personal learning". Researchers and practitioners, who process the concept accordingly, tend to be more concerned with individuals (or groups) gaining control over their (intentional) learning activities (formal and non-formal) and their instrumentation (see for example Attwell, 2007b; Downes, 2007; Johnson & Liber, 2008).

For educational theorising and research this second reading of the term seems to be far more appropriate and fruitful. First, it appears to be rather short sighted to base the further development of "personal learning environments" as a concept on the current, and certainly transient, state of the Web, as an emerging leading medium.

Second, an educational concept eventually needs to be rooted in an explicit (human) change perspective to develop and maintain any lasting, generative power for theorizing and empirical research in education.

A review of recent literature on Personal Learning Environments (Attwell, 2007a, 2007b; Bhattacharya & Dron, 2007; Chan, Corlett, Sharples, Ting, & Westmancott, 2005; Costello, 2007; Downes, 2007; Dron & Bhattacharya, 2007; Godwin-Jones, 2009; Johnson, Beauvoir et al., 2006; Johnson & Liber, 2008; Johnson et al., 2006; Kerres, 2007; Kolas & Staupe, 2007; Lubensky, 2007; Mazzoni & Gaffuri, 2009; Milligan et al., 2006; Neuhaus, 2007; Olivier & Liber, 2001; Pilkington, Meek, Corlett, & Chan, 2006; Severance et al., 2008; Taraghi et al., 2009; Tindal, Powell, & Millwood, 2007; van Harmelen, 2006, 2008; Wilson, 2005, 2008; Wilson et al., 2006;

Zubrinic & Kalpic, 2008), however, produced only a single contribution (Johnson & Liber, 2008) in which the authors make an explicit attempt to anchor an exploration of the concept of personal learning environments within a model of "the personal learner" (p. 3). Though we have referred to and made explicit use of different models (Harri-Augstein & Cameron-Webb, 1996; Harri-Augstein & Thomas, 1991; Thomas & Harri-Augstein, 1985) in earlier works (Fiedler, 2003; Sharma & Fiedler, 2007), we have recently made an explicit effort (Fiedler & Väljataga, in press) of describing our work in direct conversation with the propositions and terminological distinctions made by Johnson and Liber. While this paper is certainly not the place for a detailed description of such modelling efforts, it seems important to emphasise that there is certainly a general and somewhat discomforting lack of theorising on the "personal learning" aspect of the concept under reflection here.

CONSIDERING THE SOCIO-HISTORIC CONTEXT OF THE EMERGENCE OF THE NOTION OF PERSONAL LEARNING ENVIRONMENTS

The contradiction that we have described above in relation to the dominant (digital) instrumentation of current formal education, and the agency experienced by individuals who "live in" the digital realm, should not be seen in isolation. Rückriem (2009), for example, only recently reminded us that digitalization "has penetrated every societal process and every societal activity system" (p. 88) and that "global digitalization and networking represent the specific 'leading' and epoch-making medium of our present time and provide totally new and rather inexhaustible potentials to human practice" (p. 89). We currently cannot grasp, let alone predict, the direction and extent of all related

transformation processes. The emergence of a new "leading"- or even "dominating" - medium undoubtedly poses formidable developmental challenges for individuals and current activity systems.

Individually and collectively we seem to be living through a transition phase that produces mounting contradictions for existing activity systems and individuals. The emerging leading medium, however, is gradually changing what we perceive as a potential object of activity, or an artefact that can be turned into a helpful instrument. We see this as a co-evolutionary process, since human needs, imagination, and activity in turn will shape the further development of the leading medium and new human abilities emerge. No doubt that individual and collective learning activity (formal or non-formal) is equally affected by these transformations. Educational intervention and research needs to respond to these challenges and support the necessary individual and collective developmental moves and trajectories.

Since we are still in the early stages of a massive, co-evolutionary transition phase that will most likely result in the emergence of computation, digitisation, and the overall digital realm as *the* dominant medium, we need to expect a disparity in developmental trajectories of "living in and with the digital realm". In many ways we can currently witness how more and more areas of human activity get gradually augmented and transformed by getting "morphed" into the digital realm. In early stages of this process the dominating developmental move seems to be the search for and acquisition of functional equivalents (e-mail replaces letters or phone calls), then new configurations of instruments are explored, and finally new affordances (potentials for action) emerge through a co-evolutionary development of the dominant medium and human dispositions. Education and its digital (re-)instrumentation is no exception to this general pattern.

EDUCATIONAL WORK IN THE FACE OF THE ONGOING TRANSFORMATION

Early stages of fundamental media transformations in general seem to be dominated by the replication of old patterns within the new medium (Giesecke, 2002). Therefore, it should come with very little surprise that many educators and educational researchers seem to maintain the view that it is quite appropriate to limit their efforts on the (re-) design, (re-)instrumentation, and implementation of particular learning activities, while mostly reproducing traditional patterns of control and responsibility. In fact, this position and enactment is somewhat to be expected. However, from an educational perspective it certainly needs to be addressed.

In the light of the ongoing socio-economic developments and the emergence of digitalisation and networking as the leading or dominant medium (Rückriem, 2003, 2009) for the co-evolutionary transformation of individual and collective life (way of being) and its instrumentation, we need to scrutinize traditional patterns of control and responsibility in education, and in higher education in particular.

From an educational intervention perspective, we need to make an attempt to re-configure learning activities so that the individual personal adult learners can actualize and execute control and responsibility on that level by modelling and actively shaping their own (personal) learning activity and its specific (personal learning) environment (Fiedler & Väljataga, 2010; Väljataga & Fiedler, 2009). It is important to note here that any (intentional) learning activity, be it attached to a formal educational setting or not, can potentially benefit from the personal modelling of the activity itself and the active shaping of a specific (personal learning) environment for its execution.

We consider it as a valuable, educational goal in itself, that the individual develops personal control of different types of (intentional) learning activity (formal or not), a certain level of transitory fluency between them, and the active shaping of their specific (personal learning) environments. We think that this goal merits diverse and multi-faceted educational interventions (see for example Väljataga, 2010) that hold the potential to open up progressive, developmental moves for the personal (adult) learner.

To summarise:

- We need to scrutinise traditional patterns of control and responsibility in (higher) education.
- Personal (adult) learners need to be able to model and actively shape their own learning activities and their specific environments.
- A potential (personal learning) environment for a particular learning activity is made of all the resources (artefacts, natural objects, people) that an individual is aware of and has access to at a given point in time and that s/he can turn into instruments to mediate her actions (Fiedler & Pata, 2009).
- We need to stimulate the explicit exploration of the digital realm in relation to particular learning activities and the conscious shaping of their potential (personal learning) environments.

CONCLUSION

Since we seem to be living in an early stage of a fundamental media transformation (digitalisation and networking) (Erdmann & Rückriem, 2010) that currently can be characterized by a huge disparity and variety of developmental stages and trajectories, we should not orientate our conceptualisations of human change and development (in education, counselling, therapy, and so forth) on the current state of the leading medium and its most prominent artefacts (digital, material, or conceptual).

If we do so, we run the risk that many individuals simply engage in the temporary exploration of a succession of "new toys" without ever connecting their experiences with a wider model of themselves as personal (adult) learners (Fiedler & Väljataga, forthcoming). A simple collection of potential resources (artefacts, natural objects, people) does not make a "personal learning environment," if there is no personal model of (intentional) learning activity in the first place, or if people run on out-dated models from previous times (Thomas & Harri-Augstein, 2001).

What is currently presented as "personal learning environments" as such, or as their instantiations, obscures the fact that these collections of digital artefacts are mostly a snapshot of the current state of development of the emerging leading medium. From an (adult) educational perspective, however, we need to support individuals (and groups) to gain awareness and control over a range of learning activities and their environments, and eventually their overall development as personal (adult) learners living *in* (and not only with) the digital realm.

REFERENCES

Attwell, G. (2007a). E-portfolios - the DNA of the personal learning environment? *Journal of e-Learning and Knowledge Society, 3*(2), 39-61.

Attwell, G. (2007b). *Personal learning environments - future of eLearning?* Retrieved from http://www.elearningpapers.eu/index. php?page=doc&doc_id=8553&doclng=6

Bhattacharya, M., & Dron, J. (2007). Cultivating the Web 2.0 jungle. In *Proceedings of the 7th IEEE International Conference on Advanced Learning Technologies* (pp. 897-898). Washington, DC: IEEE Computer Society.

Chan, T., Corlett, D., Sharples, M., Ting, J., & Westmancott, O. (2005). Developing interactive logbook: A personal learning environment. In *Proceedings of the IEEE International Workshop on Wireless and Mobile Technologies in Education* (pp. 73-75). Washington, DC: IEEE Computer Society.

Costello, F. (2007). *The development of personal learning environments.* Retrieved from http://www.ericsson.com/ericsson/corpinfo/programs/resource_documents/ericsson_eden_2007.pdf

Downes, S. (2005). *E-Learning 2.0.* Retrieved from http://www.elearnmag.org/subpage.cfm?section=articles&article=29-1

Downes, S. (2007). *Learning networks in practice.* Retrieved from http://partners.becta.org.uk/f

Dron, J., & Bhattacharya, M. (2007). Lost in the Web 2.0 jungle. In *Proceedings of the 7th IEEE International Conference on Advanced Learning Technologies* (pp. 895-896). Washington, DC: IEEE Computer Society.

Engeström, Y. (1987). *Learning by expanding.* Helsinki, Finland: Orienta-konsultit.

Erdmann, J. W., & Rückriem, G. (2010). Lernkultur oder Lernkulturen - was ist neu an der, Kultur des Lernens. In Rückriem, G., & Giest, H. (Eds.), *Tätitgkeitsteorie und (Wissens-) Gesellschaft* (pp. 15–52). Berlin, Germany: Lehmans Media.

Fiedler, S. (2003). Personal webpublishing as a reflective conversational tool for self-organized learning. In Burg, T. N. (Ed.), *BlogTalks* (pp. 190–216). Norderstedt, Germany: Books on Demand.

Fiedler, S., & Pata, K. (2009). Distributed learning environments and social software: In search for a framework of design. In Hatzipanagos, S., & Warburton, S. (Eds.), *Handbook of research on social software and developing community ontologies* (pp. 145–158). Hershey, PA: IGI Global. doi:10.4018/978-1-60566-208-4.ch011

Fiedler, S., & Väljataga, T. (2010). Interventions for second-order change in higher education: Challenges and barriers. *Electronic Journal of e-Learning, 8*(2), 85-92.

Fiedler, S., & Väljataga, T. (in press). Modeling the personal adult learner: The concept of PLE re-interpreted. In Siemens, G., Downes, S., & Kop, F. (Eds.), *Personal learning environments and personal learning networks*. Athabasca, AB, Canada: Athabasca University.

Giesecke, M. (2002). *Von den Mythen der Buchkultur zu den Visionen der Informationsgesellschaft: Trendforschung zur aktuellen Medienökologie.* Frankfurt, Germany: Suhrkamp.

Godwin-Jones, R. (2009). Emerging technologies: Personal learning environments. *Language Learning & Technology, 13*(2), 3–9.

Harri-Augstein, S., & Cameron-Webb, I. M. (1996). *Learning to change. A resource for trainers, managers, and learners based on self organised learning*. London, UK: McGraw-Hill.

Harri-Augstein, S., & Thomas, L. (1991). *Learning conversations: The self-organised way to personal and organisational growth*. London, UK: Routledge.

Johnson, M., Beauvoir, P., Milligan, C., Sharples, P., Wilson, S., & Liber, O. (2006). Mapping the future: The personal learning environment reference model and emerging technology. In *Proceedings of ALT-C: The Next Generation* (pp. 182-191).

Johnson, M., & Liber, O. (2008). The personal learning environment and the human condition: From theory to teaching practice. *Interactive Learning Environments, 16*(1), 3–15. doi:10.1080/10494820701772652

Johnson, M., Liber, O., Wilson, S., & Milligan, C. (2006). *The personal learning environment: A report on the CETIS PLE project*. Retrieved from http://wiki.cetis.ac.uk/image:plereport.doc

Kerres, M. (2007). *Microlearning as a challenge to instructional design*. Retrieved from http://mediendidaktik.uni-duisburg-essen.de/system/files/Microlearning-kerres.pdf

Kolas, L., & Staupe, A. (2007). The PLExus prototype: A PLE realized as topic maps. In *Proceedings of the 7th IEEE International Conference on Advanced Learning Technologies* (pp. 750-752). Washington, DC: IEEE Computer Society.

Lubensky, R. (2007). *The present and future of personal learning environments (PLE)*. Retrieved from http://members.optusnet.com.au/rlubensky/2006/12/present-and-future-of-personal-learning.html

Mazzoni, E., & Gaffuri, P. (2009). Personal learning environments for overcoming knowledge boundaries between activity systems in emerging adulthood. *eLearning Papers, 15*.

Milligan, C., Johnson, M., Sharples, P., Wilson, S., & Liber, O. (2006). Developing a reference model to describe the personal learning environment. In W. Nejdl & K. Tochtermann (Eds.), *Proceedings of the First European Conference on Innovative Approaches for Learning and Knowledge Sharing* (LNCS 4227, pp. 506-511).

Neuhaus, W. (2007). *Personal learning environments (PLE)*. Retrieved from http://mediendidaktik.port07.de/?p=76

Olivier, B., & Liber, O. (2001). *Lifelong learning: The need for portable personal learning environments and supporting interoperability standards*. Retrieved from http://wiki.cetis.ac.uk/uploads/6/67/Olivierandliber2001.doc

Pilkington, R., Meek, J., Corlett, D., & Chan, T. (2006). Openness to electronic professional development planning: Evaluating the interactive Logbook Project. In *Proceedings of the 6th IEEE International Conference on Advanced Learning Technologies* (pp. 774-778). Washington, DC: IEEE Computer Society Press.

Rückriem, G. (2003). *Tool or medium? The meaning of information and telecommunication technology to human practice. A quest for systemic understanding of activity theory.* Retrieved from http://www.iscar.org/fi/ruckriem.pdf

Rückriem, G. (2009). Digital technology and mediation: A challenge to activity theory. In Sannino, A., Daniels, H., & Gutierrez, K. D. (Eds.), *Learning and expanding with activity theory* (pp. 88–111). Cambridge, UK: Cambridge University Press.

Severance, C., Hardin, J., & Whyte, A. (2008). The coming functionality mash-up in personal learning environments. *Interactive Learning Environments*, *16*(1), 47–62. doi:10.1080/10494820701772694

Sharma, P., & Fiedler, S. (2007). Supporting self-organized learning with personal webpublishing technologies and practices. *Journal of Computing in Higher Education*, *18*(2), 3–24. doi:10.1007/BF03033411

Taraghi, B., Ebner, M., Till, G., & Mühlburger, H. (2009). Personal learning environment - a conceptual study. *International Journal of Emerging Technologies in Learning*, *5*, 25–30.

Thomas, L., & Harri-Augstein, S. (1985). *Self-organised learning: Foundations of a conversational science for psychology*. London, UK: Routledge.

Thomas, L., & Harri-Augstein, S. (2001). Conversational science and advanced learning technologies (ALT). Tools for conversational pedagogy. *Kybernetes*, *30*(7-8), 921–954. doi:10.1108/EUM0000000005917

Tindal, I., Powell, S., & Millwood, R. (2007). *Undergraduate student researchers - the Ultraversity model for work based learning.* Retrieved from http://www.informaworld.com/smpp/content~content=a788481519~db=all~order=page

Väljataga, T. (2010). *Learner control and responsibility: Expanding the concept of self-direction in higher education*. Tampere, Finland: Tampere University of Technology.

Väljataga, T., & Fiedler, S. (2009). Supporting students to self-direct intentional learning projects with social media. *Journal of Educational Technology & Society*, *12*(3), 58–69.

van Harmelen, M. (2006). Personal learning environments. In *Proceedings of the 6th IEEE International Conference on Advanced Learning Technologies* (pp. 815-816). Washington, DC: IEEE Computer Society.

van Harmelen, M. (2008). Design trajectories: Four experiments in PLE implementation. *Interactive Learning Environments*, *16*(1), 35–46. doi:10.1080/10494820701772686

Wilson, S. (2005). *Future VLE - The visual version.* Retrieved from http://zope.cetis.ac.uk/members/scott/blogview?entry=20050125170206

Wilson, S. (2008). Patterns of personal learning environments. *Interactive Learning Environments*, *16*(1), 17–34. doi:10.1080/10494820701772660

Wilson, S., Liber, O., Beauvoir, P., Milligan, C., Johnson, M., & Sharples, P. (2006). *Personal learning environments: Challenging the dominant design of educational systems.* Retrieved from http://hdl.handle.net/1820/727

Zubrinic, K., & Kalpic, D. (2008). The Web as personal learning environment. *International Journal of Emerging Technologies in Learning*, *3*, 45–58.

This work was previously published in the International Journal of Virtual and Personal Learning Environments, Volume 2, Issue 4, edited by Michael Thomas, pp. 1-11, copyright 2011 by IGI Publishing (an imprint of IGI Global).

Chapter 15
Making it Rich and Personal:
Crafting an Institutional Personal Learning Environment

Su White
University of Southampton, UK

Hugh Davis
University of Southampton, UK

ABSTRACT

Many of the communities interested in learning and teaching technologies within higher education now accept the view that a conception of personal learning environments provides the most realistic and workable perspective of learners' interactions with and use of technology. This view may not be reflected in the behaviour of those parts of a university which normally purchase and deploy technology infrastructure. These departments or services are slow to change because they are typically, and understandably, risk-averse, the more so because the consequences of expensive decisions about infrastructure will stay with the organisation for many years. Furthermore across the broader (less technically or educationally informed) academic community, the awareness of and familiarity with technologies in support of learning may be varied. In this context, work to innovate the learning environment will require considerable team effort and collective commitment. This paper presents a case study account of institutional processes harnessed to establish a universal personal learning environment fit for the 21st century.

INTRODUCTION

Contemporary practice in the use of technology has been evolving rapidly in the early years of the 21st century. There has been considerable progress in network technologies, miniaturisation and

telephony services. These changes have made an impact on practice and thinking across all types of computer applications ranging from those which are concerned with large-scale organisational and infrastructural issues through to smaller scale personal and mobile applications.

DOI: 10.4018/978-1-4666-2467-2.ch015

The trend in business and commerce deployment of large-scale computer systems has been to move away from single centralised monolithic architectures towards shared, distributed, architectures. Individual use of technology for the majority in post-industrial countries has become widespread bringing about greater access to personal computers, laptops, netbooks and mobile devices. For many it has led to behaviours which integrate personal technology use into everyday behaviours, extending across the whole range of individual activities; life, leisure and learning. In less developed countries, mobile technologies and distributed architectures plus new business models have enabled or accelerated technology adoption because of the reduction and management of front-loaded infrastructure costs.

However, while individuals can be agile in their response to technology changes, organisations are typically more constrained by the heritage of past decisions and previous investment. In addition organisations can find that they are required to provide consistency over time (in software, platform or infrastructure) for large numbers of individuals with differing needs and requirements. For the organisation these factors can tend to slow the process of change, so that in a time of rapid technological development and adoption the gap between everyday practice and organisational provision tends to increase.

A growing understanding of these difficulties has emerged at the University of Southampton. It has fired an institutional ambition to provide a replacement for parts of the existing technology infrastructure to be known as the 'Southampton Learning Environment'.

This ambition has been influenced to some extent by contemporary development in the modelling of Personal Learning Environments (PLEs). The context is the increasingly widespread use of the social web, increasing understanding of the applications and affordances of Web 2.0, and effective use in our School of Electronics and Computer Science of 'linked data' for educational and associated administrative applications.

As well as being influenced by external technological developments, the requirements for this system have been derived following extensive analysis of existing practice across the University of Southampton. The university initially engaged in an institution-wide e-learning benchmarking exercise that was followed by a large-scale survey of the student experience of technology.

At the same time a set of colleagues concerned with the management of teaching and learning across the institution participated in a national Higher Education Academy (HEA) Enhancement Academy designed to assist organisational change. This latter initiative helped provide some additional impetus required to developed policy to bring about changes in our current practices associated with the digital learning infrastructure. This academy sponsored innovation and change was led by the university director of technology-enhanced learning (TEL) and formed part of a wider network of changes introduced under an umbrella initiative titled the 'Curriculum Innovation Programme'. Thus prepared and armed with a large amount of information the University of Southampton has begun designing the "Southampton Learning Environment" (SLE) as a virtual, adaptable, and innovative environment fit for the next ten years.

LOCAL CONTEXT

The University of Southampton was an early adopter of technology for learning and teaching based on personal computer networks. Prior to the web in the early 1990s the university made an extensive commitment to the use of a locally developed hypertext system called Microcosm. It embarked on an ambitious project to establish a 'campus-wide structure for multimedia learning' (White, 1993). Colleagues across the institution developed approaches to resource-based learning which were subsequently incorporated into mate-

Figure 1. eMM evaluation areas

- **Learning:**
  Processes that directly impact on pedagogical aspects of e-learning

- **Development:**
  Processes surrounding the creation and maintenance of e-learning resources

- **Support:**
  Processes surrounding the support and operational management of e-learning

- **Evaluation:**
  Processes surrounding the evaluation and quality control of e-learning through its entire lifecycle

- **Organisation:**
  Processes associated with institutional planning and management

(adapted from Marshall & Mitchell, 2006)

rials and instructional practice using web-based learning resources and through taught modules delivered by the institutional virtual learning environment (VLE).

Over a ten-year period academics' attitudes to and use of technology across the university were tracked and analysed. It was observed that usage grew alongside national and international trends which saw an expansion of the ownership of technology and increasing use of the web as a platform for publication (White, 2006).

Over this period university-wide commitment to a virtual learning environment was introduced to help overcome differences in technical infrastructure which existed between departments teaching (predominantly) hard, applied subjects in science and engineering compared with departments who were concerned with arts, humanities and the social science.

Using the eLearning Maturity Model

In 2007, motivated by a desire to better understand the impact of changes in practice, the university embarked on an institution-wide exercise to benchmark eLearning practice (White & Davis, 2008). The analytical approach was based on Marshall's eLearning Maturity Model (eMM)

originally developed in the New Zealand Higher Education system (Marshall & Mitchell, 2006).

The eMM method provides a framework for evaluating the current state of maturity of eLearning practices and processes. There are five broad areas for evaluation which are defined by the method outlined in Figure 1:

Within each area there is a set of questions which need to be addressed, and the items of evidence gathered in response to the questions are then evaluated across the following five areas:

- Delivery.
- Planning.
- Definition.
- Management.
- Optimisation.

When evidence has been gathered in answer to each question, that evidence is then scored on against a five-point rating as shown in Figure 2. Each score-point is assigned a different colour as is illustrated in the figure.

When all the ratings under all the headings are combined the output is a 'carpet' where the shading of the area can give a broad understanding of the level of maturity which has been achieved by the institution within a particular evaluation area.

Figure 2. eMM evaluation criteria

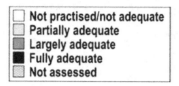

An example of part of a completed (example) carpet is illustrated in Figure 3.

At Southampton, initial planning meetings were convened where colleagues shared their understandings of the various ways in which the practices which were due to be surveyed were organised and managed.

Figure 4 shows how an initial mapping of our e-learning areas of impact and management (which we referred to as Technology Enhanced Learning Practices) was agreed and defined. At the centre we identified the management core which was concerned with policy, strategy and implementation. Surrounding this we identified:

1.   Processes which could generate evidence.
2.   Actors in the eLearning process.
3.   The structure and roles which the university had created to deliver this process.

Sources of evidence were identified, and representative academic disciplines were selected where it would be necessary to interview academic and support staff in order to gain detailed insight of current practice. Ways in which data was gathered is indicated in Figure 5.

Running this complex process and gaining an agreed understanding of the component activities of Technology Enhanced Learning at the university had an indirect benefit. An important outcome was achieved in gaining widespread institutional 'buy in' to the possibility of future change in the way we worked with and used technologies for learning. Two years later when we engaged in the activity of establishing the Southampton Learning Environment we were able to draw on the support of many individuals whose understanding of our university's needs had first been established during their participation in the benchmarking activity.

The eMM benchmarking process at Southampton was supported by the UK's HEA academy who co-ordinated a large-scale evaluation programme using a selection of methods to evaluate eLearning across a range of different institutions. Institutions using like methods were clustered into peer groups. As well as providing an opportunity

Figure 3. An example of part of an eMM carpet

Learning: Processes that directly impact on pedagogical aspects of e-learning						
L1	Learning objectives guide the design and implementation of courses					
L2	Students are provided with mechanisms for interaction with teaching staff and other students					
L3	Students are provided with e-learning skill development					
L4	Students are provided with expected staff response times to student communications					
L5	Students receive feedback on their performance within courses					
L6	Students are provided with support in developing research and information literacy skills					
L7	Learning designs and activities actively engage students					
L8	Assessment is designed to progressively build student competence					
L9	Student work is subject to specified timetables and deadlines					
L10	Courses are designed to support diverse learning styles and learner capabilities					

Figure 4. A reference framework for TEL practices across the university

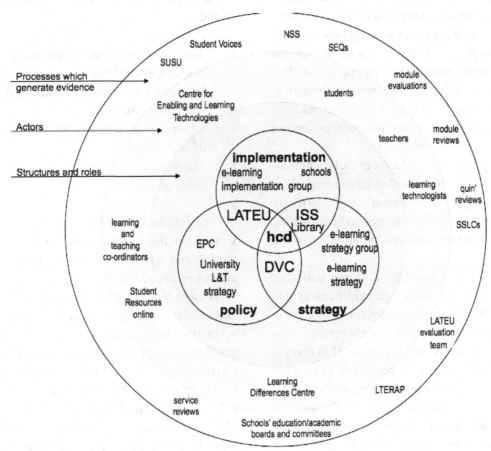

Figure 5. Details of how the data was actually collected across the university

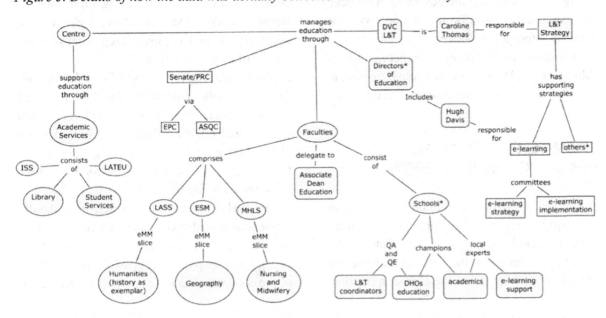

to develop internal understanding of the 'state of play' for technology enhanced learning, we were able to compare our understandings and learning at Southampton with those of other institutions using the same process. Southampton was clustered with a number of other 'research intensive' universities but we also exchanged our findings with a wider range of institutions representing differing organisational types.

A further important outcome of the benchmarking process was a formalised understanding within the university of a framework for identifying practice and information sources which enabled informed discussion and collaboration across the institution.

When the benchmarking data was collected and assembled as a 'carpet' the evidence was also evaluated by the project steering committee. It examined the evidence against the existing objectives and action points contained in the University's eLearning Strategy. This secondary evaluation process was used to establish a set of further actions which the institution agreed to follow.

An understanding of key processes, actors, structures and roles associated with Technology Enhanced Learning (TEL) in the university was achieved through the definition diagram shown in Figure 4 which has already been introduced and explained. This information along with the detailed information derived from the analysis represented by the Southampton carpet would both subsequently play an important role in helping to specify the Southampton Learning Environment.

FROM PERSONAL TO RICH LEARNING ENVIRONMENTS

A number of factors in addition to analysis of existing practice in our institution derived from the eMM benchmarking, have contributed to the growing awareness of the value of framing our models of learning technologies from a Personal Learning Environment perspective. These factors include:

- The constraints and limitations of virtual learning environments.
- Increasing independently initiated use of technology by learners.
- Observed changes in cost and availability of technology.
- Theoretical modelling of systems and behaviours.

These factors have emerged in a number of ways through external studies and discussions of the role and nature of current and future learning environments and their technological context.

A large body of work had analysed and discussed personal learning environments most often from the perspective of students and teachers. Van Harmelen's view of Personal Learning Environments (Van Harmelen, 2006), Atwell's consideration of PLEs as the future of eLearning (Attwell, 2007) and the JISC CETIS report (JISC, 2007) on Personal Learning Environments mark a clear stage in the development of ideas which had been much discussed across the learning technologies community in previous years. Such formal definitions of Personal Learning Environments largely incorporated (transitory) technological constraints which required integration of tools into third party frameworks.

Alongside the CETIS report, Scott Wilson's visualisation of the components of a PLE has formed a focus for numerous discussions. Other authors who have also been influential include Downes on eLearning 2.0 (Downes, 2005), Shaffert and Hilzensauer's discussion of personal learning environments (Shaffert & Hilzensauer, 2008).

An earlier contribution which undoubtedly influenced UK thinking took a strong systems perspective (Olivier & Liber, 2002). From the pedagogic viewpoint, it is possible to see aspects of the conceptualisation of personal learning environments in the body of work which was published around constructivist education and active learning during the early 1990's, for example the Manifesto for a constructivist education in higher education (Jonassen et al., 1993).

Conceptualizations of PLEs, discussions of their relevance, constraints, advantages and roles have continued to occupy journal editions, discussion time, conference space, and blogging posts. The approach which we have chosen to take at Southampton is from a perspective of technology affordances (Gaver, 1991, 1996). Our interest is in enabling the learner to operate within a consolidated environment where they intermix their own chosen environments with others which have functions to perform in support of the processes of learning. This has led us to articulate our idealized environment as a rich learning environment discussed within the case study details that follow.

Beyond Web 1.0

Discussions and definitions of PLEs frequently incorporate assumptions of the social web. Shirky defines the social web as 'software that supports group interaction', (Shirky, 2003). Shortly afterwards, first at conference discussions, and then formally in a published paper, O'Reilly defines web 2.0 and encapsulates his thinking through his meme map (O'Reilly, 2005, 2007). In everyday discussion the two concepts of the social web and web 2.0 have become intermingled – understandably since many of the technology affordances of web 2.0 support, or even engender Shirky's concept of the social web. It is worth observing however that social software can be seen to predate web 1.0. Social software in action has in effect been operational from the time of bulletin board forums which flourished during the 1980s in forms such as The Well.

From the point of view of the social web, discussions and definitions of personal learning environments frequently include explorations of learners' behaviours mediated by the use of social software. This realization of the social web sees social software fulfilling the requirements of the original conception of the 'read-write web' from Berners-Lee.

The social web has special value because applications such as blogs and wikis, which support writing, publishing, sharing and commenting, can also support construction-based learning activities. The affordances of social web applications which enable and encourage learners to explore ideas through engineered opportunities for reflection and engagement thereby fulfill a core role in the constructivist model. The social web is also of interest from the perspective of an affordance which supports and enables Wenger's creation of and participation in communities of practice (Wenger, 1998).

However, while these are undoubtedly educationally useful facets of personal learning environments, from the perspective of the Southampton Learning Environment, the social web is interesting in different ways. Pre-existing use of the social web in particular challenges educational assumptions which it may encounter. Learners' prior or current experience of the social web means that:

- Learners have other virtual identities via the social web which will intersect with their virtual identities in an institutional context.
- Learners may well have established (and effective) practices of virtual communications.
- Learners may feel critical of, or hostile to institutional environments because of their prior experience of social web applications.

These observations are not new and can be found in the existing literature, but do lead us towards our technology affordances-led definition of our rich learning environment. They are observations may be relevant to guiding our educational decisions in terms of how we choose to implement our environment and perhaps what affordances we particularly wish to develop, exploit, or take into account.

The Web 2.0 point of view is more relevant to articulating the technological assumptions which will underpin our conceptions of the Southampton Learning Environment. O'Reilly (2005) contrasts the software features which can be used to differentiate web 1.0 – the vanilla web, with Web 2.0. He places the following features at the core of his Web 2.0 meme map:

- The web as a platform.
- You control your own data.
- Services not packaged software.
- Architecture of participation.
- Cost-effective scalability.
- Re-mixable data source and data transformations.
- Software above the level of a single device.
- Harnessing collective intelligence.

This list provides resonances for our technical collaborators and designers who have an aspiration to "let computers do the tedious stuff". Downes provides an interesting (and prescient) outline on eLearning 2.0 (Downes, 2005) which includes references to the web of linked data and semantic technologies which Tiropanis et al. have subsequently been able to track coming into use much wider use (Tiropanis et al., 2009).

Both Downes and O'Reilly anticipate the world of mash-ups and the realization of the potential for sharing, aggregation and interoperability which can come about through the use of standards for data identification and exchange.

The Edgeless University

A more over-arching view is presented by Bradwell. When proposing an 'Edgeless University' Bradwell's report for Demos suggests that technology offers a means for institutions to find a collaborative response to external changes such as an economic downturn (Bradwell, 2009). His account tracks ways in which technology has already impacted on educational experiences using data collected from a set of interviews and group discussions. In the context of the PLE he anticipates a future with increasing volumes of open content supported by an e-infrastructure for higher education.

This authoritative report commissioned by the provider of key networked services for UK universities and further education colleges envisages a future infrastructure outside of individual institutions, and suggests a context in which future individual planning decisions can reasonably be made.

Taken together, personal learning environments, the social web, Web 2.0, linked data, the semantic web and over-arching changes in the use of technology and commonplace infrastructure communicate an inevitable future of changed technology practice in education. The challenge for institutions is to successfully anticipate the most important future changes. While continuing to meet the demands of providing day-to-day support for learning, institutions need to set in place mechanisms to update their person

DEFINING THE SOUTHAMPTON LEARNING ENVIRONMENT

During the period described the university purposefully moved away from describing the remit of this work as eLearning in preference using the phrase Technology Enhanced Learning. Throughout the period the work was led by a university director of education who was working with a group of colleagues drawn from across the academic schools and from the professional support services.

In our Benchmarking final report (January 2008) we noted that "At the University of Southampton we have reached the stage where technology is ubiquitously used by our students, who have an expectation of interacting online: for admin; for learning and for university life in general. The University has a high quality infrastructure and most modules have an on-line presence". Bur we were also aware that we needed additional insights into the everyday experience of our infrastructure from our students.

Student Survey

The provide this insight, In 2009 we carried out a major survey of the student experience of eLearning (919 students answered 34 multi-part questions), Basic demographic analysis of the data is shown in Tables 1 through 5.

Our Students' Union supported administering the survey which enabled us to draw representa-

Table 1. Respondents by academic school

School	Response
Chemistry	2
Civil Engineering & Environment	75
ECS	114
Engineering Sciences	30
Geography	38
ISVR	8
Mathematics	13
Ocean & Earth Sciences	30
Physics & Astronomy	13
Biological Sciences	25
Health Sciences	193
Medicine	43
Psychology	26
Art	48
Education	2
Humanities	151
Law	15
Management	23
Social Sciences	71
Other	3

Table 2. Respondents by year of study

Year	Response
Year 0	14
Year 1	259
Year 2	288
Year 3	210
Year 4	50
Year 5	4
Postgrad.	93

tive data from all of the University's 20 schools which were organised in three different faculties. Taken as a whole, the data returned was broadly consistent with other surveys in the sector examining the learners experience of technology; notably the findings of the JISC Learners Experience Programme (Conole et al., 2006). The data confirmed the ubiquity of personal technology. Students were asked whether they had exclusive use during term time of any of a range of different types of ICT equipment. Of all respondents, only 25 had none of the options for their exclusive use:

This data was particularly valuable in communicating student use and expectation of technology to colleagues who did not themselves make wide use of technology beyond personal computers for email and admin.

Three questions gathered qualitative data. These questions were designed to explore barriers and frustrations which learners experienced in their use of technology.

Table 3. Respondents by age group

Age	Response
Under 18	8
18-21	500
22-25	172
26-30	59
31-40	62
Over 40	73

Table 4. Ownership of personal technology

ICT Equipment	Response
Laptop	782
PC	292
PDA/Smart Phone	142
MP3 Player	289
iPod	450
None	25

The questions highlighted the range of different problems which might be encountered (Figure 6). The biggest issues were associated with connectivity. In some cases it was possible to infer that additional information and support for users might have prevented some of these problems from arising. In other instances the responses pointed to issues generated by known constraints brought about by details of software licensing and access agreements for services such as electronic journals.

This data provided a valuable backdrop to subsequent discussion when we tried to specify the proposed environment. In addition, for our support services (library and computing infrastructure) the survey was invaluable in augmenting official student feedback data on teaching with is routinely collected across the academic year.

Enhancement Academy

In parallel to the process of data collection and analysis, senior colleagues directly engaged with the management of teaching and the support of learning at the university agreed to participate in a national enhancement academy.

The enhancement academy engaged participants in a development process. The university team was given a brief to identify proposed changes. A critical friend, a senior (and external academic) with extensive experience of managing change in technology innovation was assigned to work with the management team providing on-

Table 5. Use of websites and systems

How often do you use the following tools/websites/systems?							
	> once a day	Daily	> once a week	Weekly	Monthly	Have used	Never
Blackboard	143	218	215	122	65	72	82
Online assessments	15	20	51	100	164	342	190
SUSSED Portal	312	252	102	77	54	59	30
Facebook	422	189	101	50	29	36	84
Text Messaging	571	195	71	28	11	17	19
Instant Messaging	215	128	139	75	74	142	126
Skype/VoIP etc.	99	68	82	68	69	194	320
Google	566	204	99	23	6	4	13
Google Scholar	66	57	130	91	104	176	268
Wikipedia	103	103	242	159	123	141	35
YouTube etc.	120	131	216	154	116	119	57
Flickr (or similar)	14	12	30	46	49	201	548
Del.ic.ous / DIgg or other Bookmarking sites	18	15	19	23	17	70	742
Twitter	27	18	22	16	11	70	737

Figure 6. Blockages and irritations encountered by students

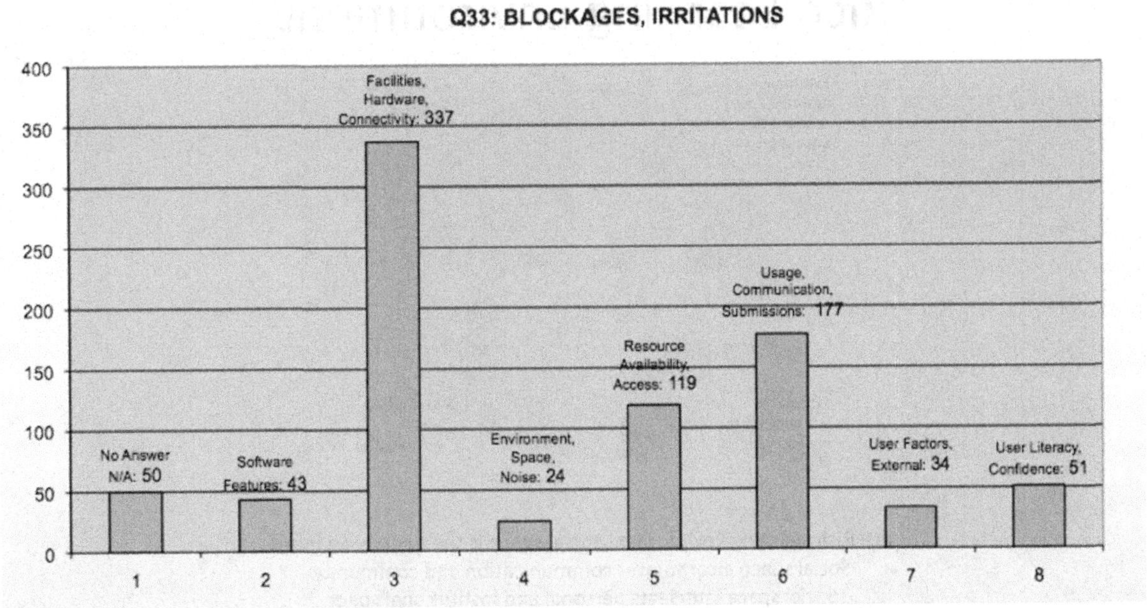

Q33: BLOCKAGES, IRRITATIONS

going support and consultancy. The role of 'critical friend' is to contribute as a trusted and respected advisor (*friend*) who can challenge the team's decisions in an objective (*critical)* manner. The projects' critical friend guided the development process and attended key meetings contributing to debate as they judged appropriate. The 'critical friend' role provided a level of objectivity beyond the university team, and also created opportunities for expert contributions and advice during critical decision making processes.

The university team created a community of champions, innovators and sponsors (the Southampton Learning Environment team) which worked in conjunction with the already established Technology Enhanced Learning Support and Innovation Group (TEL-SIG). There was some overlap between the two groups which was beneficial in retaining consistency in discussions and decision making. As was noted previously there was also consistency between this team and many of the individuals involved in establishing the earlier eMM benchmarking activity.

Facilitating Understanding

Early meetings of the Southampton Learning Environment team and TEL-SIG were concerned with ensuring that the vision for the proposed environment could address the twin aims of supporting *living and learning*. This perspective would ensure a shared vision for university support services and the academic schools which had been newly defined under the Curriculum Innovation Project.

Different specialisms and expertise contributed to the decision-making process and time was needed to develop understandings of the necessary assumptions which were associated with each specialism. Learning Environment meetings became a forum in which to communicate, share and discuss understandings which gave rise to our observation that: "Its more than a system, it's a mind-set". One example of a representation of specialist understanding, which became useful during discussions is the visualization of a Rich Learning Environment which is shown as Figure 7.

Figure 7. Components of a rich learning environment

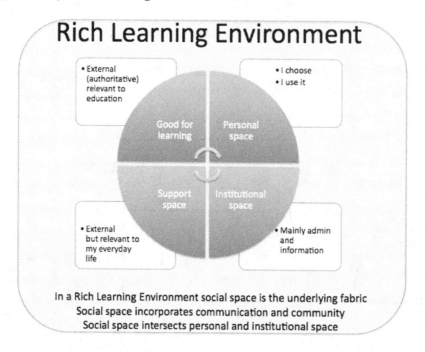

Having found the Enhancement Academy process a useful one, it was agreed that the wider learning environment group would also participate in a facilitated residential meeting in the form of a 'mini' Enhancement Academy which was organised jointly with the critical friend. The mini academy incorporated a variety of 'thinking exercises' the outputs of which were captured into documents and diagrams which have been used to take forward the specification for the Southampton Learning Environment.

The Southampton Learning Environment

We have defined the scope of the Southampton Learning Environment as:

The Virtual space with which the learner associated with Southampton University is engaged. This definition incorporates the impact of the virtual space on the Physical space utilised by these Learners.

Four fundamental drivers for change were identified. They comprise the desire to:

- Support curriculum change and innovation.
- Address student expectations.
- Enable the university to remain credible in its support for learning and teaching with a particular desire to be seen to be fluent and innovative in the use of IT.
- Facilitate the adoption of a University-wide educational style.

Working with our colleagues responsible for the technology infrastructure we were able to produce the following summary of our ambitions (Figure 8). In this diagram the boxes at the top represent the university corporate applications and existing student facing applications. The box at the bottom represents the student interface, which allows single login access to the student facing applications and to the information that the student may wish to access from the university, such as timetables, assessment records etc.

Figure 8. Proposed SLE Architecture showing personalised widget/portal front-end to SLE and the existing student facing applications and enterprise DBs

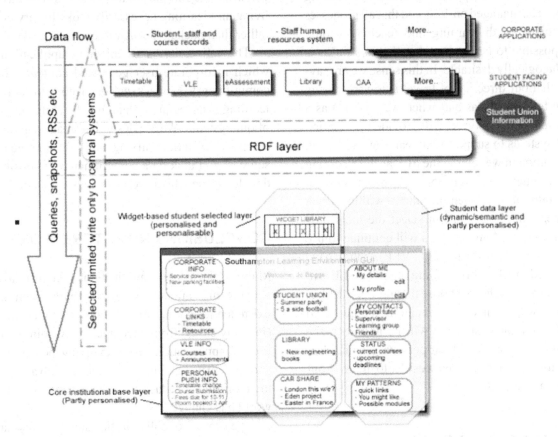

We have taken an "open data" approach in which all corporate data is now considered open and publically available unless there is a clear reason why this should not be the case. In cases where data is not open (e.g., due to privacy constraints) we have implemented a transparent access system making it clear who has view or change access to the data. In order to protect corporate systems from accidental or deliberate damage or overloading we have implemented a cached layer so that the open data which can be accessed by third party applications (widgets).

We have implemented a "Widget Store" on a similar basis to the Apple AppStore. Widgets can be registered for inclusion in this store after some basic checks to ensure they are not malicious, but the university provides no guarantee as to how useful (or stable) these widgets will be. Typical widgets might be a personal timetable display or a course news feed.

The user can select which widgets they choose to use, and can control to some extent the layout of the screens. They can also choose which sources they choose to aggregate into news feeds. (Unsurprisingly students are much keener to have information about coursework deadlines than they are to hear about prestigious prizes awarded to people they don't know). We thus describe the environment as *personalised* (the information and functionality that is available to the user is based on our knowledge of the user) and *personalisable* (the user can change the layout and choice of widgets).

It is our long term goal that all processes associated with the support of learning and teaching should be managed on-line, and that all processes associated with learning and teaching should be possible to be organised on-line, so far as is pedagogically desirable. In this sense we are saying that our direction of travel is towards being able to perform (as and when we wish to) as a "Virtual University". It will provide information and systems to support both learning and living.

Although we refer to the SLE as the "learning environment", this is to some extent a misnomer. Actually it is the environment within which students and teachers can select the tools they wish to use. Many teachers will continue to use Blackboard (our institutional VLE) as they have invested much effort in doing this. The SLE will allow each teacher to choose the appropriate tools to use with their class – including cloud-based tools. Similarly, students will be able to make their own choices for their personal leaning. It is for this reason in part that we refer to the environment as a mindset.

WHAT HAVE WE GOT?

It is interesting to observe the extent to which our collaborative workings achieve a number of the principles of web 2.0 suggested by O'Reilly's meme map.

Student feedback from the survey suggested that while we have for some time had reliable systems, they are now becoming rather "long in the tooth", and showing their age in a Web 2.0 world where everything and everyone is connected.

The vision of the Southampton Learning Environment assumes the web as a platform. Proof of concept from our school of Electronics and Computer Science has demonstrated how this is possible. Other projects around the university demonstrated the range of possible solutions.

The necessary assumptions of an environment which has the complexity to address the agenda of living and learning necessarily looks to services rather than packaged software.

The university is establishing applications which incorporate user generated content. The commitment to services such open repositories for learning is necessarily changing the architecture of our systems. We are designing in aggregation and personalisation, mixing data from a range of sources, and making a commitment to exposing data for reuse whilst preserving a secure core.

CONCLUSION AND FUTURE WORK

Many of the systems/applications that currently support the student experience have been in existence for a long time. They were configured (in many cases) from a technical viewpoint with limited appreciation of the evolving pedagogic and student needs. They do a practical job against their original production remits. However, the world has changed.

The process of collaboration supported by the working groups and enhancement academy activities has been powerful catalysts for facilitating communication across different (and sometimes disparate) specialisms.

Different understandings of Personal Learning Environments have provided a starting point which has been used to integrate differing viewpoints, technical and non technical, educational and administrative: our shared 'mindset'. The university has benefited from long established expertise, but also recognises that the purposeful engagement in developmental activities was crucial for bringing about change. It remains to be seen what the long-term impact of these plans will be, but we look forward to future implementation and further evaluation.

An interesting question that will only be resolved with time is the extent to which an institution can provide a "personal learning" environment. The tool we have initially implemented provides information and functionality that is personalized to the user, and provides the facility for the user to personalise how their environment appears and what tools to include; in reality it a 'personal environment' to support learning. However, our surveys and benchmarking show that we still have a long way to go down the digital literacies agenda before the majority of our students and teaching staff understand the meaning and implications of an environment to support 'personal learning'. It is our intention that the SLE will provide the bridge to those understandings and, like us, will adapt as we learn.

ACKNOWLEDGMENT

Thanks are due to the anonymous reviewers who directed us towards some constructive revisions of this paper based on the original version which was part of the conference proceedings. Thanks are also due to all the members of the Southampton Learning Environment and the University's Technology Enhanced Learning Strategy and Implementation Group – in particular Debra Morris and Pete Hancock with whom we collaborated extensively in developing the institutional thinking which is represented in this paper.

REFERENCES

Attwell, G. (2007). *Personal learning environments – the future of eLearning?* Retrieved from http://citeseerx.ist.psu.edu/viewdoc/download?doi=10.1.1.97.3011&rep

Bradwell, P. (2009). *The edgeless university: Why higher education must embrace technology*. London, UK: Demos.

Conole, G., de Laat, M., Dillon, T., & Darby, J. (2006). *JISC LXP: Student experiences of technologies report*. Bristol, UK: HEFCE.

Downes, S. (2005). *E-learning 2.0*. Retrieved from http://www.elearnmag.org/subpage.cfm?article=29-1&section=articles

Gaver, W. W. (1991). Technology affordances. In *Proceedings of the SIGCHI Conference on Human Factors in Computing Systems: Reaching through Technology*, New Orleans, LA (pp. 78-94).

Gaver, W. W. (1996). Situating action ii: Affordances for interaction: The social is material for design. *Ecological Psychology*, *8*(2), 111–129. doi:10.1207/s15326969eco0802_2

JISC. (2007). *A report on the JISC CETIS PLE project*. Retrieved from http://wiki.cetis.ac.uk/Ple/Report

Jonassen, D. H., Mayes, J. T., & McAleese, R. (1993). A manifesto for a constructivist approach to uses of technology in higher education. In Duffy, T. M., Lowyck, J., & Jonassen, D. H. (Eds.), *Designing environments for constructive learning* (pp. 231–247). Heidelberg, Germany: Springer-Verlag.

Marshall, S., & Mitchell, G. (2006). Assessing sector e-learning capability with an e-learning maturity model. In *Proceedings of the 13th ALT-C Conference on the Association for Learning Technologies: The Next Generation* (pp. 203-214).

O'Reilly, T. (2005). *What Is Web 2.0 – Design patterns and business models for the next generation of software*. Retrieved from http://oreilly.com/web2/archive/what-is-web-20.html

O'Reilly, T. (2007). What Is Web 2.0 – Design patterns and business models for the next generation of software. *Communications & Strategies*, *1*(1), 17–37.

Olivier, B., & Liber, O. (2002). Lifelong learning: The need for portable personal learning environments and supporting interoperability standards. In *Proceedings of the International Conference on Advances in Infrastructure for Electronic Business, Education, Science and Medicine on the Internet*, L'Aquilla, Italy.

Shaffert, S., & Hilzensauer, W. (2008). *On the way towards personal learning environments: Seven crucial aspects*. Retrieved from http://www.elearningeuropa.info/mt/node/2680

Shirky, C. (2003). A group is its own worst enemy. *Clay Shirky's writings about the Internet: Economics & culture, media & community*. Retrieved from http://www.shirky.com/writings/group_enemy.html

Tiropanis, T., Davis, H., Millard, D., Weal, M., White, S., & Wills, G. (2009). *Semantic technologies in learning and teaching (SemTech)*. Bristol, UK: JISC.

Van Harmelen, M. (2006). Personal learning environments. In *Proceedings of the 6th International Conference on Advanced Learning Technologies*, Kerkrade, The Netherlands.

Wenger, E. (1998). *Communities of practice: Learning, meaning and identity*. Cambridge, UK: Cambridge University Press.

White, S. (1993). Scholar - A campus wide structure for multimedia learning. In *Proceedings of the 27th Annual Meeting of the Association for Educational and Training Technology*, Glasgow, UK.

White, S. (2006). *Higher education and learning technologies: An organisational perspective*. Unpublished doctoral dissertation, University of Southampton, Southampton, UK.

White, S., & Davis, H. C. (2008). *eMM Benchmarking at Southampton: The carpet, observations and reflections* (Tech. Rep. No. LSL-EL-0108, ECS). Southampton, UK: University of Southampton.

This work was previously published in the International Journal of Virtual and Personal Learning Environments, Volume 2, Issue 4, edited by Michael Thomas, pp. 23-39, copyright 2011 by IGI Publishing (an imprint of IGI Global).

Chapter 16
Exploring Task-Based Curriculum Development in a Blended-Learning Conversational Chinese Program

Yao Zhang Hill
Kapiʻolani Community College, USA

Stephen L. Tschudi
University of Hawaiʻi at Mānoa, USA

ABSTRACT

This paper brings task-based language teaching (TBLT) curriculum development principles into the blended learning context, presenting processes and outcomes from a project to develop a task-based thematic unit — asking and giving directions — in a hybrid web-based university-level class focused on listening and speaking skills in Mandarin Chinese. The authors follow the principled task-based curriculum design phases informed by Long and Crookes (1993) and Long and Norris (2000). Unit-based development made the workload manageable and provided an important experimental space for the instructors to best align task-based principles with online language instruction. First, the context of the project and its theoretical TBLT curriculum development framework are established. The distinct processes of needs analysis, materials development, task sequencing and teaching methods, and assessment methods adopted to meet the special requirements of the class are presented, along with a preliminary formative and summative evaluation of the teaching model. The conclusion discusses the theoretical and practical implications of the project.

DOI: 10.4018/978-1-4666-2467-2.ch016

INTRODUCTION

This paper presents the processes and outcomes of an ongoing task-based language teaching (TBLT) curriculum development project, which focused on the development of one thematic unit: asking and giving directions. This project was implemented in a conversational Chinese program at the University of Hawai'i at Mānoa and it was delivered in a blended learning format combining asynchronous web-based and face-to-face elements. First, the context of the project and its theoretical TBLT curriculum development framework are established. Then the distinct processes of needs analysis, materials development, task sequencing and teaching methods adopted to meet the special requirements of the class are presented, along with a preliminary evaluation of our teaching model. The conclusion discusses the theoretical and practical implications of the project.

THE CONTEXT OF THE PROJECT

In the Fall 2005 academic semester, the Department of East Asian Languages and Literatures (EALL) at the University of Hawai'i at Mānoa (UHM) started offering Conversational Mandarin classes in a blended learning format (web + live meetings): Chinese 111 (CHN 111) and Chinese 112 (CHN 112) for the beginning level, and Chinese 211 (CHN 211) and Chinese 212 (CHN 212) for the intermediate level. These blended-learning conversational classes required students' daily asynchronous online participation, as well as attendance at a once-a-week 50-minute face-to-face group tutoring session (for a discussion of blended learning, see Bonk & Graham, 2006.) The majority of the students were UHM undergraduate students; there were also several graduate students and UHM faculty members. By Fall 2006, CHN 111 had fifteen students, double the size of the previous cohort (7 students); in Spring 2007, CHN 112 had eleven students.

The TBLT curriculum development project was motivated by a formative utilization-focused evaluation that was carried out by the authors in their capacity as instructors of CHN111 and 112 in the Spring 2006 semester. The results showed that students were satisfied overall with various aspects of the program: the instructors, the material, the online instruction and exercises, and the tutoring sessions. However, several concerns emerged from the students' feedback and the instructors' observations, including: (1) not all thematic topics covered in the textbook were perceived as useful by the students; (2) students seemed to have a greater desire to develop fluency in listening and speaking than to develop accuracy in grammar; (3) students expressed a strong need to practice conversational abilities to deal with real-life situations (Hill & Tschudi, 2008). The instructors' strategy for meeting students' expressed language learning and development needs was to embark on TBLT curriculum development, because it provides language teaching principles that are based on second language acquisition theories and empirical evidence and it has systematic principles for program development.

THEORETICAL FRAMEWORK OF TBLT CURRICULUM DEVELOPMENT PRINCIPLES

TBLT is a principled language teaching, learning, and program development approach. It utilizes an analytical syllabus, in which learners are presented with authentic input from a real-world task (e.g., purchasing a ticket, finding directions, etc.) as a whole. The learners need to analyze the language themselves by connecting meaning, form, and context, and produce language similar to the input in a simulated authentic context. The learning process is facilitated by pedagogical tasks that are sequenced by task complexity, not by linguistic criteria (Long & Crookes, 1993). TBLT has been actively proposed due to the relative ineffectiveness of the traditional synthetic syllabus, or Type A syllabus, in which language forms are taught piecemeal to students in the belief that they can develop native-like mastery of the language structure or the function taught, even if they are arguably not ready to integrate the language forms taught into their interlanguage system (Long & Crookes, 1993).

Definitions of task are very diverse (for overviews of different definitions that exist in the literature, see Edwards & Willis, 2005; Norris et al., 1998). In this chapter, tasks are classified into three types: real world target tasks, pedagogical tasks, and test tasks. The real world target tasks are those that learners need to carry out in real world communication situations. Pedagogical tasks may have differing degrees of authenticity. The difficulty of tasks in a specific sequence may be purposefully manipulated to promote learners' accuracy, fluency, and complexity in language performance. Pedagogical tasks are scaffolded or supported to various degrees to help learners develop the ability to accomplish real world target tasks. Test tasks are ideally types of tasks that incorporate elements of real world target tasks, so that the successful completion of the test tasks may lead to direct inference of the students' ability to accomplish real world tasks.

Contrary to many people's oversimplified understanding of TBLT as the implementation of tasks in language classes, TBLT provides guiding principles for every element in a language curriculum. It is not just another methodology in language teaching, but a *curriculum design principle*. According to Doughty and Long (2003), "Task-Based Language Teaching … constitutes a coherent, theoretically motivated approach to all six components of the design, implementation, and evaluation of a genuinely task-based language teaching program: (a) needs and means analysis, (b) syllabus design, (c) materials design, (d) methodology and pedagogy, (e) testing, and (f) evaluation." Long and Norris (2000) proposed six steps in developing a TBLT program:

1. Through a task-based needs analysis, identify real-world target tasks.
2. Classify target tasks into task-types.
3. Use task-types to develop and sequence pedagogical tasks.
4. Sequence pedagogical tasks to form a task syllabus based on non-linguistic criteria.
5. Apply TBLT methodological principles (e.g., focus on form) in a particular pedagogical procedure situated in the local context.
6. Assess students' achievement and carry out formative and summative evaluation of the TBLT program.

The general structure of the TBLT curriculum is illustrated in Figure 1 [adapted from Norris (Personal Communication) and Brown (1995)], which also demonstrates the interaction between the elements in a TBLT curriculum. For example, the target tasks identified in the *needs analysis* also represent targeted learning *outcomes*. Both task-based needs analysis and *input analysis* (used to investigate local context, constraints and resources) are to be considered in determining the *scope* of the innovation to take place in the curriculum, *sequencing* of the target task-types to form the task syllabus, and the choice of methodological principles and *pedagogical procedures*. These will in turn guide *materials development*, *teaching practice*, and *assessment*. Each step and component in program development can provide input for, and is subject to, evaluation for both formative and summative purposes.

Many of these TBLT principles for curriculum design have been successfully implemented in several language programs, such as Georgetown University's German program (Byrnes & Sprang, 2003), language programs at the California Defense Language Institute (Antokhin, Boussalhi, Chen, Combacau & Koppany, 2004); a program-level Curricular and Teacher Innovation (CATI) project in an ESL program in an American university (Markee, 1996); Dutch education programs in Flanders (Van Avermaet & Gysen, 2007); and

Figure 1. General structure of TBLT curriculum design

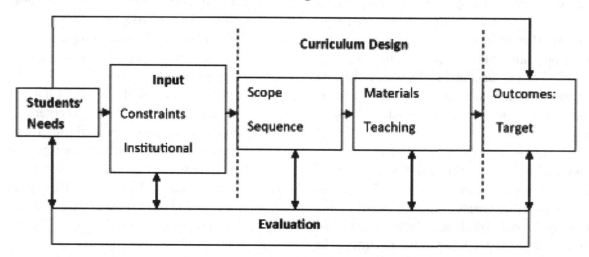

the Korean as a foreign language (KFL) program at UHM (Chaudron et al., 2005). The commonality among all these programs and their task-based curriculum development is that the innovation initiative was in all cases supported program-wide and all were well funded. Most often, the TBLT program development was led by administrators who were either TBLT researchers themselves or who hired TBLT and content area experts to construct a specific piece in a curriculum, such as assessment. All of the aforementioned programs had sufficient funding to conduct needs analysis and hire or train teaching staff.

Some task-based learning initiatives in the literature have been undertaken by language teachers (see Edwards & Willis, 2005). However, most often, teachers either have limited knowledge of TBLT curriculum development principles or limited resources and support, and frequently the result is that teachers simply replace language drills with pedagogical tasks in the classroom and do not implement needs analysis and assessment components, let alone formal evaluation and program-level application. A few exceptions (e.g., González-Lloret, 2003), though, do shine a light on the possibilities for language teachers to systematically build task-based instructional

modules (for example, on understanding and giving directions), guided by TBLT curriculum development and teaching principles, which can eventually be expanded upon to reshape teaching and assessment for all the other modules in the curriculum.

González-Lloret (2003) developed a multi-media Internet-delivered learning module, "En Busca de Esmeraldas," to teach asking and giving directions. In this module, students were given a simulated real-life task — to find a document inside a building. The module followed task-based curriculum development procedures and principles. It started from a small needs analysis, which identified the need for a medium in which students could learn giving and receiving directions in an efficient and realistic manner. Three target tasks were identified (i.e., listen and understand directions, read and understand directions, and follow directions), which were classified into more general task types: receive directions and follow directions. Pedagogical tasks were developed (e.g., listen to an answering machine message and identify what needs to be accomplished, follow the directions given orally on a tape, work with a partner in exchanging information). Finally, the tasks were sequenced in a chronological manner, following the steps for the document search. Task sequencing also considered cognitive complexity dimensions, such as planning time, number of tasks, prior knowledge, and number of elements, as proposed by Robinson (2001). The quality of the tasks and students' self-perceived learning were highly rated by the students on the post-task evaluation questionnaire. The second student reported upon in the paper also showed evidence of improved interpersonal negotiation and communication skills fostered by the designed tasks.

Following González-Lloret (2003), the research project reported in this paper is one of few examples of a bottom-up effort in TBLT curriculum innovation guided by TBLT principles (Long & Crookes, 1993; Long & Norris, 2000; Doughty & Long, 2003) in a blended-learning conversational Mandarin program (blended CMP) at UHM. The following section will summarize the authors' efforts in utilizing TBLT curriculum development principles to design one thematic unit (asking and giving directions) in the program from needs analysis to materials development, task-sequencing and pedagogical implementation, including assessment and evaluation.

NEEDS ANALYSIS

Needs analysis, sometimes also called needs and means identification in TBLT, is the first step in TBLT curriculum development as illustrated in Figure 1. A well-conducted needs analysis helps to direct limited resources toward their most effective use in the teaching and learning practices of a language program. According to Long (2005), needs analysis can be based on data from different sources (literature, the learners, applied linguistics, domain experts, triangulated sources) and can use different methods (e.g., expert and non-expert intuitions, interviews, questionnaire surveys, language audits, observation, ethnographic methods, journals and logs, and language measurements). The reliability and validity of the

needs analysis can be enhanced by triangulating different sources and methods in data collection (Chaudron et al., 2005; Long, 2005; Van Avermaet & Gysen, 2006; González-Lloret, 2003). The needs analyses conducted in this project took place at different stages and had varied scales. Just as with the entire project, it was an evolutionary process, rather than a one-time large-scale effort.

First of all, based on a motivational study of students in a previous version of the blended CMP class (Hill & Tschudi, 2005) and previous class evaluation results (Hill & Tschudi, 2008), a six-point Likert scale survey questionnaire was administered to eleven students from CHN 111 and ten from CHN 211. Among other items, the survey asked students to rate the perceived importance of content topics covered in the textbook and to suggest topics that they were interested in learning.

The results showed that students rated directions as the most important topic to learn, following which were other topics that reflect travel communication needs: shopping, food, and transportation. The ranking of the relative importance of the topics reflected that learners' chief motivation in taking the blended CMP was to fulfill interpersonal communication and travel needs. These needs and motivations were also confirmed in student interviews that were conducted in the previous semester (Hill & Tschudi, 2005).

Based on the results of this initial needs analysis, two decisions were made. The first one was to select directions as a pilot TBLT module to develop. In addition, the authors decided to conduct a larger scale needs analysis, expanding on the topics covered in the textbook and investigating a full range of language use situations that learners might consider important to learn. Investigating which language use situations were pertinent to students' needs was also the first step taken toward deciding which target real world tasks were important for students to be able to do. The resulting information would serve as a basis for future selection of thematic units for continued development. A total of 95 returned surveys were collected from representative beginning and intermediate level Chinese students at UHM. Asking directions was considered to be quite useful by the participants (a rating of 3.94 on a continuum from the lowest rating of 2.94 to the highest rating of 4.56). The results supported the decision to select directions as the first TBLT development module.

MATERIALS DEVELOPMENT

Learners are an important source of information in a needs analysis. However, language learners often do not have educated opinions of what kinds of language knowledge are most suitable for them to learn, often because they are not familiar with the language that is appropriate and pertinent in dealing with a given real world task (Long, 2005). In order to make a well informed decision on the selection of target tasks, the authors also conducted semi-structured interviews with learners who had experience visiting China and native speakers or fluent second language speakers of Mandarin who had experience dealing with non-Mandarin speakers in the target language situations. The target tasks were then classified into task types, which in a TBLT development of larger scope would then be sequenced into the TBLT syllabus. Although the semi-structured interviews, strictly speaking, belonged to the stage of needs analysis, they are presented in this section since they directly informed materials development.

Interview on Learning Needs from Experienced and Potential China Travelers

The authors interviewed three learners, two of whom had experience traveling to China and one of whom planned to visit China in the future. All the interviews were summarized to categorize language needs for specific tasks. Summaries of language needs for directions included:

- Names of landmarks (train station, bus stop, Tian'anmen Square, shopping mall, restaurant, monument).
- Immediacy of location (e.g. Is it close? Right around there. Right around the corner. Right there. Is that down there? Am I close to…?).
- Relative location: near, next to, opposite to, front, back, left, right.
- Absolute location: north, south, east, west, N miles/meters/kilometers away from.
- Sequence in giving directions: first, after that, then, go until, and finally.

Semi-Authentic Data Collection

The first author (Hill) collected discourse from four native speakers of Mandarin, two from Taiwan and two from mainland China, through a simulated direction-asking role-play. Permissions were granted by all the participants for the discourse to be used in materials development and publication. Role-plays included asking directions to (1) places that were close and familiar to them; (2) places that were far but still familiar to them; and (3) places that were both far and unfamiliar. Hill also conducted interviews with two native speakers in a northern city in China by phone.

Even though the interviews did not happen in truly authentic situations, several striking patterns in the discourse could still be observed that typify native speakers and advanced target language speakers' behavior (or knowledge of normative behavior). First, with regard to how to attract people's attention for asking directions, almost all interviewees mentioned eye contact. One female interviewee said that she would approach someone who looked nice and local, or would approach roadside vendors. If they happened to look at her, she would maintain eye contact, smile at that person, approach him/her, and then say *ni3 hao3* (hello), and then something like *Qing3wen4, ni3 zhi1buzhi4dao4 dao4… zen3me zou3?* (May I ask whether you know how to get to…?). This eye-contact – smile – approach-and-say-hello pattern was confirmed by another male participant from the southern part of mainland China. One interviewee from Harbin (a northern city in China) revealed on the phone that when one person tried to attract attention from another person to ask directions, the first person would in general first use eye contact, then the direction inquirer would call the potential direction giver by a general respectful title such as *da4ge1 / da4jie3* (older brother / sister). If the inquirer was far older than the giver, the former, often an elderly person, would call the latter *ta1 da4ge1* or *ta1 da4jie3* (his/her older brother or his/her older sister). The implied meaning is "my child/grandchild's older brother or sister."

Dialectal and gender-related differences emerged in ways of asking or giving directions in the sample. In Harbin and Beijing, in Northeast China, when people ask directions, they often say *Gen1 nin2 da3ting1 ge dao4r bei!* or *Gen1 nin2 wen4 ge dao4r bei!* (more or less "I'd like to ask a route from you!"). This is a common method of asking, understandable by every Mandarin speaker. Three of six interviewees started giving directions every time with the phrase *Na4 hen3 jian3dan1* (that's simple). The three females (two from Taiwan, one from mainland China) in general provided more details in giving directions than the three males. Social-cultural patterns and information such as those mentioned above were summarized and used as materials in the input phase as a consciousness-raising activity in the CMP course.

Discourse Analysis of Task-Essential Linguistic Elements for Materials Development

In order to develop linguistic input material, we first analyzed the linguistic features that emerged in our discourse collection data. The theoretical framework for the discourse analysis was based on the communicative competence components model proposed by Canale and Swain (1980), which includes grammatical, discourse, socio-linguistic, and strategic competence. Bartlett's (2005), Holmes's (2005), and Winn's (2005) discourse analysis studies of service encounters in coffee shops, small talk in the workplace, and US naturalization interviews with implications for language teaching also informed the discourse analysis focus of this study. The authors identified six discourse features to focus on in language teaching. They were: (1) discourse structure and components; (2) lexical chunks specific to the tasks; (3) task-essential linguistic functions; (4) speech acts; (5) features specific to naturally occurring discourse; (6) negotiation of meaning.

The authors identified the macro discourse structure from these simulated authentic discourses as follows. The direction inquirer is denoted as A and the direction giver is B. First A asks whether B knows the place (e.g., *Ni3 you3meiyou3 qu4guo…? Ni3 zhi1dao … zen3me zou3 ma?* [Have you ever been to…? Do you know the way?]). If B's answer is "Yes," before B gives directions, she asks how A wants to get there (e.g., *Zhi1dao. Ni3 shi4 zou3 zhe qu4 hai2shi4 kai1che1 / zuo4 gong1gong4 qi4che1?* [Yes, I know. Are you walking or driving / taking the bus?]). Then B gives directions according to a specific transportation mode: walking, biking, taking a bus, or driving. In the end, A thanks B for giving directions.

The authors also identified frequently occurring lexical chunks that were not covered in the textbook, such as *ran2hou4 ma3shang* (then immediately), *zou3 dao4 di3r* (go to the end), *A jiu4 bian4cheng2 le/jie1dao4 B* (X turns into or becomes Y).

Several task-essential linguistic functions were identified in direction giving, including repetition, topicalization, renomination, and the use of modals to indicate prediction. Of these, repetition and renomination serve pragmatic functions, creating discursive "landmarks" for the listener receiving the directions. Even though repetition and renomination contribute significantly to a speaker's ability to function in a colloquial register appropriate to the giving and receiving of directions, they are not available in traditional curricula. The authors' use of a TBLT curriculum development process including the collection of natural discourse enabled learners to access native-like input including these phenomena. Topicalization and the use of modals, while cited in Chinese reference grammars and learner's grammars (Yip & Rimmington, 2004; Ross & Ma, 2006), have specific roles in the giving of directions distinct from their generic usages as presented in these references. See the examples below for the four linguistic functions/forms identified.

Repetition of directional phrase meaning "keep going" was the first identified function:

- **Example 1:** *Wang3 qian2 zou3. Yi4zhi2 wang3 qian2zou3.* (Go straight ahead. Keep *going straight ahead.*)
- **Example 2:** *Yi4zhi2 zou3 yi4zhi2 zou3.* (Go straight on, go straight on.)
- **Example 3:** *Yi4zhi2 kai1, yi4zhi2 kai1.* (Drive straight on, drive straight on.)

Renomination and topicalization often occur hand in hand to enhance the mental image of the landmarks and the route given. Renomination is the phenomenon in which a noun is first mentioned in one sentence as new information, and immediately mentioned again in the next sentence as old information to bring forward other new information. Topicalization is a syntactic device bringing an element in a sentence to the beginning of the sentence to place the emphasis on a topic.

- **Example 4:** (renomination): *Zai4 wang3qian2, hui4 kan4dao yi2ge ting-2che1chang3. Na4ge* ting2che1chang3 de

pang2bian shi4 yi2ge xue2xiao. Ru2guo3 ni3 kan4dao na4ge ting2che1chang3 gen1 na4ge xue2xiao4, ni3 jiu4 zou3 dui4 fang1xiang le.

(Keep on going straight, and you will see a *parking lot.* Beside that *parking lot* is a *school.* If you see that *parking lot* and that *school*, you are headed in the right direction.)

- **Example 5:** (topicalization): *Dao4 yi2ge zhu4zhai2qu1. Zhu4zhai2qu1 de hua4, ni3 zhe4 shi2hou hui4 yu4dao yi2ge cha4lu4.*

(You will get to a residential area. *[At] the residential area [+topic marker de hua4]*, you will come to a fork in the road).

The fourth linguistic function that the authors found essential to the task was the prediction of future possibilities that one may experience, marked using the modal verbs *hui4* and *ke3yi3*. Both can be translated as "be able to," "will," "can." A sentence using *hui4* may be seen in Example 4.

- **Example 6:** (modal verb *ke3yi3*): *Ni3 yi-4zhi2 kai1 xia4qu, ni3 jiu4 ke3yi3 kai1dao dong4wu4yuan2.* ([If] you keep on driving straight on, you will arrive at the zoo.)

In terms of speech acts, the authors found that simple greetings and saying thanks were essential to the task. The authors also found some features that were specific to naturally occurring spoken Mandarin, such as the filler *na4ge* (that). Three negotiation of meaning strategies were identified: clarification request (*Qian2bian na4ge?* [The one in front?]); repetition request *(Suo3yi3 wo3 [repeat direction], ran2hou4 ne?* [So I will {repeat direction}, then what?]); and backchanneling (e.g., oh, uhm).

After the analysis, the teaching materials were then developed from the information gathered from the student interviews and semi-authentic discourse collection. A brief description of the process is provided in the next section.

Task Sequencing and Pedagogical Methods

The design of the instructional sequence and activities followed ten task-based principles of language teaching grounded in second language acquisition research by Long (1985, cited in González-Lloret, 2003). The principles have been adapted and categorized under four aspects (González-Lloret, 2003, p. 88):

1. **Activities:**
   a. Support integral education: the concept of learning by doing.
   b. Use tasks, not texts, as the units of analysis: follow TBLT curriculum development principles (Long & Norris, 2000).
2. **Input:**
   a. Elaborate input and 4. Provide rich input: use elaborated rather than simplified language or natural unmodified language. Provide synonyms, antonyms, paraphrases, definitions, or links to an on-line dictionary of the unfamiliar words to assist comprehension.
3. **Learning Processes:**
   a. Encourage inductive / "chunk" learning: encourage learning formulaic sentences and lexical "chunks."
   b. Focus on form: to briefly draw learners' attention to linguistic elements (e.g., words, collocations, syntax) while focusing on communication and meaning.
   c. Provide negative feedback: provide feedback to learners' language.
   d. Respect learner "syllabuses" / developmental processes: provide content suited to learners' needs and that learners are psycholinguistically ready for.

4. **Learners:**
   a. Promote cooperative/collaborative learning: encourage interaction and collaboration in conducting tasks.
   b. Individualize instruction: accommodate learner aptitude, motivation, learning styles and strategies.

The weekly structure of the blended CMP was as follows:

1. Student independent study of textbook, listening workbook and audio CDs.
2. Online listening exercises, in which students listened to audio recordings of words or lexical chunks and selected the image that represented what they heard. The computer gave audio feedback (i.e., correct or not correct in Chinese).
3. Online Q & A forum for checking student's completion of textbook exercises, assigning additional tasks before the tutoring sessions, and communicating problems and questions from students.
4. Face-to-face tutoring to complete the interactive tasks that students were assigned in the Q & A forum.
5. Post-tutoring performance task online in which students were given a different language task for them to respond to by recording online.
6. Focus-on-form task online, in which pedagogical tasks were given to target learning of specific linguistic forms.
7. Quiz.

Integrating TBLT Material and Task Sequence into Existing Structure of the Course

The task sequence is presented below in the form of a description of day-by-day activities. In this pedagogical approach, task – rather than syntactic or lexical forms – served as the unit of analysis. On

Day 1, the students were presented with authentic input from part of the discourse collection on "how to get to City Mill (a local hardware store)" with input enhancement. Unit structure-wise, this corresponded to Component (1). Students were provided with a video screen capture of the Google map (maps.google.com) of the area around City Mill near the university. In the video, while the dialogue on asking the directions played in the background, a little white hand moved across the map in accordance with the directions given in the dialogue. The video was created using the open source screen capture software CamStudio (http://camstudio.org/). Students viewed the video link using the Internet Explorer web browser as many times as they liked.

The second activity was for students to identify the general dialogue discourse structure. The exercise was developed through the software Hot Potatoes™ (http://hotpot.uvic.ca/), online quiz development software. In this exercise, the English translation was provided for the discourse structure. Students listened to five recorded segments of the directions dialogue and then arranged them in the correct order of discourse. See Figure 2 for a screenshot of this exercise.

On Day 2, the focus was on direction-specific vocabulary and social-cultural awareness of customs related to asking and giving directions in China compared with those in the U.S. Another several online gap-filling exercises were developed, again using Hot Potatoes™. This corresponded to unit structure Component (2). Target vocabulary items pertinent to direction / location or transitional words were left blank in the transcripts of the directions dialogue. There was one audio link beside each utterance. Students would listen to the short audio for that sentence and fill in the missing words. All the missing words were provided in a randomized menu at the top, and

Figure 2. Screenshot of the discourse structure exercise

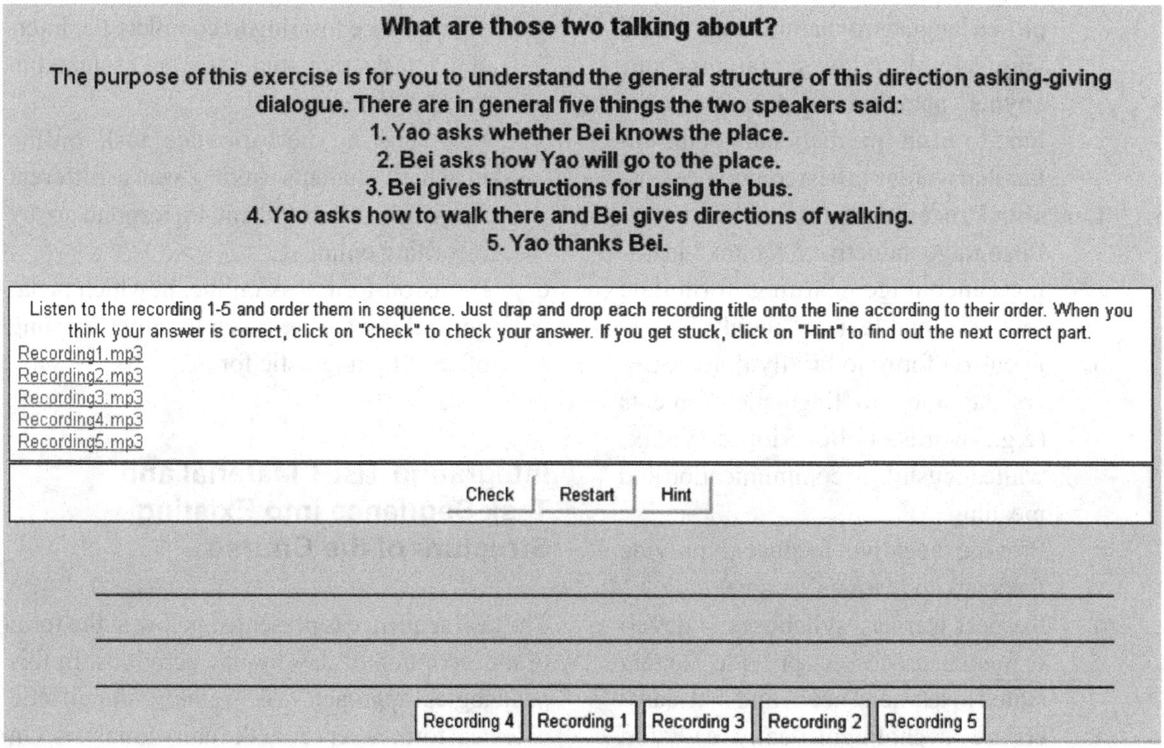

What are those two talking about?

The purpose of this exercise is for you to understand the general structure of this direction asking-giving dialogue. There are in general five things the two speakers said:
1. Yao asks whether Bei knows the place.
2. Bei asks how Yao will go to the place.
3. Bei gives instructions for using the bus.
4. Yao asks how to walk there and Bei gives directions of walking.
5. Yao thanks Bei.

Listen to the recording 1-5 and order them in sequence. Just drap and drop each recording title onto the line according to their order. When you think your answer is correct, click on "Check" to check your answer. If you get stuck, click on "Hint" to find out the next correct part.
Recording1.mp3
Recording2.mp3
Recording3.mp3
Recording4.mp3
Recording5.mp3

| Check | Restart | Hint |

| Recording 4 | Recording 1 | Recording 3 | Recording 2 | Recording 5 |

English translations of the words were provided as hints for students who clicked the hint button (labeled "?" or "Hint") in the exercise. First year students were given a simpler set of directions (to a closer location) as their listening task, and second year students were given a more complex task (to a further location). A screenshot of this exercise is presented in Figure 3.

In the Q&A forum [unit structure Component (3)], the instructors presented several consciousness-raising questions, asking students to reflect on the culture of approaching strangers and asking directions in their own country and to speculate on the culture of this social transaction in China. Students then read an informal essay summarizing the insights the authors had gained from the needs analysis interviews.

During Day 3 face-to-face tutoring [unit structure Component (4)], an information-gap map task was given to students. Each student held a map; one student designated the locations of certain landmarks (e.g., banks, hospitals) while her partner designated the locations for other landmarks given in the exercise. Then, they gave directions to each other as to where to find all the landmarks.

In the end, they compared maps to see whether they got it right. Key phrases were provided on the handout to facilitate the task.

On Day 4, students were asked to complete two tasks online [unit structure Component (5)]. One was a modeled direction-giving task, and the other was giving directions in a phone message. The modeled direction-giving task was a chain activity in which each participant depended on input from the person immediately preceding and provided input for the person immediately following. First the instructor provided a model set of directions, in the form of a recording and transcript, to a location on a map of Beijing, beginning at the railway station; the next student posting in the forum would guess where the instructor meant to go, and then this student would give directions to another location and the following students would guess this location and give directions to yet other locations, each in turn. Chain activities were often used in the online portion of this course to increase the degree of interactivity of language use and to compensate for the asynchronous format. Students were asked to record their response in an MP3

Figure 3. Screenshot of the gap filling vocabulary exercise

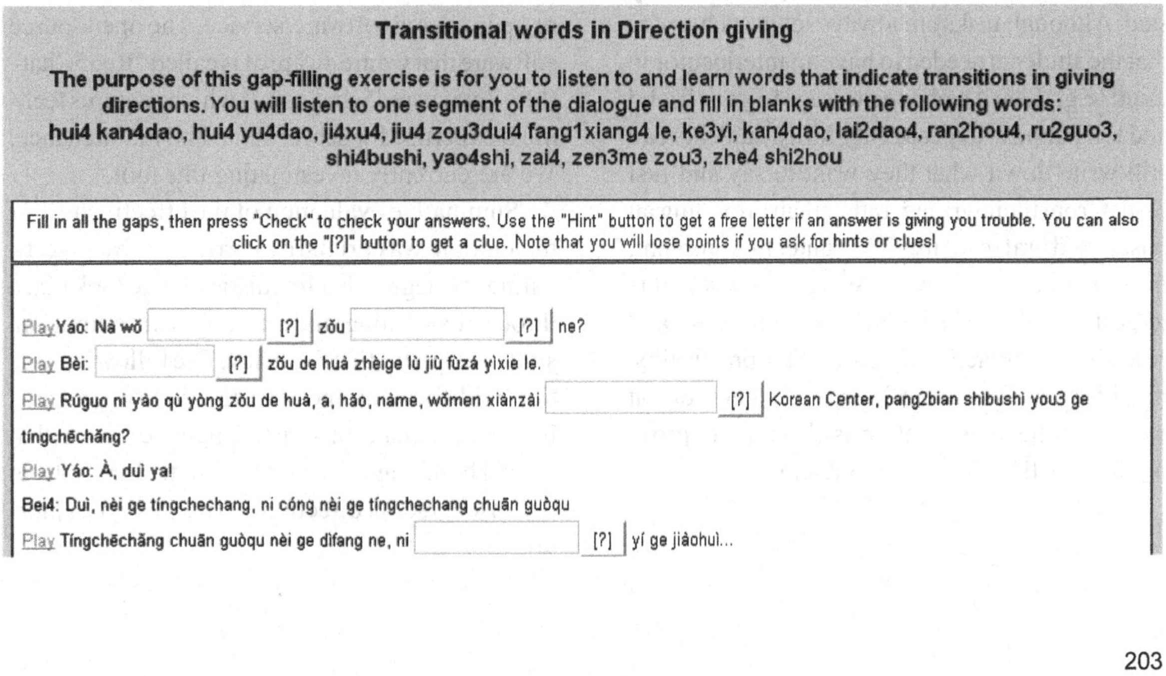

Transitional words in Direction giving

The purpose of this gap-filling exercise is for you to listen to and learn words that indicate transitions in giving directions. You will listen to one segment of the dialogue and fill in blanks with the following words: hui4 kan4dao, hui4 yu4dao, ji4xu4, jiu4 zou3dui4 fang1xiang4 le, ke3yi, kan4dao, lai2dao4, ran2hou4, ru2guo3, shi4bushi, yao4shi, zai4, zen3me zou3, zhe4 shi2hou

Fill in all the gaps, then press "Check" to check your answers. Use the "Hint" button to get a free letter if an answer is giving you trouble. You can also click on the "[?]" button to get a clue. Note that you will lose points if you ask for hints or clues!

Play Yáo: Nà wǒ [____] [?] zǒu [____] [?] ne?

Play Bèi: [____] [?] zǒu de huà zhèige lù jiù fùzá yìxie le.

Play Rúguo ni yào qù yòng zǒu de huà, a, hǎo, nàme, wǒmen xiànzài [____] [?] Korean Center, pang2bian shìbushì yǒu3 ge tíngchēchǎng?

Play Yáo: À, duì ya!

Bei4: Duì, nèi ge tíngchechang, ni cóng nèi ge tíngchechang chuān guòqu

Play Tíngchēchǎng chuān guòqu nèi ge dìfang ne, ni [____] [?] yí ge jiāohuì...

203

recording application in the courseware and to post a transcript of the recording if they chose to.

The activity in Component (6) form on the form was to leave a phone message to answer a request from the "friend" of a student for spoken directions to City Mill. Scaffolding was provided by presenting a sequenced set of pictures along with key phrases, which were target linguistic forms. The un-scaffolded version of this task was used in the final online exam.

The instructor provided ongoing feedback on students' questions, as well as explicit and implicit negative feedback. Students' recordings provided a basis for instructors to evaluate students' fluency and pronunciation accuracy, and the transcript allowed the instructors to examine students' linguistic knowledge in detail (e.g., knowledge of tone marks, spelling, and grammar).

Assessment

Currently, the Web Audio Utility, an online application which allows password-protected login and the option of private posting of audio recordings from students to instructors, is used for the final exam. Instructors can give test task instructions in written form and provide an audio prompt. Students need to respond by providing an audio recording and (if desired) a transcript of what they said. Although tasks are always set in such a way that the students needed to have an interlocutor in mind (e.g., Leave a phone message to your friend and tell her how to get to City Mill), students can still write down what they want to say and just read it from their writing, rather than providing an unscripted oral response. To counter this problem, the last tutoring class was reserved to ask students to perform test tasks with different partners and record their interactions. However, the practicality, reliability and validity of this assessment format require further investigation as a basis for improving the existing assessment system.

EVALUATION

We carried out both formative and summative evaluation of our module. The purpose of the formative evaluation was to identify the problems and challenges in the process of developing and implementing the TBLT. The purpose of the summative evaluation was for us, as developers and instructors of the TBLT module, was to judge the effectiveness of the module and to make decisions as to whether to continue the module and keep developing new modules.

Formative evaluation of our TBLT direction module was informally carried out throughout the lesson, by asking students to reflect their learning and to post questions and challenges that they were facing in the course. Instructors promptly reacted to the difficulties or questions that students had throughout the unit.

We also identified the achievement assessment system as the area most in need of future improvement. We need a system that allows live interactions between the student and the instructor or other students which can be conducted through the Internet, a system that can also record streaming audio or video for the instructors to assess students later and for the students to examine their own performance later. Although Adobe ConnectTM can serve this function, we are looking for a free or open source software/service. The open source software that we are aware of is called "Red5Chat" (http://www.red5chat.com/) which requires technical expertise for server setup and maintenance. We are currently investigating this tool.

Summative evaluation of the effectiveness of the module was primarily carried out by investigating the degree that linguistic uptake took place through examining students' linguistic output and students' qualitative feedback. The following section will focus on the investigation of students' linguistic uptake of target language forms that served both linguistic and pragmatic functions in the discourse of direction asking, as an explor-

Figure 4. Number of target linguistic form tokens from CHN 111 and 211 students' output in two language tasks

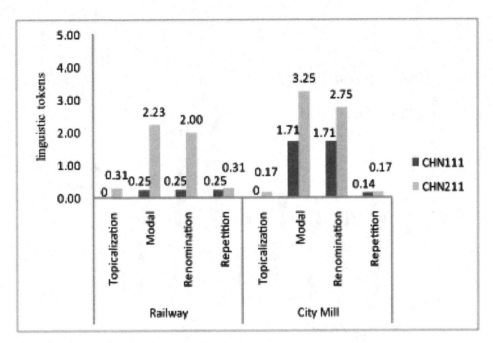

atory effort to investigate the effectiveness of the TBLT module. The authors selected four linguistic functions, namely topicalization, renomination, repetition, and modal verbs, because they were highly representative of natural discourse features, but were not covered in the textbook.

Two tasks were selected for the purpose of analysis: "Beijing Railway Station Directions" and "Directions to City Mill." Both tasks are described above under Day 4 activities. All students' recordings and forum postings for two pedagogical tasks in the BRIX courseware were transcribed. The transcription of the recording was first conducted by the first author and was verified by the second author. Target linguistic functions were identified, namely, topicalization, renomination, repetition, and modal verbs. Figure 4 shows the number of target linguistic forms that were produced per student, and Figure 5 the percentage of students who produced the forms. (The actual frequencies of the linguistic forms produced and the number of the students who produced the forms are pre-

sented in the Appendix). Coding was done by both authors, and interrater consensus was reached for the coding of each function.

Several patterns may be observed in Figures 4 and 5. First, there was an obvious developmental sequence between CHN 111 (Year 1) and CHN 211 (Year 2) students. Our sample showed that Year 2 students used a greater number of tokens of each form than Year 1 students, and a greater percentage of the second year students than first year students used the target linguistic forms (except for the repetition form produced in the Railway task). Nevertheless, Year 1 students used quite a few modal verbs and renominations, which were not observed in output from previous cohorts. Therefore, it is clear that both levels of students showed uptake of the target linguistic functions, but Year 2 students were much more ready than Year 1 students.

Another pattern observed was the suggested acquisition order of different linguistic functions. Topicalization seemed to be the hardest form for

Figure 5. Percentage of CHN 111 and CHN 211 students whose linguistic output in two language tasks contained the target linguistic forms

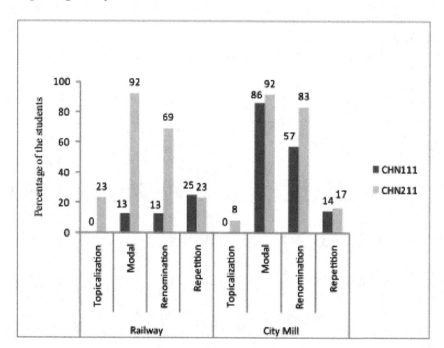

learners to acquire. Year 1 students did not use it in either task at all, and only 23% (3 out of 13) Year 2 students used it in the train station task and 8% (1 out of 12) in the City Mill task. Repetition was the second most rarely used form when the two tasks were taken together for both levels. The modal verbs *hui4* and *ke3yi3* were easiest among all the target forms and renomination was the second easiest, in terms of the average number of forms produced per student and the percentage of students who produced this form.

The third pattern observed was the task factor in the production of the target linguistic forms and its interaction with language level. The City Mill task elicited more frequent use of the modal and renomination forms per student and it elicited those two target forms from a higher percentage of students when all students from both levels were examined together. The difference between the percentage of Year 1 students and the percentage of Year 2 students who produced the modal and renomination forms in the Railway task was much

larger than the percentage difference between the Year 1 and Year 2 students in the City Mill task.

Since the purpose of output analysis was to evaluate the effect of TBLT on students' learning in these specific blended CMP classes rather than to conduct an experimental study, the generalizability is limited. However, the findings were interesting and significant in the following ways:

1. The results provided evidence that linguistic uptake of these target forms was achieved through conducting and completing pedagogical tasks, not through linguistic modeling or focus-on-forms instruction. In other words, the forms were picked up by students through their noticing and learning of the forms in naturally occurring discourse and scaffolded pedagogical tasks.

2. Student output was marked by use of natural discourse features not typically seen in output in Chinese language courses using textbook-based input. This may be credited

to the TBLT curriculum development model in which natural discourse served as input, and learning was scaffolded to achieve target tasks that were sequenced based on their cognitive complexity.

Overall, students were satisfied with the unit, including the utilization of the technology, natural discourse, and cultural components. They had comments such as:

- "I really like the [Hot Potatoes™] fill-in-the-blank format…"
- "This was a fruitful exercise but it took a while."
- "I really enjoyed the narration with the map because it really helped me to better understand how fluent Mandarin speaking people explain directions in a coherent way."

Students' linguistic and cultural awareness were activated as well. The students' feedback in the Q&A forum provided some evidence to support this claim:

- One student said "I learned *zhi2jie1* [directly], which I didn't know before…"
- Another student noticed some important phrases that he wanted help with: "Lots of interesting phrases for giving travel directions and I have some questions. What does *che1dao4* mean?…What about *qi2dao4di3*?"
- One student started noticing some discourse features of direction asking: "Yeah, I noticed she repeated everything. At first, I thought it was kind of weird but as I listened [more] I actually thought it helped in making sure I knew what area she was talking about."

All of these examples of the noticing of linguistic forms and mapping of form to function constitute evidence that TBLT and its integration with the blended CMP allowed learners to follow their own internal interlanguage syllabus and learn what they were ready to learn through noticing from input, as well as noticing the gap between their guesses and instructors' feedback.

IMPLICATIONS

It was encouraging for us to observe the positive feedback from the students and linguistic uptake analysis results. However, we acknowledge the challenges that we faced in terms of time and resource constraints. The data collection and analysis in the needs analysis and semi-authentic discourse collection were very time-consuming, and may be daunting to instructors with a full teaching schedule. For instance, in the transcription of interviews or role plays, one minute of audio recording would take 6 to 10 minutes to transcribe. All survey instruments (questionnaires and interview guiding questions) were based on literature reviews and pilot studies. We also had no budget to purchase commercial software for instrumental materials development and student assessment. We overcame some of the challenges by complementing our expertise, with Hill specializing in holistic curriculum development structuring, data collection and analysis in needs analysis, discourse analysis, and evaluation, and Tschudi being the expert in instrumental materials development and instruction delivery. We gave feedback to refine each other's work. We worked on one piece, say needs analysis, at a time, which usually took one semester. Resource-wise, we utilized many free services and open-source software applications (e.g., Google Maps, Hot Potatoes).

Figure 6. TBLT learning model in blended CMP

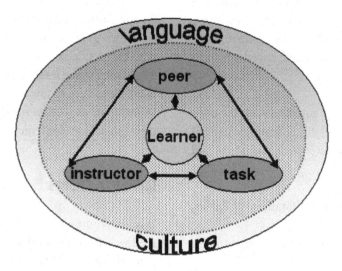

This project provides an example of a bottom-up TBLT curriculum development initiated by language teachers through the development of thematic units, which fit in the existing instruction structure and fully utilize TBLT curriculum development and task sequencing and instructional design principles. Throughout the process of needs analysis, materials development, task sequencing, and pedagogical and test task development, the authors centered their efforts around individual learners by forming interactions between learners, peers, the instructor, and the task, in learning both language and culture associated with a real life task deemed important to students. These interactions were evidenced in the needs analysis, which put learners at the center of curriculum design and innovation, and in pedagogical task engagement by learners with ongoing scaffolding and feedback from the instructor, showing both the interaction between the learners and the tasks and between learners and the instructor. Learners also interacted with their peers by providing answers to each other's questions and feedback to each other's production through the online forums, face-to-face interactions, and online chain activities. The interactions between the instructors and the tasks were ongoing from identification of target tasks

to the design and implementation of pedagogical and test tasks, which encompassed both formal and social-cultural aspects of the target tasks. This learning model and relationship between learning agents is depicted in Figure 6.

There are several characteristics of this project that may make it a unique contribution to TBLT praxis and literature: (1) This project is one of only a few examples showing how web-based language curricula can be implemented based on second language acquisition theories and TBLT teaching principles — in other words, a workable integration of TBLT principles and practices into computer assisted language learning (CALL) (for another example, see González-Lloret, 2003). (2) This project also demonstrates the possibility of TBLT curriculum design and implementation by individual language educators through constructive collaboration. (3) The current project was an example of curriculum innovation motivated by a previous evaluation effort.

The experience gained through the development of the directions unit provided great insight into the development of a systematic syllabus and online materials, and the potential extension of TBLT unit development to other important task types (e.g., transportation, shopping, restaurant dining). However, due to the intense labor demands of curriculum development through needs analysis, including assessment and evaluation, there is a need to seek collaboration with other colleagues. We hope that by providing our positive experience with TBLT curriculum development we will inspire more colleagues in and outside of our university to join us in such a rewarding endeavor.

REFERENCES

Antokhin, N., Boussalhi, A., Chen, K.-L., Combacau, P., & Koppany, S. (2004). Task-based reading activities developed for online delivery at the Defense Language Institute. In Leaver, B. L., & Willis, J. R. (Eds.), *Task-based instruction in foreign language education: Practices and programs* (pp. 181–203). Washington, DC: Georgetown University Press.

Bartlett, N. J. D. (2005). A double shot 2% mocha latte, please, with whip: Service encounters in two coffee shops and at a coffee cart. In Long, M. H. (Ed.), *Second language needs analysis* (pp. 305–344). Cambridge, UK: Cambridge University Press.

Bonk, C. J., & Graham, C. R. (2006). *The handbook of blended learning: Global perspectives, local designs*. San Francisco: Pfeiffer.

Brown, J. D. (1995). *The Elements of Language Curriculum: A Systematic Approach to Program Development*. Boston: Heinle & Heinle.

Byrnes, H., & Sprang, K. (2004). Fostering advanced L2 literacy: A genre-based, cognitive approach. In Byrnes, H., & Maxim, H. H. (Eds.), *Advanced Foreign Language Learning: A Challenge to College Programs* (pp. 47–85). Boston: Thompson-Heinle.

Canale, M., & Swain, M. (1980). Theoretical bases of communicative approaches to second language teaching and testing. *Applied Linguistics, 1*(1), 1–47. doi:10.1093/applin/1.1.1

Carless, D. R. (1997). Managing Systemic Curriculum Change: A Critical Analysis of Hong Kong's Target-Oriented Curriculum Initiative. *International Review of Education, 43*(4), 349–366. doi:10.1023/A:1003027923361

Chaudron, C., Doughty, C. J., Kim, Y., Kong, D.-K., Lee, J., & Lee, Y.-G. (2005). A Task-based needs analysis of a tertiary Korean as a foreign language program. In Long, M. (Ed.), *Second language needs analysis* (pp. 225–261). Cambridge, UK: Cambridge University Press.

Doughty, C. J., & Long, M. H. (2003). Optimal psycholinguistic environments for distance foreign language learning. *Language Learning & Technology, 7*(3), 50–80.

Edwards, C., & Willis, J. (Eds.). (2005). *Teachers exploring tasks in English language teaching*. Oxford, UK: Palgrave Macmillan.

Ellis, R. (2003). *Task-based language learning and teaching*. New York: Oxford University Press.

González-Lloret, M. (2003). Designing task-based CALL to promote interaction: En busca de esmeraldas. *Language Learning & Technology, 7*(1), 86–104.

González-Lloret, M. (2005, September). *Implementing task-based language teaching on the Web*. Paper presented at the 1st International TBLT Conference, Leuven, Belgium.

Hill, Y. Z., & Tschudi, S. (2005). *The effect of motivation and self-regulation on online language learning achievement: A preliminary research*. Honolulu, HI: University of Hawaii at Manoa. Honolulu.

Hill, Y. Z., & Tschudi, S. (2005). A utilization-focused approach to the evaluation of a Web-based hybrid conversational Mandarin program in a North American university. *Teaching English in China: CELEA Journal, 31*(5), 37–54.

Holmes, J. (2005). When small talk is a big deal: Sociolinguistic challenges in the workplace. In Long, M. H. (Ed.), *Second language needs analysis* (pp. 344–372). Cambridge, UK: Cambridge University Press.

Long, M. H. (2005). Methodological issues in learner needs analysis. In Long, M. H. (Ed.), *Second language needs analysis* (pp. 19–76). Cambridge, UK: Cambridge University Press. doi:10.1017/CBO9780511667299.002

Long, M. H., & Crookes, G. (1993). Units of analysis in syllabus design—The case for task. In Crookes, G., & Gass, S. M. (Eds.), *Tasks in a pedagogical context: Integrating theory and practice* (pp. 9–54). Clevedon, UK: Multilingual Matters.

Long, M. H., & Norris, J. M. (2000). Task-based teaching and assessment. In Byram, M. (Ed.), *Encyclopedia of language teaching* (pp. 597–603). London: Routledge.

Markee, N. (1996). *Managing curricular innovation*. Cambridge, UK: Cambridge University Press.

Norris, J. M., Brown, J. D., Hudson, T. H., & Yoshioka, J. (1998). *Designing second language performance assessments*. Honolulu, HI: National Foreign Language Resource Center.

Ross, C., & Ma, J.-H. S. (2006). *Modern Mandarin Chinese grammar: A practical guide*. London: Routledge.

Van Avermaet, P., & Gysen, S. (2006). From needs to tasks: Language learning needs in a task-based approach. In Branden, K. V. D. (Ed.), *Task-based language education: From theory to practice* (pp. 17–46). Cambridge, UK: Cambridge University Press.

Winn, M. (2005). Collecting target discourse: The case of the US naturalization interview. In Long, M. H. (Ed.), *Second language needs analysis* (pp. 265–304). Cambridge, UK: Cambridge University Press.

Yip, P.-C., & Rimmington, D. (2004). *Chinese: A comprehensive grammar*. London: Routledge.

APPENDIX

Table 1. Students' Uptake of Linguistic Functions/Forms in blended CMP direction tasks (Year 1 & 2)

			Topicalization	Modal	Renomination	Repetition
CHN Year 1	**Railway (n=8)**	*Frequency of Functions*	0	2	2	2
		Number of Students	0	1	1	2
	City Mill (n=7)	*Frequency of Functions*	0	12	12	1
		Number of Students	0	6	4	1
CHN Year 2	**Railway (n=13)**	*Frequency of Functions*	4	29	26	4
		Number of Students	3	12	9	3
	City Mill (n=12)	*Frequency of Functions*	2	39	33	2
		Number of Students	1	11	10	2

This work was previously published in the International Journal of Virtual and Personal Learning Environments, Volume 2, Issue 1, edited by Michael Thomas, pp. 19-36, copyright 2011 by IGI Publishing (an imprint of IGI Global).

Chapter 17

My Personal Mobile Language Learning Environment:
An Exploration and Classification of Language Learning Possibilities Using the iPhone

Maria A. Perifanou
National and Kapodistrian University of Athens, Greece

ABSTRACT

Mobile devices can motivate learners through moving language learning from predominantly class-room–based contexts into contexts that are free from time and space. The increasing development of new applications can offer valuable support to the language learning process and can provide a basis for a new self regulated and personal approach to learning. A key challenge for language teachers is to actively explore the potential of mobile technologies in their own learning so that they can support students in using them. The aim of this paper is first to describe the basic theoretical framework of Mobile Learning and Personal Learning Environments. Secondly, it intends to assist language teachers and learners in building their own Mobile Personal Learning Environment providing a useful classification of iPhone applications with a description and examples. The paper concludes with the proposal of ideas for practical, personal language learning scenarios, piloted in an Italian language learning context.

INTRODUCTION: THE ARRIVAL OF MOBILE LEARNING

Web 2.0 has changed the way that we communicate, get information, collaborate and learn. The increasingly ubiquitous nature of internet connectivity with the development of wireless and GSM networks, as well as the spread of broadband, has made it possible to access the web from almost everywhere. The Web has turned into a community of loosely connected participants who share their knowledge and interests (Tuchinda, Szekely, & Knoblock, 2008). Mobile devices including smartphones now include functionality for voice,

DOI: 10.4018/978-1-4666-2467-2.ch017

text, camera, video, paging and geo-location and are increasingly changing the nature of knowledge exchange and discourse in learning (Dieterle & Dede, 2006). This rich variety of platforms not only enhances the learning process but alters the nature of learning – both formal and informal- and changes the ways in which learning can be delivered (Ally, 2009). As Traxler comments, "Mlearning is uniquely placed to support learning that is personalized, authentic and situated. Formal learning is giving way to informal, mass learning to personalized learning" (Ally, 2009, p.18).

This new way of learning, assisted by mobile technologies, has opened new horizons for many fields of learning and especially for Language Learning. One of the major challenges for both foreign and second language learning is thinking about how technology can mediate or create connections between formal and more informal Personal Learning Environments (PLEs). MALL (Mobile Assisted Language Learning) is a new research field and according to research findings from several projects, mobile technologies can play an important role in foreign and second language learning. Language is about communication, and the ability to use newly acquired language skills in an authentic environment is seen as an important motivating factor for successful Language Learning.

Mobile technologies such as smartphones, can support communication, content delivery, personal learning engagement and contextual learning (Naismith, Lonsdale, Vavoula, & Sharples, 2005). Language learners can explore and choose the applications and tools that can support self-directed learning and can also assist the learner in developing a Personal Mobile Language Learning Environment (PMLLE). Language teachers can support this learning process and create their own PMLLE. Mobile devices such as smartphones can bridge the distance between learning in formal and informal contexts. These technologies have the potential to transform language learning into

an exciting lifelong learning experience. This article will explore these issues. The first section of the paper will briefly introduce the concept of Personal Learning Environments and a more open and democratic technology-assisted education and learning culture. The second section will describe the key issues in Mobile Learning and will briefly present a number of MALL projects. The following section will examine a number of Language Learning applications and services developed for the iPhone and will then propose a classification of those *'dedicated'* and those *'not dedicated'* to Language Education. The aim of this classification is to introduce language learners and educators to the rich variety of applications and services that iPhone offers, in order to become aware of the possibilities to create a rich PMLLE. The iPhone has been chosen because of the popularity of this mobile device among language learners in Greece. However other smartphones offer similar functionality. The paper will conclude with the proposal of practical, personal, collaborative Language Learning scenarios and a reflection on the benefits and implications of using the iPhone for creating a Mobile Personal Language Learning Environment (MPLLE).

OPEN EDUCATION AND PERSONAL LEARNING ENVIRONMENTS

Have new technological developments paved the way for a new more open and democratic in education and is this a new development? The vision of an open educational system was expressed many years ago by Piaget, Illich (1970) and Freire (1970) who have contributed their voices in a call to make education more equitable, more accessible, and more reflective of the nature of learning. Other researchers and educationalists have argued for reform in the balance of power between teachers and learners. Papert and Harel (1991) suggested that learning requires active doing and not lecture-based telling, while Vygotsky (1978) and Wenger (1998) emphasized the importance of social, culture, community, and history for learning.

In the digital age, new technologies can support an open educational movement that can bridge the divide between formal and informal learning, transforming this diachronic vision into a reality. The open technology-enhanced educational movement has the potential to improve access to educational media and networks and can provide standards and tools for the development of Open Educational Resources. Perhaps most importantly, the open education movement can help to reshape and transform pedagogy and educational institutions themselves (Couros, 2006). One of the challenges for educators is to develop new learning theories and methodologies that can assist learners and teachers in using increasingly powerful technological tools in formal or informal learning practice.

Connectivism (Siemens, 2005) is a learning theory that supports the idea of social and open learning enhanced by technology. It suggests that knowledge and cognition are distributed across networks of people and technology and learning is the process of connecting, growing, and navigating those networks. These on-line learning networks build on the dynamic of informal learning to transform traditional forms of knowledge acquisition and development focusing on personalized, lifelong and contextual learning. Whereas formal learning would appear to be still more important in terms of accreditation and recognition, informal learning has increasingly been acknowledged as having a greater impact within the context of lifelong development and practice (Cross, 2007).

The need for a more personalized environment for learning that can enable the learner to decide how to build knowledge, what kind of learning to pursue (formal or informal learning, social or more individual learning, short term or lifelong learning) or what to learn, has led to the development of a new learning model: the Personal Learning Environment (PLE). But what exactly are PLEs?

Personal Learning Environments (PLEs) offer a future model of learning that incorporates a greater range of tools, largely under the control of the learner. Wilson (2008) refers that PLEs are "not a piece of software... [but] an environment where people and tools and communities and resources interact in a very loose kind of way" (p. 109). According to Mark van Harmelen (2006), PLEs are systems that help learners take control of and manage their own learning. This includes providing support from learners to set their own learning goals, manage their learning, managing both content and process and communicate with others in the process of learning (para. 2). Furthermore, learners have the possibility to develop a learning environment to support their own style of learning. Attwell (2007) says the idea of a PLE recognizes that learning is continuing and contextual and will not be provided by a single learning provider. Furthermore, he explains that the PLE's idea is "to bring together all forms of learning, including informal learning, workplace learning, learning from the home, learning driven by problem solving and learning motivated by personal interest as well as learning through engagement in formal educational programmes"(p. 2).

New technologies and ubiquitous connectivity can support the idea of a PLE idea in combining situated, contextual and informal learning, and also encourage personal engagement with learning and lifelong learning experiences.

MOBILE LEARNING

The development of mobile technologies has led to the emergence of terms such as *'U-Learning'* or *'M-learning'*. Ubiquitous Learning - learning enhanced by ubiquitous devices (Zhan & Jin, 2005) is characterized by five different parameters (u-Environment, u-Contents, u-Behavior, u-Interface, u-Service). Where mobile technologies are used for educational purposes, the term *'M-learning'* (Mobile Learning) has become more common and this describes any educational interaction delivered through mobile technology and accessed at a student's convenience from any location (Educause, 2010). Bryan Alexander's (2004) descriptions of *'M-learning'* define new relationships and interactions between learners, information, personal computing devices, and the wider community. An important issue is to what extent these mobile devices have become a part of our lives or have been naturally integrated in the educational context. As long as eight years ago it was claimed that every student would have a portable wireless device (Bull, Garofalo, & Harris, 2002). According to recent research, around 2 billion cell phones are in service today compared to 700 million PCs, while most owners of cell phones who do not have PCs say that they will not purchase a PC in the foreseeable future (Katz & Yablon, 2009). Josh Dhaliwal, Director of MobileYouth, found that one in three children aged between 5 and 9 own a mobile phone and the average age of first phone ownership is now 8, while there are now a million children under the age of 10 with a mobile phone (Naish, 2009). "Students may turn up to class without an exercise book or pen, but never without the mobile phone" (May, 2005, para. 23).

Providing young children with tools to capture and organize their everyday experiences, to create and share images of their world, and to explore their surroundings can pave the way for lifetime learning. Cell phone platforms can provide flexible, user-friendly, controlled and adaptive learning (Collins, 2008). In research related to *'M-learning'*, undertaken by Roschelle (2003), it was found that some participants adapted their devices to suit their learning needs, writing new applications or tailoring existing ones, and adapted how they learned to suit the functionality available from their devices. He also identified two forms of collaborative participation: "the normal social participation in classroom discussion and the new informatic participation among connected devices", (p. 262). Those findings

not only show how mobile devices can support the personal learning needs of the learners, but also foresee how these technologies can change the way that people can learn in collaboration in different contexts and situations. Is it the device or something more that has changed and will continue to change the way we will learn? Low says that it is not about the technology, but about the mobility of the learning and what we need to do to fully exploit the use of mobile devices is look at the context and the mobility of learning, not the device itself (Downes, 2007).

One of the areas that is likely to lead the *'mobile movement'* is the field of language instruction (Wagner, 2005). Language teachers are actively exploring the potential of current mobile technologies in Language Learning. This sector is known in the language learning research community as *Mobile Assisted Language Learning* (MALL).

MOBILE ASSISTED LANGUAGE LEARNING PROJECTS

Introduction to MALL

One of the most critical factors for successful second and foreign language learning is contact and immersion in that language. Of course living in a country or region where that language and immersion in the culture of that language is a highly effective language learning strategy. But what about those students who are unable or unwilling to take advantage of opportunities to study abroad? In this situation, mobile technologies can help to provide an authentic language learning experience. Mobile learning can support learning conversations across contexts (Mohamed, 2009). Mobile learning can facilitate situated learning in a context with real interactions in the target language and not just a simple simulation of the process; can provide access to information while moving around a specific environment and information sharing in collaborative learning.

Learners are free to learn a language by gathering and processing information, while playing a role in real life locations (Meyer & Bo-Kristensen, 2008). According to Milton (2006), learning a language is very different from any other subject in the curriculum. It combines explicit learning of vocabulary and language rules with unconscious skills development in the fluent application of both these things. This can only happen when language learners are exposed to regular, authentic language use, something that mobile technologies can support. Successful learning involves a mixture of work and fun and mobile devices can motivate learners through moving language learning from predominantly classroom–based contexts into contexts that are free from time and space (Naismith et al., 2004).

However there remain issues of how best to develop the potential of mobile devices for learning and how to support students in their use. A key challenge for language teachers is to actively explore the potential of mobile technologies in their own learning in order to apply it to their teaching practice.

MALL Projects

Recent research has focused not only on the learning possibilities of mobile devices in language instruction, but also to explore how technology can mediate or create connections between the formal and informal environments. At a Japanese university, cell-phones have been used successfully for learning English as a Foreign Language (EFL), (Thornton & Houser, 2002, 2003). The TAMALLE (Television and Mobile Assisted Language Learning Environment) project at the University of Brighton developed a cross platform system, blending iTV and mobile phones, to support adult EFL learners' comprehension of television programmes and the learning of new vocabulary. TAMALLE supported learners' understanding of authentic materials broadcast on television (e.g., news, documentaries) by scaffolding difficult

language constructions with explanation, and enabled learners to construct and organize their own individual knowledge through an environment that could be also accessed anytime and anywhere via mobile phones. In another project, Katz and Yablon (2006) compared students' achievement using cell phones, email, and postal mail as learning content delivery systems. Their research findings showed that achievement in English vocabulary learning was not dependent on a particular delivery system. However, mobile phone based SMS learning appeared to lead to a greater feeling of flexibility, user-friendliness, control of learning and adaptability than email or postal mail based learning. The LinguaNet project, undertaken by the Universities of Rousse and Bulgaria, had as an objective the development of a smart, virtual space for language learning through a distributed system (Virtual Private Network), comprising of educational Language Nodes delivering learning services for mobile users through WAN or GPRS wireless connectivity to handheld devices. The second goal of the project was the improvement of the quality of service *at 'guest contact points'*, by motivating and aiding professionals in the tourism sector to learn the language of the country of their customers through their PDA, Smartphone or wireless laptop. The main target groups were personnel in the hotel and tourism industry (company managers, tourism promoters), hotel guests and travelers, European tourists and businessmen, language trainers, and young graduates. Another project at the Open University of UK has investigated how personal mobile devices are used by students and alumni from a global Masters Programme offered by the Institute of Educational Technology (Kukulska-Hulme & Pettit, 2006). BBC Wales has offered Welsh lessons (Andrews, 2003) via SMS and the BBC World Service Learning English section has provided English lessons via SMS in Francophone West Africa and in China (Godwin-Jones, 2005). The *'Mobile and Immersive Learning for Literacy in Emerging Economies'* (Educause, 2010) project undertaken by Carnegie Mellon University and the University of California, Berkeley, aimed to support a group of English teachers in rural India with m-learning applications designed for grade-school students. Students at Duke University have positively embraced the use of iPods for language courses (Belanger, 2005).

DEVELOPING A MOBILE LANGUAGE LEARNING PLE

There is increasing development of applications for mobile phones that provide challenging and authentic language learning experiences and bridge formal and informal contexts of learning. This provides opportunities for both language learners and teachers to develop a MPLLE including applications such as flashcards, quizzes, phrasebooks and tour guides.

Some researchers (Gay, Rieger, & Bennington, 2002; Roschelle, 2003; Naismith et al., 2005) have attempted to classify the variety of mobile learning applications and services that have been developed in the past few years. Patten (2006) has developed a framework dividing mobile learning applications into seven categories (collaborative, location aware, data collection, referential, administrative, interactive, and microworld applications).

This framework can be used as the basis for a classification of applications for Mobile Language Learning. Applications for the iPhone were firstly divided into two basic categories; *'dedicated'* and *'not dedicated'* to Language Education (Figure 1).

Applications created specifically for language learners or teachers and applications that even though not created for that purpose, could support the process of language learning. The classification also examines the level of flexibility or potentiality for use in language education.

The second step was to sub-divide the dedicated applications into two sub-categories based on the potential target groups of users: language learners and language teachers.

The third step was the further sub-division of the applications into nine categories. The first five categories (language courses; language courses offered by HE institutes; language learning materials and authoring tools; podcasts and audio books; data bases and portals) offered a variety of applications that could be used either by language learners to support autonomous learning or by language teachers for example to access multimedia language resources. The other four categories (assessment and management tools; course plans and material; podcasting tools; teachers' professional information, journals, magazines, etc.) comprised of applications created specifically for language teachers. This also includes the browsers offered by the iPhone, Wikitude, and Safari that can be used to access authentic language materials.

The fourth and last step in the classification was the sub-division of the 'non dedicated' applications into seven different categories (tools for vocabulary and translation; tools for data collection; location aware tools; edutainment tools; administrative tools; social networking, communication and collaboration tools; authentic material and Interaction tools) that could be used by both language learners and teachers.

The aim of this classification is to assist language learners and teachers in exploring the variety of applications and services for the iPhone as a basis developing their MPLLEs.

Table 1 in the Appendix provides a brief description of each category together with examples of applications and services.

STUDENT LED AND COLLABORATIVE MOBILE LANGUAGE LEARNING SCENARIOS

This section looks at different scenarios and examples of using Mobile Language Learning applications.

The first is a student-led quiz blog.

Figure 1. My PMLLE as a language learner and teacher

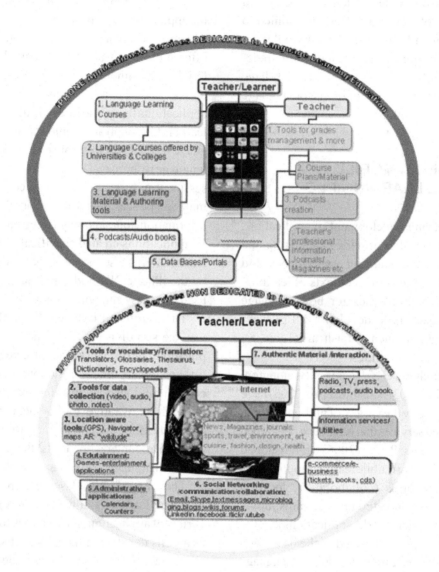

The language learner can use the *'Open Culture'* application to find a topic and then try to find related material including podcasts, audio-books and videos etc. The learner can create a blog, upload the material and then create a quiz for other students. The whole class can continue playing the game, each student choosing a topic of and creating their own quiz.

The second collaborative learning scenario is to develop a 'Wiki tourist guide' using microblogging tools and a wiki to create a tourist guide of a city and to invite students from other countries to collaborate to create a world cities guide.

This guide can be creative and interactive. Students can upload maps and geotag photos of places and people, and videos or podcasts of interviews of local people who present their city and their culture. Discussion topics could include hotels, places to visit, restaurants and entertainment, cultural events, local markets, history and traditions. Students can work in teams and use microblogging tools not only to communicate with each other but also to upload the material during the activity. Each group can work together on creating the final product on the wiki platform.

These learning scenarios have been piloted with a group of students in the second year of an Italian language course in a language school in Thessaloniki, Greece. The first research results showed that students were enthusiastic about the learning experience and impressed by the potential of the iPhone for learning. They found the classification of applications useful in accessing new applications and mobile tools for learning.

CONCLUSION

Learning a foreign language is an intensive and time consuming activity. Students are usually hard-pressed by the limited class time available and few have the opportunity to visit another country to learn a language. Immersion in the target language and learning in an enjoyable and creative way, appear to be the most critical factors for successful language learning. While mobile technologies offer rich possibilities for learning a language in an authentic environment, making the best use of these mobile technologies is a challenge for language learners and teachers.

A number of issues need to be taken into consideration. First of all, it is not the technology which is central to learning. Mobile phones are not a pedagogy, nor a means of pedagogy, but just a way of delivering learning. The development of pedagogies is a major challenge and remains a barrier to the proper integration of mobile technologies in the language learning processes.

Nevertheless, the high cost of advanced mobile phones is slowing the adoption of mobile learning. There are now a number of advanced operating systems for mobile phones with the expectation of cheaper smart phones in the near future. However the proliferation of mobile platforms is leading to

interoperability issues with different applications available for different platforms. Additionally many schools ban or restrict the use of mobile phones. This leads to a contradictory situation in which some schools are banning mobile phones while some of the world's most prestigious universities are investing resources to create free and open educational applications and materials to be accessed through mobile devices.

However, cell phones have become part of our culture, and despite the barriers mobile devices can offer valuable support to the language learning process and can provide a basis for the creation of a MPLLE. PLEs and MPLLEs are not just software applications, but represent a new model of learning. This incorporates a wide range of tools, services and applications under the control of the learner. A MPLLE can be a part of a broader PLE and can pave the way to an authentic learning experience for language learners and teachers.

REFERENCES

Ally, M. (2009). *Mobile learning: Transforming the delivery of education and training.* Athabasca, AB, Canada: Athabasca University Press.

Andrews, R. (2003, February 25). *Learn Welsh by txt msg.* Retrieved from http://news.bbc.co.uk/2/hi/uk_news/wales/2798701.stm

Attwell, G. (2007). *Personal learning environments – the future of eLearning?* Retrieved from http://citeseerx.ist.psu.edu/viewdoc/download?doi=10.1.1.97.3011&rep

Belanger, Y. (2005). *iPod first year experience* Retrieved from http://cit.duke.edu/pdf/reports/ipod_initiative_04_05.pdf

Blake, R. J. (2008). New trends in using technology in the foreign-language curriculum. *Annual Review of Applied Linguistics, 27,* 76–97.

Bryan, A. (2004). M-Learning: Emerging pedagogical and campus issues in the mobile learning environment. *EDUCAUSE Center for Applied Research (ECAR) Bulletin, 16.*

Bull, G., Garofalo, J., & Harris, J. (2002). Grand challenges: Preparing for the technological tipping point. *Learning and Leading with Technology, 29*(8).

Collins, T. G. (2008, July 5-8). *Proceedings of the Fifth IEEE International Conference on Advanced Learning Technologies*, Kaohsiung, Taiwan.

Couros, A. (2006). *Examining the open movement: Possibilities and implications for education.* Retrieved from http://www.scribd.com/doc/3363/Dissertation-Couros-FINAL-06-WebVersion

Dieterle, E., & Dede, C. (2006). Building university faculty and student capacity to use wireless handled devices for learning. In van Hooft, M., & Swift, K. (Eds.), *Ubiquitous computing: Invisible technology, visible impact.* Mahwah, NJ: Lawrence Erlbaum.

Downes, S. (2008). *Ten Web 2.0 things you can do in ten minutes to be a more successful elearning professional.* Retrieved from http://www.elearnmag.org/subpage.cfm?article=60-1&section=articles

Educause. (2010). *7 things you should know about the mobile apps for learning.* Retrieved from http://net.educause.edu/ir/library/pdf/ELI7060.pdf

Freire, P. (1970). *Pedagogy of the oppressed.* London, UK: Continuum.

Gay, G., Rieger, R., & Bennington, T. (2002). Using mobile computing to enhance field study. In Koschmann, T., Hall, R., & Miyake, N. (Eds.), *CSCL 2: Carrying forward the conversation.* Mahwah, NJ: Lawrence Erlbaum.

Godwin Jones, R. (2005). Messaging, gaming, peer-to-peer sharing: Language learning strategies and tools for the millennial generation. *Language Learning & Technology, 9*(1), 17–22.

Harmelen, V. M. (2006). Personal learning environments. In *Proceedings of the Sixth IEEE International Conference on Advanced Learning Technologies* (pp. 815-816).

Illich, I. (1970). *Deschooling society.* London, UK: Marion Boyars.

Katz Yaacov, J., & Yablon Yaacov, B. (2006, January). *Mobile learning: A major e-learning platform.* Paper presented at the LOGOS Conference, Budapest, Hungary.

Kukulska-Hulme, A., & Pettit, J. (2006, October). *Practitioners as innovators: Emergent practice in personal mobile teaching, learning, work and leisure.* Paper presented at the MLearn Conference, Banff, AB, Canada.

May, T. (2005). Thoughts about IT in language education. *Asian EFL Journal, 1*(1).

Meyer, B., & Bo-Kristensen, M. (2008). *Designing location aware games for mobile language learning.* Retrieved from http://www.formatex.org/micte2009/book/1086-1090.pdf

Milton, J. (2006). *Literature review in languages, technology and learning.* Retrieved from http://www.futurelab.org.uk/research/lit_reviews.htm

Naish, J. (2009, June 23). *Mobile phones for children: a boon or a peril?* Retrieved from http://women.timesonline.co.uk/tol/life_and_style/women/families/article6556283.ece

Naismith, L., Lonsdale, P., Vavoula, P., & Sharples, M. (2004). *Report 11: Literature review in mobile technologies and learning.* London, UK: Nesta Future Lab.

Papert, S., & Harel, I. (1991). *Situating constructionism*. Retrieved from http://papert.org/articles/SituatingConstructionism.html

Patten, B., Sanchez, I. A., & Tangney, B. (2006). Designing collaborative, constructionist and contextual applications for handheld devices. *Computers & Education, 46*(3), 294–308. doi:10.1016/j.compedu.2005.11.011

Roschelle, J. (2003). Unlocking the learning value of wireless mobile devices. *Journal of Computer Assisted Learning, 19*(3). doi:10.1046/j.0266-4909.2003.00028.x

Siemens, G. (2005). Connectivism: A learning theory for a digital age. *International Journal of Instructional Technology and Distance Learning, 2*(1).

Tuchinda, R., Szekely, P., & Knoblock, C. (2008, January 13-16). Building mahsups by example. In *Proceedings of the ACM 13th International Conference on Intelligent User Interfaces*, Canary Islands, Spain (pp. 139-148).

Vickers, H. (2009, June 17). *Augmented reality language learning – virtual worlds meet m-learning*. Retrieved from http://www.avatarlanguages.com/blog/arll/

Vygotsky, L. S. (1978). *Mind in society*. Cambridge, MA: Harvard University Press.

Wagner, E. D. (2005). Enabling mobile learning. *EDUCAUSE Review, 40*(3), 40–53.

Wenger, E. (1998). *Communities of practice: Learning, meaning, and identity*. Cambridge, UK: Cambridge University Press.

Wikipedia. (2010). *Mobile operating system*. Retrieved from http://en.m.wikipedia.org/wiki/Mobile_operating_system?wasRedirected=true

Wilson, S. (2008). Patterns of personal learning environments. *Interactive Learning Environments, 16*(1), 17–34. doi:10.1080/10494820701772660

Zhan, G., & Jin, Q. (2005). Research on collaborative service solution in ubiquitous learning environment. In *Proceedings of the 6th International Conference on Parallel and Distributed Computing, Applications and Technologies*.

APPENDIX

Table 1. Brief description of each category together with examples of applications and services

A.1)	Applications and Services dedicated to Language Learning and Education: Language Learners/ Teachers	EXAMPLES/DESCRIPTION
1.	Language learning courses	a) The Innovative Language Learning Family: A library of over 700 hundred different audio and video lessons in 14 languages at all levels. (Visit: www.innovativelanguage. com/languagelearning/new101).
		b) 24/7tutor: A multi-function language learning system with audio recording by a native speaker. (Visit: www.247tutor.com/).
		c) Bueno, entonces: A complete Spanish language course developed by 'Rosetta Stone'. A free trial is available (Visit: http://f.generallinguistics.com/learn-spanish/).
2.	Language Learning courses offered by Universities and Colleges	a) TEESP, Technology Enhanced Elementary Spanish program from Nebraska Department, U.S.A: videos with songs and translation, audio files, pdf, lesson guides for teachers. (Visit: http://manzana.esu16.org/groups/flap/).
		b) English by Southern Institute of Technology (Invercargill, New Zealand): Intensive English language program - 12 lessons of 30 minutes each. (Visit: http://www.sit.ac.nz/).
		c) Bon depart: Elementary course in French language in 19 lessons, offered by the Open University, UK. It offers also courses in French and German languages (accessible at iTunesU). (Visit: http://deimos.apple.com/WebObjects/Core.woa/Browse/itunes.open. ac.uk.2230065684).
		d) Elementary Greek language course with 161 lessons offered by Concordia seminary, University of St.Luis (Visit: www.apple.com/.../itunes-u/).
3.1.	Language Learning Material	a) Verbs: Italian, French verbs. (Visit: www.yminds.com).
		b) Idioms: English idioms. (Visit: www.eslstudyguide.com).
		c) Phrasebooks: Coolgorilla's Talking Phrasebooks (Visit: www.coolgorilla.com/iphone-applications/phrase-books.html), LingvoSoft PhraseBook. (Visit: http://www.lingvosoft.com).
		d) Translator's Practice: - odysseytransla: Use of audio flashcards for practice in a wide variety of languages. (Visit: http://odysseytranslator.com). - itranslate: Translation of words between English, Spanish, German, French, Italian and a words repetition back to the user in the target language. (Visit: http://www.appstorehq. com/itranslate-iphone-561/app). - translator. (Visit: http://coolgorilla.com).
		e) Language courses/ phrases based on travel dialogues: travelguides: Useful phrases in 23 languages (Visit:http://WorldNomads.com).
		f) Vocabulary practice: - WordPower–Lite: A new word every day with innovative, audio registration and tests with flashcards. (Visit: http://www.innovativelanguage.com/languagelearning/). - Learnlists: 10 new words every day in 24 languages, 500 common words. Functions include learn with test, listen, speak, write with translate tool and shared vocabularies. (Visit: www.Learnitlists.com). - AccelaStudy:2,100 words, 65 topic areas, different study options, exercises quiz, audio quiz, flashcard and translation tool. (Visit: www.accelastudy.com/).
		g) Games: EuroTalk: Offers greetings game in 36 languages.. (Visit: http://eurotalk.com/ utalk/en/).
3.2.	Authoring tools for creation of Language Learning material	a) Create quizzes with QuizYour Lizard: Let the user create study material and then view it in three modes: Study, Pop Quiz, and Spelling. Tool for creating language quizzes and sharing them in the language class. (Visit: http://www.downloadcheapapp.com/ quiz-your-lizard-iphone-app-45710.html). b) Tools for the creation of language learning material. (Visit: http://c4lpt.co.uk/Directory/Tools/instructional.html).

continued on following page

Table 1. Continued

4.1.	Podcasts: itunes store and iTunesU offer many podcasts of a big variety of language programs of all the levels. There is also available a category of podcasts especially for K12.	a) Dialogues: Offered in Welsh, Spanish. French, German and Italian language and developed by the University of Glamorgan, Wales, UK (Visit: http://itunes.glam.ac.uk/). b) Grammatica Italiana: Created by Luigi Gaudio, 43 audio lessons available. (Visit: http://itunes.apple.com/it/podcast/grammatica-italiana/id163792644). c) Greek vocabulary. (Visit: http://itunes.apple.com/podcast/learn-greek-vocabulary/id263942903). d) French For Kids: Developed by KidsByBaton Roug International School. (Visit: http://itunes.apple.com/us/podcast/french-for-kids-by-kids/id120975247). e) Learn to Speak Spanish. (Visit: http://itunes.apple.com/us/podcast/learn-to-speak-spanish-discover/id264318446).
4.2.	Audiobooks	a) Cross Forwarding Consulting: Free access to over 2,800 classic audiobooks (Visit: http://www.crossforward.com/). b) Hebrew Survival Phrases 'in 30 Lessons (Visit:http://www.theaudiobookstore.com/).
5.	Data Bases/Portals	a) Portales beginners Spanish-12: A portal for Spanish culture developed for language learning purposes by the Open University of UK. (Visit:http://podcast.open.ac.uk/oulearn/languages/podcast-1194-portales).
	Web browsers (internet access)	Safari: The iPhone's web browser provides access to language learning possibilities and resources through the web. Wikitude: Provides Augmented Reality (AR) for the third generation iPhone (3GS). Augmented Reality (AR) refers to the live direct or indirect view of a real-world environment whose elements are supplemented with, or augmented by, computer-generated imagery. The augmentation is conventionally in real-time and displayed through meaningful context with environmental elements (Wagner, 2005). Augmented Reality in Mobile Assisted Language Learning (ARLL) focuses on contextual learning and allows the learners to move outside of the conventional classroom and to choose locations that are relevant to their lives. It is not just a geo-tagged language learning, but as AR is developing very quickly, users will be able to interact soon with virtual objects within a real world context (Meyer & Bo- Kristensen, 2008).
A.2)	Applications and Services dedicated to Language Learning and Education: Language Teachers	EXAMPLES/DESCRIPTION
1.	Tools for grades management and more	TeacherTool One' by Learning Innovative Language: A comprehensive class management application that allows the teacher to input grades, attendance, calendar dates, and comments to students (Visit:http://itunes.apple.com/us/app/teachertool-one/id305195004?mt=8).
2.	Course Plans/Material	Manzana: Spanish language course: Language course including plans for teachers.(Visit: http://manzana.esu16.org/groups/teesplevel5/blog/).
3.	Podcasts for teachers/Podcast tools for Creation: Beyond the podcast prepared for teachers, iphone is an excellent tool to help create educational podcasts and not just find one. By having students create and record audio reports, they can further support their learning and share their knowledge with each other.	Teachers - Podcast AppBy Wizzard Media: Ed Tech Professional Development for Educators with news, views, research and resources for the teacher. (Visit: http://itunes.apple.com/us/app/teachers-podcast-app/id338117927?mt=8). AudioBoo: A social audio application and platform to record audio to the cloud. (Visit:http://audioboo.fm/). Talkshoe: The user can participate or conduct community calls and can also create podcasts. (Visit: http://www.talkshoe.com/).
4.	Teacher's professional information	Journals, magazines, newsletters, networks dedicated to language teachers (topics: teaching training, seminars, jobs etc). TeachingUk: News, ideas and twitter feed (Visit:http://www.tda.gov.uk/).
B)	Applications and Services non dedicated to Language Learning and Education	EXAMPLES/DESCRIPTION
1.	Tools for vocabulary/Translation: Translators, Glossaries, Thesaurus, Dictionaries, Encyclopedias.	a) Dictionary.com:1,000,000 words and definitions and 90,000 synonyms and antonyms. (Visit: www.dictionary.com). b) SpeechTrans Italian English Translator: Dictionary and Translator preloaded with 200 voice recognition translations (Visit: http://www.mobyware.net/iphone-os/dictionary-translator-tag/speechtrans-italian-english-translator-download-free-33227.html). c) Word Lens: Translate printed words from one language to another with a built-in video camera in real time.(Visit: http://www.mobyware.net/iphone-os/online-multi-dict-tag/word-lens-download-free-25694.html). d) Google Translate: Translate words and phrases between more than 50 languages. For most languages, users can speak several phrases and hear the corresponding translations. (Visit: http://www.mobyware.net/iphone-os/online-multi-dict-tag/google-translate-download-free-30631.html). b)Thesaurus: (Visit: www.thesaurus.com).

continued on following page

Table 1. Continued

2.	iPhone services - Tools for data collection/editing: video, audio, photo and notes	Photon by Phanfare: Allows entire photo and video collection to be stored in the cloud and to be accessed through a mobile phone with music slide shows and editing tools. (Visit: http://itunes.apple.com/app/phanfare/id285821580?mt=8). Tumblr: Quick logging of text, photo, quotes, link, chat, audio, and video. The user can keep it all in one place and use it to keep notes. (Visit:http://www.tumblr.com). iSaidWhat?!: Useful recorder that can allow the user to do some sound editing directly from a mobile phone: record, import sound file, cut, arrange snippets, duplicate, share via email, Facebook or Twitter. (Visit: http://www.tapparatus.com/isaidwhat). Photoshop: Tool to edit photos directly on a mobile phone: crop, straighten, flip, rotate, exposure, contrast, colors black and white, sketch, effects, borders, pictures can be saved, uploaded and posted to Facebook and TwitPic. (Visit: http://mobile.photoshop.com/iphone/).
3.	Location Aware Tools: (GPS), Navigator, Maps, AR (wikitude)	MobileNavigator: A GPS app providing updates on a persistent basis and supporting multi-tasking). (Visit: http://www.iphoneness.com/mobilenavigator). oMaps: Offline mapping to the iPhone. It includes GPS, multiple zoom levels, map bookmarking and search functionality. Instead of 'Google Maps' utilizes OpenStreet-Map. After purchasing the application, individual maps are free to download. (Visit: http://omapsiphone.com/).
4.	Edutainment: Games and entertainment applications	Wordlands: A treasure hunt game wrapped in a word skill game. Earn points and prizes along the way that helps the user to progress to the Promised Land. Everyone can make as many words in two minutes, but must be careful of the Word Pyramid, a special challenge that tests the speed and word-making accuracy. If the user can pass the Word Pyramid, can earn bonus themes and can continue his/her journey. Each Word Pyramid is progressively more difficult. After the five layers of Wordlands the user can reach the Promised Land. (Visit: http://www.techteam.gr/iphone/?a=wordlands).
5.	Administrative applications: Calendars, counters etc	Qwixt Calendar: An event calendar for iPhone that allows users to move events and organize their daily life. It supports category sharing and groups.(Visit: http://itunes.apple.com/us/app/qwixt-calendar/id403637861?mt=8). Boxnet: An online file sharing and collaboration service that allows users to access files from anywhere and securely share content with anyone. (Visit: http://itunes.apple.com/WebObjects/MZStore.woa/wa/viewSoftware?id=290853822&mt=8). MindMaps: Can be exported and emailed (Visit: http://www.thinkbuzan.com/).
6.	Social Networking/communication/collaboration tools	Documents: This application allows users to edit and manage spreadsheet & text files on iPhone. Works both online and offline. The user can also synchronize files to a Google Docs account to open files on PC or Mac. (Visit: http://itunes.apple.com/WebObjects/MZStore.woa/wa/viewSoftware?id=295798315&mt=8). Diigo: The user can bookmark new sites from a mobile browser although the bookmark does not allow for saving to groups. (Visit:http://www.diigo.com/). IM+ Pro: An all-in-one social networking platform. Chat on Skype, AIM, GTalk, Yahoo, ICQ, Myspace, Facebook, Twitter etc (Visit:.http://itunes.apple.com/app/im-pro/id296246130?mt=8). WikiTap: Uses tools geared towards phone-centred community participation. Community members upload relevant videos, pictures and audio-commentaries into the larger knowledge community. (Visit: http://itunes.apple.com/app/wiki-tap/id291701649?mt=8). Linkedin: A professional networking tool with a wide range of groups for linguists and teachers. (Visit: http://www.linkedin.com/). Flickr: The user can back up the photos from a phone and pictures from Flickr's favorites can also be saved onto the phone. (Visit: http://www.flickr.com/). Twitter: The user can use this micro blogging service to text messages, share audio and photo. (Visit: http://mobile.twitter.com/). Edmodo: Offer a free private microblogging service in the classroom. (Visit: http://www.edmodo.com/m/). Facebook: A popular social networking tool. (Visit http://www.facebook.com/mobile).

continued on following page

Table 1. Continued

7.	Authentic Material /interaction:	a) Internet Radio, TV, podcasts, audio books. Boombox: Built on the framework of social music website, Blip.fm. Using the free version of Boombox the user can search for and listen to songs on his/her phone, as well as create playlists. (Visit: http://itunes.apple.com/eg/app/boombox/id297648675?mt=8). ipadio: Broadcast, record, play back and share high quality audio up to 60 minutes in length. Recorded calls can be shared on Twitter, Facebook, Wordpress, Posterous, Blogger and more. (Visit: http://www.ipadio.com/).
		b) Information services-Utilities: weatherbug: Learn about the weather. (Visit: http://itunes.apple.com/app/weatherbug/id281940292?mt=8).
		c) E-commerce/E-business (example: buy tickets or books). Amazon App: Easy access to products available from Amazon.co.uk. (Visit: http://www.amazon.com/gp/feature.html?ie=UTF8&docId=1000291661)
		Stanza: A free application that anyone can used to download books and periodicals, to be read the on a phone. (Visit: http://www.lexcycle.com/).

This work was previously published in the International Journal of Virtual and Personal Learning Environments, Volume 2, Issue 4, edited by Michael Thomas, pp. 46-62, copyright 2011 by IGI Publishing (an imprint of IGI Global).

Chapter 18

Factors Affecting the Design and Development of a Personal Learning Environment:
Research on Super-Users

Helene Fournier
National Research Council of Canada, Canada

Rita Kop
National Research Council of Canada, Canada

ABSTRACT

After speculation in literature about the nature of Personal Learning Environments, research in the design and development of PLEs is now in progress. This paper reports on the first phase of the authors' research on PLE, the identification process of what potential users would consider important components, applications, and tools in a PLE. The methodology included surveying "super-users" on their use of existing tools, applications and systems and their preferences in learning, in order to enhance the development of a PLE and reach a specification that potential learners will find useful and empowering in their learning. The research resulted in suggestions on factors affecting technology use and uptake, human factors and attitudes, and interface design that need to be factored in the design and development of a PLE.

INTRODUCTION

Over the past five years the emergence of interactive social media has influenced the development of learning environments. The Virtual Learning Environment has come to maturity, but has been seen by learning technologists as not capturing the spirit and possibilities that the new media have to offer to enhance the learning process. They are controlled by educational institutions and are subsequently used to support institutional learning.

Each learner is unique and will have a unique learning experience. This has instigated the research and development of a different type

DOI: 10.4018/978-1-4666-2467-2.ch018

of learning environment, a Personal Learning Environment (PLE) that is in controlled by the learner. The needs, requirements and experience of each learner using a PLE will be different, which makes the planning and development of a PLE that serves as an aid to each possible learner a challenge. An added problem is the openness of the environment and the large number of different dimensions that can be designed and developed. Moreover, PLEs are so new that research in their development has been limited so far.

The authors are part of a team researching and developing a PLE and after scrutinizing the literature about the possible architecture of PLEs, research in the design and development of a PLE is now in progress. This paper will report on the first phase of the research; the identification of what potential users would consider important components, applications and tools in a PLE, and their learning preferences. The methodology included surveying "super-users" on their use of existing tools, applications and systems in order to develop the highest possible PLE specification.

The research paper will set out the research strategy, in addition to the results of the actual research. It will outline methodological concerns, and focus on the usability and functionality of the learning environment, the learner experience, and the minimum set of components required to facilitate quality learning. At the centre of the design and development is the premise that it should be the learner who owns the PLE and who makes the decisions about its use, not an educational institution.

PERSONAL LEARNING ENVIRONMENTS

If the learning environment moves outside the realm of educational institutions, this might affect the learning experience (Bouchard, 2011; Kop, 2010; Weller, 2010). The lack of presence of an educator to aid the learner in his or her critical engagement with resources has for instance been identified as a problem as the Web is not a power-free environment and people will have to adapt to negotiating this environment autonomously. To find the right information and to know how to access required resources, new competencies and abilities will be required from learners. Moreover, the new learning environment requires learners to be active in their learning by editing and producing information themselves in a variety of formats and by communicating and collaborating with others in new ways. People need to have a certain level of creativity and innovative thinking, in addition to feeling competent, confident and comfortable in using ICT applications to be able to do so. Learners need to be flexible, able to adapt to new situations and be able to solve problems that they come across during their learning journey. They will have to be motivated enough to take on new challenges and could use help from the system itself.

Some argue that these skills and competencies will develop while engaging in online communication with others, or via challenging feedback or recommendations through the PLE system itself (Downes, 2009). The system and technology itself, or the activity the learner is involved in, will have to be engaging and interesting enough for the learner to work his or her way through the problems that will undoubtedly come up during the learning journey. People will have to be motivated to use the environment.

Intrinsic motivation has an affective dimension and the literature highlighting the importance of affective aspects of networked learning is growing (Picard et al., 2004; Kop, 2010; Zaharias & Poylymenakou, 2009; Jones & Issroff, 2004). Other issues related to motivation have been highlighted by Lombard and Ditton (1997), and Dron and Anderson (2007) in the form of "presence". Dron and Anderson (2007) discussed the different levels of presence in different online learning 'settings'. They made the distinction between learning in 'groups', learning on 'networks', and learning by using 'collectives'. Presence and motivation would be highest in a group, which would be a typical class room or organised online educator-led learning setting, while presence in learning on an open informal network would be lower, e.g., on the 2008/2009 connectivism courses (Siemens & Downes, 2008, 2009). The connection and presence on collectives would be even lower as the connections between people and resources would be in the form of tags.

The main characteristic of presence is that of an illusion of non-mediation. In other words, there is a high level of presence when a participant in an online activity experiences the activity as if it was taking place in real life, without the mediation of the computer. Garrison et al. (2000) argued that deep and meaningful learning results if three forms of presence play a role in education. These would be "cognitive presence" that ensures a certain level of depth in the educational process and would be important in the creation of meaningful online experiences, "social presence", would also be important, and in a formal educational environment that of "teacher presence". In PLE based learning the teacher presence would not necessarily be there, but one could argue that there are knowledgeable others on the Web who would take on that teacher role to a certain extent.

A Personal Learning Environment (Downes, 2009) that would aid the learner in this endeavour could play a positive role. But which combination of components, tools and applications would form a pedagogical platform that would make learners think critically about resources accessed?

SELECTION OF SUPER-USERS TO IDENTIFY DESIRABLE COMPONENTS AND TOOLS FOR THE PLE

The Research in PLEs is only in its infancy and to know how best to research and evaluate a PLE we looked at e-learning evaluation and design-based

research literature. The literature on e-learning evaluation (Attwell, 2006) provides a variety of models ranging from comparisons with traditional learning, to benchmarking models, product evaluations, performance evaluations, program and policy evaluations, studies of metadata and more complex all encompassing design-based research (Bannan-Ritland, 2003) models. The approach to the evaluation in these models varies considerably and ranges from an emphasis on the program objectives, the management of the scheme, the outcomes for the user, the expertise required in the program to a participant oriented approach (Attwell, 2006). These are mostly related to the organization of learning, the 'input' and 'output' and lack in substance when it comes down to establishing the process taking place and the learner experience. The PLE Project research question was based not on instututional requirements, but on learner needs and learner experiences and the research approach was design-based in order to create an iterative process of research, design, testing and evaluation and further development.

The PLE project eventually decided upon three parts to the research: 1) An exploration phase: exploration of the literature and of possible components for the PLE, and close contact with other PLE research groups worldwide 2) Usability testing of Plearn, the developed learning environment, consisting of feedback from users on mock-ups of the PLE and testing of the Plearn prototype at different stages of development and 3) Educational research, consisting of a comparison of learning without and with Plearn.

This paper will report on the first phase of the research, the exploration. As the first stage of the PLE research, we asked advanced ICT users, people who are using advanced technology in their everyday life and learning, which tools they use, and how and why they choose to use them. We surveyed "super-users".

In the literature, the word "super-user" is used in different contexts and has different meanings, ranging from loyal users in social media campaigns, the user account responsible for the IT system administrator, and brand-ambassadors (Merritt, 2009). In this paper we define super-users as people who use advanced Internet tools and technologies in an educational environment. These tools would include information aggregators, editors and publishers; ones that exploratory research highlighted as possibly important to a Personal Learning Environment.

RESULTS OF THE FIRST PHASE

The first phase of the PLE research involved gathering information from potential users; what they consider to be the important components, applications and tools in a PLE. The methodology included surveying "super-users" on their use of existing tools, applications and systems in order to enhance the development of the highest possible PLE specification.

Use of Online Applications

A first survey was conducted to collect baseline information on experiences and perceptions regarding learning and use of technology by Internet users, on tools and functionalities already in use in order to learn what the important issues and features in the development of a Personal Learning Environment might be. Survey questions were developed based on knowledge and expertise within the PLE research and development team. The online survey format was tested internally amongst the NRC PLE research and development team (before it was launched at large). The survey included 28 questions and contained closed and open-ended questions; some allowed only one answer, others provided multiple options, with text boxes for additional comments and elaboration.

An invitation to participate in the online survey was advertized on the Principal Investigator's online learning daily newsletter—OLDaily (http://www.downes.ca/news/OLDaily.htm) and an email was sent to a targeted list of individuals who participated in an online symposium on Personal Learning Environments (PLEs) and Personal Learning Networks (PLNs) (http://ltc.umanitoba.ca/blogs/ples/about/). Findings from convenience sampling are usually not representative of the general population, so conclusions from this preliminary data set are limited in their generalizability. The goal was thus to derive useful information from the data to inform the PLE design and development process. In total, 204 surveys were completed. Respondents' profiles and background information provided the criteria for recruiting and retaining those who were skilled or experienced to participate in subsequent surveys and usability testing. Inclusion criteria include: adults over the age of 18; experience with computers and the Internet; and experience with social networking tools and applications (e.g., Facebook, RSS, forums, blogs etc.).

The survey was structured in several sections, starting with a section containing information on participants' background and on their use of technology, including their motivations and frustrations. Another section surveyed participants on their management of learning; where they find information and what helps them understand and combine information more specifically. Finally, the last part of the survey dealt with design issues in creating a Personal Learning Environment. The sections contained a list of suggestions for the participants to choose from, in addition to a large comment box.

Participant Demographics

The overall sample size was 204; the majority of participants in this first survey were males (55%); females (44%); missing values 0.5%. The age range of participants captured a broad spectrum of learners from young adults, middle-aged, to mature adults, with a majority between 43-48 years old (23%). Although most participants were from North America (48%), there was strong representation from both Europe (27%), and Australia (18%). The majority of participants possessed either college or university level education (90%) ranging from a Bachelor's degree (in areas such as Learning Management, Education, Distance Education), Masters (e.g., Educational Technology, Instructional and performance technology), to PhD degrees (e.g., linguistics, history and new media). A majority of respondents were employed (82%) in the following professions or areas: university instructor, departmental EdTech liaison, software designer, high school teacher, research assistant, K-12 school principal and deputy principal, and knowledge developer. Participants were also asked about their use of technology and their level of use. In general, survey participants rated their technical ability as excellent (42%) or very good (39%); we can assume that a majority of respondents were comfortable with various computer technologies. The highest percentages of technologies used where applications such as word processing (daily 86%–weekly 13%), email (daily 100%), social networking (daily 83% - weekly 12%) and searching the web (daily 97% - weekly 3%) with lower percentages of respondents using media file editing (daily 21% -Weekly 36%), and news gathering (daily 78% - weekly 12%).

Motivational factors in using computer based technology were diverse (Table 1).

Table 1. Motivational factors in using computer based technology (N=204)

Motivation factors	Number	Percentage (%)
When I learn something new	196	96
To produce something that I can be proud of	149	73
When I find a real gem of information	148	73
To see something made by others that is really amazing	129	63
When others recommend something really interesting	128	62

The motivational factors with the highest percentages were the "desire to learn something new" followed by "producing something that they can be proud of", and the lure of finding "a real gem of information". Other important motivational issues were "to see something made by others that is really amazing" and "when others recommend something really interesting".

Other comments related to motivation highlighted issues of efficiency, supporting others in their use of technology and learning, and the requirement of using the technology in the work place. Participants were also asked about their frustrations with the use of computer-based technology in general. The most common frustrations as chosen from a list of options were as follows: advertising (62%), when technologies do not work (62%) or "phishing" or identity theft (46%).

Survey questions explored the use of communication tools, with a majority (58%) of survey participants ranking email/webmail as their preferred communication tool; this was the case for a majority in North America (32%) and Europe (16%). Cell phones for texting or voice was the second most popular communication tool for 19% of respondents; social networking sites such as Facebook, MySpace or other social networks (10%) was third; Skype, Messenger, or other Internet (video) phone (4%) was the fourth most popular; web forums and discussion boards was the fifth (3%); and finally home phone (2%) rated lowest in popularity.

When using editing and publishing tools, blog publishing tools ranked highest in preference followed by online word processors and photo and video sharing sites. Real time communication/ collaboration tools were ranked 5th in the category of editing and publishing tools. Finally, with regards to the use of online services, activities or applications, participants showed a preference for several different choices. The top five choices are listed in Table 2.

Table 2. Online services, activities, or applications consulted (N=204)

Services/ Applications/ Activities	Number	Percentage (%)
Learning Management System	158	77
Internet shopping	134	66
Internet application organizing tool (iGoogle...)	128	63
Online product reviews and ratings	121	59
Leave comments and rate people's blogs	114	56

Participants identified "other" online services, activities or applications either consulted or engaged in on a regular basis, among them was Twitter, Etherpad, lino, wallwisher, Zotero, Librarything, WordPress blogging, RSS-Feedly, particular forums and Ning, just to name a few. Social networks were also consulted for sharing photos, videos, for meetings, creating and socializing in Virtual Worlds (e.g., Second Life), blog writing, and various social media.

Survey respondents provided information related to their management of learning and what helps them to learn. A majority of respondents find information on a topic of interest, with Google or other search engines (98%), the web (92%), followed by social networks (69%), RRS feeds (69%), and books (68%). Friends were also important in finding information (50%) and other options were explored as well, including: university subscription services, databases (e.g., EBSCO, Lexis/Nexis, Naxos), professors, researchers, popular media (e.g., newspapers, magazines, ads), YouTube, occasionally TV, and online library collections.

Next, the most popular modes or mechanisms used for understanding and combining information are presented. Figure 1 reveals that a majority of respondents prefer "interactive activity" (69%) for understanding and combining information, followed by "presentations using graphs and charts" (54%), or "when presented in a video podcast" (52%).

Participants expanded on their answers regarding mechanisms that help them understand and combine information. What follows is a sampling of their comments:

•   When I can discuss it with others, screencasts and slidecasts.

Figure 1. Popular means for understanding and combining information

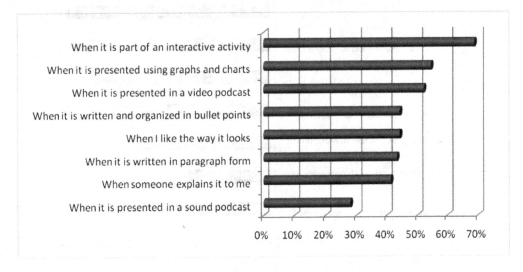

- When I can organize it so it makes sense.
- When it is posed as a challenge.
- When I take notes and rework/process them.
- When someone tweets a useful link and someone else tweets a link to a related story.
- When I can combine and check information flexibly.
- When it's blogged or op-ed'd.
- When I can do something with it.
- When it is written simply without a lot of extra words and jargon.
- Cmap, visual approaches.
- Solitude and reflection.

This information will be applied in the development of support mechanisms that will be available to learner/users of the PLE. In addition, a majority of participants indicated a preference for sharing interesting information from someone with their social network (79%) and thinking about the information (78%). Sharing the information via email (71%) was also important, while commenting (61%) and writing (57%) of blog posts

was also seen as a valuable activity related to received information. Under "other" comments, a high number of respondents indicated a preference for (social) bookmarking options to help them understand and combine information (e.g., share on Google reader, Diigo, tag it in Delicious and retweet). A majority (83%) of participants indicated a preference for talking with other people to help them reflect on a either a topic or learning activity. Receiving feedback from others, knowledgeable persons in particular, was seen as important for 56% of respondents. Writing it down in their own words (74%) was also a well-liked strategy to facilitate reflection. Several found reading related material to be helpful (58%) as well as being on their own without distractions (50%). Another important aspect of the survey was aimed at discovering features and design issues of a PLE that would be of importance to learners. The features that were viewed as highly desirable in a PLE are presented in Figure 2.

When presented with a list of possible features for a PLE, participants emphasized both the ease of navigation and the offering of a variety of tools within the PLE as key requirements. In addition,

Figure 2. Desirable design features in a PLE in general

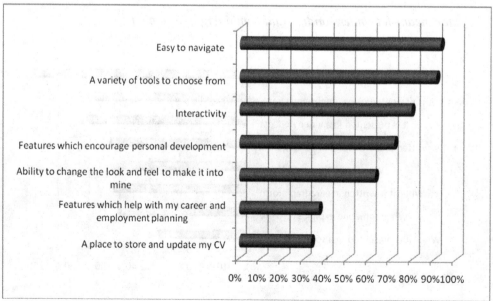

functionalities that would enable interactivity, encourage personal development, and facilitate customizability of their personal learning environment where also requested. Components to help with career and employment planning, and to write a CV were all seen as less important. Comments in the 'other' response section ranged from issues of effectiveness and organization, to flexibility, sharability and transferability.

Participants were asked which information search and organization features would be most desirable in a PLE and several options rose to the top of their priority list. The PLE should not only help learners find information relevant to them, show information in a variety of formats (e.g., text video, audio), allow learners to 'mash up' information from different sources, it should also help learners collect information, edit and produce something from it, and publish it on the internet. Responses provided under the 'other' option reflected a desire for personalization, for the integration of social bookmarking, and social networking applications. Survey respondents were also asked about required features to support their learning in a PLE. Table 3 highlights features that would support 'learning from others' and 'help manage learning activities', including structuring, organization and planning, and finally storing learning activities as a priority for a majority of respondents. Other important features for supporting learning in a PLE are presented in Table 3.

To find out if learners would object to recommendations based on data collected in their learner profile and earlier searches for finding relevant information for them in the future, respondents were asked to provide either an affirmative or negative answer. These percentages are presented in Table 4.

INFORMATION AGGREGATION

Participants from the first survey were invited to participate in a second survey which examined

Table 3. Features that support learning in a personal learning

Important features and issues	Number	Percentage (%)
Allows me to use it to learn from others	176	86.27%
Allows me to structure my learning activities (e.g., in folders)	163	79.90%
Features that help me to organize and plan my learning	162	79.41%
Provides a way to store all my learning activities	160	78.43%
Allows others to give me feedback on my learning activities	144	70.59%
Allows me to teach others	141	69.12%
Allows me to socialize with others	134	65.69%
Provides feedback on my learning activities	116	56.86%
Helps me to be critical of the information and resources I find online	107	52.45%
Teaches me about how the tool or application works	96	47.06%
Features that help me to learn about differences in quality of information sources	88	43.14%
Helps me to understand how search engines and other information sources work	62	30.39%
Other	15	7.35%

Table 4. Data collected from earlier learning projects for finding relevant information

From learner profiles	Number	Percentage (%)
No answer	12	5.88%
I would be happy	170	83.33%
I would be unhappy	22	10.78%
From earlier searches		
No answer	18	8.82%
I would be happy	120	58.82%
I would be unhappy	66	32.35%

the use of information aggregation tools and technologies, and to share issues and challenges based on their previous experience with collecting various forms of data and information from various sources. Their views would help to inform the design and development of PLE components related to information aggregation. In total, 68 participants completed the survey, with a majority of males (57%) between 43-54 years of age, with representation for groups 25-26 years of age to seniors 55+ (same characteristics as for the sample population for the online application survey, *see section on Results of the first phase*). Table 5 provides a sampling of issues and features raised by the "super-users" which should be considered in designing tools for information aggregation within a PLE.

EDITING AND PUBLISHING INFORMATION

Information and recommendations for supporting editing and publishing activities in a PLE were also gleaned from a sample of 62 respondents ("super-user") who participated in the first and second survey, with comparable demographics for age, education, and ICT skills as previously described. Table 6 presents some of the important features and issues to be consider in designing editing and publishing tools for use in a PLE, first in general, then for specific activities such as text, photo, web, video, as well as sound editing and publishing.

As represented in Table 6, survey respondents also highlighted important features and issues in web editing, video editing, sound editing which included many of the same options mentioned previously for general text and photo editing and publishing activities: namely ease of use, flexibility, capacity, variety and range of options/formats, mash up capability using a variety of applications. There was also a preference for using a combination of editors, for organizing one's own editing

Table 5. Features and issues for designing tools for information aggregation

Important features and issues
Ease of use | Tools and networking options
Loading time of the environment | options for customization
Personalization and choice over automatic inclusion of information streams
Intelligent information searching options
Some indication of trust and reputation of sources as relevant for information searching strategies used
Synergy/ integration with LMS systems
Visual representation for the organization of information— i.e., automatic tagging, ranking for quality and relevance, e.g., number of stars, flags, annotations
Cross platform environment with mobile options

Table 6. Features and issues for designing tools for editing and publishing information

General
Ease of use | Simplicity | Universality
Compatibility issues in editors
Clear and easy: menus, navigation, structure, instructions
Simple and complex tracking | advanced features| right click options: help | keyboard shortcuts | user defined styles | macros
Multimedia file inclusion options: images, video, audio
Text Editing
Various formats: brochures, newsletters, blogs, etc. | Interoperability (e.g., file format)
Online collaboration | simple and granular sharing
Indexing and cross referencing
Photo editing
Cropping | resizing (dimension and resolution) options | RAW import, non-destructive | brightness] color and exposure adjustment options; the ability to adjust hues, in addition to options to use artistic filters and to use layers
Ability to add text and shapes | add metadata | captions |label | annotations
Simplicity | ease of use | universality | level adjustment |connectivity
Options to convert and save in a variety of file formats | multiple formats | intelligent file size optimization
Extensive tutorials & help | intuitive interface | multiple import export options | low cost | open source (free) solutions
Produce mash-ups with a variety of applications | save them somehow

and publishing activities, and having an intuitive interface design. Other valuable features for editing and publishing include options that are 'handy' and 'right for me' with the option to "customize" and "refine the organization" as much as possible.

DISCUSSION AND CONCLUSION

Results of the first phase of the PLE research project provide important baseline data about user experiences with existing tools, applications, systems and desirable features for creating a new and improved personal learning environment. Participants gave high importance to social interaction in their learning and most were happy for their data to be used in information recommender systems. The surveys highlighted important factors affecting technology use and uptake, which included: demographics such as age, gender, education, experience, and specialization. Human factors such as motivation, incentive, support (organizational, social network online or in the community), perceived usefulness, ease of use, attitudes towards use, innovativeness, passed adoption behaviors, and knowledge and skill levels also need to be factored in. This research has emphasised the need for an intuitiveness and ease of use of the PLE and the tools recommended to learners. Simplicity in design features and easy navigation, as well as compatibility and interoperability of tools used and recommended were also shown to be important. Moreover, the research suggested important features for a PLE, such as an information aggregator and recommender in addition to editor, publisher and support structures, which are currently being considered as components for a PLE. Information and perceptions related to component usability along with educational research comparing learning in the context of a

Massive Open Online Course (MOOC) have also now been gathered and the concerns from this research have been tried out in the MOOC (Kop & Fournier, in press). At the centre of the design and development is the premise that it should be the learner who owns the PLE and who makes the decisions about its use, not an educational institution or organization.

REFERENCES

Attwell, G. (2006). *Evaluating e-learning: A guide to the evaluation of e-learning: Evaluate Europe handbook series volume 2.* Retrieved from http://www.pontydysgu.org/wp- content/uploads/2007/11/eva_europe_vol2_prefinal.pdf

Bannan-Ritland, B. (2003). The role of design in research: The integrative learning design framework. *Educational Researcher, 32*(1), 21–24. doi:10.3102/0013189X032001021

Bouchard, P. (2011). Network promises and their implications. In *The Impact of Social Networks on Teaching and Learning* [online monograph]. *Revistade Universidad y Sociedad del Conocimiento, 8*(1), 288-302.

Downes, S. (2009). *New tools for personal learning.* Paper presented at the MEFANET Conference, Brno, Czech Republic.

Dron, J., & Anderson, T. (2007). Collectives, networks and groups in social software for e-learning. In *Proceedings of the World Conference on E-Learning in Corporate, Government, Healthcare, and Higher Education*, Quebec City, QC, Canada.

Garrison, D. R., Anderson, T., & Archer, W. (2000). Critical inquiry in a text-based environment: Computer conferencing in higher education. *The Internet and Higher Education, 2*(2-3), 87–105. doi:10.1016/S1096-7516(00)00016-6

Jones, A., & Issroff, K. (2004). Learning technologies: Affective and social issues in computer-supported collaborative learning. *Computers & Education, 44*, 395–408. doi:10.1016/j.compedu.2004.04.004

Kop, R. (2010). *Networked connectivity and adult learning: Social media, the knowledgeable other and distance education.* Unpublished doctoral dissertation, Swansea University, West Glamorgan, UK.

Kop, R., & Fournier (2011). New dimensions to self-directed learning on open networked learning environments. In *Proceedings of the 25th Annual International Self-Directed Learning Symposium,* Coco Beach, FL.

Lombard, M., & Ditton, T. (1997). At the heart of it all: The concept of presence. *Journal of Computer-Mediated Communication, 3*(2).

Merritt, C. (2009). *The adventures of super-user.* Retrieved from http://hosteddocs.ittoolbox.com/cm120308.pdf

Picard, R., Papert, S., Bender, W., Blumberg, B., Breazeal, C., & Cavallo, D. (2004). Affective learning – a manifesto. *BT Technology Journal, 22*(4), 253–269. doi:10.1023/B:BTTJ.0000047603.37042.33

Siemens, G., & Downes, S. (2008). *Connectivism and connected knowledge.* Retrieved from http://ltc.umanitoba.ca/connectivism/

Siemens, G., & Downes, S. (2009). *Connectivism and connected knowledge.* Retrieved from http://ltc.umanitoba.ca/connectivism/

Weller, M. (2010). The centralisation dilemma in educational IT. *International Journal of Virtual and Personal Learning Environments, 1*(1), 1–9. doi:10.4018/jvple.2010091701

Zaharias, P., & Poylymenakou, A. (2009). Developing a usability evaluation method for e-learning applications: Beyond functional usability. *International Journal of Human-Computer Interaction, 25*(1), 75–98. doi:10.1080/10447310802546716

This work was previously published in the International Journal of Virtual and Personal Learning Environments, Volume 2, Issue 4, edited by Michael Thomas, pp. 12-22, copyright 2011 by IGI Publishing (an imprint of IGI Global).

Chapter 19
Developing New Literacies through Blended Learning:
Challenges and Lessons Learned in Ontario, Canada

Deborah Kitchener
York University, Canada

Janet Murphy
York University, Canada

Robert Lebans
Castlewood Consultants, Canada

ABSTRACT

This article reports on the implementation and impact of two blended models of teacher professional learning that promote innovative classroom practice and improved literacy and numeracy in six school districts in Ontario, Canada. The Advanced Broadband Enabled Learning Program (ABEL), situated at York University in Toronto, Ontario, Canada, transforms how teachers learn and teach through a strategic blend of face-to-face interaction, technological tools and resources, online interaction and support. Learning Connections (LC), its sister project, uses the same model to improve literacy and numeracy in school districts. Research into the impact of both programs reveals increased student engagement and achievement, enhanced teacher efficacy, and improved results in literacy and numeracy. This report presents the findings from two participant surveys conducted in one large suburban board just north of Toronto, and one large rural board in Northern Ontario, and demonstrates how the working definition of literacy that teachers use in the classroom is being transformed by their use of technology in the classroom.

DOI: 10.4018/978-1-4666-2467-2.ch019

DEVELOPING NEW LITERACIES THROUGH BLENDED LEARNING

When in April 2004 the International Reading Association in the United States published *Theoretical Models and Processes of Reading*, the editors included a chapter that made a cogent argument for adopting a new literacies perspective. They argued that such a perspective would recognize the wide range of skills needed to use and adapt to changing information and communication technologies and contexts that continuously emerge in our world and influence all areas of our personal and professional lives. In that chapter Leu, Kinzer, Coiro and Cammack (2004) argue that the emergence of technology in the twenty-first century has been so rapid and so continuous and the skills needed to employ this technology have become so complex that literacy had become a multimodal concept and necessitated a change in teacher roles within the new literacy classrooms of the twenty-first century. They assert that three forms of rapid change have taken place in our understanding of literacy: the transformation of the concept because of technological change; the envisioning of new literacy potentials within new technologies; and the use of efficient modes of communication that rapidly spread new literacies. They defined a new role for the teacher in the classroom as a developer of critical literacies necessary to ensure thoughtful use of the new technologies and ensure that students were prepared to live and work successfully in a new digital world.

This new role is particularly challenging for teachers and for professional programs responsible for their learning because teachers live and work in a society in transition, a society that still values the traditional literacies of the twentieth century in education while embracing the new literacies of the twenty-first in private and in public life. The problem confronting every professional learning program for teachers is how to ensure that student achievement levels in reading and writing are improved on standardized tests while at the same time recognizing that to be literate in the twenty-first century means to be skilled in the new literacies as well. This problem is far more complex than we might assume. Research (Geijsel & Meijers, 2005) indicates that change for teachers involves both the social reconstruction of their role as teachers and reflection upon what classroom instruction looks like from this new perspective. If we expect teachers to develop expertise to ensure that students master all of the multiple literacies needed in the twenty-first century, then we need to recognize how challenging that process will be and use a model of teacher in-service that is both appropriate and effective.

In this decade we have witnessed a powerful convergence of research and public policy that promises to transform teacher practice, make an expanded concept of digital literacy central to teaching and learning, and prepare students to learn, communicate and live successfully in a multi-modal digital world. With the introduction of technology into the work world, the home, and the classroom over the past twenty years our conception of literacy and literacy instruction has broadened fundamentally (Leu, Kinser, Coiro, & Carmmack, 2004). Prensky (2005) in the United States has made compelling arguments to educators to recognize and build upon the transformative influence that technology is having on learning in society and researchers from around the world are currently examining how young people use technology and experience the new literacies (Thomas, 2011). Governments in the United Kingdom, the United States, Australia, and Canada have created or are creating comprehensive policy documents on the digital economy, participation in a digital society, and the infrastructure and educational needs to be successful in a digital world. Research institutes such as the Metiri Group in the United States (Lemke, Coughlan, Thadani, & Martin, 2002) and FutureLab (Hague & Williamson, 2009) in the United Kingdom have outlined the critical literacy skills that students need to be successful in a technological world, provided pedagogical frameworks for teachers, and developed rubrics for evaluating student success. Societies such as the International Reading Association (Leu et al., 2004) have called on educators to recognize the critical literacies essential for effective information use. Meanwhile, academics have explored the positive impact of ubiquitous computing on teacher attitude, teacher belief, and teacher practice, defined the ways in which teachers in this environment are creating new forms of knowledge, and describe how students are expressing their learning using digital tools (Swan, Van't Hooft, Kratcoski, & Schenker, 2007). In addition, influential change advocates, such as Fullan (2007) in Canada and Elmore (2004) in the United States have rejected traditional forms of staff development and called for a more efficient and effective model of professional learning that promotes innovative classroom practice, engages students in authentic learning, and ensures that students will be better prepared for the technological world in which they will live and work.

The convergence of these forces has produced Learning Connections (www.learningconnections.on.ca), an exemplary model of innovation in teacher education in Ontario, Canada. This model provides dynamic personal learning environments that address the needs of teachers and students and shape a new pedagogy in the classroom. This new pedagogy acknowledges and employs the digital wisdom that students bring to learning from their private lives, engages them in rigorous and authentic activities that prepare them for success in the world, and expands and refines the concept of literacy that teachers bring to classroom planning. In this paper, we describe this exemplary model of blended professional learning, outline the research-based beliefs that inform its practice, describe the research methodology used to evaluate and direct its implementation, highlight research results in two school districts, discuss the challenges it faces, and suggest areas of future growth.

Learning Connections (LC) optimizes the use of information communications technology (ICT) for teacher professional growth, offers a blend of face-to-face and technologically mediated professional learning, and promotes innovation in classroom pedagogy. LC does this within the context of improving instruction in literacy and numeracy in addition to improving student literacy and numeracy results on standardized tests by providing a range of digital tools that teachers can use to realize student, classroom, school, and district literacy and numeracy goals. Funded by a grant from the Ministry of Education, Literacy and Numeracy Secretariat in Ontario and in partnership with York University in Toronto, Ontario, LC addresses the challenge of improving student achievement in literacy and numeracy in grades K-8 across the province of Ontario, Canada. LC employs broadband networks and leading-edge technology to foster collaboration among teachers and provides access to technology tools, funding for teacher release time, training, and just-in-time human technical support. It is available to elementary school teachers, principals, vice principals, literacy and numeracy leaders, curriculum staff, and supervisory officers in publicly funded schools across Ontario. LC employs a job-embedded professional learning program, a research and evaluation component, and a three pronged or *tri-level* implementation strategy (Barber & Fullan, 2005) for system change and capacity building. The professional learning program employs a blended learning model that combines both online professional learning and face-to-face interaction. Members access the collective wisdom of the online community for instructional improvement and leadership through asynchronous threaded discussion, synchronous discussion, video-conferences with experts and group members, relevant knowledge management practices, and reflective learning tasks. Members also attend face-to-face spring and fall conferences and an optional three-day annual summer institute at York University. Professional learning in the LC program is directed by a core group of school districts (District Champions). This group have committed to accessing and embedding the professional learning from the LC offerings into their school and district plans for continuous improvement. The District Champions group meets monthly by means of videoconference to share learning successes, discuss challenges and present evidence of improvement in student literacy and numeracy that comes as a result of their involvement in the virtual learning community. In addition, they plan for real time and virtual professional learning activities, develop strategies for building capacity within their districts, and discuss how to ensure sustainability within the shifting dynamics of district populations. By these means, the LC program ensures that students are afforded opportunities to represent their experience and knowledge using a range of multimodal digital tools as they engage in learning and communicate that learning to a wider community. Additionally this program broadens and refines the understanding of digital literacy that K-8 teachers in Ontario bring to the classroom as they experience the power of technology for learning, and shape new pedagogy that such technologies demand.

THE RESEARCH-BASED BELIEFS THAT GUIDE PRACTICE IN LEARNING CONNECTIONS

Teachers bring to their teaching an understanding of what it means to be literate derived from their own personal experiences with literacy.

In a recent submission to the Digital Economy Consultation process launched by the government of Canada, the Media Awareness Network, a Canadian not-for-profit centre for media and digital awareness, acknowledges its debt to recently published reports on digital economic strategies in the United Kingdom (2010), Australia (2009), and the United States (2009) by restating the

three principles that define digital literacy in the twenty-first century from those reports:

Established and internationally accepted definitions of digital literacy are generally built on three principles: the skills and knowledge to use a variety of digital Media software applications and hardware devices, such as a computer, a mobile phone, and Internet technology; the ability to critically understand digital media content and applications; and the knowledge and capacity to create with digital technology (Media Awareness Network, 2010, p. 1).

While these principles may seem straightforward, they nevertheless pose a challenge for classroom teachers. Classroom teachers play an ambivalent role in promoting literacy as they shape the learning environments of students and move them towards a fuller multimodal representation of experience and knowledge, a role that they themselves may not understand. They bring to their teaching an understanding of literacy that is shaped by their own experiences, an understanding that is often unarticulated, but very powerful. In a study of teacher attitudes and practice in teaching literacy, Gomez (2009) explores the powerful connection between teachers' personal experiences with literacy and the characteristics and quality of their literacy teaching. Although focused on reading the printed or written text, Gomez nevertheless makes the point that teachers bring to the classroom a sense of themselves as literate, and what and how they teach is shaped by how they view themselves as literate beings. The concept of a private literate self, shaping the professional literate self provides a significant lens through which to view literacy in the classroom. The dynamic interplay between the two selves is particularly problematic for students when only a narrow concept of literacy is praised and practiced to the exclusion of new literacies that students recognize as valuable in their literate but private selves. This interplay is particularly challenging for professional learning models that promote literacy, because developing a new sense of what it means to be literate represents a significant shift for teachers.

Using technology for professional learning transforms how teachers perceive their role, expands and refines their concept of literacy and generates new job-embedded pedagogical knowledge.

It is our belief that teachers who use technology successfully understand its efficacy, are able to reflect upon how to use it effectively in their classrooms, and begin to refine and/or expand their understanding of literacy to incorporate technology. In a comprehensive overview of how digital tools challenge traditional ways of knowing and traditional patterns of learning, Saljo (2010) points out that "the modes of relating to knowing, knowledge and social memory that are mediated by digital technology are at odds with some of the established notions of what it means to learn and know within the educational system" (Saljo, 2010, p. 56). As a result, he proposes both an epistemological and performative shift in twenty-first century teaching and learning. This shift is fully explored by Hannafin, Hannafin, and Gabbitas (2009) who analyze in some detail the cognitive demands of externally directed and student-centered learning, and describe the epistemological changes associated with learning from web-based multimedia. This new way of learning and knowing has significant implications for professional learning programs that seek to transform pedagogy in the twenty-first century classroom, expand the understanding of literacy, and improve student achievement.

These digital tools not only challenge traditional ways of learning and knowing and traditional patterns of literacy; they also expand the definition of literacy itself. Leu et al. (2004) stress that teachers are teaching in a world where new digital technologies demand new skills, new strategies, new dispositions to use them successfully, and that the introduction of new technologies throughout

the century will continue to refine and broaden our understanding of what it means to be literate in our society. They emphasize that a more precise definition of literacy may never be possible because users of new technologies go through a mechanism they call *envisionment*. This is a process in which teachers and students "imagine new possibilities for literacy, transform the function or the structure of existing technologies to construct the vision, and then share their work with others" (Leu et. al., 2004, p. 17).

The performance aspect of technology use has been documented in detail by researchers into ubiquitous computing environments, in terms of student motivation, student engagement in learning, and teacher practice. In a comprehensive study of the impact of ubiquitous computing environments on students (Swan et al., 2007) demonstrate that students engage with a variety of new representations of knowledge as a result of teacher access to technology. Although the research is focused on finding out how ubiquitous access affects students' conceptualization of knowledge, and how such access affects the ways students use knowledge and interact socially, their findings suggest significant directions for developing a teacher professional learning program that expands the concept of literacy itself. Teachers in this research study had the freedom to use all or none of the digital tools available to them in working with students over a six-week period, and were encouraged to choose those that met their curriculum goals. The students in the research study used digital photographs, print documents, objects under document camera, internet resources containing text, images, and audio/video, claymation movies, KWL charts, concept maps, Venn diagrams, multimedia presentations, video conferencing, and word processing on mobile devices to represent their new learning.

The transformative impact of ubiquitous access to technology on teacher practice, suggested by Swan et al. (2007) in their research, has been fully documented in a learning-technology-by-design experiment aimed in part at understanding of how teacher professional development moves toward rich uses of technology in the classroom. Using their experience at Michigan State University, Mishra and Koehler (2006) argue that teachers create a new type of knowledge generated by the dynamic intersections of the three areas: content, pedagogy, and technology, and they represent these intersections in a Venn diagram. They identify the intersection points as a significant area of new focus: Technological, Pedagogical, Content Knowledge or TPCK, and assert that it is a product of ICT integration into classroom practice. They argue therefore that that their framework provides a viable conceptual model for interpretation of teacher professional learning.

It may be argued that millennial students, those born since 1982, and now entering the teaching profession in significant numbers, are not immune from attention in this regard in so far as they are millennial. Although they bring experience of a wide range of digital tools into their teaching practice and are convinced of their value in their own personal learning, they too must develop pedagogical strategies that will ensure that they use these tools effectively in the context of individual learning goals and curriculum outcomes. At the same time they must become proficient at defining and articulating what the use of these ICT tools means to the concept of literacy instruction in the classroom.

Learning which is technologically mediated consequently involves a culture shift for educators. The role of the twenty-first century teacher in technologically mediated learning is no less active and demanding than it was in the twentieth-century classroom. While classroom management, relationship building, and focusing on student engagement and student achievement continue twentieth-century learning, new curriculum designs and innovative instructional strategies are needed to prepare children for success in the digitally mediated world in which we all live and work.

Innovation in classroom practice is best effected when all levels in the hierarchy of the district are aligned in their purpose and focused in their efforts.

Research into effective school improvement over the past decade reveals that a "systems thinking" approach to education is only effective if all levels of the system are aligned in their purpose and focused in their efforts. Policy implementers (Barber & Fullan, 2005) have argued for some time now that accountability and capacity building must be integrated at all levels of the system if the desired effect is to be implemented and sustained over time. They term this approach to systemic change tri-level development, because accountability and capacity building are viewed as interdependent and articulated at all levels of the system: the state, the school district, and the school community. In 2005, they called for live experiments where policy makers committed to tri-level development, learned from it, and applied that learning over time. The Literacy and Numeracy Secretariat in Ontario adopted such a tri-level model of implementation when it focused on improving literacy and numeracy in the province in 2005. In an extensive report on its effectiveness (Levin, Glaze, & Fullan, 2008) the authors argue that its effectiveness is directly attributable to its having adopted a model of implementation that embraces all levels within school districts and all educators in the province.

The informal leadership that teachers themselves provide has a strong influence on colleagues, the adoption of new pedagogy, and the expansion of the working definition of literacy in the classroom.

Teachers who develop an appreciation of digital tools and understand their power to motivate and engage students in learning bring that appreciation and understanding to their discussions of pedagogy and literacy with their colleagues. In recent studies of teacher acceptance of e-learning technology (Teo, Lee, & Chai, 2007; Yuen & Ma, 2008) used the Technology Acceptance Model (TAM) as a core framework for analysis but added additional constructs in order to find a better model to understand the attitudes of pre-service teachers. In addition to perceived usefulness and perceived ease of use, they added subjective norm, the perceived extent to which people of importance are using technology in their immediate environment, and facilitating conditions, the factors present in an environment that influence a person's desire to use technology. In their conclusions, these researchers stated that seeing other teachers using the technology in the classroom and feeling supported in their own use of technology by other teachers were significant factors in developing positive attitudes to technology use in the classroom, whether these teachers were digital natives, or digital immigrants. This subjective norm, the influence of respected colleagues demonstrating the use and effectiveness of the technology, underscores how important it is to set up a professional learning culture in which influential figures model effective technology use, discuss how to fulfill its potential for effective and engaging learning, and reflect upon its transformative impact on the definition of literacy that informs their practice.

The most efficacious model for professional learning is one that blends face-to-face interaction with online synchronous and asynchronous learning.

The past decade has seen much dissatisfaction with the traditional models for professional in-service for teachers. When Fullan stated that "professional development as a term and as a strategy has run its course" (Fullan, 2007, p. 4), he was asserting that the traditional model of delivery for teacher learning has become an obstacle to professional growth and to school improvement and that the time had come "to radically change [our] concept of what teacher learning should entail" (Fullan, 2007, p. 4). Fullan argues that "the notion that external ideas alone will result in changes in the classroom and school is deeply flawed as a theory of action" (Fullan, 2007, p. 36), and points out that we have failed to appreciate Elmore's comments that "improvement is more a

function of *learning to do the right things* in the setting where you work than it is of what you know when you start to work" (Elmore, 2004, p. 73). Fullan adds that thoughtful teachers learn every day on the job as they meet the learning needs of every student in focused and effective ways, and that the best way to ensure that teachers do so is to provide the means for teachers to reflect on their work and to collaborate with each other as they puzzle through how best to ensure that all of their students succeed.

Research indicates that the most effective model of professional learning to ensure the occurrence of reflective, collaborative learning is to take a blended or multimodal approach. One that combines face-to-face interaction at carefully selected times throughout the year with mediated learning. Such a model allows teachers to tailor personal learning environments that provide contextualized professional learning for themselves personally and meets the learning needs of their students. Dzubian, Hartman, and Moskal (2004) succinctly define the dominant characteristics of such a blended model:

Blended learning should be viewed as a pedagogical approach that combines the effectiveness and socialization opportunities of the classroom with the technologically enhanced active learning possibilities of the online environment, rather than a ratio of delivery modalities. In other words, blended learning should be approached not merely as a temporal construct, but rather as a fundamental redesign of the instructional model with the following characteristics: a shift from lecture-to student-centered instruction in which students become active and interactive learners (this shift should apply to the entire course, including face-to-face contact sessions); increases in interaction between student-instructor, student-student, student-content, and student-outside resources; and integrated formative and summative assessment mechanisms for students and instructor (Dzubian, Hartman, & Moskal, 2004, p. 3).

243

Bonk and Graham (2006) have demonstrated that there are many variations of blended learning in place in secondary schools, universities, and businesses across Canada, the United States, and the United Kingdom which combine the best elements of online and face-to-face learning. These are designed for both classroom use and professional learning, and are so varied because they meet local and national educational and professional needs. The program that has most strongly shaped the design and implementation of LC, however, is the award-winning ABEL Program: a model of blended professional learning that has been in place for the past decade at York University in Toronto, Ontario, Canada. Reported on most recently in ELEA (Murphy & Lebans, 2009), ABEL is a not for profit research and innovation program that uses broadband networks to transform teacher and faculty professional practice. ABEL maintains a learning platform that makes use of IP-based videoconferencing, video streaming, and other web based interactive and collaborative applications, and delivers a large number of videoconference and streamed video events that focus on curriculum, professional learning and community outreach throughout the year. In addition, ABEL offers a range of technological tools, support and resources of value to teachers, provides a wide-range of professional learning opportunities including an annual summer institute. The ABEL program builds networks and works with partners who add value to the program and its members, while focusing on change management and the development of innovative teaching practice. In order to build capacity for improvement, ABEL includes a research and evaluation focus for continuous improvement.

While ABEL is primarily focused on leveraging technology for pedagogical innovation, systemic change, and student achievement, LC is unique in its vision, innovative in its implementation, and transformative in its results. LC is supported by a grant from the Ministry of Education, Literacy and Numeracy Secretariat in Ontario, Canada. This is the government organization that analyzes data on student achievement in literacy and numeracy and works to build capacity province-wide to improve student achievement in these areas. Its guiding definition of literacy is "the ability to use language and images in rich and varied forms to read, write, listen, view, represent, and think critically about ideas. It involves the capacity to access, manage, and evaluate information to think imaginatively and analytically and to communicate thoughts and ideas effectively" (Literacy for Learning, 2004, p. 5). A careful reading of this definition reveals that it encompasses information literacy, the ability to retrieve information from a variety of sources, critical analysis, higher order thinking, media literacy, and the ability to both comprehend and produce multimodal representations of experience and knowledge. This definition may not directly reference digital technologies, but it is still comprehensive enough to embrace them.

THE LEARNING CONNECTIONS PROGRAM

Currently in its sixth year, LC has built upon the experience and momentum of half a decade. Its members currently include schools in ten urban and rural districts, and its purpose is to target and improve literacy and numeracy in district schools. The professional learning program that it offers includes both online and face-to-face components.

Online Components

LC offers a wide range of resources that teachers can access through the virtual community. Digital tools, tools support documents that provide both directions and strategies for use, webcasts on digital literacy, podcasts of authors, academics, consultants, streamed video events, collaborative workspaces, chat rooms, and videoconferences are all available to community members. In 2009-2010 the program provided access to and support for the use of Adobe Connect, Podcasting, Cell Phone use in classrooms, Wimba Voice Tools, Microblogging, and Digital Storytelling. Teachers use the online community to share literacy lessons with each other, create personal learning communities, engage in numeracy and literacy lesson study, participate in asynchronous professional learning, and view a range of web-based videos. In addition, regional literacy leaders from the school districts appointed at the request of the Literacy and Numeracy Secretariat have used the community to share resources and participate in asynchronous discussion and real time video conferences to build community across great distances in monthly online meetings.

Face-to-Face Components

Over the past year teachers have attended spring and fall mini conferences at York University, monthly training days at York University and in their districts, and a three-day summer institute held in August at York University in Toronto. While the mini conferences and institutes bring together learning communities in a central location, the monthly training days are delivered both live and via video-conference, and the annual summer institute is live with keynote sessions captured for viewing after the conference concludes. In the training days in 2009-2010, teachers had hands-on training in the use of a Learning Management System (Moodle), Podcasting (Audacity), Visual Thesaurus, VoiceThread, and Bitstrips, to name a few, and all instruction focused on the support of literacy and numeracy instruction in Ontario schools. At the summer institute, teachers attended sessions on Flickr, videoconferencing, Mahara and e-Pearl, interactive whiteboards, Wikis, blogs, Google docs, Comic life, Photostory, and online video and document databases.

What is significant about this professional learning program is the central role that teachers play in determining what training takes place, in designing and delivering the training and in the focus on twenty-first century literacies. Experts in using the technology are always accompanied by teachers who are using the technology in their classrooms, and the sessions are presented in the context of curriculum outcomes, classroom pedagogy, and student achievement in literacy and/or numeracy. A few descriptors from the summer institute will illustrate this point. In the LC training days in 2009-2010, the Bitstrips training session provided time for teachers to create assignments for their students and to share ideas on how the digital tools supported literacy. Additionally, teachers accessed Web 2.0 tools, using a digital graphic organizer tool to support numeracy instructional activities. During the annual summer institute in 2010, the session on Podcasting was entitled "Developing Confident Writers Using Podcasts," while the session on WriteCycle was called "Teaching the Writing Process with WriteCycle" and focused on peer editing in a digital context.

RESEARCH INTO THE IMPLEMENTATION AND IMPACT OF THE ABEL AND LC PROGRAMS

This article reports on two participant experience surveys conducted by the Institute for Research on Learning Technologies (IRLT) at York University from 2006 to 2009. The first study explored the impact of the ABEL blended learning program in the York Region District School Board (YRDSB) in 2006-2007, and the second examined the implementation and impact of the LC program in the Algoma District School Board (ADSB) in 2008-2009. We offer the results of both surveys because the ABEL research discusses the degree to which teachers in the blended learning program are creating authentic learning environments that engage students and improve student achievement in a district where the ABEL program has been institutionalized. The LC research builds upon learning from the ABEL survey and reports on a multi-level implementation and the impact of the LC program in a district where staff are beginning to create engaging and successful learning environments with a focus on improving literacy and numeracy while embedding the use of ICT in their professional learning and classroom practice.

Research Cohort

The YRDSB serves an expanding suburban population just north of Toronto, Ontario, Canada. In 2006 YRDSB operated a public school system comprised of 194 schools with an enrollment of 113,000 K-12 students and 10,000 employees. From 2007-2010 it added 20 schools to its complement. In province-wide testing in literacy and numeracy, YRDSB students have consistently performed well above the provincial average. For the past decade, this district has been committed to providing students with new opportunities to learn and grow, not only within the district, but also through the exchange of information, ideas, and experiences with communities across the world. YRDSB has maintained a strong focus on integrating technology into the classroom with a precise focus on student literacy and numeracy. In 2001 it became a founding member of ABEL; in 2004 it became a LC District Champion; and in 2009, YRDSB began to implement a blended approach to professional learning for all staff. The combination of forward looking leadership, modern infrastructure and schools designed for twenty-first century learning, participation in ABEL for a decade, and in LC for the past six years has produced a critical mass of teachers currently engaged in using digital tools that expand the working definition of literacy in the classroom.

In contrast to the YRDSB, The Algoma District School Board (ADSB) serves a large rural and small urban population along the north shore of Lake Huron and the east coast of Lake Superior in northern Ontario. In 2008-09 it operated a public school system comprised of 51 elementary and secondary schools with an enrollment of 11,250 K-12 students and 2500 employees. In 2008, its Grade 6 students showed considerable improvement in province-wide literacy and numeracy testing and one of its elementary schools was recognized as a school success story. In addition, two of its schools have been identified as Schools on the Move for staff commitment to networking and sharing of best practices, and for using research and professional expertise to inform curriculum and classroom practice. It has recently upgraded it technology infrastructure and is encouraging both teacher collaboration and a blended approach to professional learning. Staff are aligned and committed to the development of literacy and numeracy, professional learning, and the communities of professional practice at all levels of the board. The ADSB joined LC in 2008-2009 and designated three core schools as District Champions.

Research Purpose and Methodology

The main goals of the ABEL Participant Experience Evaluation (2006-2007) were to develop understanding of participating teachers' experiences with and perspectives on the ABEL blended learning program and its impacts on teaching and learning over the 2006-2007 school year, and to document the experiences of teachers in using technology in their classrooms. Forty-five teachers who were active members of the ABEL community completed an online survey that gathered rating data on their use of ABEL tools, services, and resources, changes in their teaching practice, technology use, and student outcomes consequent to ABEL participation. An additional eight teachers from YRDSB who were recognized by ABEL program leaders as exemplary users of the ABEL tools and services were studied in more detail by means of open-ended interviews to examine how these teachers implemented their ABEL initiatives, and understood the outcomes of these initiatives for students and for their own professional growth.

The main goals of the LC evaluation (2008-2009) were to document teacher understandings of how and to what extent their participation in the LC program had developed their professional capacity to promote literacy and numeracy in their schools, and to create a richly contextualized and nuanced portrayal of the ADSB's uptake and participation in LC as it unfolded throughout the year. Sixty-one respondents completed an online survey which included multiple choice questions designed to provide quantifiable data on narrowly specified issues of interest, as well as open-ended queries designed to allow for a full range of in-depth responses. For ADSB specifically, a qualitative research design was developed. This employed as its primary data source extensive group and individual interviews with relevant district personnel and participating principals and teachers from three elementary schools.

Research Findings for the ABEL Program

Research into the efficacy and impact of the ABEL by the IRLT at York University (Wideman, 2007) reveals that its model of blended professional learning is highly effective in developing innovative classroom pedagogy, engaging students in authentic learning, and fostering continuous improvement in the school. Statistical research into the impact of blended learning revealed that it had expanded teacher use of Web 2.0 tools in classrooms, increased teacher collaboration, produced innovative classroom pedagogy, and increased student engagement in authentic learning (Tables 1 through 3).

Wideman (2007) also states that seventy-eight percent of teachers surveyed had incorporated a range of digital media (graphs, images, sound files, and video clips) into their teaching somewhat more frequently or much more frequently, and seventy-one percent had encouraged students to use digital media in their projects to represent

Table 1. Percentage changes in teacher practice

Changes in Teacher Practice	Somewhat more frequently or much more frequently
Teachers sought new ways of teaching content	93%
Teachers rethought some of their ideas about teaching and learning	91%
Teachers provided more opportunities for students to take the initiative in their learning	69%
Teachers put more emphasis on engaging students' interest in their academic work	68%
Teachers had students work collaboratively to develop joint projects and to solve problems	64%

Wideman (2007)

ideas in various ways somewhat more frequently or much more frequently.

The anecdotal research gathered in YRDSB interviews reinforced these findings, but also documented unexpected outcomes as well. Reported on by Murphy and Lebans (2008), teachers revealed that their use of Web 2.0 tools and resources in their classrooms had increased student interactivity, enhanced cultural awareness

Table 2. Changes in student behaviour and academic achievement

Student Behavior and Academic Achievement	Agreed or strongly agreed
Students tended to be more engaged and on task	76%
Students engaged in a wider range of learning	76%
The quality of student work remained constant or was higher overall	66%
Students took more initiative and demonstrated better self-management	55%
Less time had to be devoted to classroom management	40%

Wideman (2007)

Table 3. Teacher collaboration and professional learning

Collaboration and Professional Learning	More frequently or much more frequently
Teachers learned from the experience of other teachers	80%
The use of Web 2.0 tools and resources made their professional lives more rewarding.	78%
Teachers collaborated with colleagues to develop new teaching strategies	78%
The content of lessons was deeper when teachers used Web 2.0 tools and resources in the classroom.	67%
The use of Web 2.0 tools and resources changed teacher perceptions of students and the nature of their achievements.	42%

Wideman (2007)

and sensitivity, promoted higher order thinking, increased opportunities for students to practice French as a second language, expanded student research, encouraged more self-editing of writing for real audiences, provided more opportunities for second language students to practice English, and improved both their vocabulary and grammatical use.

Research Findings for the Learning Connections Program

Statistical data from the research into the efficacy and impact of the LC program in 2008-2009 reveals the extent to which student use of technology increased, teachers focused on critical thinking and inquiry, and teacher understanding of literacy expanded (Table 4).

In addition, teachers reported they had greater opportunities to differentiate learning, had witnessed increased levels of student engagement, had changed their perceptions of what students could achieve, and had an expanded knowledge of how to use technology to facilitate literacy development (Table 5).

Anecdotal information into the Algoma District School Board's first year of participation, gathered through a series of lengthy interviews in 2009, revealed both increased teacher collaboration, and deeper understanding of how to use technology

Table 4. Assessed effects of LC participation on use of teaching strategies: Percentage of responses by use category

Teaching strategy	Substantially less use	Slightly less use	Same level of use	Slightly more use	Substantially more use
Ongoing assessment and feedback	4	7	33	41	15
Project-based learning	7	4	59	22	7
Student-initiated learning	4	4	48	33	11
Collaborative learning	4	4	33	26	33
Discovery learning	4	7	52	26	11
Critical thinking and inquiry	4	0	33	30	33
Integration of digital literacy into literacy program	4	4	52	26	15
Use of cognitively demanding tasks	8	4	33	33	22
Student use of technology	4	4	48	26	19

Wideman (2009)

Table 5. Respondent rating of LC participation impacts: Percentage of responses by category

Impact area	Not at all	Slightly	Moderately	Extensively
It has increased my sense of efficacy as a teacher.	22	22	30	26
It has made me feel part of a larger community of learners.	7	22	22	48
It has led to a greater professional satisfaction with teaching.	26	14	30	30
It has altered my perceptions of student abilities.	26	15	37	22
It has given me a greater opportunity to differentiate learning.	19	26	37	19
It has heightened my concern about student assessment/evaluation.	30	22	37	11
It has increased levels of student engagement with learning.	22	22	26	30
It has increased student collaboration in the classroom.	22	26	22	30
It has increased levels of student independence	26	15	41	19
It has improved student results.	26	19	37	19
It has expanded my knowledge of literacy teaching strategies.	15	31	26	28
It has expanded my knowledge of how technology can be used to facilitate literacy development.	28	21	33	18

Wideman (2009)

to facilitate literacy and numeracy development in the three schools in the case study. Wideman (2009) reports that as a result of their participation in the LC program, teachers had become more reflective about their approaches to teaching literacy and numeracy, had engaged students in "robust thinking" activities, and had provided students with tools and resources needed to represent their learning and experience using digital media. Additionally, teachers had witnessed how effective it was to use digital media for differentiated instruction, and in some cases had seen their students write with greater confidence, depth, and maturity.

It is significant that the LC model allows teachers the freedom to choose digital tools according to curriculum goals specific to their classroom context. Classroom teachers have a degree of autonomy that many other professionals would envy, but at the same time they face challenges in promoting the new literacies. Equitable access to computer technology is just one challenge, and government and district expectations for student achievement provide ongoing impetus. To address these issues in a model of professional learning that promotes a deeper appreciation and awareness of digital literacy requires understanding the concept of literacy that teachers bring to their teaching practice. Developing an appreciation in teachers of how the digital tools afford new opportunities for student engagement with learning, helps teachers to develop expertise in the use of these new digital tools themselves, and creates a thoughtful and reflective culture of professional learning. This culture of learning helps teachers to develop the pedagogical strategies that meet the demands of the curriculum and that are appropriate for use with classroom learners.

However, this process takes time and patience. It has taken almost a full decade of focused tri-level commitment to develop a critical mass of teachers who use ICT effectively in their classrooms in the YRDSB. The lessons learned from that implementation, in particular the importance of engaging all levels in the hierarchy and the influence that teacher practitioners exert in determining what colleagues do are being put to good effect as the ADSB moves into its second year as a committed member of LC. One of the greatest challenges in a programme of this nature is to continue to maintain purpose and focus over time.

WHAT MAKES LEARNING CONNECTIONS EFFECTIVE

LC is effective because it is supported by an at-arms-length government agency charged with the responsibility of improving student literacy and numeracy. In almost every industrialized nation across the world governments are marshalling resources and setting up agencies and projects to promote the use of technology in classrooms and to ensure improvement in student literacy. LC is effective because it employs the best practices in implementation, change management, and sustainability that have been identified by research over the past twenty years, and because it is guided by ongoing research into its implementation and impact. LC is also effective because it recognizes that:

- Teachers are the true agents of change in the classrooms of the nation and that they must first be comfortable with using and understanding the power of digital tools for learning before they employ them in the classroom.
- Teachers are the designers of change and must have access to a wide range of digital tools and resources that they can use in the

context of their own classroom to motivate students, engage them in learning, and develop higher order thinking.

- A job-embedded approach to professional learning recognizes both the specific contexts in which teachers teach and learn, and the autonomy that they have in making informed choices as they plan to meet curriculum expectations and develop effective pedagogy.
- A blended model of online learning and face-to-face interaction makes these choices more informed, encourages collaboration and sharing, and allows teachers to create personal learning environments that support their own learning needs and make a positive impact on student achievement.
- Teachers who are using technology for learning, making digital tools and resources available to students, and encouraging multimodal representations of learning and experience are validating the new literacies that have evolved as technology has evolved, refining their own definition of what it means to be literate, and expanding the working definition of literacy in their classrooms to reflect the needs and skills of the twenty-first century.

These statements are supported by research into the impact of the LC program on teacher efficacy. Wideman (2009) reports that as a result of their participation in this blended learning model staff in the ADSB welcomed the opportunity to design their own professional learning, appreciated escaping from the isolation of their own classrooms either virtually or in real time, and participated enthusiastically in a learning community supported by the Literacy and Numeracy Secretariat. They also valued connecting with educators in the province in ways that could never have happened if they were not part of the LC community and recognized that the new classroom strategies that they employed were beginning to have a positive impact on overall student achievement. Additionally, teachers felt empowered by the experience and gratified to be part of the larger provincial learning community.

LESSONS LEARNED AND FUTURE RESEARCH

Delivering technologically mediated professional learning that focuses on literacy and numeracy over the past six years has taught us much about digital literacy instruction. The concept of what it means to be literate in the twenty-first century is evolving even as the more traditional literacies of the twentieth century continue to be prominent in government policy and standardized tests. What we are learning is that the new literacies of the twenty-first century have not displaced traditional text-bound literacies; they augment them and indeed enrich and encourage greater literacy development. While this needs more detailed research, educators in both the ABEL and LC programs are increasingly stating that the use of digital tools for multimodal expression improves student motivation, increases student engagement with learning, develops higher order thinking skills, and improves overall achievement in both reading and writing.

At the same time, as teachers in ABEL and LC classrooms are using digital tools with students to communicate their learning, they are exploring the power of multimodal representations and validating the use of these digital tools for learning in general. Through their use of these tools to learn professionally, they are refining their own understanding of what it means to be literate in twenty-first century society, and through their use of these tools with their students, they are expanding the concept of what it means to be literate in their classrooms. This too needs further research. Much nuanced study has already been completed on teacher attitudes to technology, the transformative effects of technology on teacher knowledge and practice, and the impact of technology on student motivation and engagement with learning. The time has come to explore how the use of digital technologies is broadening the working concept of literacy in education and changing traditional definitions about what it means to be literate.

In 2010-2011 LC and ADSB will continue to build capacity by including additional schools and teachers in this professional learning program, continue to support teacher and student use of videoconferencing, and provide more widespread and easier access to a greater range of digital tools and resources. Learning Connections fully appreciates the focus on literacy and numeracy, the tri-level support and alignment of implementation efforts in its six Champion Districts: at the Secretariat for Literacy and Numeracy, the district, and the school. In all participating boards, improvement plans in literacy and numeracy have been aligned with Ministry of Education expectations, data on student achievement is used to inform planning and practice, and board staffs at all levels are aligned and focused on professional learning and classroom practice to support student success. Through the development of both real and virtual learning communities, LC is eliminating teacher isolation and deprivatizing teaching; teachers are sharing best practice across distances, responding to expert presentations on literacy and numeracy, using resources provided by and through the Literacy and Numeracy Secretariat, and aligning classroom activities with Ministry of Education expectations. This process is essentially flattening the leadership hierarchy in school districts in the interest of student achievement. In LC informal leaders are emerging in participating school districts, leaders who are influencing colleagues as they focus on the new literacies in their classrooms. Research into the extent to which informal leadership is emerging in these schools and school boards, and the manner in which this informal leadership is broadening the concept of literacy in the classroom will provide valuable insights into how to promote the new literacies in education without ignoring the old.

CONCLUSION

In response to the research conducted in 2009, LC set out to increase membership by twenty percent, develop the leadership of LC within each school district and expand the digital tools and resources available to the community. Additionally LC determined to increase the number of face-to-face Professional Learning Opportunities and real time virtual sessions for District Champions, system leaders and classroom teachers throughout 2010-2011. The LC program is determined to develop and implement a teacher learning strategy that supports job-embedded collaborative activities and existing board priorities, to ensure that direct links to resources are available at the Literacy and Numeracy Secretariat and to prominently display accountability data available from the Secretariat in the Learning Connections community. Given the involvement of participating boards and the enthusiasm of staff, there is sufficient evidence to confirm that new digital tools will increasingly engage students in authentic twenty-first-century learning. Our work confirms that teachers will continue to realize the value of these tools and engage in self-directed job-embedded professional learning that supports student achievement. Finally, our research supports the idea that the classroom concept of literacy will continue to evolve to include a vision of multiple literacies for a digital age, and that digital literacies will find their rightful place as instructional learning outcomes in Ontario classrooms.

REFERENCES

Barber, M., & Fullan, M. (2005). *Tri-level development it's the system*. Retrieved from http://www.michaelfullan.ca/

Bonk, C. J., & Graham, C. R. (2006). *The handbook of blended learning global perspectives local designs*. Hoboken, NJ: John Wiley & Sons.

Commonwealth of Australia. (2009). *Australia's digital economy: future directions*. Retrieved from http://www.dbcde.gov.au/digital_economy/final_report

Dzubian, C. D., Hartman, J. L., & Moskal, P. D. (2004). Blended learning. *Educause Center for Applied Research, 7*, 2–12.

Elmore, R. (2004). *School reform from the inside out*. Cambridge, MA: Harvard University Press.

Federal Communications Commission. (2009). *National broadband plan connecting America*. Retrieved from www.broadband.gov

Fullan, M. (2007). The road ahead. *Journal of Staff Development, 28*(3), 35–36.

Geijsel, F., & Meijers, F. (2005). Identity learning: The core process of educational change. *Educational Studies, 31*(4), 419–430. doi:10.1080/03055690500237488

Gomez, K. (2009). Living the literate life: How teachers make connections between the personal and professional literate selves. *Reading Psychology, 30*, 20–50. doi:10.1080/02702710802271990

Hague, C., & Williamson, B. (2009). *Digital participation, digital literacy, and school subjects: A review of the policies, literature, and evidence*. Retrieved from http://www.futurelab.org.uk

Hannafin, M., Hannafin, K., & Gabbitas, B. (2009). Re-examining cognition during student-centered, web-based learning. *Educational Technology Research and Development, 57*(6), 767–785. doi:10.1007/s11423-009-9117-x

Lemke, C., Coughlin, E., Thadani, V., & Martin, C. (2002). *enGauge 21st century skills: Literacy in the digital age.* Retrieved from http://www.metiri.com

Leu, D. J. Kinzer, Charles, K., Coiro, J. L., & Cammack, D. W. (2004). Toward a theory of new literacies emerging from the internet and other information and communication technologies. In R. B. Ruddell & N. J. Unrau (Eds.), *Theoretical models and processes of reading* (pp. 1570-1613). Newark, DE: International Reading Association.

Levin, B., Glaze, A., & Fullan, M. (2008). Results without rancor and ranking Ontario's success story. *Phi Delta Kappan, 90*(4), 273–280.

Media Awareness Network. (2010). *Digital literacy in Canada: From inclusion to transformation.* Retrieved from http://www.mediaawareness.ca

Mishra, P., & Koehler, M. (2006). Technological pedagogical content knowledge: A framework for teacher knowledge. *Teachers College Record, 108*(6), 1017–1054. doi:10.1111/j.1467-9620.2006.00684.x

Murphy, J., & Lebans, R. (2008). Unexpected outcomes: Web 2.0 in the secondary school classroom. *International Journal of Technology in Teaching and Learning, 4*(2), 137–147.

Murphy, J., & Lebans, R. (2009). Leveraging new technologies for professional learning in education: Digital literacies as culture shift in professional development. *E-learning, 6*(3), 275–280. doi:10.2304/elea.2009.6.3.275

Ontario Ministry of Education. (2004). *Literacy for learning: The report of the expert panel on literacy in grades 4 to 6 in Ontario.* Retrieved from http://www.edu.gov.on.ca/eng/publications/

Prensky, M. (2005). Listen to the natives. *Educational Leadership, 63*(4), 8–13.

Saljo, R. (2010). Digital tools and challenges to institutional traditions of learning: Technologies, social memory and the performative nature of learning. *Journal of Computer Assisted Learning, 26*, 53–64. doi:10.1111/j.1365-2729.2009.00341.x

Swan, K., Van 't Hooft, M., Kratcoski, A., & Schenker, J. (2007). Ubiquitous computing and changing pedagogical possibilities: Representations, conceptualizations and uses of knowledge. *Journal of Educational Computing Research, 36*(4), 481–515. doi:10.2190/B577-7162-2X11-17N5

Teo, T., Lee, C. B., & Chai, C. S. (2008). Understanding pre-service teachers' computer attitudes: Applying and extending the technology acceptance model. *Journal of Computer Assisted Learning, 24*, 128–143. doi:10.1111/j.1365-2729.2007.00247.x

Thomas, M. (Ed.). (2011). *Deconstructing digital natives: Young people, technology and the new literacies.* London, UK: Routledge.

UK Department for Business Innovation and Skills. (2009). *Digital Britain final report.* Retrieved from http://www.official-documents.gov.uk

Wideman, H. (2007). *ABEL participant experience evaluation.* Toronto, ON, Canada: Institute for Research on Learning Technologies.

Wideman, H. (2009). *Evaluation of the learning connections program 2008-2009: Summary report.* Toronto, ON, Canada: Institute for Research on Learning Technologies.

Yuen, A. H. K., & Ma, W. W. K. (2008). Exploring teacher acceptance of e-learning technology. *Asia-Pacific Journal of Teacher Education, 36*(3), 229–243. doi:10.1080/13598660802232779

This work was previously published in the International Journal of Virtual and Personal Learning Environments, Volume 2, Issue 3, edited by Michael Thomas, pp. 32-49, copyright 2011 by IGI Publishing (an imprint of IGI Global).

Chapter 20
Creative Networks of Practice Using Web 2.0 Tools

Jukka Orava
Media Centre, Finland

Pete Worrall
Media Consultant, UK

ABSTRACT

This paper examines the professional implications for teachers and managers in new and evolving forms of professional development using Web 2.0 tools in a European context. Research findings are presented from the "Creative Use of Media" learning event developed through a European eTwinning Learning Lab initiative in spring of 2009. The Creative use of the Media online learning event supported a series of initiatives celebrating the European Year of Creativity and Innovation and involved 135 participants from 27 countries. The key objective was to introduce a range of learning themes constructed around a phenomenon-based inquiry model, which supported interdisciplinary approaches and collaborative online learning methodologies to stimulate new teaching and learning rationales. Digital Web 2.0 technology was used as an independent creative medium and as a powerful facilitating tool to enhance and blend with the more traditional forms of visual, audiovisual and multimedia inquiry. In developing models encapsulating risk taking and experimentation this online learning project supported a general principle that future education models and professional development would be based on social learning and "customer-driven collaborative knowledge building" in relation to open source materials.

INTRODUCTION

Web-based learning has made rapid advances over the last decade with the development of interactive communication tools permitting computer users to move from passive receivers and consumers of information to critical co-creators and producer-consumers (Toffler, 1970; Bruns, 2008; Baldwin, 2009). The use of Web 2.0 applications has enabled users to participate in a social communication networking revolution on a global scale. Mobile technologies are transforming professional com-

DOI: 10.4018/978-1-4666-2467-2.ch020

petencies through the use of personalised virtual spaces and these are developing new pathways for screenbased experiential learning (Redecker et al., 2009; Pascu, 2008). Global educational policies reflect these changes, advocating the use of Virtual Learning Environments incorporating eportfolios, for students' to access information, interact with others using (blogs, forums and wikis) and co-construct and publish within local, national and international communities.

Social computing and Web 2.0 applications are merging with pedagogical approaches across both formal and informal educational contexts, however it remains important that the construction of technological solutions are based on pedagogical imperatives (models and concepts), rather than the reverse. New media courses incorporating elearning also require robust technological infrastructures, to enable fast networked internet access, to multimedia content streams. There is also a well-recognised need (and challenge) to modernise current curriculum content, due to these rapid technological advances. Reconceptualising curriculum models to include digital literacies will support employability and prosperity in the emerging national and global information economies (European Commission, 2006, 2007).

COMMUNITIES OF PRACTICE AND ONLINE LEARNING

Although Web 2.0 applications were not widely available in 1998, the theoretical concept and pedagogical models applied using ICT were learner oriented, focusing on collaborative and co-operative learning. Between 1998 and 2005 Jukka Orava coordinated the European Schoolnet's Virtual School Art Department developing an extensive range of online projects in cross cultural contexts (Orava, 2006). During this time early theoretical concepts were built around experiential learning (Kolb, 1984; Räsänen, 1997) and problem based learning, in a socio-constructivist knowledge paradigm.

A web-based online learning structure had also been developed in 1998 for the University of Art and Design Helsinki (UIAH) as a learning model and concept for media education and web-based media related studies (1998-2007) for teacher training in art. These learning models and structures were further developed and implemented through international curriculum development partnerships between Schools' of Art at the University of Art and Design Helsinki (UIAH), the University of Central England in Birmingham (UCE) and the Federal University of Minas Gerais in Belo Horizonte, Brazil (Worrall, 2000; Davies, et al., 2003; Orava, 2006). In contrast to the popular models of online learning developed over the last ten years, that could be described as highly organized and reliant on the use of professional learning management systems, our models harnessed the web based sources and built upon specifically tailored structures using ordinary web pages (Orava, 2006). The use of web pages and standard code, (HTML, PHP and CGI-programming) kept the focus away from the learning management system, allowing users to concentrate fully on the learning process and develop online learning as a collaborative, holistic and integrated process resulting in collaborative knowledge creation.

INTRODUCTION TO THE LEARNING LAB WORKSHOPS

In 2009 we were invited by Anne Gilleran, Pedagogical Manager, European Schoolnet to design and coordinate an online, eTwinning event for European teachers. It is worth noting that eTwinning is an online resource within the European Schoolnet, representing a hub for schools in Europe to exchange ideas and engage in online projects. We based the pedagogical concept for the eTwinning course, entitled the Creative use of Media on previously designed and trialed models of experimental workshops in Europe and Brazil, exploring the interface between Creative Arts practice across the curriculum and the use of ICT in an intercultural context (Orava, 2006).

The workshops were designed for European teachers to explore the creative and innovative use of Web 2.0 applications in teaching, learning and for professional development. The event encapsulated a model that encouraged the participants to critically experience and contextualise the potential for the use of social media within their own domain of skills' development. The key components of the Creative use of Media learning event were:

1. **A Pedagogical Model:** The workshops were introduced through a flexible pedagogical model to scaffold the learning process around the core phenomena of the creative use of media. The model provided a structure for the professional and collaborative development of skills and competences and also introduced and implemented the use of Web 2.0 applications in a developmental context.

2. **Online Resources:** Exploring the creative use of media in learning and teaching through the use of a range Web 2.0 applications including Flickr (image sharing and discussion), Youtube (video sharing) and Ning (social networking). Visual resources and websites were also provided by the course designers to introduce each workshops.

3. **Scaleable Thematic Content:** The participants could personalise and adapt exemplar workshop content for teaching and learning for use in the school curriculum, in different subject areas, with any age group and in a cross curricular context.

4. **Interconnected Modules:** The workshops introduced themes through a carefully structured series of activities incorporating visual media and timebased media, designed to develop metacognitive and communication skills.

5. **Differentiated Tasks:** Each workshop included extension tasks to enable the participants to develop higher level skill sets.

6. **An Ementoring Infrastructure:** Our transparent online support-line provided the scaffold to participants progress. Emphasis was placed on encouraging the co-creation of ideas through social interaction and through discussing the intercultural value of the workshops.

135 teachers were accepted for the Creative use of Media learning event and they were selected by the eTwinning Central Support Service from a total of 581 applications (Crawley et al., 2009). The age range of the participants was between 25 and 55 evenly distributed between primary, middle secondary and upper secondary teachers. There were 117 women and 18 men and 67% had prior experience of online training and 19% had none. It is also worth noting that prior to the start of the course it was not possible to gain a full understanding of the participants' technological infrastructures such as internet connectivity, English language understanding and the different levels ICT skills and competences.

WORKSHOP CONTEXT AND STRUCTURE

The key components underpinning the learning event reflected the eTwinning rational for Learning Labs, i.e., short experimental "taster" workshops that would sample online media and develop new competencies (Gilleran, 2008). It was essential that a carefully constructed infrastructure would support self guided study in a collaborative setting and that outcomes could be adapted in a wide range of professional and personal contexts. The Learning Lab workshops took place during the school term, consequently the workshop activity for the majority of the teachers took place outside school hours, although a small number of teachers were able to share the activities with pupils in real time using interactive whiteboards. Establishing a clear routine for the participants was important and ementor participation in discussion areas such as Flickr and Ning during the day and engaging in Question / Answer sessions at the end of the day were essential in establishing professional online social relationships with the participants.

Every eTwinning participant was provided with a professional virtual learning environment (Liferay.com) for the workshops, consisting of a sophisticated learning management system (portal) and an online personal space (social office). Liferay is an open source product providing the functionality of popular Web 2.0 apps with its own set of message boards, blogs, forums, wikis, RSS feeds, image archives, shared document library and calendar showing the events for the day. The blogs provided tools that allowed dynamic RSS feeds to email and a "Recent Blogs" display. Forum tools included RSS alerts, email-based subscriptions and replies and an activity tracking feature. This meant activities of each participant could be located from their personal pages "activity history" list and it also located comments and activity wall postings, including the participants active friends. This made collaboration between participants much easier, as team work could be supported and made visible without separate documents or workspaces. The personal pages were transformed by activity tracking into a virtual portfolio, tracking down all activities and user submissions creating a perfect node to all submissions (documents, comments, messages etc.).

At the start of the learning event each participant completed an online resumé-style profile on their personal pages providing information about the school, age group taught, subject specialism and interests, hobbies and aims relating to the learning event. Everyone created a link to the ementors as "friends" so that their personal pages could be used for tutoring and mentoring (i.e., a

direct access to personal Wall-to-Wall messaging) and the Friends / Contacts feature allowed users to keep track of people participating in the event. It was also possible to email the whole group of members and Instant Messaging (chat) enabled instant access to all logged-in participants. The Learning Lab acted as a collective hub for all participants to share their biographies (through personal pages), meet with their peers, experts and mentors, present outcomes and link to the creative use of the Web 2.0 applications which is the central focus of this paper.

THE PROGRESSIVE INQUIRY MODEL

The etwinning Liferay Learning environment presented contextual information about the workshops including a conceptual rationale to support problem-based learning, the *Progressive Inquiry* model (Hakkarainen et al., 1999). The phenomenon-based model describes the critical elements of collaborative knowledge-advancing inquiry and highlighting the pragmatic and socio-cultural aspects of inquiry, aiming at facilitating the same kind of productive practices of working with knowledge in education that characterizes scientific research communities (Figure 1).

Stage 1: Setting up the Learning Context: Each learning event starts with setting up the context to investigate online. This stage is prepared by the course designers.

Stage 2: Setting the Learning Goal: The second step involves setting the objectives and research problem, (learning goal). This stage is prepared by the course designers.

Stage 3: Creating Working Theories: The third step is to realize and become aware of our own intuitive conceptions and prior knowledge. This stage involves the participants preliminary responses to Stage 1.

Figure 1. Diagram of the progressive inquiry learning model used in the workshops

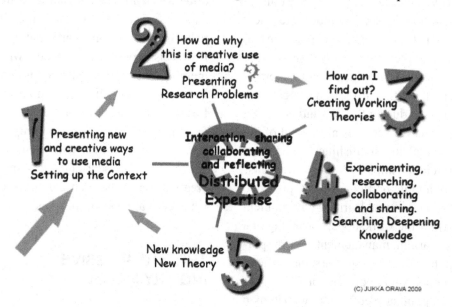

Stage 4: Searching for Deeper Knowledge: The fourth step is to search and create new information by experimenting and collaborating. This stage involves discussion regarding the preliminary responses in Stage 3.

Stage 5: New Theory: The fifth step is the creation of new knowledge and new theory. In this case participants take ownership of their learning process through developing authentic personalised outcomes. This stage involves participants creating new interpretations through shared knowledge.

Stage 6: Distributed Expertise: The core function in Progressive Inquiry is distributed expertise. Sharing and reflecting experiences help to create structure for new knowledge within a dynamic community.

The model emphasizes shared expertise for knowledge building and inquiry, by setting up the context, using questions, explanations, theories, and scientific information in the cycle of deepening inquiry (Hakkarainen et al., 1999). In a progressive inquiry process, the teacher or learning facilitator creates a context for inquiry by presenting a multidisciplinary approach applied to a theoretical or real-life phenomenon, after which the learners start defining their own questions and intuitive working theories about it. Participants' questions and explanations are then shared and evaluated together, which directs the utilization of authoritative information sources and iterative elaboration of subordinate study questions towards more advanced theories, explanations and writings.

It is important to note that distributed expertise can take place at any point of the working model. It can happen between each step or stage depending on the problem at hand. During the learning event blogs, forums, web forms, email and messaging were used as tools to distribute expertise among participants, but we also developed intermedia expertise / literacy through the use of audio, visual and time based media. Distributed expertise can have many forms but when it is interactive and in real time it creates a new spatial learning dimension.

INTRODUCTION TO THE WORKSHOP MODULES

Our objective as course designers and ementors was to provide a sequential set of structured on-line activities that would progressively develop participants' media and digital literacy in a social context. Careful consideration was given to introduce universal themes that could be used in a cross curricular context to teachers of different age-groups and specialisms. In addition, it was important to provide participants with information rich content to act as a starting point for each workshop to inspire and provoke discussion threads. After careful consideration two modules were designed that incorporated our (ementor) different strengths and expertise in elearning (Figure 2).

The modules were designed to incrementally develop media literacy through social interaction, as the participants progressed through a series of interrelated workshops. Module 1 "Interaction through Visual Media" introduced the online learning model in practice and it was extremely important to develop the participants trust and motivation on the first day by engaging with the workshop, monitoring participants progress and responding to specific questions. During this time the ementors used the Personal Page Blog and Activity Wall and the public discussion forums

as a diagnostic resource for feedback and to discuss issues that related to the learning event workshops.

Module 2 "Social Networking and Cultural Contexts" was designed to develop participants" autonomy through setting up and managing an individual social environment and use the customisable features such as photo and video sharing, forums and blogs. Participants also created and shared videos that could be used in the curriculum using Youtube and these were embedded in the social site Ning which was also used to present their work. The process of evaluation and dissemination was also completed during this module.

MODULE 1: INTERACTION THROUGH VISUAL MEDIA

The first module introduced the interpretation and meaning of images and texts was designed in three interrelated stages. Image Reading (Workshop 1) initially developed participants shared understanding of the importance of deconstructing images. Impossible Images (Workshop 2) addressed the phenomenon of the manipulation of visual information through altering the composition of an image for subversive or political purposes.

Figure 2. Workshop module structure

Etwinning Learning Labs VLE (Liferay) – used for Personal Profiles, Message Boards, Communication and Online learning				
Module 1 - Interaction through Visual Media			Module 2 - Social Networking and Cultural Contexts	
Workshop 1	Workshop 2	Workshop 3	Workshop 4	Workshop 5
Image Reading	Impossible Images	Frontpage News	Ning / Shared Space Video	Creative Media Friday
Visual Literacy	Media Literacy	Online Publishing	Networked Communities	Shared outcomes and Evaluation

Frontpage News (Workshop 3) introduced the phenomenon of texts and images in newspapers.

Image Reading - Day 1

In preparation for the workshop a set of images were uploaded into Flickr, an online image and video sharing website. Subject matter included cities, eco issues, identity, human conflict, faith, science and technology. The "image reading" activity provided the opportunity for teachers to deconstruct of images through the inherent formal qualities of line, tone, texture, colour and emotional content whilst sharing initial responses to the images in a social context. It also acted as an icebreaker for a group of teachers who had never met before online.

Here is an extract from the task script submitted online for the participants:

Figure 3. Image reading – faith

- **Please select 6 images and write down your comments – this could include:**
  ◦ Your first response to the image (please give your reason).
  ◦ A description of the image.
  ◦ The meaning of the image? (for you).
  ◦ The use of the image in the curriculum.

In addition, please show the images to your pupils and ask them to write down their responses.

The following represents a section from **8** participants discussion thread, related to the Faith image (Figure 3):

- A collection of symbols. The message could be related to the efforts of human vanity in front of the divine will.
- In the Orthodox culture, the image of Christ is placed to a clean wall, usually on the East side, because there is light which is giving color to the other things. It is a privileged place, to which people were educated, and used to watch every day, even in times of tribulation, or when Time is hardly touching them. Today their faith, or what was left of it, is an image that are undistinguished from background, suffocating crowd of other things that have gained in value today. Under the sway of a time that took it crazy (the clock up the Christ) or other threats (gun), faith gradually loses strength and distinction.
- Yes, impious as it may seen to a strictly orthodox Christian (broadly speaking) I can see piety, bitterness, an outcry to all things that re-cruxify Christian spirit of love and humanism: Violence, materialism, hedonism, whathaveyou. Christ's arm is missing. Very forceful use of a broken religious item.
- This image is symbolic in many ways: there are numerous of mixed up objects around Christ; chaos of modern society is rather intense and Christ is incapable of

helping: he lost his left arm just as people lost their faith in him. But maybe people are not responsible for loosing their faith, maybe it is only because they got tired of religion in every aspect of it (that's why there are numerous objects) and the way in which religion perpetual repeats-recycles the same old patterns for social plagues (besides, it is a recycled art image).

- The image is representative for the place religion and faith have in our life, surrounded by money, violence, trifles, running against time, being a victim of this modern world (one-handed Christ).

- Well! I think that is a picture of our times. Christ, the only standing point in chaos. Or Christ part of chaos. We are used to see Him standing above the people trying to close the world into His arms. But as our lifes are upside down probably He will come down.

- Hi everyone,
  ○ Your comments are make me realise that there are so many ways to look at images. So thank you for your comments. You may be interested to know that this is a mixed media artwork that was for sale outside a Baroque Church in Ouro Preto, Brazil. Pete Worrall.

- Ja, thank you for telling us the location, Pjaworrall. I think it is interesting, but catholic people have always been courageous to express their faith in different way (even ex-centric), but for sure I never seen something like that...

The discussion thread (above) relates to the image titled "Faith" and this is the only information the participants are provided with to begin with, although as with many of the images offered for this first workshop the criteria for the selection was the universal, provocative and multi-textural qualities of the images. The participants' discus-

sion thread includes a mixture of objective and subjective responses including the composition of the artwork, historical contexts, the contemporary message within the artwork and broader concerns regarding a society in chaos. It is also worth noting the ementors' penultimate contribution provides additional contextual information regarding the provenance of the image.

After investigating the Flickr content stream of images, the participants curated an online exhibition of six images from the Flickr set with alternative titles uploaded into Flickr or in the learning event VLE. This was followed by an extension task, inviting the participants to present a second set of their own personal images that could be used in a school project. During the workshop a number of participants, who had prior experience of using Flickr in an informal context reported that they would now begin to use Flickr as a resource in school. It also transpired that other participants shared the learning event workshop with their students in real-time in school through interactive whiteboards. In addition many participants curated their own sets of thematic resources and uploaded their images into their Flickr accounts.

Impossible Images – Day 2

"The growing circulation of the new graphic currency that digital imaging technology mints is relentlessly destabilizing the old photographic orthodoxy, denaturing the established rules of graphic communication, and disrupting the familiar practices of image production and exchange. This condition demands, with increasing urgency, a fundamental critical reappraisal of the uses to which we put graphic artifacts, the values we therefore assign to them, and the ethical principles that guide our transactions with them" (Mitchell, 1994)

The re-presentation of all forms of digital information through the use of software by news organisations, advertising companies and political parties result in increasingly cohersive montages of images that distort realities to sell "messages" and product brands. A critical visual methodology regarding "viewing" the prevailing "digital styles" involves and understanding the formal elements of the medium, the technology used and the intention of the maker. During this workshop the social, cultural and ethical implications of image manipulation were introduced to participants though specific contextual websites (Figure 4).

Here is an extract from the task script submitted online for the participants:

In this workshop we will be learning about image manipulation beginning with a short history of image manipulation (i.e., http://www.cs.dartmouth.edu/farid/research/digitaltampering/).

1. Share and post your ideas using the Message Boards (here you can see what is said, please comment on different discussion threads).
2. You can download articles into the Image Manipulation Document archive.
3. Download Images into the Image Gallery. Impossible Images or curate your own set of impossible images in Flickr.
4. Link videos relating to image manipulation using the Message Boards.

To reinforce skills developed in the first workshop participants curated an exhibition of manipulated images in Flickr. As an extension task they were invited to manipulate their own digital images using free open source graphics tools such as Gimp (gimp.org), Picasa (picasa.google.com) and Picnik (picnik.com).

Here is an extract from a participants post, for the ementors:

while reading down the thread of your posts on the message board I thought that, despite our geographical distances, we share a COMMON way of thinking and fear the same things: propaganda, dishonesty, fake and lies. The Impossible Images task was really insightful about our everyday life because we are surrounded by images: in magazines, newspapers, on TV, on the WWW, everywhere. In this way, the development of media literacy seems obligatory. The more knowledge and information is growing, the less time we have at our disposal to access all these sources and make our own unique picture of the world. So, we resort to images to understand what's happening around. And this is where danger is lurking... Image manipulation, apart from its artistic and entertaining side, can easily bias our perceptions

Figure 4. Schematic concept map of the image reading and impossible images workshops

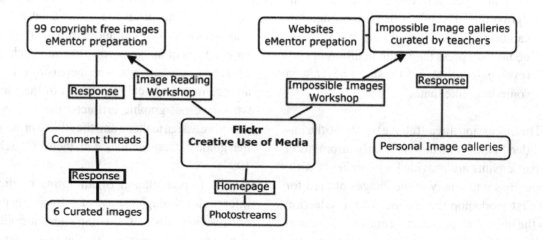

of life. By reading the history of image tamper-ing, I was intimidated and frustrated because I realized that facts and truth don't exist. We're simply aware of the reality shown to us, but not the hidden one. As a result, we and our students should be cautious enough and ready to question the truth of certain issues, especially when chances of personal experience are rare. The ethics behind altering the authenticity of photograph could be discussed in class and certain proposals to minimize the harm can be suggested. As you've already discussed relevant things for this task in great detail, I'll illustrate my points by pasting the link to what mostly impressed me...

It is informative to summarise key sections of this "longer than usual" post. The participant has clearly been reading reading discussion threads on the message board and these have reinforced common concerns despite our geographic dis-tances apart. The impossible image workshop post also raises issues about the importance of teach-ing media literacy because image manipulation can bias our perceptions of life. The participant clearly values the website link (history of image tampering), and (she states) on this evidence (teachers and students) should question the truth and authenticity of digital representation and this should be discussed in class. At the end of the post extract the ementors involvement in discussion is noted and a further link is indicated to key points. In this discussion extract the social construction of knowledge related to the exemplar resources and through the discussion group develops a model for the participant to develop in the curriculum.

Frontpage News – Day 3

With the multimedia 'text' the consumer or user is seen to be empowered by being able to navigate through a potentially immense range of knowledge and information. In making their own connections, choosing their own pathways, by being active in making their own sense of the material, they are

thought to be newly included in the construction of meaning (Lister, 2001).

The Frontpage design brief completed module 1, further extending the image reading and Impos-sible Image workshops through the design of a newspaper frontpage. This authentic 'real world' activity introduced participants to multimedia juxtaposition of text and image in the format of an online front page newspaper broadsheet.

The participants were invited to design the frontpage of a newspaper for the date on which the workshop took place (April 1st) and a key objective was to introduce online publishing skills related to web based resources and information. The end result was a published frontpage with nine news items and participants were responsible for sourcing articles, prioritising news items, and justifying their selection. The workshop was also designed to extend skills consolidated during the previous two tasks, through taking ownership of the activity by making objective decisions on the relevance and value of live news information and by presenting this to different audiences (students and teachers) for review and discussion.

Here is an extract from the task script submit-ted online for the participants:

1. Browse one of these sites: CNN Europe or BBC Europe.
    a. Choose 3 news items that are relevant to your students and explain why you selected them.
    b. Decide which one of the 3 should be the headline. Please include the URL of each news item.
2. Browse Icom Virtual Museums online.
    a. Choose 3 exhibitions that are relevant to your students and explain why you selected them. Decide which one of the 3 should be the headline. Please include the URL of each exhibition item.
3. Choose 3 more websites sites of your choice to include additional articles.

a. Explain why you like the website, share the URL and explain why you selected them.
4. Extension Task. Time permitting, you might want to try constructing your newspaper frontpage, using programs like OpenOffice or Word.

The submission of articles (above) has a significant number of references to curriculum development in school, for example, "Thousands protest ahead of G-20" article could be used by her students to explore other protest movements in Europe and the Twitter Traveller article could introduce a class discussion on the advantages and disadvantages of belonging to a social net and "a report about the main ideas in the group could be written afterwards." In her role as an online journalist she selects a breadth of news items including The UN Human Rights Council, International Women's Day, The Saatchi Gallery plus a link to the Independent newspaper cartoon to provide a balance for her readers, in this context the other course participants and her students.

The sharing of useful websites using the VLE message boards was a frequent occurrence throughout the course. On the morning of April 1st one participant shared a Web 2.0 site that provided a tool to create and publish an online newspaper and some participants used this site to submit their newspaper designs, whilst others submitted their designs in full desktop (text and image) format, using Word and Publisher, however the majority were submitted in tables, as in Figure 5.

This multi-layered design brief modeled professional competences in the form of critical thinking, applying selection criteria and publishing online to an audience. On a broader level the task introduced the use of local, national, international sources of information and introduced bias in reporting using different websites including CNN and BBC. In an educational context, it was also evident that interdisciplinary, collaborative and intercultual activites could be transferred

to a student production team of editors, journalists and news photographers to engage directly in a 21st Century workplace scenario.

MODULE 2: SOCIAL NETWORKING AND CULTURAL CONTEXTS

The underlying themes developed in Module 2 were time based media in the curriculum, sustainability through social networking and self evaluation. In this module participants were introduced to the Web 2.0 resource Ning, a social networking service and social platform with customisable features, such as photo and video galleries, forums and blogs. A brief introduction to digital video using Youtube provided opportunities for participants to upload and embed digital video into Ning for use in the curriculum. Evaluation and self reflection using a range of diagnostic tools completed the Learning Lab week.

Ning And Shared Space Video – Day 4

The focus on interaction and social collaboration using new media continued through the introduction to the contrasting online environments of Ning and Youtube. Ning was selected because it offered a functional solution for the social networking with an easy-to-use interface that could be used to embed audio visual media, including digital video. The interrelationship between Ning, Youtube and the range of Web 2.0 media explored during the week provided opportunities for participants to present workshop outcomes in a new format.

Forty five participants signed up for the social platform immediately and for the majority, the Ning site was a new experience. By the end of the day the Ning environment had grown to more than 56 blog entries and 40 forum entries, 45 videos, animations, slideshows and concept maps with many participants experimenting with new Web

Figure 5. Frontpage News – participant submission

Main News Items	Reason for Selection
1. US seeks seat on UN Human Rights Council	'Education in Values is one of the aims of the school, so reading about Human Rights situation is always good'.
2. Thousands protest ahead of G-20	'There is a protest movement against Bolonia Agreement for University. With the news about protests in London they (students) will explore other protest movements in Europe'.
3. Man completes world trip relying on Twitter friend	'The one about the twitter traveller connects with one of their leisure time activities: social nets. It could be followed by a discussion on advantages and disadvantages of belonging to a social net. A report about the main ideas in the group could be written afterwards'.
Museums	
1. The Saatchi Gallery	'Contemporary art will be explored. I think this is very important for our students because they live in an ancient town where artistic examples are Romanes, Renaissance. So, a comparison would open their minds.
2. Welcome to the Women's Library	As a way to finish celebrations for International Women's Day to know about women's magazines have influenced of have been influenced by society'.
3. Museo Vostell Marlpartida. Wolf Vostell	It is not a famous museum but it is important for Modern Art. Happenings, Conceptual Art, Video-Art. I find it interesting for our students who are used to visiting, if any, painting museums.
Other Sites	
1. The Guardian	It gives student a different point of view for news. Besides it has an educational section for languages.
2. BBC	Learning English It contains articles for students with vocabulary and grammar structure study, so

2.0 applications (through suggestions posted on message boards).

The Shared Space design brief was designed to introduce the use of digital video in teaching and learning. The participants searched for creative videos that had potential for use in their subject areas using Blip.tv, Youtube, TeacherTube and YouTubeEDU and after locating 3 examples, they were invited to write a short explanation (including the url) about how they would develop the use of the videos in the curriculum and submit this in their blog and / or Ning site. An additional option was to create a 1 minute film called Shared Space Video introducing a snap shot of local cultural space (classroom activity, local environment or interview) and upload it into Youtube, the VLE blog or the Ning network.

Here is an extract from the task script submitted online for the participants:

1. We invite everyone to join this totally open social network even only for one day. Follow the link to the page: Sign Up and fill in the personal data and passwords etc., follow the process and you will be granted access immediately. There is no validation process.

2. Explore the site, it's post's and discuss whether you could see yourself using this type social network tool / area using the forum.

3. You can upload materials such as videos, images and post messages, write blogs etc. and you can link these materials to the Liferay VLE.

4. Search for 3 videos you could use in the curriculum using Youtube, Teachertube or YoutubeEDU add the link to the video in your blog or Ning area and explain why you would use it in your curriculum area.

5. As an optional task is to create a one minute film called Shared Space Video, introducing a snapshot of your local space and upload this into Youtube, Ning or the Learning Lab (Figure 6).

This workshop was more demanding than the previous days, however it was encouraging to observe that participants suggested numerous Web 2.0 sites for use in the curriculum and engaged in

Figure 6. Schematic Diagram showing the key areas used by participants using the in Module 2

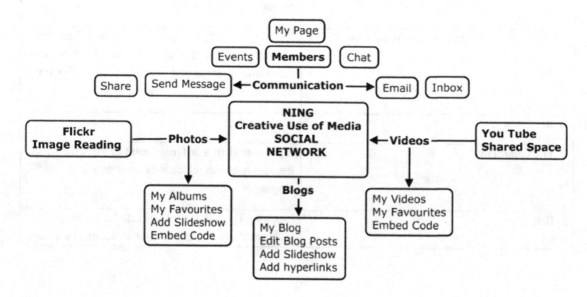

extended discussions regarding the use of digital video in learning and teaching. Ning was also used as a dual purpose social facility to develop educational partnerships and as a multimedia presentation resource to present the previous workshop outcomes. Ning was an appropriate resource to complete the week's activities as the eTwinning Labs would close a month after the event had finished. As a postscript it is worth noting that The Creative use of Media Ning social network is still active in 2010 with over 120 members.

Creative Media Friday – Day 5

The final workshop was reserved for reflection and evaluation, with the main task was to use Web 2.0 applications to capture the experiences and responses of the learning event. Each participant wrote a hundred words "event summary" in a Creative Friday Blog, however participants also used different multimedia forms to present the past weeks online activities using Jingproject.com (sound / video recording), Slide.com, (slideshows), Wordle.net (word maps) and Bubbl.us (concept maps). A formal evaluation was also completed by each participant and the main criticism related to the design and usability of the eTwinning Liferay Learning Lab platform. The user interface and lack of any kind of "help" or guidance materials made the navigation and use of the virtual environment challenging for some participants.

The range of evaluation data gathered from this event was challenging for the ementors to process, due to the volume and the multi-layered forms of responses and it is worth noting here that they will be the subject of a second paper. In general terms the Creative Media Friday (according to the end of the week event polls) was the most valuable workshop with 26% of the total votes, next was the Creative Friday online discussion with 22% of the votes, followed 13% for both the Impossible Images and the Ning Social network with Image

Reading gaining 9% of the votes. Another proof of learning and actionable knowledge creation (albeit difficult to document) was through the changes in practice that many of the participants displayed during the event (Dewey, 2003).

Here is an extract from a blog comment written on day 5:

The second day was a continuation of the first one, going deeper and deeper into the world of images. Re-writing history through images is a dangerous issue, but there is always somebody to teach us how to find out ... I never read the 'or' in the activity description. I only saw 'and,' so I entered every link we were suggested and kept on reading and reading. I went to bed at 2:00 in the morning ... But I can use slide.com and other tools to create short things to express my feelings. It was very funny. And signing up for the social net was the best way to finish a working day. I've participated in other social nets but yesterday I joined new ones and even created my own social net for the school. I have invited all the departments, let's see what happens. Such as I posted, sometimes, working with ICT at school is not very popular. The new links we have been given today are very useful I knew the one to create concept maps, in fact I started using it with my youngest students as a research and reinforcement vocabulary exercise. I'm looking forward to the live discussion. It's been a tiring lab... Thank you very much for giving me this possibility. See all of you in the Net and thanks for sharing. Bye.

The post is both personal and reflective regarding the value of online collaboration using Web 2.0 tools to express her feelings. There is an underlying sense of achievement and autonomy combined with a real need to translate the learning labs experience for her students. What is clear here is that through the process of experimenting with new media pedagogies in a practical workshop context the teacher is now empowered to transfer and blend this new elearning process with her students in the classroom.

CONCLUSION

The eTwinning learning event, The Creative use of Media introduced a phenomenon-based progressive inquiry model for participants from 27 different European countries to learn and experiment with digital media in a collaborative knowledge building context. The event was structured to encourage experimentation and creativity, whilst developing the participants shared interests in particular domains and areas (Lave & Wenger, 1991). The event was time intensive from an ementoring perspective, however a coherent course structure ensured that the participants learnt together and developed new professional skills.

The Virtual Learning Environment (Liferay) used in the Creative use of Media learning event, allowed and hosted fluid and transparent interactions with Web 2.0 applications in a very demanding intercultural and cross-disciplinary training context. During the course of the week, it is worth noting that the ementors were working in their respective countries and engaged in full-time jobs, so most of the course planning and ementoring took place in the evenings. In this context the Liferay VLE was well designed and provided excellent open source management tools to facilitate our own ementoring needs and to easily locate and 'monitor the participants' activities in the VLE.

The cyclic structure of the progressive inquiry model and learning process was successfully implemented into the event structure and target audience. The pedagogical model scaffolded fluid knowledge development through sharing of experiences and social networked collaboration. Synergies were created between participants as insights were shared. The feeling of belonging to a 'real' knowledge sharing and knowledge building European community of professionals (teachers) was articulated in the evaluations and the desire

to continue and preserve this network of practice was realised as the participants transferred from the Liferay VLE to the social network Ning.

Monitoring the participants engagement, motivation and commitment during the eTwinning event was only possible after the event had been completed through the recording of individual audit trails across a range of online locations. Solutions to these problems are perhaps easier to resolve when sustainable forms of collaborative knowledge construction models are established. In this field we have much to learn from the open source communities and their culture of engagement Improvements to the next learning event will include instructional design through developing multiple media forms such as video and sound files complemented by embedded translation tools to enhance social and cultural inclusion.

Social Software and Web 2.0 tools can enhance and gain value from social interactions and behaviour, and can provide opportunities for collective intelligence, so adding value to data and concepts (Becta, 2006). Online exchanges of information and knowledge enable participants to begin to form an initial understanding of the person and personality 'behind the screen' through the value judgments expressed. From an ementoring perspective a diagnostic analysis of discussion thread data informed decisions regarding the second Learning Lab course in November 2009.

The Web 2.0 tools also provided new opportunities for the collaborative creation and sharing of knowledge, providing new means for fostering lifelong learning and supporting the ongoing vision of personalized learning spaces in the knowledge society. In educational contexts it also raised issues relating to professional development (Redecker et al., 2006). We believe that social computing and Web 2.0 applications and services can be and need to be utilized for professional development in a wide range of education contexts. The need and reasoning comes from the simple realization that social computing and Web 2.0 is an integrated part of the new global knowledge paradigm and as such it part of the active reality today.

Ementoring is a new role for many teachers who may require new professional competencies to manage future online learning initiatives. Elearning courses should, as a minimum requirement, support "blended" learning methods to enable teachers to manage course content delivery and the student interface between physical experience (tactile sensory and manipulative) and the virtual online world of audio visual information. The effective balance of the virtual / physical experience is complex and variable, however this is often the creative key to success. The social learning taking place during the workshops was externalised in thousands of discussion threads and in this context the role of the ementors was to make the social learning taking place "visible" through discussion discuss the value of this new learning. Social learning will provide further challenges for teachers as long as traditional curriculum infrastructures and course requirements do not adapt to embrace these new conceptual collaborative tools.

The potential for events such as these to develop local, national and international communities of practice are enormous (and the tools are there), but as yet the vision is unrealized. It was clear that the group of teachers who enrolled for the learning event shared an interest in elearning and creative practice and by the end of the event they had formed a creative "community of practice" in Ning that continues today. A dedicated and mobile network of pedagogical experts and e-mentors is required in order to develop social learning hubs in Europe at all levels. In this context Etwinning learning events provide natural opportunities to identify individual participants as potential ementors. In times of austerity and economic problems, it would seem obvious for politicians to prioritise on maximising the development and implementation of online communities:

The contribution of ICT to the European economy is fundamental for the development of productivity and knowledge-intensive products and services. There is an important need to address ICT-related skills (e-skills) issues in order to respond to the growing demand for highly-skilled ICT practitioners and users, meet the fast-changing requirements of industry, and ensure that every citizen is digitally literate in a lifelong learning context requiring the mobilisation of all stakeholders (European Commission, 2007)

REFERENCES

Baldwin, C. Y., & Von Hippel, E. A. (2009). *Modeling a paradigm Shift: From producer innovation to user and open collaborative innovation.* Cambridge, MA: Harvard.

Becta. (2006). *Becta schools: Social networking.* Retrieved January 6, 2010, from http://schools.becta.org.uk/index.php?section=lv&catcode=ss_lv_com_02&rid=12065&pagenum=1&NextStart=1&print=1

Bruns, A. (2008). *Blogs, Wikipedia, Second Life, and beyond: From production to produsage.* New York: Peter Lang.

Crawley, C., Gilleran, A., Scimeca, S., Vuorikari, R., & Wastiau, P. (2009). *Beyond school projects: A report on eTwinning 2008-2009.* Retrieved February 4, 2010, from http://resources.eun.org/etwinning/25/EN_eTwinning_165x230_Report.pdf

Davies, T., Forrest, E., & Worrall, P. (2003). *A critical context: Art and design education on the edge.* Birmingham, UK: Cascade Publications.

Davies, T., & Worrall, P. (1999). *Electric studio.* Manchester, UK: Granada.

Dewey, J. (2004). *Perspectives on learning.* New York: Teacher's College, Columbia University.

European Commission. (2006). *Delivering on the modernisation agenda for universities: Education, research and innovation.* Retrieved February 16, 2010, from http://eur-lex.europa.eu/LexUriServ/site/en/com/2006/com2006_0208en01.pdf

European Commission. (2007). *e-Skills for the 21st Century: Fostering competitiveness, growth and jobs.* Retrieved March 3, 2010, from http://ec.europa.eu/enterprise/sectors/ict/files/comm_pdf_com_2007_0496_f_en_acte_en.pdf

European Commission. (2007). *Action plan on adult learning: It is always a good time to learn.*

Gilleran, A. (2008). *Online learning in eTwinning.* Brussels, Belgium: European Schoolnet.

Hakkarainen, K., Lipponen, L., Järvelä, S., & Niemivirta, M. (1999). The interaction of motivational orientation and knowledge-seeking inquiry in computer-supported collaborative learning. *Journal of Educational Computing Research, 21,* 263–281. doi:10.2190/C525-TDYQ-WWKY-87CB

Kolb, D. A. (1984). *Experiential Learning: Experience as the source of learning and development.* Englewood Cliffs, NJ: Prentice-Hall.

Kress, G., & van Leeuwen, T. (2005). *Reading images: Grammar of visual design.* London: Routledge.

Lave, J., & Wenger, E. (1991). *Situated learning: Legitimate peripheral participation.* Cambridge, UK: Cambridge University Press.

Lister, M. (2005). *The photographic image in digital culture.* London: Routledge.

Mitchell, W. J. (1994). *The reconfigured eye: Visual truth in the post-photographic era.* Cambridge, MA: MIT Press.

Orava, J. (2006). *Virtuaalikoulun taidekasvatuksen luokka.* Opetushallitus.

Pascu, C. (2008). *An empirical analysis of the creation, use and adoption of social computing applications.* Retrieved March 3, 2010, from http://ftp.jrc.es/EURdoc/JRC46431.pdf

Räsanen, M. (1997). *Building bridges, experiential art understanding: A work of art as a means of understanding and constructing self.* Helsinki, Finland: University of Art and Design Helsinki.

Redecker, C. AlaMutka, K., & Punie, Y. (2009). *Learning 2.0 – the use of social computing to enhance lifelong learning.* Seville, Spain: European Commission, Joint Research Centre, Institute for Prospective Technological Studies (IPTS).

Scardamalia, M., & Bereiter, C. (2003). Knowledge building. In *Encyclopedia of Education* (2nd ed., pp.1370-1373). New York: Macmillan Reference, USA.

Toffler, A. (1970). *Future shock.* New York: Random House.

This work was previously published in the International Journal of Virtual and Personal Learning Environments, Volume 2, Issue 1, edited by Michael Thomas, pp. 37-53, copyright 2011 by IGI Publishing (an imprint of IGI Global).

Compilation of References

Agostini, A., De Michelis, G., & Loregian, M. (2009). Using blogs to support participative learning in university courses. *International Journal of Web Based Communities, 5*(4), 515–527. doi:10.1504/IJWBC.2009.028087

Alicea, B., Biocca, F., Bohil, C., Owen, C., & Xiao, F. (2006). Targeting and motor learning in augmented reality: optimal spatial positions for remembering. In *Proceedings of the Annual Meeting of the International Communication Association,* Dresden Germany. Retrieved July 10, 2010, from http://www.allacademic.com/meta/p93545_index.html

Ally, M. (2009). *Mobile learning: Transforming the delivery of education and training.* Athabasca, AB, Canada: Athabasca University Press.

American Historical Association. (1998). *Statement of excellence in classroom teaching of history.* Retrieved from http://www.historians.org/teaching/policy/ExcellentTeaching.htm

Amory, A., Naicker, K., Vincent, J., & Adams, C. (1999). The use of computer games as an educational tool: Identification of appropriate game types and game elements. *British Journal of Educational Technology, 30*(4), 311. doi:10.1111/1467-8535.00121

Anderson, T. (2006). *PLEs versus LMS: Are PLEs ready for prime time? Virtual Canuck – Teaching and Learning in a Net-Centric World.* Retrieved from http://terrya.edublogs.org/2006/01/09/ples-versus-lms-are-ples-ready-for-prime-time/

Anderson, C., & Hounsell, D. (2007). Knowledge practices: 'Doing the subject' in undergraduate courses. *Curriculum Journal, 18*(4), 463–478. doi:10.1080/09585170701687910

Anderson, J. L. (1998). Embracing uncertainty: The interface of Bayesian statistics and cognitive psychology. *Conservation Ecology, 2*(1), 2.

Andrews, R. (2003, February 25). *Learn Welsh by txt msg.* Retrieved from http://news.bbc.co.uk/2/hi/uk_news/wales/2798701.stm

Antokhin, N., Boussalhi, A., Chen, K.-L., Combacau, P., & Koppany, S. (2004). Task-based reading activities developed for online delivery at the Defense Language Institute. In Leaver, B. L., & Willis, J. R. (Eds.), *Task-based instruction in foreign language education: Practices and programs* (pp. 181–203). Washington, DC: Georgetown University Press.

Apter, M. J. (2007). *Reversal theory: The dynamics of motivation, emotion and personality.* Oxford, UK: Oneworld Publications.

Armitage, J. (2003). *An exploratory study on the benefits of a thinking skills programme, cognitive enrichment advantage, informed by the needs of pupils identified with special educational needs.* London: Institute of Education University of London.

Armitage, J., & Scott-Saunders, R. (2007). From questions to cartoons. *Teaching Thinking and Creativity, 8*(24), 54–57.

Armitage, J., & Scott-Saunders, R. (2007). The primary mystery challenge. *Teaching Thinking and Creativity, 8*(24), 48–53.

Arskey, H., & Knight, P. (1999). *Interviewing for social scientists.* London, UK: Sage.

Asai, K., Kobayashi, H., Kondo, T., & Takase, N. (2007). Learning molecular structure using augmented reality. In T. Hirashima, U. Hoppe, & S. S. Young (Eds.), *International Conference on Computers in Education* (pp. 569-572). Amsterdam, The Netherlands: IOS Press.

Asai, K., Kondo, T., Kobayashi, H., & Takase, N. (2006). Augmented instructions for learning molecular structures. In Tzafestas, E. (Ed.), *EUROMEDIA* (pp. 63–68). Ostend, Belgium: EUROSIS Publication.

Attewell, J., Savill-Smith, C., & Douch, R. (2009). *The impact of mobile learning; examining what it means for teaching and learning*. London, UK: LSN.

Attewell, J., Savill-Smith, C., Douch, R., & Parker, G. (2010). *Modernising education and training: Mobilising technology for learning*. London, UK: LSN.

Attwell, G. (2006). *Evaluating e-learning: A guide to the evaluation of e-learning: Evaluate Europe handbook series volume 2*. Retrieved from http://www.pontydysgu.org/wp-content/uploads/2007/11/eva_europe_vol2_pre-final.pdf

Attwell, G. (2007). *Personal learning environments – the future of eLearning?* Retrieved from http://citeseerx.ist.psu.edu/viewdoc/download?doi=10.1.1.97.3011&rep

Attwell, G. (2007). E-portfolios - the DNA of the personal learning environment? *Journal of e-Learning and Knowledge Society, 3*(2), 39-61.

Attwell, G. (2007). *Personal learning environments - future of eLearning?* Retrieved from http://www.elearningpapers.eu/index.php?page=doc&doc_id=8553&doclng=6

Attwood, R. (2010). *Changed utterly: Cuts expected to transform the teaching landscape*. Retrieved from http://www.timeshighereducation.co.uk/story.asp?sectioncode=26&storycode=414005

Azuma, R. T. (1997). A survey of augmented reality. *Presence (Cambridge, Mass.), 6*, 355–385.

Badderley, A. D. (2000). The episodic buffer: A new component of working memory? *Trends in Cognitive Sciences, 4*, 417–423. doi:10.1016/S1364-6613(00)01538-2

Baldwin, C. Y., & Von Hippel, E. A. (2009). *Modeling a paradigm Shift: From producer innovation to user and open collaborative innovation*. Cambridge, MA: Harvard.

Bampton, R., & Cowton, C. J. (2002). The e-interview. *FQS Forum: Qualitative . Social Research, 3*(2).

Bannan-Ritland, B. (2003). The role of design in research: The integrative learning design framework. *Educational Researcher, 32*(1), 21–24. doi:10.3102/0013189X032001021

Barber, M., & Fullan, M. (2005). *Tri-level development it's the system*. Retrieved from http://www.michaelfullan.ca/

Barr, P. (2007). *Video game values: Play as human computer interaction*. Unpublished doctoral dissertation, Victoria University, Wellington, New Zealand.

Barras, J.-L., & Petko, D. (2007). *School and Internet in Switzerland: Overview and developments between 2001 and 2007*. Retrieved from http://doebe.li/t07870

Bartlett, N. J. D. (2005). A double shot 2% mocha latte, please, with whip: Service encounters in two coffee shops and at a coffee cart . In Long, M. H. (Ed.), *Second language needs analysis* (pp. 305–344). Cambridge, UK: Cambridge University Press.

Baxter, G. J., Connolly, T. M., & Stansfield, M. (2009). How can organisations learn: An information systems development perspective. *Learning Inquiry, 3*(1), 25–46. doi:10.1007/s11519-009-0038-8

Baxter, G. J., Connolly, T. M., & Stansfield, M. (2009). The use of blogs as organisational learning tools within project-based environments. *International Journal of Collaborative Enterprise, 1*(2), 131–146. doi:10.1504/IJCENT.2009.029285

Beaufort, A. (2004). Developmental gains of a history major: A case for building a theory of disciplinary writing expertise. *Research in the Teaching of English, 39*(2), 136–185.

Becta. (2006). *Becta schools: Social networking*. Retrieved January 6, 2010, from http://schools.becta.org.uk/index.php?section=lv&catcode=ss_lv_com_02&rid=12065&pagenum=1&NextStart=1&print=1

Becta. (2008). *Personalising learning in a connected world: A guide for school leaders.* Coventry, UK: Becta

Becta. (2009). *Enabling next generation learning: Enhancing learning through technology A guide for those who work with schools.* Coventry, UK: Becta

Belanger, Y. (2005). *iPod first year experience* Retrieved from http://cit.duke.edu/pdf/reports/ipod_initiative_04_05.pdf

Bhattacharya, M., & Dron, J. (2007). Cultivating the Web 2.0 jungle. In *Proceedings of the 7th IEEE International Conference on Advanced Learning Technologies* (pp. 897-898). Washington, DC: IEEE Computer Society.

Billinghurst, M., Kato, H., & Poupyrev, I. (2001). The MagicBook: a traditional AR interface. *Computers & Graphics, 25*(5), 745–753. doi:10.1016/S0097-8493(01)00117-0

Blackman, S. (2005). Serious games …and less! *Computer Graphics, 39*(1), 12–16. doi:10.1145/1057792.1057802

Blake, R. J. (2008). New trends in using technology in the foreign-language curriculum. *Annual Review of Applied Linguistics, 27*, 76–97.

Blenkharn, L., Carlisle, P., Charlton, J., Hollins, P., Ranyard, R., & Williams, A. (2006). *Engagement and motivation in games development processes.* Retrieved from http://www.freewebs.com/pamsgamelearning/BECTA-games.pdf

Blood, R. (2002). Weblogs: A history and perspective . In Rodzvilla, J. (Ed.), *We've got blog: How weblogs are changing our culture* (pp. 7–16). Cambridge, MA: Perseus Publishing.

Boateng, R. (2010). When Web 2.0 becomes an organizational learning tool: Evaluating Web 2.0 tools. *Development and Learning in Organizations, 24*(3), 17–20. doi:10.1108/14777281011037254

Bogost, I. (2007). *Persuasive games: The expressive power of videogames.* Cambridge, MA: MIT Press.

Bonk, C. J., & Graham, C. R. (2006). *The handbook of blended learning global perspectives local designs.* Hoboken, NJ: John Wiley & Sons.

Bouchard, P. (2011). Network promises and their implications. In *The Impact of Social Networks on Teaching and Learning* [online monograph]. *Revistade Universidad y Sociedad del Conocimiento, 8*(1), 288-302.

Bourdieu, P. (1984). *Distinction: A social critique of the judgment of taste.* Cambridge, MA: Harvard University Press.

Bowman, D. A., Kruijff, E., LaViola, J. J., & Poupyrev, I. (2004). *3D user interfaces: theory and practice.* Boston: Addison-Wesley.

Boyd, D. M., & Ellison, N. B. (2007). Social networks: Definition, history, and scholarship. *Journal of Computer-Mediated Communication, 13*(1). doi:10.1111/j.1083-6101.2007.00393.x

Boyle, E., & Connolly, T. (2008, October 16-17). A review of theories of player enjoyment in playing computer games. In *Proceedings of the 2nd European Conference on Games-Based Learning*, Barcelona, Spain (pp.59-67).

Bradley, L., & Bryant, P. E. (1983). Categorising sounds and learning to read: A causal connection. *Nature, 310*, 419–421. doi:10.1038/301419a0

Bradshaw, G. A., & Borchers, J. G. (2000). Uncertainty as information: narrowing the science-policy gap. *Conservation Ecology, 4*(1), 7.

Bradwell, P. (2009). *The edgeless university: Why higher education must embrace technology.* London, UK: Demos.

Bricken, M., & Byrnes, C. M. (1993). Summer students in virtual reality: a pilot study on educational applications of virtual reality technology . In Wexelblat, A. (Ed.), *Virtual reality: Applications and explorations* (pp. 199–217). Boston: Academic.

Britt, M. A., & Aglinskas, C. (2002). Improving students' ability to identify and use source information. *Cognition and Instruction, 20*(4), 485–522. doi:10.1207/S1532690XCI2004_2

Brown, A. (1992). Design experiments: Theoretical and methodological challenges in creating complex interventions in classroom settings. *Journal of the Learning Sciences, 2*(2), 141–178. doi:10.1207/s15327809jls0202_2

Brown, J. D. (1995). *The Elements of Language Curriculum: A Systematic Approach to Program Development.* Boston: Heinle & Heinle.

Brown, J. S., & Duguid, P. (1991). Organizational learning and communities-of-practice: Toward a unified view of working, learning, and innovation. *Organization Science, 2*(1), 40–57. doi:10.1287/orsc.2.1.40

Brown, R. E. (2001). The process of community-building in distance learning classes. *Journal of Asynchronous Learning Networks, 5*(2), 18–35.

Bruns, A. (2008). *Blogs, Wikipedia, Second Life, and beyond: From production to produsage.* New York: Peter Lang.

Bryan, A. (2004). M-Learning: Emerging pedagogical and campus issues in the mobile learning environment. *EDUCAUSE Center for Applied Research (ECAR) Bulletin, 16.*

Bryant, P. E., MacLean, M., Bradley, L. L., & Crosssland, J. (1990). Rhyme and alliteration, phoneme detection, and learning to read. *Developmental Psychology, 26,* 429–438. doi:10.1037/0012-1649.26.3.429

Bull, G., Garofalo, J., & Harris, J. (2002). Grand challenges: Preparing for the technological tipping point. *Learning and Leading with Technology, 29*(8).

Busuu. (2010). *busuu.com enters into strategic partnership with leading language learning publisher Collins.* Retrieved from http://blog.busuu.com/busuu-com-enters-into-strategic-partnership-with-leading-language-learning-publisher-collins/

Butterworth, B. (2005). The development of arithmetical abilities. *Journal of Child Psychology and Psychiatry, and Allied Disciplines, 46*(1), 3–18. doi:10.1111/j.1469-7610.2004.00374.x

Butterworth, B. (2008). Developmental Dyslexia . In Reed, J., & Warner-Rogers, J. (Eds.), *Child neuropsychology concepts: Theory and practice.* West Sussex, UK: Wiley-Blackwell.

Byrnes, H., & Sprang, K. (2004). Fostering advanced L2 literacy: A genre-based, cognitive approach . In Byrnes, H., & Maxim, H. H. (Eds.), *Advanced Foreign Language Learning: A Challenge to College Programs* (pp. 47–85). Boston: Thompson-Heinle.

Calleja, G. (2007). *Digital games as designed experience: Reframing the concept of immersion.* Unpublished doctoral dissertation, Victoria University, Wellington, New Zealand.

Calleja, G. (2007). Digital game involvement: A conceptual model. *Games and Culture, 2,* 236–260. doi:10.1177/1555412007306206

Canale, M., & Swain, M. (1980). Theoretical bases of communicative approaches to second language teaching and testing. *Applied Linguistics, 1*(1), 1–47. doi:10.1093/applin/1.1.1

Carless, D. R. (1997). Managing Systemic Curriculum Change: A Critical Analysis of Hong Kong's Target-Oriented Curriculum Initiative. *International Review of Education, 43*(4), 349–366. doi:10.1023/A:1003027923361

Cavaglioli, O., & Harris, I. (2004). *Reaching out to all thinkers.* Stafford: Network Educational Press Ltd.

Chan, T., Corlett, D., Sharples, M., Ting, J., & Westmancott, O. (2005). Developing interactive logbook: A personal learning environment. In *Proceedings of the IEEE International Workshop on Wireless and Mobile Technologies in Education* (pp. 73-75). Washington, DC: IEEE Computer Society.

Chan, T.-W., Roschelle, J., Hsi, S., Sharples, K. M., Brown, T., & Patton, C. (2006). One-to-one technology enhanced learning – An opportunity for global research collaboration. *Research and Practice in Technology Enhanced Learning, 1*(1), 3–29. doi:10.1142/S1793206806000032

Chaudron, C., Doughty, C. J., Kim, Y., Kong, D.-K., Lee, J., & Lee, Y.-G. (2005). A Task-based needs analysis of a tertiary Korean as a foreign language program . In Long, M. (Ed.), *Second language needs analysis* (pp. 225–261). Cambridge, UK: Cambridge University Press.

Chen, Y.-C. (2006). A study of comparing the use of augmented reality and physical models in chemistry education. In *Proceedings of ACM International Conference on Virtual Reality Continuum and its Applications* (pp. 369-372). New York: ACM Press.

Choi, J., & Nesi, H. (1999). *An account of a keypal project for Korean children.* The Internet TESL Journal.

Clark, D. (2003, November 20). *Computer games in education and training.* Paper presented at the LSDA Seminar: Learning by Playing: Can Computer Games and Simulations Support Teaching and Learning for Post-16 Learners in Formal, Workplace and Informal Learning Contexts? London, UK.

Claxton, G. (2002). *Building learning power.* Bristol, UK: TLO Ltd.

Clyde, J., & Wilkinson, G. (2009, Fall). *The digital mode of history.* Paper presented at Seventy Years On: New Perspectives on the Second World War, Lake Louise, AB, Canada.

Clyde, J., & Thomas, C. (2008). Building and information literacy first person shooter. *RSR. Reference Services Review, 36*(4), 366–380. doi:10.1108/00907320810920342

Cobb, P., Confre, J., diSessa, A., Lehrer, R., & Schauble, L. (2003). Design experiments in education research. *Educational Researcher, 32*(1), 9–13. doi:10.3102/0013189X032001009

Cohen, L., & Manion, L. (1995). *Research methods in education* (4th ed.). London, UK: Routledge.

Cohen, M. D., & Sproull, L. S. (1991). Editors' introduction. *Organization Science, 2*(1), 1–3.

Collins, T. G. (2008, July 5-8). *Proceedings of the Fifth IEEE International Conference on Advanced Learning Technologies,* Kaohsiung, Taiwan.

Collins, A. (1992). Toward a design science of education . In Scanlon, E., & O'Shea, T. (Eds.), *New directions in educational technology* (pp. 15–22). New York, NY: Springer.

Commonwealth of Australia. (2009). *Australia's digital economy: future directions.* Retrieved from http://www.dbcde.gov.au/digital_economy/final_report

Conole, G., & Alevizou, P. (2010). *A literature review of the use of Web 2.0 tools in Higher Education.* Retrieved from http://www.heacademy.ac.uk/assets/EvidenceNet/Conole_Alevizou_2010.pdf

Conole, G., de Laat, M., Dillon, T., & Darby, J. (2006). *JISC LXP: Student experiences of technologies report.* Bristol, UK: HEFCE.

Consalvo, M. (2007). *Cheating: Gaining advantage in videogames.* Cambridge, MA: MIT Press.

Cordova, D. I., & Lepper, M. R. (1996). Intrinsic motivation and the process of learning: Beneficial effects of contextualization, personalization, and choice. *Journal of Educational Psychology, 88,* 715–730. doi:10.1037/0022-0663.88.4.715

Costello, F. (2007). *The development of personal learning environments.* Retrieved from http://www.ericsson.com/ericsson/corpinfo/programs/resource_documents/ericsson_eden_2007.pdf

Council of Australian Governments. (2008). *Council of Australian Governments' Meeting.* Retrieved March 10, 2009, from http://www.coag.gov.au/coag_meeting_outcomes/2008-11-29/attachments.cfm

Couros, A. (2006). *Examining the open movement: Possibilities and implications for education.* Retrieved from http://www.scribd.com/doc/3363/Dissertation-Couros-FINAL-06-WebVersion

Crawford, C. (2003). *Chris Crawford on games design.* Indianapolis, IN: New Riders Publishing.

Crawley, C., Gilleran, A., Scimeca, S., Vuorikari, R., & Wastiau, P. (2009). *Beyond school projects: A report on eTwinning 2008-2009.* Retrieved February 4, 2010, from http://resources.eun.org/etwinning/25/EN_eTwinning_165x230_Report.pdf

Csikszentmihalyi, M. (1988). The flow experience and human psychology . In Csikszentmihalyi, M., & Csikszentmihalyi, I. S. (Eds.), *Optimal experience* (pp. 15–35). Cambridge, UK: Cambridge University Press.

Csikszentmihalyi, M. (1990). *Flow: The psychology of optimal experience.* New York, NY: Harper & Row.

Daneshkhah, A. R. (2004). *Psychological aspects influencing elicitation of subjective probability.* Retrieved from http://www.sheffield.ac.uk/content/1/c6/03/09/33/Psychologypapers.pdf

Davies, T., & Worrall, P. (1999). *Electric studio.* Manchester, UK: Granada.

Davies, T., Forrest, E., & Worrall, P. (2003). *A critical context: Art and design education on the edge.* Birmingham, UK: Cascade Publications.

Dawid, A. P. (1982). The well-calibrated Bayesian. *Journal of the American Statistical Association, 77*, 605–613. doi:10.2307/2287720

Dawid, A. P. (1997). The well-calibrated Bayesian . In Hamouda, O. F., & Rowley, J. C. R. (Eds.), *Probability concepts, dialogue and beliefs* (pp. 165–173). Cheltenham, UK: Edward Elgar.

Dawid, P. (2007). The geometry of proper scoring rules. *Annals of the Institute of Statistical Mathematics, 59*, 77–93. doi:10.1007/s10463-006-0099-8

De Castell, S., & Jenson, J. (2003). Serious play. *Journal of Curriculum Studies, 35*(6), 649–665. doi:10.1080/0022027032000145552

De Freitas, S. (2006). *Learning in immersive Worlds: A review of game-based learning.* Retrieved from http://www.jisc.ac.uk/media/documents/programmes/elearninginnovation/gamingreport_v3.pdf

De Freitas, S., Savill-Smith, C., & Attewell, J. (2006). *Computer games and simulations for adult learning. Case studies from practice.* London, UK: LSN.

Dede, C., Salzman, M. C., & Bowen Loftin, R. (1996). ScienceSpace: virtual realities for learning complex and abstract scientific concepts. In *Proceedings of the IEEE Virtual Reality Annual International Symposium* (pp. 246-252). Washington, DC: IEEE Computer Society Press.

Dede, C. (1995). The evolution of constructivist learning environments; immersion in distributed virtual worlds. *Educational Technology, 35*(5), 46–52.

Del Gaudio, J. J. (2002). Creating simulations for use in teaching lower division U.S. History. *History Computer Review, 18*(1), 37–52.

Delazer, M., Domahs, F., Bartha, L., Brenneis, C., Lochy, A., & Trieb, T. (2003). Learning complex arithmetic- an fMRI study. *Brain Research. Cognitive Brain Research, 18*, 76–88. doi:10.1016/j.cogbrainres.2003.09.005

Dempsey, J. V., Haynes, L. L., Lucassen, B. A., & Casey, M. S. (2002). Forty simple computer games and what they could mean to educators. *Simulation & Gaming: An Interdisciplinary Journal, 33*(2), 157–168.

Department for Education and Skills. (2006). 2020 *vision report of the teaching and learning in 2020 review Group.* Nottingham, UK: DfES Publications.

Design-Based Research Collective (DBRC). (2003). Design-based research: An emerging paradigm for educational inquiry. *Educational Researcher, 32*(1), 5–8. doi:10.3102/0013189X032001005

DEST. (2009). *National Goals of Schooling in the 21ˢᵗ Century.* Retrieved March 25, 2009, from http://www.dest.gov.au/sectors/school_education/policy_initiatives_reviews/national_goals_for_schooling_in_the_twenty_first_century.htm#Goals

Dewey, J. (2004). *Perspectives on learning.* New York: Teacher's College, Columbia University.

Dickey, M. (2007). Game design and learning: A conjectural analysis of how massively multiple online role-playing games (MMORPGs) foster intrinsic motivation. *Educational Technology Research and Development, 55*(3), 253–273. doi:10.1007/s11423-006-9004-7

Dickey, M. D. (2005). Engaging by design: How engagement strategies in popular computer and video games can inform instructional design. *Educational Technology Research and Development, 53*(2), 67–83. doi:10.1007/BF02504866

Dickey, M. D. (2005). Three-dimensional virtual worlds and distance learning: two case studies of Active Worlds as a medium for distance education. *British Journal of Educational Technology, 36*, 439–451. doi:10.1111/j.1467-8535.2005.00477.x

Dieterle, E., & Dede, C. (2006). Building university faculty and student capacity to use wireless handled devices for learning. In van Hooft, M., & Swift, K. (Eds.), *Ubiquitous computing: Invisible technology, visible impact.* Mahwah, NJ: Lawrence Erlbaum.

diSessa, A. A. (2000). *Changing minds: Computer, learning, and literacy.* Cambridge, MA: MIT Press.

Döbeli Honegger, B. (2009). *Wann wird telefoniert? Nicht im Unterricht!* Retrieved from http://www.projektschule-goldau.ch/permalink/757

Döbeli Honegger, B. (2010). *Beats Biblionetz: Begriffe: Personal Learning Environment (PLE)*. Retrieved from http://doebe.li/w01997

Döbeli Honegger, B. (2010) *iPhone-Weiterbildung für PH-Dozierende*. Retrieved from http://www.projektschule-goldau.ch/permalink/869

Dormans, J. (2008, July 22-27). Beyond iconic simulation. In *Proceedings of Gaming: Designing for Engaging Experience and Social Interaction*, Amsterdam, The Netherlands.

Douch, R., Attewell, J., & Dawson, D. (2010). *Games technologies for learning; more than just toys*. London, UK: LSN.

Douch, R., Savill-Smith, C., Parker, G., & Attewell, J. (2010). *Work-based and vocational mobile learning: Making IT work*. London, UK: LSN.

Doughty, C. J., & Long, M. H. (2003). Optimal psycholinguistic environments for distance foreign language learning. *Language Learning & Technology, 7*(3), 50–80.

Dowker, A. (2009). *What works for children with mathematical difficulties?* Retrieved from http://jumpmath.org/00086-2009BKT-EN.pdf

Downes, S. (2005). *E-learning 2.0*. Retrieved from http://www.elearnmag.org/subpage.cfm?article=29-1&section=articles

Downes, S. (2007). *Learning networks in practice*. Retrieved from http://partners.becta.org.uk/f

Downes, S. (2008). *Ten Web 2.0 things you can do in ten minutes to be a more successful elearning professional*. Retrieved from http://www.elearnmag.org/subpage.cfm?article=60-1&section=articles

Downes, S. (2009). *New tools for personal learning*. Paper presented at the MEFANET Conference, Brno, Czech Republic.

Driver, R., Mortimer, E., Asoko, H., Leach, J., & Scott, P. (1994). Constructing scientific knowledge in the classroom. *Educational Researcher, 23*(7), 5–12.

Dron, J., & Anderson, T. (2007). Collectives, networks and groups in social software for e-learning. In *Proceedings of the World Conference on E-Learning in Corporate, Government, Healthcare, and Higher Education*, Quebec City, QC, Canada.

Dron, J., & Bhattacharya, M. (2007). Lost in the Web 2.0 jungle. In *Proceedings of the 7th IEEE International Conference on Advanced Learning Technologies* (pp. 895-896). Washington, DC: IEEE Computer Society.

Drucker, P. F. (1993). *Post-capitalist society*. New York, NY: HarperBusiness.

Duenser, A., Steinbugl, K., Kaufmann, H., & Gluck, J. (2006). Virtual and augmented reality as spatial ability training tools. In B. Plimmer (Eds.), *Proceedings of the ACM SIGCHI New Zealand Chapter's International Conference on Human-Computer Interaction: Designed-Centered HCI* (pp. 125-132). New York: ACM Press.

Duffy, T. M., & Jonassen, D. H. (1992). Constructivist: New implications for instructional technology . In Duffy, T., & Jonassen, D. (Eds.), *Constructivist and the Technology of Interaction: A Conversation*. Hillsdale, NJ: Lawrence Erlbaum Associates.

Du, H. S., & Wagner, C. (2006). Weblog success: Exploring the role of technology. *International Journal of Human-Computer Studies, 64*(9), 789–798. doi:10.1016/j.ijhcs.2006.04.002

Dzubian, C. D., Hartman, J. L., & Moskal, P. D. (2004). Blended learning. *Educause Center for Applied Research, 7*, 2–12.

Ebner, M., & Holzinger, A. (2007). Successful implementation of user-centered game based learning in higher education: An example from civil engineering. *Computers & Education, 49*(3), 873–890. doi:10.1016/j.compedu.2005.11.026

Educause. (2010). *7 things you should know about the mobile apps for learning*. Retrieved from http://net.educause.edu/ir/library/pdf/ELI7060.pdf

Edwards, C., & Willis, J. (Eds.). (2005). *Teachers exploring tasks in English language teaching*. Oxford, UK: Palgrave Macmillan.

Egenfeldt-Nielsen, S. (2006). Overview of the research on the educational use of video games. *Digital Kompetanse, 1*, 184–213.

Egenfeldt-Nielsen, S., Smith, J. H., & Tosca, S. P. (2008). *Understanding video games: The essential introduction.* London, UK: Routledge.

Elliott, D. (2009). Internet technologies and language teacher education . In Thomas, M. (Ed.), *Handbook of research on Web 2.0 and second language learning* (pp. 432–450). Hershey, PA: IGI Global. doi:10.4018/978-1-60566-190-2.ch023

Ellis, R. (2003). *Task-based language learning and teaching.* New York: Oxford University Press.

Elmore, R. (2004). *School reform from the inside out.* Cambridge, MA: Harvard University Press.

Engeström, Y. (1987). *Learning by expanding.* Helsinki, Finland: Orienta-konsultit.

Erdmann, J. W., & Rückriem, G. (2010). Lernkultur oder Lernkulturen - was ist neu an der, Kultur des Lernens . In Rückriem, G., & Giest, H. (Eds.), *Tätitgkeitsteorie und (Wissens-) Gesellschaft* (pp. 15–52). Berlin, Germany: Lehmans Media.

eTandem. (2001). *Brammerts Ruhr-Universität Bochum.* Retrieved from http://www.telecom-paristech.fr/

European Commission. (2006). *Delivering on the modernisation agenda for universities: Education, research and innovation.* Retrieved February 16, 2010, from http://eur-lex.europa.eu/LexUriServ/site/en/com/2006/com2006_0208en01.pdf

European Commission. (2007). *Action plan on adult learning: It is always a good time to learn.*

European Commission. (2007). *e-Skills for the 21st Century: Fostering competitiveness, growth and jobs.* Retrieved March 3, 2010, from http://ec.europa.eu/enterprise/sectors/ict/files/comm_pdf_com_2007_0496_f_en_acte_en.pdf

Facer, K., Joiner, R., Stanton, D., Reidt, J., Hull, R., & Kirk, D. (2004). Savannah: mobile gaming and learning? *Journal of Computer Assisted Learning, 20*, 399–409. doi:10.1111/j.1365-2729.2004.00105.x

Federal Communications Commission. (2009). *National broadband plan connecting America.* Retrieved from www.broadband.gov

Feiner, S., MacIntyre, B., & Seligmann, D. (1993). Knowledge-based augmented reality. *Communications of the ACM, 36*, 52–62. doi:10.1145/159544.159587

Ferrer, E., Shaywitz, B. A., Holahan, J. M., Marchione, K., & Shaywitz, S. E. (2010). Uncoupling of reading and IQ over time: empirical evidence for a definition of dyslexia. *Psychological Science, 21*(1), 93–101. doi:10.1177/0956797609354084

FiatLux. (n.d.). *MolFeat.* Retrieved from http://www.fiatlux.co.jp/product/lifescience/molfeat/mol-index.html

Fiedler, S., & Väljataga, T. (2010). Interventions for second-order change in higher education: Challenges and barriers. *Electronic Journal of e-Learning, 8*(2), 85-92.

Fiedler, S. (2003). Personal webpublishing as a reflective conversational tool for self-organized learning . In Burg, T. N. (Ed.), *BlogTalks* (pp. 190–216). Norderstedt, Germany: Books on Demand.

Fiedler, S., & Pata, K. (2009). Distributed learning environments and social software: In search for a framework of design . In Hatzipanagos, S., & Warburton, S. (Eds.), *Handbook of research on social software and developing community ontologies* (pp. 145–158). Hershey, PA: IGI Global. doi:10.4018/978-1-60566-208-4.ch011

Fiedler, S., & Väljataga, T. (in press). Modeling the personal adult learner: The concept of PLE re-interpreted . In Siemens, G., Downes, S., & Kop, F. (Eds.), *Personal learning environments and personal learning networks.* Athabasca, AB, Canada: Athabasca University.

Fiol, C. M., & Lyles, M. A. (1985). Organizational learning. *Academy of Management Review, 10*(4), 803–813.

Fjeld, M. Fredriksson, Ejdestig, M., Duca, F., Botschi, K., Voegtli, B., & Juchli, P. (2007). Tangible user interface for chemistry education: comparative evaluation and redesign. In B. Begole, S. Payne, E. Churchill, R. S. Amant, D. Gilmore, & M. B. Rosson (Eds.), *ACM Conference of Human Factors in Computing Systems* (pp. 805-808). New York: ACM Press.

Fjeld, M., Juchli, P., & Voegtli, B. M. (2003). Chemistry education: a tangible interaction approach. In Rauterberg, M., Menozzi, M., & Wesson, J. (Eds.), *INTERACT* (pp. 287–294). Amsterdam, The Netherlands: IOS Press.

Fluent in 3 months. (2010). *Busuu & LiveMocha: review of pros and cons.* Retrieved from http://www.fluentin-3months.com/busuu-livemocha-review/

Freire, P. (1970). *Pedagogy of the oppressed.* London, UK: Continuum.

Fullan, M. (2007). The road ahead. *Journal of Staff Development, 28*(3), 35–36.

Furman, N., Goldberg, D., & Lusin, N. (2007). *Enrollments in languages other than English in United States institutions of higher education, Fall 2006.* Retrieved from http://www.mla.org/pdf/06enrollmentsurvey_final.pdf

Futurelab. (2009). *Using digital technologies to promote Inclusive Practice in Education.* Bristol, UK: Futurelab.

Gabbard, J. L., Hix, D., & Swan, J. E. (1999). User-centered design and evaluation of virtual environments. *IEEE Computer Graphics and Applications, 19*(6), 51–59. doi:10.1109/38.799740

Garrison, D. R., Anderson, T., & Archer, W. (2000). Critical inquiry in a text-based environment: Computer conferencing in higher education. *The Internet and Higher Education, 2*(2-3), 87–105. doi:10.1016/S1096-7516(00)00016-6

Garris, R., Ahlers, R., & Driskell, J. E. (2002). Games, motivation, and learning: A research and practice model. *Simulation & Gaming, 33*(4), 441–467. doi:10.1177/1046878102238607

Garvin, D. A., Edmondson, A. C., & Gino, F. (2008). Is yours a learning organization? *Harvard Business Review,* 109–116.

Gathercole, S. E., & Alloway, T. P. (2008). *Working memory and learning: A practical guide for teachers.* London, UK: Sage.

Gathercole, S. E., Pickering, S. J., Knight, C., & Stegmann, Z. (2004). Working memory skills and educational attainment: Evidence from National curriculum assessments at 7 and 14 years of age. *Applied Cognitive Psychology, 40*, 1–16. doi:10.1002/acp.934

Gaver, W. W. (1991). Technology affordances. In *Proceedings of the SIGCHI Conference on Human Factors in Computing Systems: Reaching through Technology,* New Orleans, LA (pp. 78-94).

Gaver, W. W. (1996). Situating action ii: Affordances for interaction: The social is material for design. *Ecological Psychology, 8*(2), 111–129. doi:10.1207/s15326969eco0802_2

Gay, G., Rieger, R., & Bennington, T. (2002). Using mobile computing to enhance field study. In Koschmann, T., Hall, R., & Miyake, N. (Eds.), *CSCL 2: Carrying forward the conversation.* Mahwah, NJ: Lawrence Erlbaum.

Gee, J. P. (2003). *What video games have to teach us about learning and literacy.* New York, NY: Palgrave Macmillan.

Gee, J. P. (2005). Good video games and good learning. *Phi Kappa Phi Forum, 85*(2), 33–37.

Gee, J. P. (2010). *New digital media and learning as an emerging area and "worked examples" as one way forward.* Cambridge, MA: MIT Press.

Geijsel, F., & Meijers, F. (2005). Identity learning: The core process of educational change. *Educational Studies, 31*(4), 419–430. doi:10.1080/03055690500237488

Gelman, R., & Gallistel, C. R. (1978). *The child's understanding of number.* Cambridge, MA: Havard University Press.

Giesecke, M. (2002). *Von den Mythen der Buchkultur zu den Visionen der Informationsgesellschaft: Trendforschung zur aktuellen Medienökologie.* Frankfurt, Germany: Suhrkamp.

Giles, J. (2009). *Physios recommend a healthy dose of gaming.* Retrieved from http://www.newscientist.com/article/mg20227145.700-physios-recommend-a-healthy-dose-of-gaming.html

Gilleran, A. (2008). *Online learning in eTwinning.* Brussels, Belgium: European Schoolnet.

Gillet, A., Sanner, M., Stoffler, D., Goodsell, D., & Olson, A. (2004). Augmented reality with tangible auto-fabricated models for molecular biology applications. In *Proceedings of the IEEE Visualization Conference* (pp. 235-242). Washington, DC: IEEE Computer Society Press.

Godwin Jones, R. (2005). Messaging, gaming, peer-to-peer sharing: Language learning strategies and tools for the millennial generation. *Language Learning & Technology, 9*(1), 17–22.

Godwin-Jones, B. (2005). Emerging technologies: Skype and Podcasting: Disruptive technologies for language learning. *Language Learning & Technology, 9*(3), 9–12.

Godwin-Jones, R. (2009). Emerging technologies: Personal learning environments. *Language Learning & Technology, 13*(2), 3–9.

Gomes, M. J. (2008). Blogs: A teaching resource and a pedagogical strategy . In Jose Mendes, A., Pereira, I., & Costa, R. (Eds.), *Computers and education: Towards educational change and innovation* (pp. 219–228). London, UK: Springer.

Gomez, K. (2009). Living the literate life: How teachers make connections between the personal and professional literate selves. *Reading Psychology, 30*, 20–50. doi:10.1080/02702710802271990

González-Lloret, M. (2005, September). *Implementing task-based language teaching on the Web*. Paper presented at the 1st International TBLT Conference, Leuven, Belgium.

González-Lloret, M. (2003). Designing task-based CALL to promote interaction: En busca de esmeraldas. *Language Learning & Technology, 7*(1), 86–104.

Goswami, U. (2008). Reading . In Reed, J., & Warner-Rogers, J. (Eds.), *Child neuropsychology concepts, theory, and practice*. West Sussex, UK: Wiley-Blackwell.

Grippa, F., & Secundo, G. (2009). Web 2.0 project-based learning in higher education: Some preliminary evidence. *International Journal of Web Based Communities, 5*(4), 543–561. doi:10.1504/IJWBC.2009.028089

Grosseck, G. (2009). To use or not to use Web 2.0 in higher education? *Procedia Social and Behavioral Sciences, 1*, 478–482. doi:10.1016/j.sbspro.2009.01.087

Groundwater-Smith, S. (2007). *Supporting Student Learning in a Digital Age*. Sydney, Australia: NSWDET.

Guo, S. (2010). From printing to Internet, are we advancing in technological application to language learning? *British Journal of Educational Technology, 41*(2), 10–16. doi:10.1111/j.1467-8535.2008.00867.x

Habgood, M. P. J., Ainsworth, S. E., & Benford, S. (2005, July 5). Intrinsic fantasy: Motivation and affect in educational games made by children. In *Proceedings of the AIED Workshop on Motivation and Effect in Educational Software*.

Habgood, M. P. J., Ainsworth, S. E., & Benford, S. (2005). Endogenous fantasy and learning in digital games. *Simulation & Gaming, 36*, 483–498. doi:10.1177/1046878105282276

Hague, C., & Williamson, B. (2009). *Digital participation, digital literacy, and school subjects: A review of the policies, literature, and evidence*. Retrieved from http://www.futurelab.org.uk

Hakkarainen, K., Lipponen, L., Järvelä, S., & Niemivirta, M. (1999). The interaction of motivational orientation and knowledge-seeking inquiry in computer-supported collaborative learning. *Journal of Educational Computing Research, 21*, 263–281. doi:10.2190/C525-TDYQ-WWKY-87CB

Hall, H., & Davison, B. (2007). Social software as support in hybrid learning environments: The value of the blog as a tool for reflective learning and peer support. *Library & Information Science Research, 29*(2), 163–187. doi:10.1016/j.lisr.2007.04.007

Hannafin, M., Hannafin, K., & Gabbitas, B. (2009). Re-examining cognition during student-centered, web-based learning. *Educational Technology Research and Development, 57*(6), 767–785. doi:10.1007/s11423-009-9117-x

Harmelen, V. M. (2006). Personal learning environments. In *Proceedings of the Sixth IEEE International Conference on Advanced Learning Technologies* (pp. 815-816).

Harpercollins. (2010). *Collins language and Livemocha sign multi-language online learning agreement*. Retrieved from http://www.harpercollins.co.uk/News_and_Events/News/Pages/Collins-Language-and-Livemocha-Sign-Multi-Language-Online-Learning-Agreement.aspx

Harri-Augstein, S., & Cameron-Webb, I. M. (1996). *Learning to change. A resource for trainers, managers, and learners based on self organised learning.* London, UK: McGraw-Hill.

Harri-Augstein, S., & Thomas, L. (1991). *Learning conversations: The self-organised way to personal and organisational growth.* London, UK: Routledge.

Harris, I., & Caliglioli, O. (2004). *Reaching out to all thinkers.* Stafford: Network Educational Press Ltd.

Harrison, R., & Thomas, M. (2009). Identity in online communities: Social networking sites and language learning. *International Journal of Emerging Technologies & Society, 7*(2), pp, 109-124.

Hayden, K. A. (2003). *Lived experience of students searching for information.* Unpublished doctoral dissertation, University of Calgary, Alberta, Canada.

Hayden, K. A., Rutherford, S., & Pival, P. (2006). Workshop on the information search process for research in the library. *Journal of Library Administration, 45*(3), 427–443. doi:10.1300/J111v45n03_08

Hazlett, R. L. (2008). Using biometric measurement to create emotionally compelling games . In Isbister, K., & Schaffer, N. (Eds.), *Game usability: Advice from the experts for advancing the player experience* (pp. 187–206). San Francisco, CA: Morgan Kauffman.

Hedberg, B. (1981). How organizations learn and unlearn . In Wystrom, C. P., & Starbuck, W. T. (Eds.), *Handbook of organizational design* (*Vol. 1*, pp. 3–27). Oxford, UK: Oxford University Press.

HEFCE. (2009). *The national student survey.* Retrieved from http://www.hefce.ac.uk/learning/nss/data/2009/

Herring, S. C., Scheidt, L. A., Bonus, S., & Wright, E. (2004). Bridging the gap: A genre analysis of weblogs. In *Proceedings of the 37th Hawaii International Conference on System Sciences* (pp. 1-11).

Hill, Y. Z., & Tschudi, S. (2005). A utilization-focused approach to the evaluation of a Web-based hybrid conversational Mandarin program in a North American university. *Teaching English in China: CELEA Journal, 31*(5), 37–54.

Hill, Y. Z., & Tschudi, S. (2005). *The effect of motivation and self-regulation on online language learning achievement: A preliminary research.* Honolulu, HI: University of Hawaii at Manoa. Honolulu.

History Channel. (2003-2006). *Battlefield Detectives.* USA: The A & E Network.

HITLab. (n.d.). *ARToolkit.* Retrieved from http://www.hitl.washington.edu/artoolkit/

Holmes, J. (2005). When small talk is a big deal: Sociolinguistic challenges in the workplace . In Long, M. H. (Ed.), *Second language needs analysis* (pp. 344–372). Cambridge, UK: Cambridge University Press.

Howard-Jones, P. A. (2009). *Neuroscience, learning and technology (14-19).* Cheshire, UK: Becta.

Hoyrup, S. (2004). Reflection as a core process in organisational learning. *Journal of Workplace Learning, 16*(8), 442–454. doi:10.1108/13665620410566414

Huh, J., Bellamy, R., Jones, L., Thomas, J. C., Erickson, T., & Kellogg, W. A. (2007). BlogCentral: The role of internal blogs at work. In *Proceedings of the Conference on Human Factors in Computing Systems* (pp. 2447-2452).

Hunter, J. (2007). Fresh equation: quality digital resources + interactive whiteboards + collaborative tools = engaging pedagogy for the classroom. *Learning, Media and Technology, 32*(3), 245–260.

Hunter, J. (2008). *Video conferencing and students: Listening to State Student Representative Council voices in NSW.* Sydney, Australia: NSWDET.

Hurter, S. R. (2003). Elusive or illuminating: Using the web to explore the Salem witchcraft trials. *OAH Magazine of History, 17*(4), 60–61. doi:10.1093/maghis/17.4.60

Iacovides, I. (2009, September 1-5). Exploring the link between player involvement and learning within digital games. In *Proceedings of the 23rd Conference on Human Computer Interaction*, Cambridge, UK (pp.29-34).

Ibrahim, J. (2008). The new risk communities: Social networking sites and risk. *International Journal of Media and Cultural Politics, 4*(2), 245–253. doi:10.1386/macp.4.2.245_3

IDEO. (2009). *Human centered design toolkit (2nd ed.)*. Retrieved from http://www.ideo.com/work/item/human-centered-design-toolkit/

Illich, I. (1970). *Deschooling society*. London, UK: Marion Boyars.

Interdepartementaler Ausschuss Informationsgesellschaft (IDA IG). (2008). *Informationsgesellschaft Schweiz in Zahlen. In Bericht des Interdepartementalen Ausschusses Informationsgesellschaft für die Jahre 2006 - 2008 zur Umsetzung der Strategie des Bundesrates für eine Informationsgesellschaft in der Schweiz*. Retrieved from http://doebe.li/t09186

International Telecommunication Union (ITU). (2009). *Measuring the information society*. Retrieved from http://doebe.li/b04033

Ireson, J., Hallam, S., & Plewis, I. (2001). Ability grouping in secondary schools: Effects on pupils' self-concepts. *The British Journal of Educational Psychology, 71*(2), 315–326. doi:10.1348/000709901158541

Iwata, S. (2008). *Keynote address: Nintendo Fall Conference*. Retrieved from http://www.nintendo.co.jp/n10/conference2008fall/presen/e/index.html

Jackson, A., Yates, J., & Orlikowski, W. (2007). Corporate blogging: Building community through persistent digital talk. In *Proceedings of the 40th Hawaii International Conference on System Sciences* (pp. 1-10).

Javis, H. L., & Gathercole, S. E. (2003). Verbal and non-verbal working memory and achievements on national curriculum tests at 11 and 14 years of age. *Educational and Child Psychology, 20*, 123–140.

Jee, M. J., & Park, M. J. (2009). *Livemocha as an online language-learning community, Calico software reviews*. Retrieved from https://calico.org/p-416-livemocha%20as%20an%20online%20language-learning%20community%20%28012009%29.html

Jenkinson, D. (2005). *The elicitation of probabilities: A review of the statistical literature*. Yorkshire, UK: University of Sheffield.

Jenson, J., & de Castell, S. (2008, October 16-17). From simulation to imitation: New controllers, new forms of play. In *Proceedings of the 2nd European Conference on Games-Based Learning*, Barcelona, Spain (pp. 213-218).

JISC. (2007). *A report on the JISC CETIS PLE project*. Retrieved from http://wiki.cetis.ac.uk/Ple/Report

JISC. (2009). *Effective practice in a digital age: A guide to technology-enhanced learning and teaching*. Bristol, UK: JISC.

Johnson, M., Beauvoir, P., Milligan, C., Sharples, P., Wilson, S., & Liber, O. (2006). Mapping the future: The personal learning environment reference model and emerging technology. In *Proceedings of ALT-C: The Next Generation* (pp. 182-191).

Johnson, M., Liber, O., Wilson, S., & Milligan, C. (2006). *The personal learning environment: A report on the CETIS PLE project*. Retrieved from http://wiki.cetis.ac.uk/image:plereport.doc

Johnson, L. F., Levine, A., & Smith, R. S. (2009). *Horizon report*. Austin, TX: The New Media Consortium.

Johnson, M., & Liber, O. (2008). The personal learning environment and the human condition: From theory to teaching practice. *Interactive Learning Environments, 16*(1), 3–15. doi:10.1080/10494820701772652

Jonassen, D. H., Mayes, J. T., & McAleese, R. (1993). A manifesto for a constructivist approach to uses of technology in higher education . In Duffy, T. M., Lowyck, J., & Jonassen, D. H. (Eds.), *Designing environments for constructive learning* (pp. 231–247). Heidelberg, Germany: Springer-Verlag.

Jones, A., & Issroff, K. (2004). Learning technologies: Affective and social issues in computer-supported collaborative learning. *Computers & Education, 44*, 395–408. doi:10.1016/j.compedu.2004.04.004

Jones, A., & Issroff, K. (2005). Learning technologies: Affective and social issues in computer supported collaborative learning. *Computers & Education, 44*(4), 395–408. doi:10.1016/j.compedu.2004.04.004

Juul, J. (2009). *A casual revolution: Reinventing video games and their players*. Cambridge, MA: MIT Press.

Kahneman, D., Slovic, P., & Tversky, A. (Eds.). (1982). *Judgment under uncertainty: Heuristics and biases*. Cambridge, UK: Cambridge University Press.

Kaiser, S., & Muller-Seitz, G. (2009). Acknowledging the innate impact of an information technology for engaging people in knowledge work: The case of weblog technology. *International Journal of Networking and Virtual Organisations, 6*(1), 4–21. doi:10.1504/IJNVO.2009.022480

Kalla, H. K. (2005). Integrated internal communications: A multidisciplinary perspective. *Corporate Communications: An International Journal, 10*(4), 302–314. doi:10.1108/13563280510630106

Karras, R. W. (1994). Writing essays that make historical arguments. *OAH Magazine of History, 8*(4), 54–57. doi:10.1093/maghis/8.4.54

Kato, H., Billinghurst, M., Poupyrev, I., Imamoto, K., & Tachibana, K. (2000). Virtual object manipulation on a table-top AR environment. In *Proceedings of the International Symposium on Augmented Reality* (pp. 111-119). Washington, DC: IEEE Press.

Kato, P. M., Cole, S. W., Bradlyn, A. S., & Pollock, B. H. (2008). A video game improves behavioural outcomes in adolescents and young adults with cancer: A randomised trial. *Paediatrics, 122*(2), 305–317. doi:10.1542/peds.2007-3134

Katz Yaacov, J., & Yablon Yaacov, B. (2006, January). *Mobile learning: A major e-learning platform*. Paper presented at the LOGOS Conference, Budapest, Hungary.

Kaufmann, H. (2002). Construct3D: an augmented reality application for mathematics and geometry education. In *Proceedings of the International Conference on Multimedia* (pp. 656-657). New York: ACM Press.

Kaufmann, H., & Duenser, A. (2007). Summary of usability evaluation of an educational augmented reality application. In R. Shumaker (Ed.), *Proceedings of the Human-Computer Interaction International Conference* (pp. 660-669). Berlin: Springer-Verlag.

Kay, A. (1972, August). A personal computer for children of all ages. In *Proceedings of the Annual ACM National Conference*, Boston, MA (p. 1).

Kearns, P. (2002). *Towards a connected learning society*. Canberra, Australia: Global Services.

Kee, K., Graham, S., Dunae, P., Lutz, J., Large, A., & Blondeau, M. (2009). Towards a theory of good history through gaming. *The Canadian Historical Review, 90*(2), 303–326. doi:10.3138/chr.90.2.303

Kelly, L. G. (1969). *25 centuries of language teaching*. Rowley, MA: Newbury House.

Kember, D. (2000). *Action learning and action research: Improving the quality of teaching & learning*. London, UK: Kogan Page.

Kennison, M. M., & Misselwitz, S. (2002). Evaluating reflective writing for appropriateness, fairness and consistency. *Nursing Education Perspectives, 23*(5), 238–242.

Kerres, M. (2007). *Microlearning as a challenge to instructional design*. Retrieved from http://mediendidaktik.uni-duisburg-essen.de/system/files/Microlearning-kerres.pdf

Kim, D. H. (2004). The link between individual and organizational learning . In Starkey, K., Tempest, S., & McKinlay, A. (Eds.), *How organizations learn: Managing the search for knowledge* (pp. 29–50). London, UK: Thomson Learning.

Kirriemuir, J., & McFarlane, A. (2003). *Use of computer and video games in the classroom*. Retrieved from http://www.slideshare.net/silversprite/use-of-computer-and-video-games-in-the-classroom

Kirriemuir, J., & McFarlane, A. (2004). *Literature review in games and learning*. Retrieved from http://www.futurelab.org.uk/resources/documents/lit_reviews/Games_Review.pdf

Kiyokawa, K., Billinghurst, M., Hayes, S. E., Gupta, A., Sannohe, Y., & Kato, H. (2002). Communication behaviors of co-located users in collaborative AR interfaces. In *Proceedings of the International Symposium on Mixed and Augmented Reality* (pp. 139-148). Washington, DC: IEEE Computer Society Press.

Klemmer, S., Nartmann, B., & Takayama, L. (2006). How bodies matter: five themes for interaction design. In J. M. Carroll, S. Bodker, & J. Coughlin (Eds.), *Proceedings of the ACM Conference on Designing Interactive Systems* (pp. 140-149). New York: ACM Press.

Klopfer, E., Squire, K., & Jenkins, H. (2002). Environmental detectives: PADs as a window into a virtual simulated world. In *Proceedings of the IEEE International Workshop on Wireless and Mobile Technologies in Education* (pp. 95-98). Washington, DC: IEEE Computer Society Press.

Knowles, M. S., Holton, E. F., & Swanson, R. A. (1998). *The adult learner*. Oxford, UK: Gulf Professional Publishing.

Koepp, M. J., Gunn, R. N., Lawrence, A. D., Cunningham, V. J., Dagher, A., & Jonnes, T. (1988). Evidence for striatal dopamine release during a video game. *Nature, 392*, 266–268.

Kolas, L., & Staupe, A. (2007). The PLExus prototype: A PLE realized as topic maps. In *Proceedings of the 7th IEEE International Conference on Advanced Learning Technologies* (pp. 750-752). Washington, DC: IEEE Computer Society.

Kolb, D. A. (1984). *Experiential Learning: Experience as the source of learning and development*. Englewood Cliffs, NJ: Prentice-Hall.

Kop, R. (2010). *Networked connectivity and adult learning: Social media, the knowledgeable other and distance education.* Unpublished doctoral dissertation, Swansea University, West Glamorgan, UK.

Kop, R., & Fournier (2011). New dimensions to self-directed learning on open networked learning environments. In *Proceedings of the 25th Annual International Self-Directed Learning Symposium*, Coco Beach, FL.

Kosonen, M., Henttonen, K., & Ellonen, H. K. (2007). Weblogs and internal communication in a corporate environment: A case from the ICT industry. *International Journal of Knowledge and Learning, 3*(4-5), 437–449. doi:10.1504/IJKL.2007.016704

Koster, R. (2004). *A theory of fun*. New York, NY: Parglyph Press.

Kress, G., & van Leeuwen, T. (2005). *Reading images: Grammar of visual design*. London: Routledge.

Kukulska-Hulme, A., & Pettit, J. (2006, October). *Practitioners as innovators: Emergent practice in personal mobile teaching, learning, work and leisure.* Paper presented at the MLearn Conference, Banff, AB, Canada.

Kuutti, K. (1996). Activity theory as a potential framework for human computer interaction research . In Nardi, B. A. (Ed.), *Context and consciousness: Activity theory and human-computer interaction* (pp. 17–44). Cambridge, MA: MIT Press.

Latour, B. (1999). *Pandora's hope: Essays on the reality of science studies*. Cambridge, MA: Harvard University Press.

Latour, B., & Woolgar, S. (1986). *Laboratory life: The construction of scientific facts* (2nd ed.). Princeton, NJ: Princeton University Press.

Lave, J., & Wegner, E. (1991). *Situated learning: Legitimate peripheral participation*. Cambridge, UK: Cambridge University Press.

Learning and Teaching Scotland. (2009). *Game-based learning.* Retrieved from http://www.itscotland.org.uk/

Leddo, J. (1996). An intelligent computer game to teach scientific reasoning. *Journal of Instruction Delivery Systems, 10*(4), 22–25.

Lee, G. A., Nelles, C., Billinghurst, M., & Kim, G. J. (2004). Immersive authoring of tangible augmented reality applications. In *Proceedings of the IEEE/ACM International Symposium on Mixed and Augmented Reality* (pp. 172-181). Washington, DC: IEEE Computer Society Press.

Lee, H. H., Park, S. R., & Hwang, T. (2008). Corporate-level blogs of the Fortune 500 companies: An empirical investigation of content and design. *International Journal of Technology Management, 7*(2), 134–148. doi:10.1504/IJITM.2008.016601

Lee, S. M., & Trimi, S. (2008). Editorial: organisational blogs: Overview and research agenda. *International Journal of Information Technology and Management, 7*(2), 113–119.

Lemke, C., Coughlin, E., Thadani, V., & Martin, C. (2002). *enGauge 21st century skills: Literacy in the digital age.* Retrieved from http://www.metiri.com

Leu, D. J. Kinzer, Charles, K., Coiro, J. L., & Cammack, D. W. (2004). Toward a theory of new literacies emerging from the internet and other information and communication technologies. In R. B. Ruddell & N. J. Unrau (Eds.), *Theoretical models and processes of reading* (pp. 1570-1613). Newark, DE: International Reading Association.

Levin, B., Glaze, A., & Fullan, M. (2008). Results without rancor and ranking Ontario's success story. *Phi Delta Kappan*, *90*(4), 273–280.

Levitt, B., & March, J. G. (1988). Organizational learning. *Annual Review of Sociology*, *14*, 319–340. doi:10.1146/annurev.so.14.080188.001535

Lindley, C. A., Nacke, L., & Sennersten, C. C. (2008, November 3-5). Dissecting play: Investigating the cognitive and emotional motivations and affects of computer gameplay. In *Proceedings of the CGAMES*, Wolverhampton, UK (pp. 9-16).

Lindley, D. V. (2006). *Understanding uncertainty*. Cambridge, UK: Cambridge University Press. doi:10.1002/0470055480

Lister, M. (2005). *The photographic image in digital culture*. London: Routledge.

Little, D. (2003). Tandem language learning and learning autonomy. In Lewis, T., & Walker, L. (Eds.), *Autonomous language learning in tandem*. Sheffield, UK: Academy Electronic Publications.

Livemocha. (2009). *Livemocha and Pearson announce partnership for online language learning*. Retrieved from http://www.livemocha.com/pages/pr/03102009

Livemocha. (2010). *What makes Livemocha so popular?* Retrieved from http://www.livemocha.com/language-learning-method

Lombard, M., & Ditton, T. (1997). At the heart of it all: The concept of presence. *Journal of Computer-Mediated Communication*, *3*(2).

Long, M. H. (2000). Second language acquisition theories. In Byram, M. (Ed.), *Encyclopedia of language teaching* (pp. 527–534). London, UK: Routledge.

Long, M. H. (2005). Methodological issues in learner needs analysis. In Long, M. H. (Ed.), *Second language needs analysis* (pp. 19–76). Cambridge, UK: Cambridge University Press. doi:10.1017/CBO9780511667299.002

Long, M. H., & Crookes, G. (1993). Units of analysis in syllabus design—The case for task. In Crookes, G., & Gass, S. M. (Eds.), *Tasks in a pedagogical context: Integrating theory and practice* (pp. 9–54). Clevedon, UK: Multilingual Matters.

Long, M. H., & Norris, J. M. (2000). Task-based teaching and assessment. In Byram, M. (Ed.), *Encyclopedia of language teaching* (pp. 597–603). London: Routledge.

Lubensky, R. (2007). *The present and future of personal learning environments (PLE)*. Retrieved from http://members.optusnet.com.au/rlubensky/2006/12/present-and-future-of-personal-learning.html

Lund, H. H., Klitbo, T., & Jessen, C. (2005). Playware technology for physically activating play. *Artificial Life and Robotics Journal*, *9*(4), 165–174. doi:10.1007/s10015-005-0350-z

Lynch, M., & Woolgar, S. (1990). Introduction: Sociological orientations to representational practice in science. In Lynch, M., & Woolgar, S. (Eds.), *Representation in scientific practice*. Cambridge, MA: MIT Press.

Maclure, M. (2009). Livemocha creates an online language learning platform. *Information Today*, 10.

Maggioni, L., VanSledright, B., & Alexander, P. A. (2009). Walking on the borders: A measure of epistemic cognition in history. *Journal of Experimental Education*, *77*(3), 187–213. doi:10.3200/JEXE.77.3.187-214

Magnussen, R. (2008). *Representational inquiry in science learning games*. Unpublished doctoral dissertation, Aarhus University, Copenhagen, Denmark.

Magnussen, R. (2007). Games as a platform for situated science practice. In de Castell, S., & Jenson, J. (Eds.), *Worlds in play: International perspectives on digital games research* (pp. 301–311). New York, NY: Peter Lang.

Magnussen, R. (2009). Representational inquiry competences in science games. In Rodrigues, S. G. A. (Ed.), *Multiple literacy and science education: ICTs in formal and informal learning environments* (pp. 360–370). Hershey, PA: IGI Global. doi:10.4018/9781615206902.ch017

Mallon, B., & Webb, B. (2000). Structure, causality, visibility and interaction: Propositions for evaluating engagement in narrative multimedia. *International Journal of Human-Computer Studies*, *53*, 269–287. doi:10.1006/ijhc.2000.0387

Mallon, B., & Webb, B. (2005). Stand up and take your place: Identifying narrative elements in narrative adventure and role-play games. *ACM Computers in Entertainment*, *3*(1), 6–6. doi:10.1145/1057270.1057285

Malone, T. W. (1981). Toward a theory of intrinsically motivating instruction. *Cognitive Science: A Multidisciplinary Journal, 5*, 333-369.

Malone, T. W., & Lepper, M. R. (1987). Making learning fun: A taxonomy of intrinsic motivations for learning. *Aptitude . Learning and Instruction, 3*, 223–253.

Malone, T. W., & Lepper, M. R. (1987). Making learning fun: A taxonomy of intrinsic motivations for learning . In Snow, R. E., & Farr, M. J. (Eds.), *Aptitude, learning and instruction III: Conative and affective process analyses.* Mahwah, NJ: Erlbaum.

Mandryk, R. L., & Inkpen, K. M. (2004). Physiological indicators for the evaluation of co-located collaborative play. In *Proceedings of the ACM Conference on Computer Supported Cooperative Work*, Chicago, IL (pp. 102-111).

Mandryk, R. L., & Atkins, M. S. (2007). A fuzzy physiological approach for continuously modeling emotion during interaction with play environments. *International Journal of Human-Computer Studies, 6*(4), 329–347. doi:10.1016/j.ijhcs.2006.11.011

Margerison, A. (1996). Self-esteem: Its effect on the development and learning of children with EBD. *Support for Learning, 11*(4), 176–180. doi:10.1111/j.1467-9604.1996.tb00256.x

Markee, N. (1996). *Managing curricular innovation.* Cambridge, UK: Cambridge University Press.

Marshall, S., & Mitchell, G. (2006). Assessing sector e-learning capability with an e-learning maturity model. In *Proceedings of the 13ᵗʰ ALT-C Conference on the Association for Learning Technologies: The Next Generation* (pp. 203-214).

Martensson, M. (2000). A critical review of knowledge management as a management tool. *Journal of Knowledge Management, 4*(3), 204–216. doi:10.1108/13673270010350002

Martin, M. (2005). Seeing is believing: the role of video conferencing in distance learning. *British Journal of Educational Technology, 36*(3), 397–405. doi:10.1111/j.1467-8535.2005.00471.x

Maxwell, A. (2010). Assessment strategies for a history exam, or, why short-answer questions are better than in-class essays. *The History Teacher, 43*(2), 233–245.

May, T. (2005). Thoughts about IT in language education. *Asian EFL Journal, 1*(1).

Mazzoni, E., & Gaffuri, P. (2009). Personal learning environments for overcoming knowledge boundaries between activity systems in emerging adulthood. *eLearning Papers, 15*.

McAfee, A. P. (2006). Enterprise 2.0: The dawn of emergent collaboration. *MIT Sloan Management Review, 47*(3), 21–28.

McBride, K. (2009). Social-networking sites in foreign language classrooms . In Lomicka, L., & Lord, G. (Eds.), *The next generation: Social networking and online collaboration in foreign language learning.* San Marcos, TX: CALICO Book Series.

McClymer, J. F., & Moynihan, K. J. (1977). The essay assignment: A teaching device. *The History Teacher, 10*(3), 359–371. doi:10.2307/491847

McFarlane, A., Sparrowhawk, A., & Heald, Y. (2002). *Report on the educational use of games.* Retrieved from http://www.teem.org.uk/resources/teem_gamesined_full.pdf

McGinn, M. K., & Roth, W. M. (1999). Preparing students for competent scientific practice: Implications of recent research in science and technology studies. *Educational Researcher, 28*(3), 14–24.

McLoughlin, C., & Lee, M. J. W. (2008). Future learning landscapes: Transforming pedagogy through social software. *Innovate, 4*(5).

McNab, F., Varrone, A., Farde, A., Jucaite, A., Bystitsky, P., & Frossberg, H. (2009). Changes in cortical dopamine D1 receptor binding associated with cognitive Training. *Science, 323*, 800–802. doi:10.1126/science.1166102

Media Awareness Network. (2010). *Digital literacy in Canada: From inclusion to transformation.* Retrieved from http://www.mediaawareness.ca

Medienpädagogischer Forschungsverbund Südwest (MPFS). (2008). *KIM-Studie 2008.* Retrieved from http://doebe.li/b03536

Merritt, C. (2009). *The adventures of super-user.* Retrieved from http://hosteddocs.ittoolbox.com/cm120308.pdf

Meyer, B., & Bo-Kristensen, M. (2008). *Designing location aware games for mobile language learning.* Retrieved from http://www.formatex.org/micte2009/book/1086-1090.pdf

Meyler, A., Keller, T. A., Cherkassky, V. L., Gabrieli, J. D. E., & Just, M. A. (2008). Modifying the brain activation of poor readers during sentence comprehension with extended remedial instruction: A longitudinal study of neuroplasticity. *Neuropsychologia, 46*(10), 2580–2592. doi:10.1016/j.neuropsychologia.2008.03.012

Milgram, P., & Kishino, F. (1994). A taxonomy of mixed reality visual displays. *IEICE Transactions on Information and Systems, 12,* 1321–1329.

Milligan, C., Johnson, M., Sharples, P., Wilson, S., & Liber, O. (2006). Developing a reference model to describe the personal learning environment. In W. Nejdl & K. Tochtermann (Eds.), *Proceedings of the First European Conference on Innovative Approaches for Learning and Knowledge Sharing* (LNCS 4227, pp. 506-511).

Milton, J. (2006). *Literature review in languages, technology and learning.* Retrieved from http://www.futurelab.org.uk/research/lit_reviews.htm

Ministerial Council on Education and Employment Training and Youth Affairs. (2005). *Learning in an online world.* Canberra, Australia: DEST.

Ministerial Council on Education and Employment Training and Youth Affairs. (2006). *Report of the ICT in schools taskforce.* Canberra, Australia: DEST.

Ministerial Council on Education and Employment Training and Youth Affairs. (2008). *Digital Education: Making Change Happen.* Canberra, Australia: DEWAR.

Mishra, P., & Koehler, M. (2006). Technological pedagogical content knowledge: A framework for teacher knowledge. *Teachers College Record, 108*(6), 1017–1054. doi:10.1111/j.1467-9620.2006.00684.x

Mitchell, A., & Savill-Smith, C. (2004). *The use of computer and video games for learning: A review of the literature.* Retrieved from http://www.m-learning.org/archive/docs/The%20use%20of%20computer%20and%20video%20games%20for%20learning.pdf

Mitchell, W. J. (1994). *The reconfigured eye: Visual truth in the post-photographic era.* Cambridge, MA: MIT Press.

Miyazaki, H., Takeuchi, M., & Nakajima, E. (2009). *Demon's Souls.* Foster City, CA: Atlus & Sony Computer Entertainment.

Monahan, G., W. (2002). Acting out Nazi Germany: A role-play simulation for the history classroom. *Teaching History, 27*(2), 74–85.

Moser, T., & Petko, D. (2007). Lerntagebuch.ch, Lernstrategien mit Weblogs fördern. *Unterricht Konkret 2007*(6), 44.

Mullen, T., Appel, C., & Shanklin, T. (2009). Skypebased tandem language learning and web 2.0 . In Thomas, M. (Ed.), *Handbook of research on Web 2.0 and second language learning* (pp. 101–118). Hershey, PA: IGI Global. doi:10.4018/978-1-60566-190-2.ch006

Munslow, A. (2003). *The new history.* Toronto, ON, Canada: Pearson Longman.

Munslow, A. (2007). *Narrative and history.* New York, NY: Palgrave MacMillan.

Murphy, J., & Lebans, R. (2008). Unexpected outcomes: Web 2.0 in the secondary school classroom. *International Journal of Technology in Teaching and Learning, 4*(2), 137–147.

Murphy, J., & Lebans, R. (2009). Leveraging new technologies for professional learning in education: Digital literacies as culture shift in professional development. *E-learning, 6*(3), 275–280. doi:10.2304/elea.2009.6.3.275

Muzzy, L. (2007, 2010). *Making history: The calm and the storm & making history II: The war of the world.* Retrieved from http://making-history.com

Naish, J. (2009, June 23). *Mobile phones for children: a boon or a peril?* Retrieved from http://women.timesonline.co.uk/tol/life_and_style/women/families/article6556283.ece

Naismith, L., Lonsdale, P., Vavoula, P., & Sharples, M. (2004). *Report 11: Literature review in mobile technologies and learning*. London, UK: Nesta Future Lab.

Nardi, B. A., Schiano, D. J., Gumbrecht, M., & Swartz, L. (2004). Why we blog. *Communications of the ACM, 47*(12), 41–46. doi:10.1145/1035134.1035163

Navab, N. (2004). Developing killer apps for industrial augmented reality. *IEEE Computer Graphics and Applications, 24*, 16–20. doi:10.1109/MCG.2004.1297006

Neff, C. (2009). *iMemento – Effektiv lernen mit Karteikarten.* Retrieved from http://www.projektschule-goldau.ch/permalink/314

Neff, C. (2009). *Kopfrechnen – da wird geübt!* Retrieved from http://www.projektschule-goldau.ch/permalink/478

Neff, C. (2009). *Vertrag – gemeinsam erarbeitet.* http://www.projektschule-goldau.ch/permalink/624

Neff, C. (2009). *Kalender – Agenda für die ganze Klasse.* Retrieved from http://www.projektschule-goldau.ch/permalink/473

Neff, C. (2010). *Diktat ohne stress.* Retrieved from http://www.projektschule-goldau.ch/permalink/857

Neff, G. (2009). *iMotion – Trickfilme machen.* Retrieved from http://www.projektschule-goldau.ch/permalink/736

Neff, G. (2010). *Kunst mit iPhone.* Retrieved from http://www.projektschule-goldau.ch/permalink/978

Neuhaus, W. (2007). *Personal learning environments (PLE).* Retrieved from http://mediendidaktik.port07.de/?p=76

Neumann, U., & Majoros, A. (1998). Cognitive, performance, and systems issues for augmented reality applications in manufacturing and maintenance. In *Proceedings of the IEEE Virtual Reality Annual International Symposium* (pp. 4-11). Washington, DC: IEEE Computer Society Press.

New South Wales Government. (2009). Connected Classrooms Program. Retrieved March 25, 2009 from https://www.det.nsw.edu.au/strat_direction/schools/ccp/index.htm

New South Wales Institute of Teachers. (2006). *Handbook of professional teaching standards.* Sydney, Australia: NSWDET.

Nielsen, J., Bærendsen, N. K., & Jessen, C. (2009). Music-making and musical comprehension with robotic building blocks. In *Proceedings of the 4th International Conference on E-Learning and Games: Learning by Playing. Game-based Education System Design and Development* (pp. 399-409).

Norris, C., & Soloway, E. (2004). Envisioning the handheld-centric classroom. *Journal of Educational Computing Research, 30*(4), 281–294. doi:10.2190/MBPJ-L35D-C4K6-AQB8

Norris, J. M., Brown, J. D., Hudson, T. H., & Yoshioka, J. (1998). *Designing second language performance assessments.* Honolulu, HI: National Foreign Language Resource Center.

NSW Department of Education and Training. (2005). *Micro trial of LAMS report.* Sydney: Centre for Learning Innovation.

NSW Department of Education and Training. (2007). *Engaging pedagogy: Teachers in the field.* Sydney, Australia: Centre for Learning Innovation.

NSW Department of Education and Training. (2007). *Report on how DET teachers discover, access and use online learning resources in their practice.* Sydney, Australia: Centre for Learning Innovation.

NSW Public Schools. (2009). *Home.* Retrieved March 24, 2009, from http://www.schools.nsw.edu.au/

O'Neil, H. F., Wainess, R., & Baker, E. L. (2005). Classification of learning outcomes: Evidence from the computer games literature. *Curriculum Journal, 16*(4), 455–474. doi:10.1080/09585170500384529

Oblinger, D. (2004). The next generation in educational engagement. *Journal of Interactive Media in Education, 8*.

OECD (Ed.). (2005). *Are students ready for a technology-rich world? – What PISA studies tell us* (p. 37). Paris, France: OECD.

OECD. (2000). *Knowledge management in the learning society*. Paris, France: OECD Publications.

Olivier, B., & Liber, O. (2001). *Lifelong learning: The need for portable personal learning environments and supporting interoperability standards*. Retrieved from http://wiki.cetis.ac.uk/uploads/6/67/Olivierandliber2001.doc

Olivier, B., & Liber, O. (2002). Lifelong learning: The need for portable personal learning environments and supporting interoperability standards. In *Proceedings of the International Conference on Advances in Infrastructure for Electronic Business, Education, Science and Medicine on the Internet*, L'Aquilla, Italy.

Online Education. (2009). *Videogame statistics*. Retrieved from http://www.onlineeducation.net/videogame

Ontario Ministry of Education. (2004). *Literacy for learning: The report of the expert panel on literacy in grades 4 to 6 in Ontario*. Retrieved from http://www.edu.gov.on.ca/eng/publications/

Orava, J. (2006). *Virtuaalikoulun taidekasvatuksen luokka*. Opetushallitus.

O'Reilly, T. (2005). *What Is Web 2.0 – Design patterns and business models for the next generation of software*. Retrieved from http://oreilly.com/web2/archive/what-is-web-20.html

O'Reilly, T. (2007). What Is Web 2.0 – Design patterns and business models for the next generation of software. *Communications & Strategies, 1*(1), 17–37.

Oreskes, N. (2004). Beyond the ivory tower: The scientific consensus on climate change. *Science 3, 306*(5702), 1686

Oretnblad, A. (2005). Of course organizations can learn! *The Learning Organization, 12*(2), 213–218. doi:10.1108/09696470510583566

Ortenblad, A. (2001). On differences between organizational learning and learning organization. *The Learning Organization, 8*(3), 125–133. doi:10.1108/09696470110391211

Ortenblad, A. (2002). Organizational learning: A radical perspective. *International Journal of Management Reviews, 4*(1), 87–100. doi:10.1111/1468-2370.00078

Overly, S. (2010). *Q&A with Rosetta Stone chief: In using social media for education, it needs to serve learning goals, not just be a "time sink"*. Retrieved from http://www.washingtonpost.com/wp-dyn/content/article/2010/09/24/AR2010092405995.html

Pace, D. (2004). Decoding the reading of history: An example of the process. *New Directions for Teaching and Learning, 98*, 13–21. doi:10.1002/tl.143

Pachler, N., & Bachmair, B. (2010). *Mobile learning*. New York, NY: Springer. doi:10.1007/978-1-4419-0585-7

Papert, S., & Harel, I. (1991). *Situating constructionism*. Retrieved from http://papert.org/articles/SituatingConstructionism.html

Pascu, C. (2008). *An empirical analysis of the creation, use and adoption of social computing applications*. Retrieved March 3, 2010, from http://ftp.jrc.es/EURdoc/JRC46431.pdf

Patten, B., Sanchez, I. A., & Tangney, B. (2006). Designing collaborative, constructionist and contextual applications for handheld devices. *Computers & Education, 46*(3), 294–308. doi:10.1016/j.compedu.2005.11.011

Pelletier, C., & Oliver, M. (2006). Learning to play in digital games. *Learning, Media and Technology, 31*, 329–342. doi:10.1080/17439880601021942

Petersen, S. A., Divitini, M., & Chabert, G. (2009). Sense of community among mobile language learners: Can blogs support this? *International Journal of Web Based Communities, 5*(3), 428–445. doi:10.1504/IJWBC.2009.025217

Pettit, J., & Street, K. (2007). *Heaven & hell on earth: The massacre of the "Black" Donnellys: Great unsolved mysteries in Canadian history*. Retrieved from http://www.canadianmysteries.ca/sites/donnellys/home/indexen.html

Phillips, J. (2002). The dinosaurs didn't see it coming, but Historians had better: Computer-aided activities in the history classroom. *History Computer Review, 18*(1), 27–36.

Picard, R., Papert, S., Bender, W., Blumberg, B., Breazeal, C., & Cavallo, D. (2004). Affective learning – a manifesto. *BT Technology Journal, 22*(4), 253–269. doi:10.1023/B:BTTJ.0000047603.37042.33

Pilkington, R., Meek, J., Corlett, D., & Chan, T. (2006). Openness to electronic professional development planning: Evaluating the interactive Logbook Project. In *Proceedings of the 6th IEEE International Conference on Advanced Learning Technologies* (pp. 774-778). Washington, DC: IEEE Computer Society Press.

Pivec, P. (2009). *Game-based learning or game-based teaching?* Retrieved from: http://emergingtechnologies. becta.org.uk/upload-dir/downloads/page_documents/research/emerging_technologies/game_based_learning.pdf

Poland, R., LaVelle, L. B., & Nichol, J. (2003). The Virtual Field Station (VFS): using a virtual reality environment for ecological fieldwork in A-Level biological studies – Case Study 3. *British Journal of Educational Technology, 34*, 215–231. doi:10.1111/1467-8535.00321

Poupyrev, I., Tan, D. S., Billinghurst, M., Kato, H., Regenbrecht, H., & Tetsutani, N. (2002). Developing a generic augmented reality interface. *Computers, 35*, 44–50. doi:10.1109/2.989929

Prensky, M. (2001). *Digital game-based learning.* New York, NY: McGraw Hill.

Prensky, M. (2003). Computer games and learning—digital game-based learning . In Goldstein, J., & Raessens, J. (Eds.), *Handbook of computer game studies* (pp. 97–122). Cambridge, MA: MIT Press.

Prensky, M. (2005). Listen to the natives. *Educational Leadership, 63*(4), 8–13.

Prensky, M. (2006). *'Don't bother me mom – I'm learning!' How computer and video games are preparing your kids for 21st century success—and how you can help!* St. Paul, MN: Paragon House.

Prensky, M. (2007). *Digital game-based learning.* St Paul, MN: Paragon House Publishers.

Pulman, A. (2008). *Mobile assistance – the Nintendo DS Lite as an assistive tool for health and social care students.* Retrieved from http://www.swap.ac.uk/docs/casestudies/pulman.pdf

QCA. (2008). *Personal learning and thinking skills: Supporting successful learners, confident individuals and responsible citizens.* London: Qualifications and Curriculum Authority.

QCA. (2009). *Functional skills: Essential for life, learning and work.* London: Qualifications and Curriculum Authority.

Räsanen, M. (1997). *Building bridges, experiential art understanding: A work of art as a means of understanding and constructing self.* Helsinki, Finland: University of Art and Design Helsinki.

Redecker, C. AlaMutka, K., & Punie, Y. (2009). *Learning 2.0 – the use of social computing to enhance lifelong learning.* Seville, Spain: European Commission, Joint Research Centre, Institute for Prospective Technological Studies (IPTS).

Reed, J., & Warner-Rogers, J. (2008). *Child neuropsychology concepts, theory, and practice.* West Sussex, UK: Wiley-Blackwell.

Regenbrecht, H., Baratoff, G., & Wagner, M. T. (2001). A tangible AR desktop environment. *Computer Graphics, 25*, 755–763. doi:10.1016/S0097-8493(01)00118-2

Rekimoto, J. (1998). Matrix: a realtime object identification and registration method for augmented reality. In *Proceedings of the Asia Pacific Computer Human Interaction* (pp. 63-68). Washington, DC: IEEE Computer Society Press.

Robertson, J., & Howells, C. (2008). Computer game design: Opportunities for successful learning. *Computers & Education, 50*(2), 559–578. doi:10.1016/j.compedu.2007.09.020

Robson, P. J. A., & Tourish, D. (2005). Managing internal communication: An organizational case study. *Corporate Communications: An International Journal, 10*(3), 213–222. doi:10.1108/13563280510614474

Rogers, P. C., Liddle, S. W., Chan, P., Doxey, A., & Isom, B. (2007). A Web 2.0 learning platform: Harnessing collective intelligence. *Turkish Online Journal of Distance Education, 8*(3), 16–33.

Rogers, Y., Scaife, M., Gabrielle, S., Smith, H., & Harris, E. (2002). A conceptual framework for mixed reality environments: designing novel learning activities for young children. *Presence (Cambridge, Mass.), 11*, 677–686. doi:10.1162/105474602321050776

Roll, M. (2004, July 5-6). Distributed KM – improving knowledge workers' productivity and organizational knowledge sharing with weblog-based personal publishing. In *Proceedings of the BlogTalk 2.0 European Conference on Weblogs*, Vienna, Austria (pp. 1-12).

Roschelle, J. (2003). Unlocking the learning value of wireless mobile devices. *Journal of Computer Assisted Learning, 19*(3). doi:10.1046/j.0266-4909.2003.00028.x

Rose, J. (2006). *Independent review of the teaching of reading*. Retrieved from http://media.education.gov.uk/assets/files/pdf/i/independent%20review.pdf

Rosenbloom, A. (2004). The blogosphere. *Communications of the ACM, 47*(12), 31–33.

Ross, C., & Ma, J.-H. S. (2006). *Modern Mandarin Chinese grammar: A practical guide*. London: Routledge.

Royle, K. (2009). Computer games and realising their learning potential: Crossing borders, blurring boundaries and taking action. Retrieved from http://www.game-basedlearning.org.uk/content/view/67/

Royle, K., & Clarke, R. (2003). *Making the case for computer games as a learning environment*. Retrieved from http://citeseerx.ist.psu.edu/viewdoc/download?doi=10.1.1.110.2561&rep=rep1&type=pdf

Rückriem, G. (2003). *Tool or medium? The meaning of information and telecommunication technology to human practice. A quest for systemic understanding of activity theory*. Retrieved from http://www.iscar.org/fi/ruckriem.pdf

Rückriem, G. (2009). Digital technology and mediation: A challenge to activity theory . In Sannino, A., Daniels, H., & Gutierrez, K. D. (Eds.), *Learning and expanding with activity theory* (pp. 88–111). Cambridge, UK: Cambridge University Press.

Russell, W. B. III, & Pellegrino, A. (2008). Constructing meaning from historical content: A research study. *Journal of Social Studies Research, 32*(2), 3–15.

Salen, K., & Zimmernam, E. (2004). *Rules of play: game design fundamentals*. Cambridge, MA: MIT Press.

Saljo, R. (2010). Digital tools and challenges to institutional traditions of learning: Technologies, social memory and the performative nature of learning. *Journal of Computer Assisted Learning, 26*, 53–64. doi:10.1111/j.1365-2729.2009.00341.x

Salzman, M., Dede, C., Loftin, R., & Chen, J. (1999). A model for understanding how virtual reality aids complex conceptual learning. *Presence (Cambridge, Mass.), 8*, 293–316. doi:10.1162/105474699566242

Sandford, R., & Williamson, B. (2005). *Games and learning*. Bristol, UK: Nesta Futurelab.

Sawyer, R. K. (2006). Educating for innovation. *Thinking Skills and Creativity, 1*(1), 41–48. doi:10.1016/j.tsc.2005.08.001

Scardamalia, M., & Bereiter, C. (2003). Knowledge building. In *Encyclopedia of Education* (2nd ed., pp. 1370-1373). New York: Macmillan Reference, USA.

Schein, E. H. (1993). On dialogue, culture, and organizational learning. *Organizational Dynamics, 22*(2), 40–51. doi:10.1016/0090-2616(93)90052-3

Schmid, C. (1999). Simulation and virtual reality for education on the Web . In Hahn, W., Walther-Klaus, E., & Knop, J. (Eds.), *EUROMEDIA* (pp. 181–188). Amsterdamn, The Netherlands: SCS Publication.

Schon, D. (1983). *Reflective practitioner: How professionals think in action*. New York, NY: Basic Books.

Schuck, S., & Kearney, M. (2006). *Exploring pedagogy with interactive whiteboards: A case study of six schools*. Sydney, Australia: UTS Press.

Schulmeister, R. (2009). *PLE zwischen Alltäglichem und Besonderem – Was konstituiert eigentlich eine LERNumgebung?* Paper presented at the Conference Personal Learning Environments in der Schule, Goldau.

Sclater, N. (2010). eLearning in the cloud. *International Journal of Virtual and Personal Learning Environments, 1*(1), 10–19.

Severance, C., Hardin, J., & Whyte, A. (2008). The coming functionality mash-up in personal learning environments. *Interactive Learning Environments, 16*(1), 47–62. doi:10.1080/10494820701772694

Seymore, P. H. K., Aro, M., & Erskine, J. M. (2003). Foundation literacy acquisition in European orthogphies. *The British Journal of Psychology*, *94*, 143–174. doi:10.1348/000712603321661859

Shaffer, D. W., & Gee, J. P. (2005). *Before every child is left behind: How epistemic games can solve the coming crisis in education* (Tech. Rep. No. 2005-7). Madison, WI: University of Wisconsin-Madison, Center for Education Research.

Shaffer, D. W. (2006). Epistemic frames for epistemic games. *Computers & Education*, *46*(3), 223–234. doi:10.1016/j.compedu.2005.11.003

Shaffer, D. W. (2007). *How computer games help children learn.* New York, NY: Palgrave Macmillan.

Shaffert, S., & Hilzensauer, W. (2008). *On the way towards personal learning environments: Seven crucial aspects.* Retrieved from http://www.elearningeuropa.info/mt/node/2680

Sharma, P., & Fiedler, S. (2007). Supporting self-organized learning with personal webpublishing technologies and practices. *Journal of Computing in Higher Education*, *18*(2), 3–24. doi:10.1007/BF03033411

Sharma, R., & Molineros, J. (1997). Computer vision-based augmented reality for guiding manual assembly. *Presence (Cambridge, Mass.)*, *6*, 292–317.

Sharples, M. (2005). *Big issues in mobile learning.* Retrieved from http://mlearning.noe-kaleidoscope.org/repository/BigIssues.pdf

Sharples, M., Taylor, J., & Vavoula, G. (2005). Towards a theory of mobile learning. In *Proceedings of the Mobile Learning Conference*, Birmingham, AL.

Shawitz, S. (2003). *Overcoming dyslexia.* New York, NY: Vintage.

Sheely, S. (2006). Persistent technologies: Why can't we stop lecturing online? In *Proceedings of the 23rd ASCI-LITE Conference on Who's Learning? Whose Technology?* Sydney, Australia (pp. 769-774).

Shelton, B. E., & Hedley, N. R. (2002). Using augmented reality for teaching Earth-Sun relationships to undergraduate geography students. In *Proceedings of the International Augmented Reality Toolkit Workshop.* Washington, DC: IEEE Press.

Shelton, B. E., & Hedley, N. R. (2003). Exploring a cognitive foundation for learning spatial relationships with augmented reality. In *Technology, Instruction, Cognition, and Learning.* Philadelphia: Old City Publishing.

Shepard, R. N., & Metzler, J. (1971). Mental rotation of three-dimensional objects. *Science*, *191*, 952–954. doi:10.1126/science.1251207

Shirky, C. (2003). A group is its own worst enemy. *Clay Shirky's writings about the Internet: Economics & culture, media & community.* Retrieved from http://www.shirky.com/writings/group_enemy.html

Siemens, G., & Downes, S. (2008). *Connectivism and connected knowledge.* Retrieved from http://ltc.umanitoba.ca/connectivism/

Siemens, G., & Downes, S. (2009). *Connectivism and connected knowledge.* Retrieved from http://ltc.umanitoba.ca/connectivism/

Siemens, G. (2005). Connectivism: A learning theory for a digital age. *International Journal of Instructional Technology and Distance Learning*, *2*(1).

Sims, R. (2006). Online distance education: New ways of learning, new modes of teaching? *Distance Education*, *27*(2), 3–5.

Singh, R. P., & Singh, L. O. (2008). Blogs: Emerging knowledge management tools for entrepreneurs to enhance marketing efforts. *Journal of Internet Commerce*, *7*(4), 470–484. doi:10.1080/15332860802507305

Smith, A. (1973). *Symbol digit modalities test.* Los Angeles, CA: Western Psychological Services.

Soloway, E. (1998). Learner-centered design: the challenge of HCI in the 21st century. *Interaction*, *1*, 36–48. doi:10.1145/174809.174813

Soloway, E., Becker, H. J., Norris, C., & Topp, N. (2001). Handheld devices are ready-at-hand. *Communications of the ACM, 44*(6), 15–20. doi:10.1145/376134.376140

Somekh, B. (2000). New technology and learning: Policy and practice in the UK, 1980-2010. *Education and Information Technologies, 5*(1), 19–37. doi:10.1023/A:1009636417727

Squire, K. (2004). *Changing the game: What happens when video games enter the classroom? Innovate.* Retrieved from http://www.innovateonline.info/index.php?view=article&id=82

Squire, K. (2005). Changing the game: What happens when video games enter the classroom? *Innovate: Journal of Online Education, 1*(6).

Squire, K. (2005). *Game-based learning: Present and future state of the field.* Retrieved from http://www.mendeley.com/research/gamebased-learning-present-and-future-state-of-the-field/

Squire, K., & Barab, S. (2004). Replaying history: Engaging urban underserved students in learning world history through computer simulation games. In *Proceedings of the 6th international conference on Learning sciences,* Santa Monica, CA (pp. 505-512).

Squire, K., Giovanetto, L., Devane, B., & Durga, S. (2005). From users to designers: Building a self-organizing game-based learning environment. *TechTrends, 49*(5), 34–74. doi:10.1007/BF02763688

Squire, K., & Klopfer, E. (2007). Augmented reality simulations on handheld computers. *Journal of the Learning Sciences, 16*(3), 371–413. doi:10.1080/10508400701413435

Stake, R. E. (2008). Qualitative case studies . In Denzin, N. K., & Lincoln, Y. S. (Eds.), *Strategies of qualitative inquiry* (pp. 119–149). London, UK: Sage.

Stevick, E. (1971). Evaluating and adapting language materials . In Allen, H., & Campbell, R. (Eds.), *Teaching English as a second language* (pp. 102–107). New York, NY: McGraw-Hill.

Street-Smart Language Learning. (2010). *Livemocha review: Love the native speakers, the method not so much.* Retrieved from http://www.streetsmartlanguagelearning.com/2009/01/livemocha-review-love-native-speakers.html

Swan, K., Van 't Hooft, M., Kratcoski, A., & Schenker, J. (2007). Ubiquitous computing and changing pedagogical possibilities: Representations, conceptualizations and uses of knowledge. *Journal of Educational Computing Research, 36*(4), 481–515. doi:10.2190/B577-7162-2X11-17N5

Tang, A., Owen, C., Biocca, F., & Mou, W. (2003). Comparative effectiveness of augmented reality in object assembly. In V. Bellotti, T. Erickson, G. Cockton, & P. Korhonen (Eds.), *Proceedings of the ACM Conference on Human Factors in Computing Systems* (pp. 73-80). New York: ACM Press.

Taraghi, B., Ebner, M., Till, G., & Mühlburger, H. (2009). Personal learning environment - a conceptual study. *International Journal of Emerging Technologies in Learning, 5,* 25–30.

Teo, T., Lee, C. B., & Chai, C. S. (2008). Understanding pre-service teachers' computer attitudes: Applying and extending the technology acceptance model. *Journal of Computer Assisted Learning, 24,* 128–143. doi:10.1111/j.1365-2729.2007.00247.x

Tey, J. (1968). *The daughter of time.* Scarborough, ON, Canada: Bellhaven House.

Thomas, L., & Harri-Augstein, S. (1985). *Self-organised learning: Foundations of a conversational science for psychology.* London, UK: Routledge.

Thomas, L., & Harri-Augstein, S. (2001). Conversational science and advanced learning technologies (ALT). Tools for conversational pedagogy. *Kybernetes, 30*(7-8), 921–954. doi:10.1108/EUM0000000005917

Thomas, M. (Ed.). (2011). *Deconstructing digital natives: Young people, technology and the new literacies.* London, UK: Routledge.

Tindal, I., Powell, S., & Millwood, R. (2007). *Undergraduate student researchers - the Ultraversity model for work based learning.* Retrieved from http://www.informaworld.com/smpp/content~content=a788481519~db=all~order=page

Tiropanis, T., Davis, H., Millard, D., Weal, M., White, S., & Wills, G. (2009). *Semantic technologies in learning and teaching (SemTech).* Bristol, UK: JISC.

Tobin, K. (2001). To think on paper: Using writing assignments in the world of history survey. *The History Teacher, 34*(4), 497–508. doi:10.2307/3054202

Toffler, A. (1970). *Future shock.* New York: Random House.

Tsui, L. (1999). Courses and instruction affecting critical thinking. *Research in Higher Education, 40*(2), 185–200. doi:10.1023/A:1018734630124

Tuchinda, R., Szekely, P., & Knoblock, C. (2008, January 13-16). Building mahsups by example. In *Proceedings of the ACM 13th International Conference on Intelligent User Interfaces*, Canary Islands, Spain (pp. 139-148).

Turner, M., & Risdale, J. (1984). *Turner and Risdale digit span test.* Retrieved from http://www.dyslexiaaction.org.uk/

UK Department for Business Innovation and Skills. (2009). *Digital Britain final report.* Retrieved from http://www.official-documents.gov.uk

Ullmer, B., & Ishii, H. (1997). The metaDesk: models and prototypes for tangible user interfaces. In *Proceedings of the ACM Symposium on User Interface Software and Technology* (pp. 223-232). New York: ACM Press.

Väljataga, T. (2010). *Learner control and responsibility: Expanding the concept of self-direction in higher education.* Tampere, Finland: Tampere University of Technology.

Väljataga, T., & Fiedler, S. (2009). Supporting students to self-direct intentional learning projects with social media. *Journal of Educational Technology & Society, 12*(3), 58–69.

Valve Corporation. (2007). *Source SDK.* Bellevue, WA: Valve Corporation.

Van Avermaet, P., & Gysen, S. (2006). From needs to tasks: Language learning needs in a task-based approach. In Branden, K. V. D. (Ed.), *Task-based language education: From theory to practice* (pp. 17–46). Cambridge, UK: Cambridge University Press.

van Harmelen, M. (2006). Personal learning environments. In *Proceedings of the 6th IEEE International Conference on Advanced Learning Technologies* (pp. 815-816). Washington, DC: IEEE Computer Society.

van Harmelen, M. (2008). Design trajectories: Four experiments in PLE implementation. *Interactive Learning Environments, 16*(1), 35–46. doi:10.1080/10494820701772686

Vavoula, G., Scanlon, E., Lonsdale, P., Sharples, M., & Jones, A. (2005). *Report on empirical work with mobile learning and literature on mobile learning in science (Tech. Rep. No. IST 507838).* Brussels, Belgium: The European Commission.

Vickers, H. (2009, June 17). *Augmented reality language learning – virtual worlds meet m-learning.* Retrieved from http://www.avatarlanguages.com/blog/arll/

Vie, S. (2007). *Engaging others in online social networking sites: Rhetorical practices in MySpace and Facebook.* Unpublished doctoral dissertation, University of Arizona, Tucson, AZ.

Vince, J. (1998). *Essential virtual reality fast: how to understand the techniques and potential of virtual reality.* London: Springer-Verlag.

Voelker, D. J. (2008). Assessing student understanding in introductory courses: A sample strategy. *The History Teacher, 41*(4), 506–518.

Vygotsky, L. (1978). *Mind in society: The development of bigger psychological processes.* Boston, MA: Harvard University Press.

Vygotsky, L. S. (1978). *Mind in society.* Cambridge, MA: Harvard University Press.

Wagner, C. (2003). Put another (b)Log on the wire: Publishing learning logs as weblogs. *Journal of Information Systems Education, 14*(2), 131–132.

Wagner, E. D. (2005). Enabling mobile learning. *EDUCAUSE Review, 40*(3), 40–53.

Waldner, M., Hauber, J., Zauner, J., Haller, M., & Billinghurst, M. (2006). Tangible tiles: design and evaluation of a tangible user interface in a collaborative tabletop setup. In J. Kjeldskov & J. Paay (Eds.), *Proceedings of the Australia Conference on Computer-Human Interaction: Design: Activities, Artefacts, and Environments* (pp. 151-158). New York: ACM Press.

Wallace, B. (2002). *Teaching thinking skills across the middle years.* London: David Fulton.

Wallace, B., Maker, J., Cave, D., & Chandler, S. (2004). *Thinking skills and problem solving an inclusive approach.* London: David Fulton.

Wallop, H. (2009). Video games bigger than film. Retrieved from http://www.telegraph.co.uk/technology/video-games/6852383/Video-games-bigger-than-film.html

Wang, X., Gu, N., & Marchant, D. (2008). An empirical study on designers' perceptions of augmented reality within an architectural firm. *Journal of Information Technology in Construction, 13*, 536–552.

Warriner-Burke, H. P. (1990). Distance learning: "What we don't know can't hurt us. *Foreign Language Annals, 23*(2), 131. doi:10.1111/j.1944-9720.1990.tb00351.x

Watts, M., & Ebbutt, D. (1987). More than the sum of the parts: Research methods in group interviewing. *British Educational Research Journal, 13*(1), 25–34. doi:10.1080/0141192870130103

Webber, A. M. (1994). Surviving in the new economy. *Harvard Business Review*, 76–92.

Wechsler, D. (1967). *Wechsler preschool and primary scale of intelligence.* San Antonio, TX: The Psychological Corporation.

Wechsler, D. (1992). *Wechsler Individual Achievement Test.* San Antonio, TX: Harcourt Assessments.

Wegner, E. (1998). *Communities of practice: Learning, meaning and identity.* Cambridge, UK: Cambridge University Press.

Weller, M. (2010). The centralisation dilemma in educational IT. *International Journal of Virtual and Personal Learning Environments, 1*(1), 1–9. doi:10.4018/jvple.2010091701

Wellner, P., Mackay, W., & Gold, R. (1993). Computer-augmented environments: back to the real world. *Communications of the ACM, 36*, 24–27. doi:10.1145/159544.159555

Wenger, E. C. (1991). Communities of practice: Where learning happens. *Benchmark*, 1-6.

Wenger, E. (1998). *Communities of practice: Learning, meaning and identity.* Cambridge, UK: Cambridge University Press.

Wenger, E. C. (2000). Communities of practice and social learning systems. *Organization, 7*(2), 225–246. doi:10.1177/135050840072002

Wenger, E. C., & Snyder, W. M. (2000). Communities of practice: The organizational frontier. *Harvard Business Review, 78*(1), 139–145.

Whately, D., & Harris, N. (2010) *Hero engine simutronics corporiation.* Paper presented at the Harris at Game Developers Conference, San Francisco, CA.

Whelchel, A. (2007). Using civilization simulation video games in the world history classroom. *World History Connected, 4*(2), 1–14.

White, S. (1993). Scholar - A campus wide structure for multimedia learning. In *Proceedings of the 27th Annual Meeting of the Association for Educational and Training Technology*, Glasgow, UK.

White, S. (2006). *Higher education and learning technologies: An organisational perspective.* Unpublished doctoral dissertation, University of Southampton, Southampton, UK.

White, S., & Davis, H. C. (2008). *eMM Benchmarking at Southampton: The carpet, observations and reflections* (Tech. Rep. No. LSL-EL-0108, ECS). Southampton, UK: University of Southampton.

Whitton, N. (2007). *An investigation into the potential of collaborative computer game-based learning in higher education.* Unpublished doctoral dissertation, Napier University, Edinburgh, UK.

Whitton, N. (2007, December 2-5). *Motivation and computer game based learning.* Paper presented at the Ascilite Workshop on Providing Choices for Learners and Learning, Singapore.

Whitton, N., & Hynes, N. (2006). Evaluating the effectiveness of an online simulation to teach business skills. *E-Journal of Instructional Science and Technology, 9*(1).

Whitton, N. (2010). *Learning with digital games.* New York, NY: Routledge.

Whitty, M., & Gavin, J. (2001). Age/sex/location: Uncovering the social cues in the development of online relationships. *Cyberpsychology & Behavior, 4*, 623–630. doi:10.1089/109493101753235223

Wideman, H. (2007). *ABEL participant experience evaluation*. Toronto, ON, Canada: Institute for Research on Learning Technologies.

Wideman, H. (2009). *Evaluation of the learning connections program 2008-2009: Summary report*. Toronto, ON, Canada: Institute for Research on Learning Technologies.

Wiedenmaier, S., Oehme, O., Schmidt, L., & Luczak, H. (2003). Augmented reality (AR) for assembly processes design and experimental evaluation. *Journal of Human-Computer Interaction, 16*, 497–514. doi:10.1207/S15327590IJHC1603_7

Wikipedia. (2010). *Mobile operating system*. Retrieved from http://en.m.wikipedia.org/wiki/Mobile_operating_system?wasRedirected=true

Williams, P. (2008). *Independent review of mathematics teaching in early years settings and primary schools*. Retrieved from http://www.education.gov.uk/publications//eOrderingDownload/Williams%20Mathematics.pdf

Wilson, S. (2005). *Future VLE - The visual version*. Retrieved from http://zope.cetis.ac.uk/members/scott/blogview?entry=20050125170206

Wilson, S. (2008). Address to the Connected Learning Conference. In *Side by Side*. Sydney, Australia: DET School Newspaper Pty Ltd.

Wilson, S., Liber, O., Beauvoir, P., Milligan, C., Johnson, M., & Sharples, P. (2006). *Personal learning environments: Challenging the dominant design of educational systems*. Retrieved from http://hdl.handle.net/1820/727

Wilson, S. (2008). Patterns of personal learning environments. *Interactive Learning Environments, 16*(1), 17–34. doi:10.1080/10494820701772660

Winkler, K. (2010). *The new CEO of Livemocha goes mobile and looks out for the best customer*. Retrieved from. http://www.kirstenwinkler.com/the-new-ceo-of-livemocha-goes-mobile-and-looks-out-for-the-best-customer/

Winn, M. (2005). Collecting target discourse: The case of the US naturalization interview . In Long, M. H. (Ed.), *Second language needs analysis* (pp. 265–304). Cambridge, UK: Cambridge University Press.

Winn, W., & Jackson, R. (1999). Fourteen propositions about educational uses of virtual reality. *Educational Technology, 39*(2), 5–14.

Wolfe, J., & Crookall, D. (1998). Developing a scientific knowledge of simulation/gaming. *Simulation & Gaming, 29*(1), 7–19. doi:10.1177/1046878198291002

World of Uncertainty. (n. d.). *Welcome to the World of Uncertainty*. Retrieved from http://www.worldofuncertainty.org

Xu, F., & Spelke, E. S. (2000). Large number discrimination in 6-month-old infants. *Cognition, 74*, 1–11. doi:10.1016/S0010-0277(99)00066-9

Yee, N. (2006). The labor of fun: How video games blur the boundaries of work and play. *Games and Culture, 1*, 68–71. doi:10.1177/1555412005281819

Yin, R. K. (2008). *Case study research: Design and methods*. Thousand Oaks, CA: Sage.

Yip, P.-C., & Rimmington, D. (2004). *Chinese: A comprehensive grammar*. London: Routledge.

Ylvisaker, M., Adelson, D., Braga, L. W., Burnett, M., Glang, A., & Feeney, T. (2005). Rehabilitation and ongoing support after pediatric TBI: Twenty years of progress. *The Journal of Head Trauma Rehabilitation, 20*, 95–109. doi:10.1097/00001199-200501000-00009

Yuen, A. H. K., & Ma, W. W. K. (2008). Exploring teacher acceptance of e-learning technology. *Asia-Pacific Journal of Teacher Education, 36*(3), 229–243. doi:10.1080/13598660802232779

Zaharias, P., & Poylymenakou, A. (2009). Developing a usability evaluation method for e-learning applications: Beyond functional usability. *International Journal of Human-Computer Interaction, 25*(1), 75–98. doi:10.1080/10447310802546716

Zhan, G., & Jin, Q. (2005). Research on collaborative service solution in ubiquitous learning environment. In *Proceedings of the 6th International Conference on Parallel and Distributed Computing, Applications and Technologies*.

Zhao, Y. (2003). *What teachers should know about technology: Perspectives and practices*. Greenwich, CT: Information Age Publishing.

Ziegler, J. C., & Goswami, U. C. (2005). Reading acquisition, developmental dyslexia and skilled reading across languages: A psycholinguistic grain size theory. *Psychological Bulletin, 131*(1), 3–29. doi:10.1037/0033-2909.131.1.3

Zubrinic, K., & Kalpic, D. (2008). The Web as personal learning environment. *International Journal of Emerging Technologies in Learning, 3*, 45–58.

Zuckerman, O., Arida, S., & Resnick, M. (2005). Extending tangible interfaces for education: digital Montessori-inspired Manipulatives. In W. Kellogg, S. Zhai, C. Gale, & G. van der Veer (Eds.), *Proceedings of the ACM Conference of Human Factors in Computing Systems* (pp. 859-868). New York: ACM Press.

About the Contributors

Michael Thomas, BA (Hons), M.Ed., MBA, Ph.D., FHEA, is Senior Lecturer in Language Learning Technologies at the University of Central Lancashire, United Kingdom. He has taught at universities in the United Kingdom, Germany, and Japan. His research interests are in task-based learning, digital technologies in education, and online and distance learning. He is lead editor of three book series, "Digital Education and Learning" (with J. P. Gee and J. Palfrey), "Advances in Digital Language Learning and Teaching" (with M. Peterson and M. Warschauer), and "Advances in Virtual and Personal Learning Environments." He has published over ten books including Handbook of Research on Web 2.0 and Second Language Learning (2009), Interactive Whiteboards for Education: Theory, Research and Practice (2010), Task-Based Language Learning & Teaching with Technology (with H. Reinders) (2010), Digital Education: Opportunities for Social Collaboration (2011), Deconstructing Digital Natives: Young People, Technology and the New Literacies (2011), and Online Learning: Volumes I-IV (2011). He has completed funded research projects and consultancies on digital gaming, open educational resources, mobile learning and blended learning. Dr. Thomas is a Fellow of the Higher Education Academy.

* * *

James Aczel's research at The Open University explores how learning occurs when people use digital technologies, with a particular focus on novel research methods and strategic models of learning. Recent topics include pedagogical knowledge sharing, climate change policy negotiation, institutional ICT strategies, multiple mathematical representations, collaborative design, and intermediate steps in educational software. James has played a leading role in several international research collaborations and led the team that won the 2005 International Information Industry Award for innovation in knowledge management. He has chaired the examination of the OU's social sciences research masters degrees and developed the OU's course on educational technology research.

Jo Armitage has taught in secondary schools and in higher education. She has worked with the Open University in the UK, presenting courses on-line and has developed materials to improve study skills and access to higher education. Work with Kingston University resulted in programmes to promote wider participation, including the development of on-line support materials. As an adviser for E-Learning in Hounslow, Jo Armitage promotes inclusion across all key stages of education, supported by ICT and thinking skills. This work formed the basis of research for a doctorate. She works closely with teachers to integrate thinking skills across the curriculum within media rich learning environments. She develops flexible learning spaces, which meet teaching and learning needs that are enquiry based, mobile, and adaptable, in order to support formal, informal, virtual and non-virtual learning.

Kikuo Asai received a B.E. degree in Electric and Electronic Engineering from Meijo University, Japan and his M.E. and Ph.D. degrees in Electrical Engineering and Electronics from Nagoya University, Japan in 1993 and 1998, respectively. He joined the National Institute of Multimedia Education in 1996. He was a visiting researcher at University of Illinois at Chicago in 2000, at University of Alberta in 2002-2003, and at University of Canterbury in 2009-2010. He has been engaged in research and development on communication networks, multimedia systems and human computer interaction. He is a member of ACM, IEICE, IEEJ and VRSJ.

Jill Attewell is the Programme Manager for MoLeNET. She also manages LSN's Technology Enhanced Learning Research Centre. This involves designing and managing research and development projects. Jill has contributed to the implementation of UK national e-learning initiatives including the Quality in Information and Learning Technology (QUILT) staff development programme and the National Learning Network (NLN). Between 2001 and 2004 Jill was the Programme Manager of the EC 5th framework research and development programme "m-learning" which explored, with partners, practitioners and learners in the UK, Italy and Sweden, the use of mobile phones and palmtop computers to engage young people in learning and help to develop their literacy and numeracy skills. Jill is Vice President of the International Association for Mobile Learning (IAMLearn) and she co-chaired MLEARN2003 and MLEARN2004 conferences.

Gavin Baxter is a research assistant in the School of Computing at the University of the West of Scotland. His research focuses on the implementation of Web 2.0 technologies in organisations for the purposes of organisational learning. His other research areas include: the applicability of blogs as communication and knowledge sharing tools in organisational project-based environments. He has also published works about organisational blogging in *The Learning Organization* and *IJCEnt*. He researches about the application of Web 2.0 technologies in educational contexts and is presently involved on the 'Web 2.0 European Resource Centre' project.

Billy Brick is Languages Centre Manager and principal lecturer in the Department of English and Languages at Coventry University. He teaches Multimedia in Language Teaching and Learning to undergraduate students and Computer-Assisted Language Learning at Masters level and has been involved with numerous JISC/HEA projects including the Coventry On-line Writing Lab (COWL) and the Humbox, an Open Educational Resource project for the humanities. Billy is a member of the Coventry University's English Language in the Professions and Higher Education (Elphe) research group, is a member of Evaluation of Learners' Experiences of e-learning Special Interest Group (ELESIG) and sits on the Languages, Literature and Area Studies Advisory Group. In addition to his research in Social Networking and language learning, Billy's interests include using Turnitin as a tool to improve students' writing and providing feedback to students with screen capture software.

Jerremie Clyde is the librarian for History, Greek and Roman studies and the Digital Video Games collection at the University of Calgary. He has published articles on the use of digital video games in education and creation of games specifically for the educational environment. His current research interests continue to focus on games, education, and scholarly communication. He collaborates with Glenn Wilkinson and Chris Thomas of the University of Calgary in his research.

Thomas Connolly is Chair of the ICT in Education Research Group at the University of the West of Scotland and Director of the Scottish Centre for Enabling Technologies. His specialisms are online learning, games-based learning, Web2.0 technologies and database systems. He has published papers in a number of international journals as well as authoring the highly acclaimed books *Database Systems: A Practical Approach to Design, Implementation, and Management, Database Solutions* and *Business Database Systems*, all published by Addison Wesley Longman. Professor Connolly also serves on the editorial boards of many international journals, as well as managing several large-scale externally funded research projects.

Hugh Davis is Professor of Learning Technology and Director of the Learning Societies Lab (LSL) within the School of Electronics and Computer Science (ECS) at the University of Southampton. He is also the University Director of Education with responsibility for Technology Enhanced Learning. He has been involved in hypertext research since the late 1980's and has publications in the areas of hypertext for learning, open hypertext systems and architectures for adaptation and personalisation, and he has experience of starting a spin-off company with a hypertext product. His recent research interests focus on technology enhanced learning, revolving around Web service frameworks for e-Learning, personal learning environments, educational repositories (EdShare) and semantic applications in education. He is a passionate believer in the importance of sharing and open data. He has led many projects focusing on both the technology and application of e-learning. He has over 200 publications at http://www.ecs. soton.ac.uk/people/hcd/.

Sebastian H. D. Fiedler is a researcher and project manager at the Centre for Social Innovation in Vienna, Austria. Sebastian is an educational psychologist (Dipl.-Psych. (Univ.), University of Erlangen-Nürnberg, Germany) who also holds a degree in Instructional Design & Technology (MEd, University of Georgia, USA). He has worked for industry on numerous human-centered design and information architecture projects and lectured in Media Pedagogy graduate programs at various universities. Since 2005 he has worked mainly on international research and development projects in educational technology. His main research interests are related to adult education, self-direction and self-organization in education, and the role of social media and networked technology within the ongoing (digital) transformation of human activities.

Helene Fournier is a Research Officer with the National Research Council of Canada's Institute for Information Technology. Dr. Fournier joined the NRC in 2002 and holds a Ph.D. in Educational Psychology from McGill University. Her research area is education and technology and she has participated in several research projects focused on the application and evaluation of advanced technologies in the training sector, in distance education, and more recently in learner-centered research and development of a Personal Learning Environment. She has contributed to the advancement of research in the field of distance education, online learning, adult learning, and more recently to educational learning analytics in the context of Massive Open Online Courses. She has published widely in peer reviewed journals and at international conferences.

Yao Zhang Hill has worked as an Institutional Researcher at Kapiʻolani Community College since 2008, actively involved in faculty development, grant and program evaluations, and quantitative and qualitative survey research. Before that, she taught Chinese and English as second languages for eight years, and served as summer research intern at Educational Testing Service in 2008. In 2010, she completed her Ph.D. degree in Second Language Studies at the University of Hawaii at Manoa, with specializations in language assessment, program evaluation, CALL and task-based language curriculum development.

Beat Döbeli Honegger is Professor at the University of Teacher Education Central Switzerland (PHZ) in Goldau. He acquired a masters degree and a PhD in computer science at the Swiss Federal Institute of Technology Zürich (ETHZ). His current research fields are personal mobile learning, knowledge management in a network society and didactics of computer science. He is the scientific leader of the smartphone project described in this issue.

Jane Louise Hunter is an academic in teacher education in the School of Education at the University of Western Sydney. Her professional background is in pedagogy and technology, new media, teacher professional learning, HSIE curriculum especially civics and citizenship. She has previously taught in schools, in teacher education at the University of Sydney, and her most recent appointment was as a senior officer in a number of large technology projects in the NSW Department of Education and Training. Jane has written scholarly articles for journals and books, and regularly presents at education conferences both nationally and internationally.

Misbah Mahmood Khan graduated from the University of Leicester with a BSC degree in Psychology with Neuroscience. She then completed a MSC Research in cognitive Neuropsychology degree at the University of Hertfordshire. She has worked as an honouree assistant psychologist at Guys and St Thomas hospital. She has also undertaken an apprenticeship within the University of Hertfordshire looking at current research on the role of gestures in learning. Misbah is currently working as a cancer and palliative care services audit facilitator.

Deborah Kitchener is Program Manager of the Learning Connections program based at York University and funded by a grant from the Ministry of Education, Literacy & Numeracy Secretariat of Ontario, Canada. Deborah has 20 years of teaching and leadership experience in both elementary and secondary schools in the York Region District School Board, Ontario, Canada. She is an experienced adult educator in both online and blended learning environments. Deborah holds a graduate degree in Educational Technology and has presented at conferences in the United States and Canada about effective models of professional learning integrating information computer technologies.

Rita Kop has been a researcher at the National Research Council of Canada's Institute for Information Technology since September 2009 and holds a Ph.D. in Adult Continuing Education. Her current research focuses on human learning in advanced networked learning environments, and her recent teaching took place in massive open online events. Before she joined the NRC she was an assistant professor at Swansea University in the UK after a career as teacher and head-teacher in Dutch primary education. Her research interests are adult learning and open educational practice, self-directed learning, widening access to Higher Education, networked learning, and learning analytics and e-research methods.

Jyldyz Tabyldy Kyzy is a final year PhD student in Queens University Belfast, working on a research project developing and testing a computer game aimed at improving decision-making under uncertainty. It is designed to change people's perception of uncertainty and to improve their skills in estimating, quantifying and communicating subjective probabilities and degrees of confidence. The game is available at http://quiz.worldofuncertainty.org/. We have a multidisciplinary team between Queens University Belfast, Cambridge and Brunel universities. It is an exciting project for me. Hopefully, the game is useful and fun to play, but it is also a valuable research instrument to study people's choices and confidence. My interests: cognitive and educational psychology; educational games; chance games, betting and forecasting; decision-making under uncertainty; Bayesian approach; reasoning, rationality and intuition.

Ioanna Iacovides is a second year PhD student looking at digital games and learning within the Institute of Educational Technology at the Open University, UK. She is particularly interested in how interview and observational case studies (including the use of physiological data) can be used to explore the relationship between motivation, engagement and informal learning in games. She previously worked as a research assistant at the University of Bath on the JISC funded "Racing Academy" project in collaboration with Futurelab and Lateral Visions. She also has a BSc in Psychology from the University of Nottingham and an MSc in Human Communication and Computing from the University of Bath. For more information visit: http://iet.open.ac.uk/people/i.iacovides.

Robert Lebans is a staff development consultant with Castlewood Consultants who has worked with the ABEL program since its creation in 2002. He was a staff development consultant with the Toronto District School Board for 5 years and a teacher and Head of English in secondary schools in Southern Ontario for over 30 years. He has a keen interest in implementation theory and change management and a passion for exploring how technological knowledge and instructional intelligence can most effectively inform each other for student engagement in learning and academic achievement.

Rikke Magnussen is an Assistant Professor at the Department of Curriculum Research at Aarhus University in Copenhagen where she is currently part of the research project 'Serious Games on a Global Marketplace'. The subject of her research concern creative and innovative learning processes in game-based science and technology education. Rikke Magnussen has worked as a game researcher and designer for several years and has been an active part in establishing the learning game research group at Aarhus University where researchers and game developers design and study new types of game-based learning spaces. Rikke Magnussen holds a M.Sc.in molecular biology and science communication and has worked as a science TV producer before doing game studies.

Janet Murphy directs the Advanced Broadband Enabled Learning (ABEL) program for York University's Office of the Vice President Research and Innovation and the York Region District School Board in Toronto, Ontario, Canada. Janet has received provincial and national awards recognizing her leadership in the use of information communications technology for education, including two ORION awards for Learning and for Leadership (2006); the Learning Partnership Technology Innovation Award (2005 and 2003); the Information Highways e-Content Award for Education (2002); the Prime Minister's Award of Excellence (2001); and, the Roberta Bondar Millennium Award of Excellence (January 2000). Janet has presented papers on the effective use of technology for professional learning at conferences and events around the world.

Christian Neff is class teacher and ICT manager at the primary school of Goldau, where he teaches the smartphone class described in this issue. He uses ICT in education since he began as a teacher 18 years ago.

Jukka Orava is an eLearning Specialist and currently a Special Planner and Media Literacy Specialist and Medius Team Leader at the Media Centre Education Department in the City of Helsinki. He also works as private consultant and expert in the fields of media education, collaborative knowledge building and art education. His past roles have included Researcher at the University of Art and Design (UIAH) in Helsinki, Cumulus Art Education working group member and steering committee member at UIAH Virtual University. On an International level Jukka has worked as Coordinator for the Art Department in the European Schoolnet Virtual School initiative (1999-2005) and as Steering Committee member in EU Prometheus Initiative. He has ten years experience in international collaboration and curriculum development. He is currently working on his doctoral thesis about developing media education and elearning.

Maria A. Perifanou received her Bachelor Degree in Italian Language and Literature from the Aristotle University of Thessaloniki in 1999. She continued her Masters studies at the University of Venice, Ca'Foscari, Science of Language Department, Laboratory ITALS (2001-2003). For the last six years she has been a PhD candidate in the field of Applied Linguistics at the National Kapodistrian University of Athens, Faculty of Italian Studies. Currently, she works as an Italian lecturer at the European Institute of Vocational Training AKMI, Greece, and as a senior researcher at the Research Institution 'Pontydysgu', Wales, UK. Her main practice and research concerns Web 2.0, TELL, Mobile learning, Collaborative Learning, Web2Quests, PLEs, CALL, and Blended Learning. She is an experienced e-learning teacher trainer and has worked as a co-editor and a reviewer with 3 TEL journals. She has also taken part in organising, programme development and academic committees of international conferences and other international TEL events.

Rebecca Petley is a Senior Researcher in the Technology for Learning team, currently working alongside Carol Savill-Smith on the MoLeNET project. Rebecca has a first degree in Psychology and has previously worked as a researcher for the University of Kent. Her research focussed on social and developmental psychology, specifically investigating interpersonal relations and prejudice reduction. In addition Rebecca has a PGCE and has taught in both the primary and adult education sectors.

Jonathan Reed is a Chartered Clinical Psychologist and full practitioner paediatric neuropsychologist. He has worked as a senior paediatric neuropsychologist at Guy's Hospital London and as a Specialist Paediatric neuropsychologist at the Royal London Hospital. He has also held positions in child development, child mental health services and was a researcher on the National Traumatic Brain Injury Study. He is currently a director of Recolo, which provides child neuropsychological rehabilitation and Neurogames, which develops computer games to help children develop. He is co editor of *Child Neuropsychology Theory, Concepts and Practice* (Wiley-Blackwell 2008).

Carol Savill-Smith, together with Jill Attewell, leads the Research and Evaluation strand of the MoLeNET Support and Evaluation Programme. She is a senior researcher in the Technology Enhanced Learning Research Centre at the LSN, where she has principally worked in the field of mobile learning and computer games including the m-learning project and the mobile learning teachers toolkit project which enabled teachers and tutors to author or adapt mobile learning materials for the specific needs of their students in their particular context.

Eileen Scanlon is Professor of Educational Technology and Associate Director Research and Scholarship in the Institute of Educational Technology at the Open University in the UK. She is also Visiting Professor in Moray House School of Education, University of Edinburgh. Her research interests in the area of Information and Communication Technologies are wide-ranging. She is currently directing projects on science learning in formal and informal settings concentrating on the development of an inquiry learning pedagogy and innovative approaches to evaluation. She has extensive research experience on educational technology projects including mobile learning.

Mark Stansfield is a Reader in Learning Technologies in the School of Computing at the University of the West of Scotland. He has written and co-written more than 80 refereed papers in areas that include e-learning, games-based e-learning and virtual campuses. He also serves on the editorial boards of several international journals that include the *International Journal of Information Management*, *Journal of Information Systems Education*, *ALT-J* and the *Journal of IT Education*, as well as being an Editor of the *Interdisciplinary Journal of E-Learning and Learning Objects*. He was Project Coordinator of the European Commission co-financed project Promoting Best Practice in Virtual Campuses and is currently working on the Web 2.0 European Resource Centre project.

Norio Takase received his B.S. degree in Physics from Kyushu Institute of Technology, Japan in 1997, after which he joined the Solidray Co., Ltd. In 2001 he joined the FiatLux Corporation where he is currently the head of a section in the R&D Section. His interests have focused on research and development in bio-science software, visual simulators using virtual reality, and stereoscopic systems.

Josie Taylor is Professor of Learning Technologies, and Director of the Institute of Educational Technology (IET) at the Open University. Josie has a bachelor's degree in Dance, Drama and Psychology (University College, Worcester) and a D.Phil in Cognitive Sciences (University of Sussex). Her research focuses on understanding the ways in which people learn from complex media (traditional and digital) and how best to design those media to support learning. This spans system design, interface design, interaction design, user requirements, and evaluation, and entails understanding user psychology, the nature of learning and the contexts of learning.

Stephen L. Tschudi, Specialist in Technology for Language Education, has developed models for distance education in less commonly taught languages using interactive television and Web technologies, and has also authored self-instructional software for intermediate-to-advanced Mandarin Chinese. He is particularly interested in the effective integration of spoken communication into Web-based language instruction.

Terje Väljataga is a researcher and lecturer at Tallinn University in the Centre for Educational Technology. She holds a Doctor of Science in Technology from Tampere University of Technology, Finland. Her background is teacher education, natural sciences (MSc, Tallinn Pedagogical University, Estonia) and telematics application in education and training (MSc, University of Twente, The Netherlands). She has experience in teaching at secondary school and university. She has been involved in various educational research projects both local and international since 2004. Her research interests are related to adult education and media pedagogy, social media implementation in higher education, personal learning environments in formal and informal educational settings and competence advancement for self-directing intentional learning projects.

Su White as an associate professor who researches within the Learning Societies Lab (LSL) and the Web and Internet Science Group within the School of Electronics and Computer Science (ECS) at the University of Southampton. She has been involved research at the intersection of institutional change and technology innovation research since the early 1990s and has publications across the areas of institutional change, educational innovation and the educational use of technology for learning. Her recent research activities have focused on drivers and barriers for the adoption of open technologies facilitated by semantic enhancement and educational innovation via institutional adoption of technology infrastructure such as the EdShare educational repository. She has over 80 publications at http://www. ecs.soton.ac.uk/people/saw/.

Glenn Wilkinson is an Adjunct Assistant Professor in History and Communication and Culture at the University of Calgary, Alberta, focusing on British and European cultural history, film and history, and military history. His book, *The Depiction and Images of War in Edwardian Newspaper, 1899-1914*, published by Palgrave, combined media studies, cultural studies, and military history. Current research interests include the digital mode of history, with Jerremie Clyde; the utopian vision in Rev. W. Awdry's *Railway Series*; and a study of post-war British war films (1945-1960). He was elected Fellow to the Royal Historical Society in 2009 and lives with his activist wife and five children (daughter, son and set of identical triplet girls) in chaotic bliss.

Will Woods is Senior Learning and Teaching Technologies Manager in the Institute of Educational Technology at the Open University. He has an honours degree in Computer Science and further professional qualifications including MCSE (Microsoft Certified Systems Engineer) and is a Chartered IT Provider (British Computer Society accredited). Will has worked in the Open University for seventeen years and has a background in researching technologies in the support of education and as part of the Electronic Media in Education Research Group he developed innovative online multimedia courses. Will is an active participant on a number of enterprise initiatives and is Technical Director on a number of e-learning projects. His current role is largely in the exploration, development and management of systems for learning and teaching. Will has published and presented papers on knowledge systems, Learning Design and online course presentation. For more information visit his website at http://iet. open.ac.uk/people/w.i.s.woods.

Pete Worrall is an Independent Consultant in Art and Design, New Media and eLearning in the United Kingdom and Finland. His past roles have included Senior Lecturer (Initial Teacher Training, Art and Design) at University of Central England in Birmingham, LEA Advisor and UK Representative in the Virtual School Art Department, European Schoolnet. He has also worked with National Agencies including the Qualifications and Curriculum Development Agency (QCDA), the British Educational Communications and Technology Agency (Becta) and the Training and Development Agency (TDA). His publications include Electric Studio, A Critical Context: Art and Design Education on the Edge and Cultural Identity (Brazil), Digital Media and Art (International Case Studies). He has also coordinated new media projects in Brazil, Holland, Portugal and Finland.

Index